Vision and narrative in Achilles Tatius' *Leucippe and Clitophon*

Achilles Tatius' *Leucippe and Clitophon*, long regarded as the most controversial of the ancient Greek novels, is an outrageous tale of love and loss, of Phoenicians and philosophers, virginity tests and snuff dramas. This book, the first published monograph on Achilles Tatius, is a study of *Leucippe and Clitophon* in its literary and visual contexts. It presents fresh insights into the work's narrative complexities and interpretative difficulties. It is particularly concerned with the novel's obsessions with the eye, with theories, descriptions and metaphorics of the visual. It advances a reading that gives full play to the narrative's 'digressions' – *ekphrasis, sententia, blason* and spectacle – and discusses the politics of digressivity. This book is written to be accessible to non-specialists and all Greek is translated or paraphrased. It aims to contribute to a cultural history of viewing and to feminist literary criticism, as well as to the study of the ancient novel.

HELEN MORALES lectures in Classics at the University of Cambridge and is a Fellow of Newnham College. She is co-editor of *Intratextuality: Greek and Roman Textual Relations* (OUP, 2000).

CAMBRIDGE CLASSICAL STUDIES

General Editors
R. L. HUNTER, R. G. OSBORNE, M. D. REEVE,
P. D. A. GARNSEY, M. MILLETT, D. N. SEDLEY,
G. C. HORROCKS

VISION AND NARRATIVE IN ACHILLES TATIUS'
LEUCIPPE AND CLITOPHON

HELEN MORALES
*Lecturer in Classics in the University of Cambridge,
and Fellow of Newnham College*

CAMBRIDGE
UNIVERSITY PRESS

University Printing House, Cambridge CB2 8BS, United Kingdom

Cambridge University Press is part of the University of Cambridge.

It furthers the University's mission by disseminating knowledge in the pursuit of education, learning and research at the highest international levels of excellence.

www.cambridge.org
Information on this title: www.cambridge.org/9780521642644

© Faculty of Classics, University of Cambridge 2004

This publication is in copyright. Subject to statutory exception and to the provisions of relevant collective licensing agreements, no reproduction of any part may take place without the written permission of Cambridge University Press.

First published 2004

A catalogue record for this publication is available from the British Library

Library of Congress Cataloguing in Publication data
Morales, Helen.
Vision and narrative in Achilles Tatius' Leucippe and Clitophon / Helen Morales.
p.   cm. – (Cambridge classical studies)
Includes bibliographical references and index.
ISBN 0 521 64264 7
1. Achilles Tatius. Leucippe and Clitophon.   2. Love stories, Greek – History and criticism.   3. Digression (Rhetoric) in literature.   4. Visual perception in literature.   5. Loss (Psychology) in literature.   6. Vision in literature.   7. Narration (Rhetoric).   8. Rhetoric, Ancient.   9. Eye in literature.   I. Title.   II. Series.
PA3819.Z5M67   2004
883'.01 – dc22   2004045655

ISBN 978-0-521-64264-4 Hardback

Cambridge University Press has no responsibility for the persistence or accuracy of URLs for external or third-party internet websites referred to in this publication, and does not guarantee that any content on such websites is, or will remain, accurate or appropriate.

CONTENTS

Preface		*page* ix
List of abbreviations		xii
1	Introduction	1
	Achilles Tatius	1
	Vision and visuality	8
2	Readers and reading	36
	Open(ing) readings	36
	Theatricality and reading	60
	Characterisation and viewing	77
3	Description, digression and form	96
	Sightseeing in Alexandria	100
	Sententiousness and the arrested eye	106
	Vision and the eye	130
	The ending of the novel	143
4	Gender, gaze and speech	152
	Looking at Leucippe	156
	Sweet-talking Melite	220
5	Conclusion	227
References		232
Index locorum		259
General index		265

PREFACE

This book is about desire, knowledge and sight. It is a literary study of Achilles Tatius' novel, and its configurations of the eye. The gaze is an organising principle in *Leucippe and Clitophon*. As the ego-narrator's gaze, it directs the unfolding of events in the narrative and inserts a gnomic perspective on love and life. As the subject of sententious pronouncements, the mechanics of the gaze constitute a theorising of the visual. With the characters' gazes, the narrative reveals its emphatic concern with how people view and the relations between viewers. Thematically, the desiring eye and the sorrowful eye are repeated objects of interest and serve to initiate narrative action. As an icon, the eye is present as an image and the subject of ekphrastic description. Through its strategies of revelation and concealment, particularly in relation to the female body, the narrative solicits the reader's gaze. *Leucippe and Clitophon* is profoundly ocularcentric; it is a scopophiliac's paradise.

The primary aim of this book is to further our appreciation and understanding of this novel through a series of close readings of the narrative, and discussion of its texture and structure, themes and ideology. The introductory chapter seeks to explain what is involved in approaching the two central concerns of this book: vision and narrative. It introduces some of the complexities and problems in interpreting Achilles' novel and provides some contextualisation of his representations of vision through a discussion of visuality in Greek literature (and art), particularly that of the Roman Imperial period. Chapter 2 considers ways of reading the novel, taking as its point of departure three programmatic 'beginnings' of the novel and the different, but related, filters they suggest: erotic, philosophical and Phoenician. It goes on to examine readers in the novel and their employment of different and distinctive ways of viewing. Chapter 3 looks at 'digressions' in the novel and questions what sort of knowledge is displayed in *Leucippe and Clitophon* and how it is communicated. It reconsiders the controversial ending of the novel and analyses descriptions of the eye throughout the narrative. The fourth chapter, informed by feminist criticism, argues that the novel's representations of the gaze, and speech, operate as 'technologies of gender'. All five chapters concern themselves with the novel's constructions of visuality: with how vision is perceived and socialised. This book thus also aims to make a contribution to the cultural history of viewing.

I have quoted from Jean-Philippe Garnaud's Budé edition of Achilles Tatius, and Tim Whitmarsh's excellent translation in the Oxford World's Classics series. Sometimes I have felt the need to adapt the translation to make my point more clearly or directly. I have drawn attention to this, and to variant textual readings, only when it is germane to my argument. All other translations are adapted from the Loeb editions, unless I have indicated otherwise in the footnotes. I have been eclectic with the transliteration of names, in general preferring the more familiar latinised versions.

The first section of Chapter 3 is a revised version of my essay in *Intratextuality: Greek and Roman Textual Relations*, edited by Alison Sharrock and Helen Morales. In Chapter 4, the section 'Women and other animals' is a revised version of 'The Taming of the View: Natural Curiosities in Achilles Tatius' *Leukippe and Kleitophon*', *GCN* vol. 4 (1995). My thanks to Oxford University Press and Heinz Hoffman for permission to republish.

The illustration on page iv is a mosaic from a house in Antioch known as 'The House of the Man of Letters', published by kind permission of the Princeton University Art Museum.

This book originated in my 1997 Cambridge doctoral thesis, but it has been revised and altered (in places substantially) as my thinking about the novel has developed. It is a pleasure to thank all those who have helped in that development. I am grateful to friends and colleagues at the universities of Reading, Arizona State and Cambridge, and for a year at the Center for Hellenic Studies under the gracious directorship of Deborah Boedeker and Kurt Rauflaab. I have benefited in particular from the intellectual environment of two great institutions dedicated to promoting women's education: New Hall and Newnham College, Cambridge. Thanks to both

Colleges and especially to M. M. McCabe, who started me on my way, and to Mary Beard, whose recent encouragement has been invaluable.

John Henderson supervised my first year of doctoral research: he was, and is, an inspiring guide. My thesis examiners, Simon Goldhill and John Morgan, gave detailed and incisive criticisms, as did Pat Easterling and Series Editors Richard Hunter and Michael Reeve. Tony Boyle, Jaś Elsner, and Tim Whitmarsh also read and commented on my work. Heartfelt thanks to all. Richard Hunter supervised my doctoral thesis and has read and criticised my work many times since, always with characteristic care and generosity. It is to him that I owe my greatest debt.

Thanks to David Sedley and James Warren for answering specific questions, and to Lyn Bailey and Stephen Howe for superb library support. My copy-editor, Susan Moore, has saved me from many an error; any that remain are, of course, my responsibility.

Thanks to all those who have given other forms of encouragement and help: Annie Castledine, Richard Fletcher, Shoshana Goldhill, Kristina Milnor, Katherine Rainwood, Ian Rutherford, Caroline Vout, Sheila Watts, Liz Watson, Kent Wright, Maria Wyke, and (impossible without) Katie Fleming and Miriam Leonard. Rachel Wingfield has discussed feminism with me since we were undergraduates together: she and Hilary McCollum have been true friends. Finally, special thanks to my mother, Sara Castledine, who first read me stories about Greece.

This book is dedicated to my partner, Tony Boyle, whom I love and honour.

Cambridge Helen Morales
August 2003

ABBREVIATIONS

AJPh	*American Journal of Philology*
AN	*Ancient Narrative*
AncSoc	*Ancient Society*
Anc. Phil.	*Ancient Philosophy*
ANRW	*Aufstieg und Niedergang der römischen Welt*
A&R	*Atene e Roma*
BICS	*Bulletin of the Institute of Classical Studies, London*
BMGS	*Byzantine and Modern Greek Studies*
CA	*Classical Antiquity*
CPh	*Classical Philology*
CQ	*Classical Quarterly*
CR	*Classical Review*
CW	*Classical World*
DHA	*Dialogues d'Histoire Ancienne*
FGrHist	F. Jacoby (1923–58), ed. *Die Fragmente der griechischen Historiker.* Berlin and Leiden
GCN	*Groningen Colloquia on the Novel*
G&R	*Greece and Rome*
GRBS	*Greek, Roman, and Byzantine Studies*
HSPh	*Harvard Studies in Classical Philology*
JHS	*Journal of Hellenic Studies*
JRS	*Journal of Roman Studies*
K–A	R. Kassel and C. Austin eds. (1983–) *Poetae Comici Graeci.* Berlin
KRS	G. S. Kirk, J. E. Raven, and M. Schofield, eds. (1983) *The Presocratic Philosophers: a critical history with a selection of texts.* Cambridge
L&S	A. A. Long and D. N. Sedley, eds. (1987) *The Hellenistic Philosophers* vol 1. Cambridge
LIMC	*Lexicon Iconographicum Mythologiae Classicae* (1981–1999) Zurich, Munich and Dusseldorf

ABBREVIATIONS

MD	*Materiali e Discussioni Materiali per l'analisi dei testi classici*
MLN	*Modern Language Notes*
PAPhS	*Proceedings of the American Philosophical Society*
PCPS	*Proceedings of the Cambridge Philological Society*
PLL	*Proceedings of the Leeds Philosophical and Literary Society*
PMG	D. L. Page, ed. (1962) *Poetae Melici Graeci*. Oxford
PSN	*The Petronian Society Newsletter*
QUCC	*Quaderni urbinati di cultura classica*
REG	*Revue des Etudes Grecques*
RhM	*Rheinisches Museum*
SIFC	*Studi Italiani di Filologia Classica*
SLG	D. L. Page, ed. (1974) *Supplementum Lyricis Graecis*. Oxford
SVF	H. von Arnim, ed. (1903–5) *Stoicorum Veterum Fragmenta* vols. 1–3; M. Adler, ed. (1924) vol. 4. Leipzig
TGF	R. Kannicht and B. Snell, eds. (1981) *Tragicorum Graecorum Fragmenta* vol. 2. Gottingen
YCS	*Yale Classical Studies*
YFS	*Yale French Studies*
WS	*Wiener Studien*
ZPE	*Zeitschrift für Papyrologie und Epigraphik*

I

INTRODUCTION

Achilles Tatius

Despite the explosion of interest in ancient fiction over the last few decades, *Leucippe and Clitophon* remains the least studied of the five major Greek novels. To my knowledge, this is the first published monograph on Achilles; so far *Leucippe* has been left on the shelf. 'Most moderns,' explains Ewen Bowie in his entry on Achilles Tatius in the *Oxford Classical Dictionary*, 'uncertain how to evaluate him, prefer Longus and Heliodorus.'[1] Graham Anderson concurs: 'Even at the lowest level of literary criticism, at which writers receive one-word adjectives, one can do something for the rest of the extant novelists: Xenophon of Ephesus is naïve, Heliodorus cleverly convoluted, Longus artfully simple: yet what is one to say about Achilles?'[2] Scholarship on the novel is moving forward so quickly that these comments will soon seem dated. Nevertheless, they are symptomatic of a fundamental difficulty: there is no consensus about what to make of Achilles Tatius; at the most basic level, about how to read him. Parody? Pastiche? Pornography? It is, as John Morgan puts it, a 'hyper-enigmatic' novel.[3]

Part of the problem is that Achilles Tatius is frequently evaluated against the norms of the genre (often as the Joker in the pack: '[Achilles Tatius] inverse systématiquement les conventions du genre';[4] 'He conducts a prolonged guerrilla war against the conventions of his own genre'[5]), and the norms and the genre are themselves problematic to define.[6] It is important to note that recent approaches to the genre have been driven by the last few decades'

---

[1] *OCD*, 3rd edn (1996), 7.   [2] Anderson (1997), 2279.   [3] Morgan (1996b), 188.
[4] Plazenet (1997), 322   [5] Morgan (1995), 142.
[6] The bibliography on this is considerable. I have found of particular use or interest Kuch (1989a), 11–51 for a discussion of the ancient terminology, Winkler (1994), Fusillo (1991), Sandy (1994), Selden (1994), Doody (1996) who all, in their different ways, take

intense interest in the novels' representations of sexuality, sparked in part by Michel Foucault's focus on the ancient novel in the third volume of his *History of Sexuality*.[7] The result has been to privilege those novels that evince similar patterns regarding gender – Chariton, Xenophon of Ephesus, Longus, Achilles Tatius and Heliodorus – and to downplay those which do not. A more inclusive circumscription, which is encouraged by the variety of content and style in the material collated by Stephens and Winkler and identified as fragments of novels, would obviously set different generic standards and expectations within and against which to judge *Leucippe and Clitophon*.[8]

Several scholars have argued that the readership of the novels in the ancient world largely consisted of women.[9] Of course, many of the arguments for a female readership of the novel are primarily indicative of scholars' own prejudices. When the novels were considered hackneyed, sentimental, pulp fiction, it followed only women and other undiscerning communities of readers would be entertained by them. Recently, more positive reasons have been proposed for a mainly female readership. Focusing on the novels' representations of strong and erotically powerful women, Brigitte Egger has argued that the five 'ideal' Greek novels operate on a principle of 'practical androcentrism' but 'emotional gynocentrism'.[10] Her analyses, drawing on the reader-response

---

a quite relaxed or inclusive view of genre and Branham (2002), who argues instead for the value of more, and more refined, generic distinctions.

[7] Foucault (1984), on which see especially Konstan (1994), Goldhill (1995) and Morales (forthcoming).

[8] Stephens and Winkler (1995).

[9] Many held the view that because the novels were poor literary works, it followed that they were intended to be read by women. Cf. Altheim (1948), esp. 42 and Scobie (1973a), esp. 93–5, who compared the Greek novels to stories in women's magazines. Perry famously defined the audience as 'the poor-in-spirit': Perry (1967), vii. Rohde (1914) reasons that, as the Greek romance is a decadent genre, indicative of a society in moral decline in which women were assuming more power, it was most likely intended for women. Hägg (1983) and Holzberg (1996) view the prominent role given to women as evidence of a largely female readership: 'Most of the surviving texts offer a strikingly large variety of opportunities for women readers to identify with the characters in the story . . . [o]f great[ ] interest for women readers was probably the frequent portrayal of heroines as more active, more intelligent and more likeable than their often almost colourless lovers', Holzberg (1996), 35. For further discussion and reviews of the scant ancient testimony on readership see: Egger (1988) and (1990), esp. 1–20 and appendix; Wesseling (1988); Bowie (1994); Stephens (1994); Morgan (1995).

[10] Egger (1990), 365.

theories of Jauss and Iser, of how the internal structures of the texts might invite interest and identification from women readers, are significant contributions to our appreciation and understanding of the narratives' textual strategies. However, attempting to identify what characteristics of a narrative might be more attractive to a female than a male audience still proves a hazardous enterprise. For Egger, Melite is one of the characters whose individuality, independence and humour, demonstrated in her skilful seduction of Clitophon, make her most likely to appeal to women readers.[11] In contrast, Ewen Bowie considers Melite's conquest of Clitophon 'a male orientation which should give pause to theories of a chiefly female readership'.[12]

The trend at the moment is to assume an exclusively, or largely, male readership.[13] Literacy rates are the chief reason for suggesting that the readers of the novels were the same community of readers who read Homer, Thucydides, Plato, Plutarch and other literature, though possibly in smaller number, and that this community consisted of a small number of elite men and a much smaller number of elite women.[14] Seven papyri of *Leucippe and Clitophon* have been found, more than of any other Greek novel, but still far fewer than works by authors on school curricula. However, when the evidence is as exiguous as it is in this case, it can easily be framed to argue for a number of different positions. Thus, the answer to the question of who read the ancient novels is even more likely than usual to reflect the politics of the academy, rather than to construct a 'true' picture. As Margaret Anne Doody points out: 'The tendency to remasculinize the ancient novels in the 1990s is not so much any new discovery as a register of the fact that the Greek novel is going up in academic estimation, and is now to be reclaimed by mainstream classicists.'[15] It is significant that both male and female characters in the novels read and write. If Achilles Tatius' internal readership is in any way indicative of his actual readership, then women are likely to have been included.

---

[11] Egger (1990), 75–6. On Melite's (subversive) appeal, see Cresci (1978) and below, Ch. 4.
[12] Bowie (1989), 134.
[13] Wesseling (1988); Stephens (1994); Bowie (1994) and see also Morgan (1995), 143.
[14] See Stephens (1994). [15] Doody (1996), 24.

When Clitophon comments that 'the female of the species is rather fond of myths' (5.5), it is inviting to read this not only as an ironic reflection on the misogynist tale he is about to tell Leucippe, but also as a self-conscious nod to some of Achilles' readers. All of this is far from conclusive, but on balance, I am assuming a largely elite readership which included men and women. An equally inconclusive, but potentially more interesting question is how that audience may have been *positioned* by the text, with regard to gender. This is a subject briefly addressed in the final section of my second chapter.

We have very little certain information about the author of *Leucippe and Clitophon* (Τὰ κατὰ Λευκίππην καὶ Κλειτοφῶντα), which was possibly simply known by the title *Leucippe*. The author does not reveal any information about himself in the text of the novel itself.[16] Even his name is in dispute; the vast majority of manuscripts have Tatios, but a few, like the tenth-century encyclopaedia *Suda*, refer to him as Statios. A connection between his name and the Egyptian god Tat has been suggested.[17] The name Achilles Tatius indicates that he was a Greek who had Roman citizenship (Achilles is a famous Greek name and Tatius and Statius are common Roman names). According to the manuscripts and the Byzantine testimonia, Achilles was a native of Alexandria (and so would be a Greek Roman Egyptian) and, according to the *Suda*, also wrote works *On the Celestial Sphere*, *Etymology*, and a *Miscellaneous History of Many Great and Illustrious Men*.[18] The lexicographer Thomas Magister refers to Achilles as a *rhetor*, a professional orator, but we have no further evidence for this. The *Suda*'s assertion that he later became a Christian and a bishop seems (at best) unlikely.[19] A similar path was said to have been chosen by

---

[16] Unlike Chariton and Heliodorus. All known testimonia on him are collected in Vilborg (1955), 163–8.

[17] Cf. Vilborg (1962), 7.

[18] ἔγραψε δὲ περὶ σφαίρας καὶ ἐτυμολογίας καὶ ἱστορίαν σύμμικτον, πολλῶν καὶ μεγάλων καὶ θαυμασίων ἀνδρῶν μνημονεύουσαν (*Suda* s.v. Ἀχιλλεὺς Στάτιος ed. A. Adler, vol. 1, 439). If the *Suda* is correct that Achilles Tatius the novelist is also the Achilles Tatius who wrote *On the Sphere*, then fragments of the work on the sphere survive in *An Introduction to Aratus' Phaenomena*, ed. Maass (1898). Some scholars, however, place the author of *On the Sphere* later, probably in the 3rd century CE.

[19] *Suda* s.v. Ἀχιλλεὺς Στάτιος: γέγονεν ἔσχατον χριστιανὸς καὶ ἐπίσκοπος.

Heliodorus,[20] and it is very doubtful that both (if either) novelists became bishops. Even less probable is the story in the *Acta Sanctorum* that the parents of St Galaktion were called Leucippe and Clitophon.[21] These anecdotes are most likely part of a strategy of appropriation of the novels into a Christian agenda, without which they might never have been preserved.[22]

The date of the novel is also disputed. A papyrus published in 1938 and dated to the second century CE made scholars reassess the general consensus that *Leucippe and Clitophon* was an imitation of Heliodorus' *Aethiopika*, and might have been written as late as the sixth century CE.[23] Another recent papyrus find confirms the second century date.[24] We have, then, a *terminus ante quem*, but it is hard to be any more precise than to place Achilles Tatius somewhere in the second century CE, possibly not later than the middle of that century.[25] This means he was writing during the time known as 'The Second Sophistic', the modern term for the cultural characteristics of the first three centuries CE, and which is increasingly (if erroneously) used to denote that whole historical period. 'Second Sophistic' is a term originally coined by Philostratus in the third century CE, who uses it to refer to a style of oratory *in persona* – improvisations based on historical figures – which was inaugurated

---

[20] Socrates *Hist. Eccl.* 5.22. See Sandy (1982), 3 for discussion of testimonia on Heliodorus as bishop.

[21] Cf. Delahaye (1921), 33ff., Dörrie (1938), Plepelits, 411.

[22] Garland (1990), 65: 'Significantly, the Byzantines tended to ignore the innately erotic qualities of the novels . . . it was this belief [i.e. that Heliodorus and Achilles Tatius provided models of good conduct] that enabled the Byzantines to peruse the romances without shame and consider them allegories of the virtues of the soul and its mystical union with God.' Allegorical interpretations of the novels were proposed by Psellos, Phillipos da Ceranii and Joannes Eugenikos; see Wilson (1983), 186, 217.

[23] Vogliano (1938). The general consensus that Heliodorus came before Achilles in fact only crystallised in the early seventeenth century. In the sixteenth century, the majority of editors and translators reflected the order given by the *Suda*. As the estimation of Heliodorus' aesthetic importance steadily increased, the chronological classification of the novels began to be questioned, until in 1625, in an epitaph to the reader in his translation of *Leucippe and Clitophon*, A. Rémy suggested that Achilles Tatius imitated Heliodorus. This became the new orthodoxy: Plazenet (1997), 143. On Achilles Tatius as a parody of Heliodorus, see Durham (1938). More generally on Achilles and parody see Fusillo (1991), 97–108.

[24] See Laplace (1983b).

[25] As Willis (1990) argues, from his dating of the Robinson-Cologne papyrus. The papyri of AT 3.17–25 (P. Duk. Inv. 772) formerly P. Rob. Inv. 35 can at the time of writing be viewed on the web at http://scriptorium.lib.duke.edu/papyrus/records/772.html. See also Plepelits (1996), 388–90.

by Aeschines.[26] It has, however, come to refer to the resurgence of interest in Greek education and values under the Roman Empire.[27] The forces behind this glorification of Greece are complex, but factors include increased economic prosperity as a result of the Pax Augusta, and the enthusiasm of Hellenophile emperors like Nero and Hadrian.[28] That there was a marked interest in sophistry during this period is not in question, but 'Second Sophistic' can be an unhelpful historiographical heuristic.[29] 'Second', in particular, has the pejorative associations of the sequel. Many of the theories of the 'origins' of the ancient novel have been influenced by the ideology informing this periodisation, and posit the novel as derivative of, or a degraded version of, other genres.[30] Like the novels of Longus and Heliodorus, *Leucippe and Clitophon* is conventionally called 'sophistic' because of its paraded *paideia* and ostentatious use of rhetoric. For Achilles, *eros* (desire) is himself a sophist: 'a self-taught sophist' (1.10.1) and a 'resourceful, improvising sophist' (5.27.4).[31] One of the broad aims of this book is to consider what sort of knowledge is being proffered here: does this sophistic work have anything to teach us?

Leucippe and Clitophon does not appear to have had a great influence on the literature of late antiquity, with the notable exception of Musaeus' poem *Hero and Leander* (c. fifth–sixth century CE),[32] and, to a lesser extent, Nonnus' fifth-century epic *Dionysiaca*.[33] It appealed, however, to Byzantine writers and was imitated in the first Byzantine novel, *Hysmine and Hysminias*, written in the eleventh century by Eustathius Macrembolites.[34] The ancient Greek novel re-entered the critical discourse for the first

---

[26] *Lives of the Sophists* 481.
[27] On the term and the period it denotes, see Anderson (1993), Bowersock (1969) and (1974), Bowie (1974) and (1982), Brunt (1994), Goldhill (2001a), esp. 14–15, Reardon (1971), Schmitz (1997), Swain (1996), esp. 1–6, and Whitmarsh (2001), 41–5.
[28] The best discussion is that of Schmitz (1997).
[29] Whitmarsh gives an excellent discussion of the history and politics of the phrase: Whitmarsh (2001), 41–5.
[30] Useful discussions are found in Stephens and Winkler (1995), 11–18 and Doody (1996).
[31] The idea that *eros* was a sophist has a long literary history. Especially important are episodes in Xenophon's *Cyropaedia* 6.1.41 and Plato's *Symposium* 203d.
[32] On which see Morales (1999).   [33] On which see Shorrock (2001).
[34] On the reception of *Leucippe and Clitophon* in Byzantine writing, see Alexiou (1977); Dyck (1986); Beaton (1988b); Garland (1990); Wilson (1983); Plepelits (1996), 411–14; Beck (1976).

time since antiquity in sixteenth-century France, when Hellenism was very much in vogue on the literary scene.[35] Its complex role in the development of the modern novel and theories of fictionality has been the subject of extensive debate and two important recent studies.[36]

Two sixteenth-century translations (or, more properly, adaptations) of *Leucippe and Clitophon* expurgate and alter the text of Achilles in a way which provides a good illustration of some of the problems that faced, and still face, readers of Achilles Tatius. The first is that of Jacques de Rochemaure in 1556, which was one of the first published translations of Achilles Tatius and followed the Latin text of Annibale della Croce published in 1544.[37] Della Croce's Latin translation and its French adaptations comprise only the last four books of *Leucippe and Clitophon* (i.e. it starts after Leucippe willingly goes to bed with Clitophon and then, thwarted, elopes with him) and it also cuts the scene where Clitophon and Melite make love.[38] For these readers, it seems, the novel can be read as a story which promotes good, honest values if, and only if, various episodes are excised. The emphasis in these adaptations is upon chastity and the union of marriage. Uncertainty about how to understand the moral attitudes of *Leucippe and Clitophon*, and whether or not it has a coherent moral agenda, is at the heart of debates about the extent to which Achilles strains the conventions of the genre or breaks them. It is an issue to which this book repeatedly returns. How to decide what is parenthetical or ornamental,

---

[35] Plazenet (1997), 18. For the influence of the novels on French literary criticism, particularly the *Parnasse reformé* of Gueret (1647), the *Lettre-traité* of Pierre Daniel Huet (circulated in 1666) and two works of Abbé Prévost (*Le Pour et Contre* and *Histoire d'une Grecque moderne*) from the eighteenth century, see Létoublon (1993), ch. 2 and Plazenet (1997). Plazenet provides a comparative study of the reception of the Greek novels in France and England in the sixteenth and seventeenth centuries and her work shows just how complex a process appropriation can be. See also Sandy (1996) and, more generally on Achilles' *Nachleben*, Plepelits (1980), 48–61. The *Editio Princeps* of Achilles Tatius was Heidelberg 1601. It was preceded by Latin translations: Della Croce, 1544 (partial), 1554 (complete), and first translated into French in 1545, then into Italian in 1546, into English in 1597, Spanish in 1617 and German in 1626.

[36] Doody (1996) and Plazenet (1997).

[37] *Les quatre derniers livres des propos amoureux contenans le discours des amours et mariage du seigneur Clitophont et de damoiselle Leucippe*. Lyon, C. Marchant (1556). Reprinted in 1572 and 1573.

[38] It took another decade before della Croce published a translation which included the first half of the novel.

and what then to do with those divisions, are the central concerns of my third chapter, which analyses 'digressions' in the novel.

The second French adaptation that deserves mention is that of J. Hérembert, published in 1599 as *Les advantureuses et fortunées amours de Pandion et d'Yonice*. A considerable amount of Achilles Tatius is closely translated, but the crucial modification is that Hérembert starts the narrative with Clitophon's narration (cutting all the narration of the anonymous traveller who begins Achilles' novel, including his stunning *ekphrasis* of the painting of Europa). It ends with the marriage of Leucippe and Clitophon. This narrative organisation betrays (and solves) another problem commonly identified by Achilles Tatius' readers: what to make of the failure of the narrative to return to the opening frame and the problems of interpretation that this raises. The beginning of the novel, and the various reading strategies that it might demand of its readers, is the subject of the first part of my second chapter and the problem of the ending of the novel is discussed in Chapter 3. Narrative, then, and how one reads it, are one of the two central concerns of this book. The other, to which I shall now turn, is vision and visuality.

Vision and visuality

There is a considerable and sophisticated body of scholarship on ancient visuality and the works of Jaś Elsner, Françoise Frontisi-Ducroux, Simon Goldhill, and Andrew Stewart have been particularly important in showing just how complex and varied this field is.[39] Greek literature has always been

---

[39] Elsner (1995) is fundamental reading; see also Elsner (1992), (1994), (1996b), (1998), (2000a) and (2000b) on a whole variety of aspects of Roman and Graeco-Roman visuality; Frontisi-Ducroux (1994), (1996) on Greek art and vision; Frontisi-Ducroux and Vernant (1997) on Graeco-Roman visuality especially specularity; Goldhill (1994) on the Hellenistic viewer; (1996) on the discontinuities in visuality between the classical city, Hellenistic Alexandria and the Second Sophistic; (1998) on viewing and Xenophon's *Memorabilia*, and (2001b) on vision and cultural identity in Second Sophistic texts; Stewart (1997) on ancient visuality, with a focus on ancient Greek art and the body. Also important are Bartsch (2000) on vision, sexuality and philosophy in classical antiquity; Bryson (1990) and (1994) on classical art and the gaze; Barton (1993) and (2002), and all the essays in Fredrick (2002a) on 'the Roman gaze'; the essays in Richlin (1992b) on pornography in antiquity; Simon (1988) on ancient optics; Bettini (1992) and Steiner (2001) on statues and visuality; Vernant (1998) and (1991), 141–85 on the gaze in Greek myth and ritual; and Zeitlin (1994) on visuality and Euripidean drama.

ocularcentric.[40] The Homeric epics provide abundant attestation to the power of vision. The *Odyssey* is energised by curiosities, revelations, and epiphanies. When the Iliadic hero is repeatedly displayed as 'a wonder to behold', *thauma idesthai*, or when Priam calls Helen, that iconic beauty, to witness with him the great spectacle of war fought over her, 'we the audience become', as Segal says, 'spectators of the power of vision itself'[41]. Helen's lust-lure dazzles throughout Greek literature.[42] The sight of her transfixes and destroys. The vengeful posse in Stesichorus 'at the sight of Helen dropped their stones to the ground'.[43] In Euripides' *Women of Troy*, Hecuba begs Menelaus to kill Helen without looking at her, 'lest she seize you by desire, for she takes the eyes of men, destroys cities, burns houses: such charms does she have' (890–3). This most displaced and displayed female, with her inescapable force-field of desirability, shines through in the portrayals of Leucippe and the heroines of the other Greek novels.[44]

'Among mankind, the ears are less trusting than the eyes', says a character in Herodotus (1.8.3), whose *Histories* are a 'display', *apodeixis* (1.1), of the things which he considers 'worth seeing', *axiotheeton*.[45] This statement of the supremacy of sight is spoken by the Lydian king Candaules (in a tale that the character Clinias will use, in a highly partial interpretation, as an illustration of the evils, for men, of marriage in the first book of *Leucippe and Clitophon* (1.8.5)). 'Enamoured of his own wife' and thinking her 'the most beautiful woman in the world' (1.8) Candaules coerces his friend Gyges to see his wife naked. Gyges is horrified by his own (unwilling) voyeurism ('There are long established truths for us to learn from, and one of them is that everyone should look to his own'); it offends against *nomos* and *aidos*. The transgression is noticed by Candaules' wife who insists that Gyges murder her husband ('on the very spot where he showed me to you naked') and marry her, thereby excising a corrupt king and restoring the

---

[40] Ocularcentrism (also spelt oculocentrism) is a term coined by Jay to refer to the hegemony of vision in modernity: Jay (1988) and (1993).
[41] Segal (1995), 185. See also Prier (1989), 25–117.
[42] The best discussion is Austin (1994).   [43] Stesichorus, frg. 201 *PMG*.
[44] On Helen and Callirhoe, see Laplace (1980b).
[45] On Herodotus and vision see in particular Hartog (1988).

stability of her *oikos*.[46] This programmatic tale[47] is constructed through and against the many mythological accounts which tell of visual infringements, such as Teiresias catching sight of Athena bathing and being struck blind as a punishment;[48] and Actaeon glimpsing Artemis naked and being ripped to pieces by his own hounds as a result.[49] All these tales are ways of thinking about and controlling scopic protocols.

Visual relations – central to the works of these two great storytellers, Homer and Herodotus – play a privileged role throughout Greek literature and, as we shall see, Achilles Tatius' novel is conscious of its place in a long literary and mythic tradition of thinking about sight. Moreover, although *Leucippe and Clitophon*'s exclusion of Rome and Latin literature is as conspicuous as its insistent reference to Greek literature, the novel is none the less a product of the Roman Empire. Rome, and its visual operations, necessarily forms part of the cultural and historical contexts of Achilles, even though our inability precisely to pinpoint a specific historical moment for this author frustrates any attempt to site him with precision. I shall return to particular Roman genres, especially the mime and *controversiae*, during the course of the book; suffice it to note for now that *Leucippe and Clitophon* was written and first read in a supremely spectacular society. It is the product of a visually voracious and violent world, in which there was a heightened, sometimes paranoid, awareness of the pleasures and dangers of spectatorial relations.[50]

The novel is, therefore, grounded in both a Greek literary tradition of writing about vision and in contemporary Roman visual

---

[46] There is a papyrus fragment of a fourth- or third-century BCE tragedy on this theme, which includes a speech by the queen herself (called Nysia in later sources): P. Oxy 2382; *TGF* no. 664 (pp. 248–51), translated and discussed in Page (1951). See Hall (1989), 65 with n. 37. Obviously, staging the myth as a drama in which the queen is named and speaks for herself, involves very different framing and focalisation from that in Herodotus' version.

[47] The Candaules episode is the first episode to be narrated in detail and sets in motion the chain of obligation and revenge which runs through the text.

[48] As told in Callimachus' Hymn 5. This poem is very much concerned with vision, with how we see gods, and whether or not we *choose* to see, as Hunter (1992) discusses.

[49] Heath (1992) discusses the full range of sources for this myth. On the various penalties for mortals who look upon goddesses, see Buxton (1980) and further Vernant (1991), 27–49 and Steiner (1995).

[50] See especially Bartsch (1994); Barton (1993) and (2002); Boyle (2003), 59–67; Elsner (1998); Fredrick (2003a) and Gunderson (2003).

practices. This is a particularly exciting juncture, and, before I move on to a close examination of visuality in Achilles, I want first to look more closely at how vision was being illustrated, written, and thought about at the time when the novel was first written and read. In order to help negotiate this vast field, I have chosen to focus my discussion around (but not limit it to) three representations of vision: a work of art, a fragment from an intellectual discussion, and a poem. I have not selected these because they are particularly privileged representations, rather my broad aim is to show what sorts of things were being thought and written about vision in the early empire, and thus to give a little more substance to the contextualisation of Achilles. This should enable us to set down some axioms of visuality in Graeco-Roman imperial culture and also to trace some important continuities and differences between ancient and modern theories and representations of the gaze.

The Antioch mosaic and configurations of vision

My first representation is almost certainly one of the few visual illustrations of a scene from a novel which survive from antiquity. It is a domestic floor mosaic found in Daphne, a region of Antioch-on-the-Orontes in Syria, and is thought to date to about 200 CE (see frontispiece, page iv).[51] It depicts a man reclining on a couch in a bedroom. In his right hand he is holding outstretched a framed picture or pinax of a portrait. To the right stands a young woman who offers him a goblet. The mosaic is commonly thought to illustrate a lost episode from the Ninus romance, though this identification is not certain.[52] However, it is most likely an illustration from a novel, which seemed to be popular with the

---

[51] For a detailed description of the mosaic, see Levi (1944). See also Maehler (1976) and the excellent discussion of Quet (1992).
[52] This identification is based on the resemblance of this mosaic to another, found at Iskenderun (and now in the museum of Antakaria), which depicts a seated man holding a portrait under the inscription 'Ninus'. The similarity between the two mosaics has led to the conclusion that the one at Antioch also illustrates Ninus: see Quet (1992), 128–9. It was originally thought that the Iskenderun mosaic illustrated the early legend of Ninus and Semiramis, from which the novel fragments differ considerably: see Perry (1967), 153–66; Sandy (1989), 803–4.

householder, who had another depicting the Parthenope and Metiochus novel.[53]

The image is an arresting example of the thematisation of the gaze that so fascinates the Greek and Roman novelists. The extant Greek erotic novels, and the Latin novels of Petronius and Apuleius, are all interested in the power of sight. They feature breathtaking spectacles, characters spying at doors, descriptions of love at first sight, and discourses on the appearance and mechanics of the eye.[54] Achilles Tatius is the most eye-intense of all of the novelists, but Heliodorus boasts the most extraordinary description of optical phenomena in Calasiris' explanation of the Evil Eye.[55] Chariton stages a scene where the heroine has a debate between herself, her unborn child and her absent husband, whose presence is conjured when she looks at a picture of him. Perhaps something of this kind is happening in the mosaic image.

The central dynamic of the mosaic is not the man, nor the woman, nor the portrait, but the relations between the three, relations which are constructed by an interplay of looks staged within the image. The interaction of gazes generated between the viewers in the mosaic is complex and unstable. Both the man's and the woman's arm are extended in the same direction, gestures which operate as internal focalisers and direct the trajectory of the spectator's eye towards the portrait. In turn, the portrait's status as an object to be looked at is intensified. The man is in a privileged position of spectatorship, gazing with concentration upon the image in his possession. The impression is created by his posture and by the fact that,

---

[53] It has been suggested that the mosaics in fact depict scenes from mimes, but the arguments are inconclusive: cf. Bowie (1994), 448–9. Illustrations of mimes typically include theatrical paraphernalia, which these do not. Moreover, as Doody reminds us, at stake in the identification of the mosaics is the confirmation (or not) of certain theories of the readership and nature of the ancient novel: 'Any discussion of mosaic illustration is wrapped up in the contest over "popularity". If the novels were *too* popular, that militates against their true classicism', Doody (1996), 490, n. 10 *contra* Bowie (1994), 453–9. Like the readership of the novels, it is a political issue.

[54] There are some perceptive, though undeveloped, insights on vision in the novels in Wolff (1912) and Heiserman (1977). On vision in Petronius and Apuleius, see Slater (1997). On Petronius, see Sullivan (1968) with the comments of Gill (1973), and Elsner (1993). On vision in Apuleius, see Too (1996) and Slater (1998). On display in Chariton, see Elsom (1992) and Hunter (1994).

[55] *Aeth.* 3.7–9, an account very similar to one found in Plutarch (*Mor.* 680C–83B); see Dickie (1991) and Goldhill (2001b), 170–2.

in the moment captured by the mosaic, the entrance of the woman with the cup does not distract his gaze. Her gaze is catoptric, mirroring that of the spectator of the mosaic who also observes the man and his scrutiny. Indeed, there is a relay of catoptric relations; the spectator of the mosaic beholds the woman looking at the man looking at the figure in the portrait. Thus the viewer in the mosaic becomes the viewed and as the man becomes the object of our look, his position as subject and master of the gaze is displaced.

At the same time as we behold the character in the mosaic looking at the picture, we are made aware of ourselves as viewers similarly poised in the act of viewing. This *mise-en-abîme* effect operates to accentuate the spectator's awareness of his or her role as spectator and invites a self-conscious reflection upon the act of viewing.[56] This prompts a consciousness of what Claude Gandelman describes as 'the dialectic of seeing, which always implies a being-seen relationship'.[57] All visual works of art declare to their spectators: 'I am watching you watching me.'[58] Visual images can act like mirrors, reflecting an awareness that they are seen and in turn looking back at the spectator. One viewer of the Antioch mosaic suggests that the pinax does not frame a painted image, but instead consists of a mirror that reflects the likeness of the reclining man.[59] On this reading, the viewing relations become literally as well as figuratively catoptric. Now the man is both beholder and beheld, as he views himself in the act of viewing and, in a dizzying relay of looks, the spectator of the mosaic views him viewing himself viewing. The object of his look is a kind of picture, as it frames his reflected image like a portrait, but it has the power actively to return his gaze. Like the painting in Gandelman's formulation, the mirror declares: 'If you look at me I look at you too' ("Αν μ'ἐσίδῃς, καὶ ἐγὼ σέ).[60]

Like the novels, the mosaic is theatrical and stages relations between viewers. The bedroom setting also reflects another aspect of the novels: their concern with intimacy and privacy. There have been two main interpretations of the mosaic. The first, which takes the man to be holding a picture, is that it represents a scene of desire,

---

[56] On this device, see Steiner (1988), 43–55.   [57] Gandelman (1991), 43.
[58] Gandelman (1991), 48.   [59] Downey (1941).
[60] *Pal. Anth.* Epigram 56: Εἰς εἴσοπτρον.

perhaps incipient desire, or desire for an absent beloved.[61] The second, which understands the object to be a mirror, reads the mosaic as representing a scene of philosophical reflection.[62] In general, the mirror was considered to be a feminine object that was thought to feminise men who used it.[63] However, it also had a philosophical construction as an instrument for acquiring self-knowledge.[64] In response to the taunt 'You look in a mirror!', Apuleius fired back, 'A philosopher should!'[65] Seneca tells us mirrors were invented *ut homo se nosset* ('so that man should know himself') and Socrates was reputed by an imperial source to have recommended its use to his disciples.[66] The connection between vision, mirroring and self-knowledge is most dramatically illustrated in the Platonic dialogue, *Alcibiades 1*. This dialogue, thought to be one of Plato's earliest works, but possibly spurious, ranges widely, exploring the natures of justice, leadership and statecraft.[67] In the third section (128–35) it deals with the question of how the Delphic maxim, 'Know Thyself', is to be interpreted:

SOCRATES: I rather think that there are not many illustrations of it to be found, but only in the case of sight.
ALCIBIADES: What do you mean by that?
SOCRATES: Consider in your turn: suppose that, instead of speaking to a man, it said to the eye of one of us, as a piece of advice – 'See Thyself' – how should we comprehend the meaning of this admonition? Would it not be, that the eye should look at something in looking at which it would see itself?
ALCIBIADES: Clearly . . .   (132C–D)

This turns out to be 'mirrors and things like them'. This quite extraordinary exegesis of the Delphic maxim – one of the most famous tenets in Greek thought and at the heart of the philosophical project – takes as its paradigm for self-knowledge the faculty of

---

[61] Hägg (1983), 19.   [62] Downey (1941).
[63] Frontisi-Ducroux and Vernant (1997), 61. Seneca's account of Hostius Quadra's misuse of mirrors is perhaps the most lurid cautionary tale of the danger mirrors pose to men (*NQ* 1.12, 2–5): cf. Frontisi-Ducroux and Vernant (1997), 177–81 and *passim* on the symbolic function of the mirror as a means of thinking about the relationship between the sexes; Myerowitz (1992) and Bartsch (2000) *passim* and 88, n. 7 for further bibliography.
[64] Frontisi-Ducroux and Vernant (1997) ch. 8; McCarty (1989); Bartsch (2000).
[65] *Apology* 15. For Apuleius' defence of the mirror see *Apology* 13–16 and Too (1996).
[66] Diogenes Laertius, *Lives of the Philosophers* 2.33.
[67] For general discussion of the dialogue see the introduction to Denyer (2001).

sight: *opsis*. The mirror will enable the eye to see itself, just as philosophical dialectic will reflect the soul to itself.[68]

Sight is a privileged sense not just here, but throughout Plato's work. It is worth pausing for a moment to consider the significance of vision in Platonic thought and other philosophical schools, not least because their constructions of visuality are of some importance in Achilles Tatius. Achilles was writing at or around the time of Ptolemy, 'the greatest optician of antiquity'.[69] Ptolemy, writing in Alexandria between 146 and c. 170 CE, was responsible for some major advances in the science of optics, which were massively influential on medieval and later optics through the work of ibn al-Haytham.[70] His work *Optics* survives only in fragmentary form and is hopelessly refracted: it is a Latin translation of an Arabic translation of the Greek original. However, from Albert Lejeune's reconstruction of the work and from other testimonia, we can tell that Ptolemy analysed the physical, physiological and psychological elements of vision, building primarily on Euclid's mathematical analysis of vision.[71] He was also influenced by Stoic theories of vision. Stoicism was the philosophical *koine* of the early empire.[72] Stoic concepts of vision, so far as we can reconstruct a basic picture from the fragmentary evidence, are materialist.[73] In essence, a visual effluence (*pneuma*), or perhaps more specifically fire, radiates from the eyes and imposes on the air (providing it is illuminated) a suitably tensioned cone with its apex at the eye. The cone senses distant objects by touch and transmits the data back to the eye, in a way which they compare to feeling distant objects with a rod. In essence, Ptolemy attributed sight to a *pneuma* that flowed conically from the eye of the viewer and interacted with the colour of the object which was viewed, aided by a source of light such as the sun. The polymath Galen (c. 129–c. 199 CE) was also concerned with the anatomy and physiology of the eye and

---

[68] On *Alcibiades* 1 and self-knowledge see Soulez-Luccioni (1974).
[69] Lindberg (1976), 15. [70] Lejeune (1948) and (1989); Lindberg (1976).
[71] Euclid's *Optics* (third century BCE), the first extant collection of optical theories, was commented upon and extended by Pappus of Alexandria (early fourth century CE); cf. Simon (1988), 129–85; Lejeune (1989).
[72] Perkins (1995), 77–103.
[73] *SVF* 2.866 (*Aet.* 4.15.3) and *SVF* 2.867 (Diog. Laert. 7.157) There is little secondary literature on the subject. I am grateful to David Sedley and James Warren for clarification of the material here.

blended elements of Aristotelian and Stoic theories of vision.[74] In his work *On the Opinions of Hippocrates and Plato* he argues that vision involves the extension of a visual flux (*pneuma*) sent from the brain, through the optic nerves, through the eye of the observer to the object to be viewed by means of the air which was itself, he contended, an instrument of vision.[75]

There is much that could be said about these fascinating theories, but there are three observations of concern to me here. The first is simply to note that in Achilles Tatius' time the eye was a hot topic. The novelist's interest in the mechanics of vision is symptomatic of his period; he is in tune with the *Zeitgeist*. The second point I wish to make is that visual theory in the Roman Empire is strikingly syncretistic. Both Ptolemy and Galen blend and fuse previous theories of vision. As I shall discuss later, it is too fast a leap to read a description of vision in Achilles Tatius and assume it must be Platonic or Stoic; optical theory at this time is complex and hybrid. My third point is that optical theory constructs vision as corporeal and haptic. Viewing is an active, bodily encounter. The optics of the Stoics, and of Ptolemy and Galen, involve extramission, where rays issue forth from the eye of the viewer and, directly or indirectly, come into contact with the thing that is viewed. Extramission and intromission (where rays emanate from the object and flow into the eye) are processes central to ancient optics. The atomists, Leucippus, Democritus, Epicurus and Lucretius (with different variations) all advocated a theory of intromission, where tiny particles, or corpuscles (*eidola* or *simulacra*), stream off objects and enter into the eye.[76] As Lindberg comments: 'Vision, then, is reduced to a species of touch.'[77]

Plato's theory of vision as outlined in the *Timaeus* suggests that the eye contains a stream of fire which issues forth and coalesces with sunlight. Vision is produced when this visual current (*tes opsis rheuma*) mixed with the daylight, meets an emanation from the object which it is viewing and is able to transmit these

---

[74] Simon (1988), 35.   [75] Cf. Meyering (1989), 26; Siegel (1970), Simon (1988), 33–5.
[76] Epicurus' *Letter to Herodotus* (Sections 46–53 = passage 15A in L&S); Lucretius, *De Rerum Natura* book 4. Cf Lindberg (1976), 2–3; von Fritz (1953), Simon (1988), 36–41, Taylor (1999).
[77] Lindberg (1976), 3.

impressions to the body and into the soul of the viewer.[78] This account combines the two theories of intromission and extramission and, like the theories of the atomists, is tactile. Aristotle, who produced the first systematic theory of vision, rejected extramission and the idea that vision is analogous to touch. His account of the 'visual medium' in *De Sensu*, in which the viewing eye passively receives light, is much more abstract and detached than most other ancient theories of optics.[79] Vision, 'the sharpest of the senses',[80] is a supreme metaphor for Plato, despite the fact that in the *Protagoras* and *Theaetetus* he shows that basing knowledge on sense-perception is a fallacy. Famously, in the parable of the cave in the *Republic*, the ascent of the soul to acquire knowledge in the luminous realm of the Forms is couched in terms of moving from blindness to sight.[81] But the most important Platonic description of vision, for our purposes, is an extraordinary account of intromission that connects it to desire, mirroring and self-knowledge – the subjects which arose in relation to the Antioch mosaic. Here Socrates describes what happens when the lover and his beloved are aroused by physical contact at the gymnasium and other events:

Then it is that the springs of that stream which Zeus as lover of Ganymede named 'desire' flow in abundance upon the lover, some sinking within him, and so flowing off outside him as he brims over; and as a breath of wind or an echo rebounds from smooth hard surfaces and returns to the source from which it issued, so the stream of beauty passes back into its possessor through his eyes, which is its natural route to the soul; arriving there and setting him all of a flutter, it waters the passages of the feathers and causes the wings to grow, and fills the soul of the loved one in his turn with love. So he is in love, but with what, he does not know; and he neither knows what has happened to him, nor can he even say what it is, but like a man who has caught an eye-disease from someone he can give no account of it, and is unaware that he is seeing himself in his lover as if in a mirror. (*Phaedrus* 255c–d)[82]

---

[78] Possibly adapting a theory of ocular fire by Empedocles; cf. Lindberg (1976), 4. It is still a matter for debate whether what is described in Empedocles DK 31B84 is a mechanism of extramission, as Aristotle interpreted it to be. Theophrastus, on the other hand, understood the visual process described by Empedocles to be located on the surface of the eyeball, a position defended by Sedley (1992). Part of the difficulty lies in whether *kore* here denotes the iris of the eye or the whole eyeball, as it can mean either.
[79] See also *De Anima* 2.7.418b and Johansen (1997).   [80] *Phaedrus* 250d.
[81] Book 7 514a–521c. See also *Republic* 9 586a; *Phaedo* 109b–110.
[82] The translation is that of C. J. Rowe in his Aris and Phillips edition.

This splendid and sumptuous description of erotic arousal is an imaginative elaboration of the commonplace that sexual desire was primarily a visual impulse. Ὁρᾶν (to see) and ἐρᾶν (to desire) were closely associated, both linguistically and conceptually.[83] However, Plato's account is unusual in that it involves the beloved seeing an image of his own beauty *mirrored* in the eyes of his lover. The effluences and eroticised language recall an earlier description of what happens to the soul when it sees divine beauty:

> After he has seen him, the expected change comes over him following the shuddering – sweating and a high fever; for he is warmed by the reception of the effluence of beauty through his eyes, which is the natural nourishment of his plumage, and with that warmth there is a melting of the parts around its base, which have long since become hard and closed up, so preventing it from sprouting, and with the incoming stream of nourishment the quills of the feathers swell and set to growing from their roots under the whole form of the soul; for formerly the whole of it was winged. (251a–c)

We shall return to the *Phaedrus* frequently during the course of this book, as it is a major intertext for Achilles Tatius. Suffice it to note for now the strong and important connection between erotics, viewing and the philosophical quest for self-knowledge. The sight of the Form is at the same time a source of desire and of understanding of the soul itself. The ambiguity of the Antioch mosaic – whether or not it is a scene of erotic or philosophical reflection – is an ambiguity that is built into ancient visuality. Sight is a source of desire *and* of self-knowledge; both of which, as we shall see, play a role in *Leucippe and Clitophon*.

Plutarch On Love, *Lucian* On the Hall, *and the objectivity of* opsis

My second representation of contemporary visuality takes a philosophical discussion of *eros* as its starting point. It is an extract from Plutarch's work *On Love*, of which only a few fragments survive (and which is not to be confused with his *Amatorius*). Here Plutarch

---

[83] Hence the (fallacious) etymology of *eros* proposed in the *Cratylus*: '*Eros* is so called because it flows in (*esrei*) from without and this flowing is not inherent in him who has it, but is introduced through the eyes' (420b) – recognisably an image of intromission. On *eros* and vision see Calame (1992); Cline (1972); Ogle (1920); Walker (1992).

is taking issue with a passage from one of Menander's plays (which unfortunately is also lost to us). He prefaces his discussion by commenting that it is *eros* which is the unifying factor in all Menander's plays; *eros* which, comments Plutarch (using Stoic terminology), 'pervades them like a universal spirit', ὡς πνεῦμα κοινὸν διαπεφοιτηκώς.[84] He considers Menander a particular devotee of *eros*, 'since he has also talked about the passion quite philosophically', ἐπεὶ καὶ λελάληκε περὶ τοῦ πάθους φιλοσοφώτερον. He then quotes the following extract:

> Of what are they the slaves?
> Their eyes? What nonsense! All men would then love
> The same girl, since sight's judgement is impartial.
> Some pleasure then in her company draws men
> To love? Then why does one, enjoying her company,
> Come off untouched and ridicule her charms,
> And yet another's lost? No, this disease
> Comes when the soul is ready, and a man,
> Struck at the critical time, is wounded to the quick.[85]

At stake here is the subjectivity or objectivity of sight, *opsis*. According to the passage from Menander (we do not know which character is speaking), *opsis* is equal; an objective faculty. If sight does not allow for discrimination, then all men would see in the same way. It follows that all men would be attracted to the same woman, for if sight is objective, then aesthetic judgement must also be standardised. As this is not the case, and men are not all attracted to the same woman, the speaker rejects the claim that sight is the impetus for love (any more, he says, than 'enjoying her company' is). This might raise some interesting questions about the agency of *the viewer* in the viewing process. If *opsis* is capable of *krisis*, where does the person as viewing subject fit in? However, this is not Plutarch's objection; he takes issue with the claim that sight is impartial: 'The proof here given has little weight, or is even false. It is not true that sight has impartial judgement any more than taste (τὸ γεύεσθαι) does.' His reasoning: 'one man's sight

---

[84] Cf. Ovid on Menander: *fabula iucundi nulla est sine amore Menandri* (*Tristia* 2.369).
[85] Menander, frg. 568 = K–A 791), surviving in Plutarch's *On Love*, cited in Stobaeus 4.20.34. Not in Lamprias' Catalogue. The last line and a half of the Menander are also quoted in Plutarch's *Amatorius*, 763b.

and one hearer's hearing is more developed by nature (*phusis*) and more trained by art (*techne*) to recognise beauty than another's'. He gives as examples the hearing of the musician who can deal with harmonies and melodies better and the sight of the painter who is concerned with shapes and forms. Painters are professional viewers and therefore are better trained to appreciate beauty than ordinary men. This is supported by an anecdote:

> For example, there is a story that when some man with no professional knowledge of art told Nicomachus that he had not thought Zeuxis's Helen beautiful, the painter replied: 'Take my eyes, and she will seem like a goddess.'

There can be few more striking ways to make someone see things 'from your point of view' than literally to offer them your eyes, Graiae-like. But what this illustrates is that for Plutarch, sight is not impartial or objective; it is biologically and culturally determined.

This chimes with Diogenes Laertius' account of Stoic *phantasia*: 'some [of their impressions – *phantasiai*] are expert, others are not: at all events an image is viewed in a totally different way by someone who is trained and by someone who is untrained'.[86] But it is in Lucian's *On the Hall*, a brilliant and comic meditation on viewing and *ekphrasis* (the verbal depiction of what is viewed), that the idea is most fully articulated.[87] The narrator stresses the differences in viewing between the ordinary and the cultured man:

> There is not the same law about looking at sights for ordinary people and for educated people. No, for the ordinary man the usual thing is enough, just to see, and to look round about, and to cast his eyes around and peer up at the ceiling and wave his hand, and to take pleasure silently because of his fear of not being able to say anything worthy of the things being looked at. But when a man looks with education at beautiful things, he will not be content, I am sure, to harvest their delight through sight alone, and will not endure being a dumb spectator of their beauty, but will try as hard as he can to linger there and reciprocate the sight with speech. (2)

These differences are not arbitrary; there is a law or code (νόμος) about things which are seen (περὶ τὰ θεάματα). Here the crucial

---

[86] *Lives and Opinions of Eminent Philosophers* 7.51.
[87] See Goldhill (2001b), 160–7 and Newby (2002) who reconstructs the viewers' experiences as they progress around the hall, and discusses how visuality in *De Domo* and in Philostratus' *Imagines* provides models that usefully reflect upon visual dynamics in the Spada reliefs.

factor differentiating ways of seeing is *paideia*, 'education' or 'culture', which was 'the central cultural capital of Greek society under Roman rule'.[88] *Paideia* sorted the men from the boys,[89] the elite from the ordinary,[90] the Greeks from the non-Greeks,[91] and – here – the critics from the gawpers. Sorting the Greeks from the non-Greeks is how the cultured gaze functions later in the work. The Arsacids are distinguished from (presumably) Greeks, because, says Lucian, the barbarians look for signs of wealth in their displays, whereas the Greeks appreciate beauty. Lucian comments:

The beauty of this house has nothing to do with barbarian eyes, Persian hypocrisy, or regal boasting (οὐ κατὰ βαρβαρικούς τινας ὀφθαλμοὺς οὐδὲ κατὰ Περσικὴν ἀλαζονείαν ἢ βασιλικὴν μεγαλαυχίαν). Instead of a poor man, it needs a cultured spectator (εὐφυοῦς θεατοῦ), for whom the judgement is not in the sight (μὴ ἐν τῇ ὄψει ἡ κρίσις), but a certain reasoned opinion (λογισμός) also accompanies what is looked at. (6)

This can function as a gloss on Plutarch's challenge to Menander. Plutarch argued that *opsis* does not have equal judgement (*krisis*); it is more developed in some than in others. For Lucian's speaker, to rely on the judgement (*krisis*) of *opsis* alone is in itself a sign of impoverishment. It is the application of thought or logic (*logismos*) to what is seen that makes for a cultivated (and Greek) spectator. In these texts, what and how a person sees is a function of who they are. As Anthony Synnott writes, 'Sight is individually subjective and culturally relative. What we see and do not see, and how we define what we see, the meanings we impose on our visual reality, reflect our personal values and interests as well as our cultural norms.'[92] It is a cultural norm that barbarians behave differently to Greeks, and Lucian affirms this when he represents them viewing differently.

Ways of seeing are determined not just by ethnicity, status and education, but by all aspects of a person's identity,

---

[88] Whitmarsh (2001), 90–129. See also Bowersock (1969), 21–3; Bowie (1982), 30–2; Gleason (1995), 159–68; Morgan (1998). On Longus and *paideia* see Hunter (1983) *passim*; Swain (1996), 115–16.
[89] Gleason (1995) on *paideia* as a mark of virility; Whitmarsh (2001), 109–15.
[90] Bowersock (1969); Morgan (1998), Schmitz (1997), 39–66.
[91] Notoriously, Favorinus the Gaul 'became Greek' through becoming *pepaideumenos*; see Gleason (1995).
[92] Synnott (1993), 219; Whitmarsh (2001), 116–29.

including mortality, gender and sexuality. Gods are characteristically omnivoyent, 'for we ascribe to the gods the power of seeing everything' (ἅπαντα γὰρ ἀποδίδομεν τοῖς θεοῖς ὁρᾶν) writes Aristotle.[93] Likewise, it is a mark of their mortality that humans cannot see gods, when they appear in their true form. For men, glimpsing a goddess naked results in severe punishment, most commonly involving loss of eyesight, madness and death. Policing the scopic is one means by which the fundamental boundaries between mortals and immortals are demarcated and regulated.

The different positions in the scopic order are culturally determined, but throughout antiquity were often couched in, and given authority by, the discourse of science, or pseudo-science. Aristotle writes that a woman looking into a mirror while menstruating could make its clean surface 'bloody dark, like a cloud' because the menstrual blood passed through her eyes onto the mirror.[94] This 'observation' exemplifies the close and determining relationship between biology and ways of seeing.[95] Eyes were physiognomic markers and how one looked was an index to identity.[96] The gaze, therefore, had to be strictly controlled. Maidens and ashamed men lowered their gaze, a sign of *aidos*. As Jan Bremmer writes: 'as rolling eyes denoted the madman and those in despair, squinting eyes treacherous persons, and looking around the passive homosexual, we may safely assume that a "proper" male looked steadfastly at the world'.[97] Indeed, for one writer, 'males with languishing

---

[93] Aristotle, *Poetics* 1454b. On the eyes of the gods see Detienne and Vernant (1978), 101; Steiner (2001), 168–72.

[94] Aristotle, *On Dreams* 459b–460a. Similar accounts are found in Pliny, *NH* 7.15.64; 28.79 and Columella, *On Agriculture* 11.3.64; cf. Frontisi-Ducroux and Vernant (1997), 147–54.

[95] Galen uses vision as a metaphor with which to explain a woman's reproductive organs. He argues that a woman's reproductive organs are like a man's but, because they are internalised, work less effectively. They are like the eyes of the mole, which are similarly undeveloped and function poorly; see Harvey (1992), 88; Laqueur (1986), 5.

[96] Polemo devoted a third of his physiognomical treatise to the importance of the eye; cf. Gleason (1995), 32.

[97] Bremmer (1991), 23 and for further references to ancient sources, 32–3 nn. 24 and 25. See also Gleason (1995), ch. 3. The extent to which we can discern distinctive homoerotic and lesbian gazes from our extant material is the subject of considerable debate. DeJean (1987) and Stehle (1990) argue for Sappho's disruption of the scopic economy. Hubbard (2002) from his analysis of Pindar's Theoxenus poem (frg. 123 S-M) argues not only that scopic relations between men and boys were configured differently to those between men and women, but also that the visual interactions in the poem indicate that paederasty is a more reciprocal and less objectifying relationship than is typically understood.

eyes and women with militant gaze' (τις ἄρρην ἔβλεψεν ὑγρὸν καὶ γυναῖκες γοργὸν προσεῖδον) are on a par with 'beardless men and bearded women' (ἄνδρες μὴν ἀγένειοι καὶ γενειάσκουσι γυναῖκες).[98] However, social identity and scopic order operate in a dialectical relation; each informs the other. Ways of seeing are not merely indicative of social roles, but actively define them; influencing and systematising cultural constructions of self and other. The gaze is thus, to extend Teresa de Lauretis' formulation, a technology of social position, an organising principle of, most importantly, gender and ethnicity.[99]

Philostratus, Epistle 26 and the gendered gaze

My third and final text, one of Philostratus' *Erotic Epistles*, presents a stark example of the gaze as a technology of gender:

> You bid me not to look and I bid you not to let yourself be seen (Κελεύεις μοι μὴ βλέπειν κἀγὼ σοὶ μὴ βλέπεσθαι). Who is the lawgiver (νομοθέτης) who orders this, and who that? If neither act is prohibited, don't deprive yourself of distinction for display nor me of the authority to enjoy (μήτε σεαυτὴν ἀφαιροῦ τῆς ἐς ἐπίδειξιν εὐδοκιμήσεως μήτε ἐμὲ τῆς ἐς τέρψιν ἐξουσίας). A fountain does not say, 'Don't drink', nor does fruit say, 'Don't take'; nor a meadow, 'Don't come near.' Do you too, woman, observe nature's laws and put a stop to my thirsting.[100] (Letter 26)

The letter is written in response to an unnamed woman who has asked its author not to look at her. We are given no insight into her reasons, but her discomfort constitutes an interesting counterpoint to the opinions of those (like Achilles' character Clinias)[101] who expect women to appreciate the visual attentions of men. His brusque retort is that if she does not like him looking, she should

---

[98] Aristides Quintilianus, *De Musica* 2.8.30. This treatise on music, possibly written in the third or fourth century CE, contains a fascinating discussion of 'male' and 'female' styles.

[99] De Lauretis (1987). In her book *Technologies of Gender*, de Lauretis discusses the cinema and how its scopic regime constitutes gendered subjects of vision. bell hooks has demonstrated how the gaze has functioned as a technology of race and how policing the scopic has contributed to racism throughout Western history. She argues that black people must now reclaim the gaze and look 'against the grain': hooks (1992), 116 and 126.

[100] Several manuscripts continue the line: ὁδοιπόρον, ὃν τὸ σὸν ἄστρον ἀπώλεσεν so the last phrase would read 'quench the thirst of a wayfarer whom your star has parched'. I find this rendition less attractive, but it would not alter my line of argument.

[101] See below 152–65.

not be looked at (implying that she lets herself be seen). This brief interchange quickly establishes the viewing relationship with the man as viewing subject and the woman as viewed object. The writer then makes an appeal to cultural codes of behaviour; is there anyone who forbids looking or being looked at? An answer to the contrary is tacitly understood; there is no one laying down the law about viewing, and the writer urges the woman not to deprive both of them of the benefits of this activity. For the woman, this involves distinction for exhibiting herself whereas the man gains the authority to enjoy (*exousia* here tropes this as a social and political right). The terms of the viewing contract are clearly gendered. There is no mention of there being any *pleasure* to be gained for the woman, but pleasure, more pointedly the pleasure in feeling powerful, is precisely the reason why the man looks at her. Instead, the woman can expect renown for her exhibition, a dubious dividend, since display is more likely to compromise a woman's reputation[102] and, in any case, we already know that exposure is the last thing she desires, possibly for that very reason.

The woman's resistance is then compared to the imagined refusals of a series of anthropomorphised inanimate objects. Despite the textual uncertainty of the final line, the meaning is apparent. It is inconceivable for fountains, fruit and meadows to make such refusals and so it should be for a woman to refuse to be looked at. It is, of course, a dishonest argument. The reason a fountain doesn't say, 'Don't drink' is that fountains cannot speak, nor can fruit or meadows. Nor, incidentally, can they look. These analogies are very telling about the scopic economy envisaged by Philostratus in this letter. Gazing at a woman is sited in paradigmatic relation to drinking, plucking fruit and invading territory. This is reinforced by the suggestion that by revealing herself the woman will quench the writer's thirst, just like drinking at a fountain. This gaze is consumptive, possessive and intrusive. The imagery also emphasises the eroticism inherent in viewing. Drinking from fountains is a symbol of desire

---

[102] See e.g. the anecdote told about Pythagoras' wife Theano, who unwittingly exposed her arm in public and when complimented upon it, retorts 'Not public property!' 'The arm of a virtuous woman', concurs Plutarch, 'should not be public property': Plut. *Mor.* 142D.

common in Philostratus and other writers[103] and plucking fruit has a long tradition in amatory literature.[104] Λειμών has clear erotic connotations; it frequently symbolises the female (usually virginal) body,[105] and often represents female genitalia in particular. The analogies reduce the woman to the status of object, inanimate, passive and inherently desirable. More pointedly, it is a fountain's 'purpose' to be drunk from, an apple's 'function' to be eaten, a meadow's *raison d'être* to be walked upon. By analogy, therefore, it is a woman's purpose, function and *raison d'être* to be put on display. That is, runs the logic, what she is *there for*. These are the laws (τοῖς νόμοις), the laws, it is implied, somewhat paradoxically, of nature, and with these comparisons the writer naturalises the male gaze.

I have three points to make before moving on to some more general concluding remarks about these representations of visuality. First, this letter shows an awareness of the gendered investments viewer and viewed make in the gaze. The benefits and pleasures afforded by the viewing relationship are subject to challenge and scrutiny. This finds striking precedence in an episode in an earlier work, the third book of Xenophon's *Memorabilia*.[106] Socrates has already visited luminaries of several professions, including the painter Parrhasius, the sculptor Cleiton and the armourer Pistias, with whom he discussed various aspects of the ethics and lures of representation.[107] These exchanges frame his next encounter which is with an artist's *model*, a beautiful woman called Theodote. She is a hetaira, God's Gift (to men). Socrates is told that artists visit her to paint her portrait and that her beauty is too great to be put

---

[103] In the erotic setting of Clitophon's garden a fountain bubbles up (1.15.1), see also Walker (1992), 139 on the metaphor of the fountain in Philostratus, Epistle 32: 'In employing the metaphor of the fountain, the passage [in Philostratus] appeals to the archaic notion of beauty as a physical substance, a liquid that is "poured out" from the body or eye of the beloved, inspiring desire in those who see'; and Walker (1992), 146 n. 32 on the 'visual stream' (πηγή) of beauty in Plato's *Phaedrus* 255c1–3.
[104] For example, Daphnis plucks the apple for Chloe at Longus 3.33.4–34, echoing Sappho, frg.105a LP on which see Hunter (1983), 73–6 and 122, n. 4 for further bibliography; Carson (1986), 87–90 on Longus and 26–9 on Sappho.
[105] As in the episode where Leucippe is compared to the meadow in Achilles Tatius 1.15–19, (especially 1.19.1). On meadows more generally see Littlewood (1977).
[106] See Goldhill (1998) which analyses this episode and sites the passage in its social and political contexts.
[107] On which see Rouveret (1989), 15; Steiner (2001), 33–5.

INTRODUCTION

into words (an ironic dig at, and *topos* of, *ekphrasis*). It is established that (unlike the reluctant addressee of Philostratus' letter) exhibitionism is Theodote's *forte*: 'she let them see as much of her as was proper' (οἷς ἐκείνην ἐπιδεικνύειν ἑαυτῆς ὅσα καλῶς ἔχοι).[108] Socrates and his companions go to see her and find her posing for a painter, where they wait and watch (ἐθεάσαντο), paralleling the artist's gaze. When the painter has finished, Socrates begins his questioning:

"Ὦ ἄνδρες," ἔφη ὁ Σωκράτης, "πότερον ἡμᾶς δεῖ μᾶλλον Θεοδότῃ χάριν ἔχειν, ὅτι ἡμῖν τὸ κάλλος ἑαυτῆς ἐπέδειξεν, ἢ ταύτην ἡμῖν, ὅτι ἐθεασάμεθα; ἆρ' εἰ μὲν ταύτῃ ὠφελιμωτέρα ἐστὶν ἡ ἐπίδειξις, ταύτην ἡμῖν χάριν ἐκτέον, εἰ δὲ ἡμῖν ἡ θέα, ἡμᾶς ταύτῃ;"

'Ought we men', said Socrates, 'to be more grateful to Theodote for letting us see her beauty, or she to us for looking at her? I suggest that, if the display has been more beneficial to her, she ought to be grateful to us, and if the sight has been more beneficial to us, we ought to be grateful to her.' (3.11.2)

Socrates makes some suggestions in answer to his questions, all of which indicate that the woman gets the better end of the bargain. She has already won the praise of her audience and will gain even more when they spread news of her: αὕτη μὲν ἤδη τε τὸν παρ' ἡμῶν ἔπαινον κερδαίνει καὶ ἐπειδὰν εἰς πλείους διαγγείλωμεν, πλείω ὠφελήσεται (3.11.3). The men, he implies, get a raw deal because they are left unsatisfied, longing to touch what they have seen and leaving in a state of heightened desire: ἡμεῖς δὲ ἤδη τε ὧν ἐθεασάμεθα ἐπιθυμοῦμεν ἅψασθαι καὶ ἄπιμεν ὑποκνιζόμενοι καὶ ἀπελθόντες ποθήσομεν (3.11.3). 'The likelihood is', concludes Socrates, 'that we take care of her, she is taken care of by us': ἐκ δὲ τούτων εἰκὸς ἡμᾶς μὲν θεραπεύειν, ταύτην δὲ θεραπεύεσθαι. 'If that is so', interjects Theodote, 'of course I ought to be grateful for you for looking' (ἐμὲ ἂν δέοι ὑμῖν τῆς θέας χάριν ἔχειν).

The account continues with further interrogation of the erotics and economics involved in viewing the hetaira, but this is not the

[108] This phrase is more ambiguous than is conveyed in Marchant and Todd's translation, 'she showed them as much as decency allowed'. It is not clear how much Theodote showed her beholders. What would be *kalon* for a hetaira to reveal? More than that which would be acceptable for a 'respectable' woman, to be sure. What might be *kalon* ('fine', 'beautiful') for Theodote to reveal might well not be *kalon* ('decent') for her do so.

26

place for an extended analysis.[109] What I first want to emphasise is that at stake here is the same question that is posed by Philostratus' Letter 26: where is the benefit, τό ὠφέλημα, for both viewer and viewed in display, ἡ ἐπίδειξις? The heroines of the ancient novels are repeatedly put on display and the question of who benefits from these exhibitions – the viewers or the viewed – is, as we shall see later, at the heart of how to read Leucippe and the gender dynamics of *Leucippe and Clitophon*.

My second point about Philostratus' letter is that (like the Xenophon episode) it represents an emphatically gendered scopic regime. The woman is the object of *epideixis* and the man its viewing subject.[110] This is symptomatic of Graeco-Roman visuality. Rarely are men displayed for women and rarely do women gaze upon men. The most significant site of what we might call the oppositional gaze – the gaze that disrupts this economy – is myth, for example in the figures of Baubo and Medusa. Baubo displays herself, but it is not a typical *epideixis*. Baubo flashed her genitalia to the grieving Demeter, who 'feasted her eyes' and cheered up.[111] Deliberate exposure of one's genitals – *anasurmos* or *anasurma* – is sometimes deemed shameful (*aiskhune*), and an act of crudeness (*agroikia*) and grossness (*bdeluria*),[112] but can also be a positive, political gesture.[113] As Helen King writes, 'What is

---

[109] For which see Goldhill (1998).
[110] E.g. in the myth of Pygmalion, on which see Elsner (1991); Freedberg (1989), 341–4; Gross (1992). It is a *topos* in Greek tragedy that women are compared to works of art: Aeschylus, *Agam.* 240: πρέπουσα θ' ὡς ἐν γραφαῖς; Eur. *Hec.* 521–69; see below 196. See the collection of essays in Richlin (1992b).
[111] Clem. Alex. *Protrep.* 2.21 = Orph. *Fr.* 52 (Kern); Arnob. *Adv. Nat.* 5.25 = Orph. *Fr.* 52 (Kern). Statuettes from Priene show a female figure who exposes herself, but has her face where we would expect her genitals to be; see Raeder (1983). Olender (1985) is a sensitive analysis of the texts and images which represent Baubo.
[112] E.g. in Theophrastus, *Characters* 11.1–2 when the gross man (ὁ βδελυρός) exposes himself to women.
[113] Plutarch reports two incidents of (collective) female *anasurma*: the Persian women prevent their men from fleeing home by lifting up their skirts and chiding them with the words: οὐ γὰρ ἐνταῦθά γε δύνασθε καταδῦναι φεύγοντες, ὅθεν ἐξεγένεσθε; and the Lycian women shame Bellerophon and repel a tidal wave by lifting up their garments; *Mor.* 247F–248D. In other cultures, revealing their sexual parts is a strong means of political protest for women; Ardener (1975b). King (1986) discusses the story of Agnodike, a woman who dressed as man in order to practise medicine, but lifts up her garments and reveals herself to be a woman to modest female patients (Hyginus, *Fabulae* 274.10–13). The story possibly derived from a Greek novella; King (1986), 54, 69 n. 4. Phryne, the Athenian hetaira who inspired a statue of Praxiteles and modelled for Apelles' painting

specific to *anasurmos* is that it is spontaneous, frontal, temporary and directional; not the female body displayed to the voyeur, but women deliberately aiming a gesture at a known target.'[114] *Anasurmos* is thus very different from exhibitionism, which is 'predicated upon a form of identification with the voyeur' and so 'shares in the eroticism of sight'.[115] It is thought that in some, especially ritual contexts, *anasurmos* may have been an apotropaic gesture, which would give it an affinity with the gaze of the Gorgon.[116]

Medusa, notoriously, is the bearer of an oppositional gaze and it is one which directly reverses and literalises the normative male gaze. She does not just see men as statues, she turns them into statues: ζῳπλαστῶν ἄνδρας ... ἀγαλματώσα.[117] Medusa dramatises male fear of the woman's active gaze. But she inhabits the realm of the monstrous and is no role model for women. Moreover, the power in her gaze brings her no pleasure; it is inflicted upon her as a punishment.[118] The Gorgon is a recurring image in *Leucippe and Clitophon* and is an important figure for one recent critic of the ancient novels who reads the exhibitionist female characters in the novels as powerfully Medusan.[119] So I shall return to the Gorgon's gaze when discussing gender and display in Chapter 4.

There are many other texts we could turn to through which to discuss visuality in the first few centuries CE. What I hope is clear from my analyses of the Antioch mosaic, the fragment of Plutarch's *On Love*, and Lucian's *On the Hall* and the letter of Philostratus, and the tour that these have taken us on around configurations of vision in philosophy, science and myth, is the amount of interest, across

---

of Venus, was reputed to have used her powers of display to save herself from conviction (for unrecorded crimes) in the lawcourt. When the eloquence of her defence lawyer, Hyperides, failed to persuade the jurors, Phryne stripped off and allowed her beauty to close the case. (Athenaeus, *Deipno.* 13 605F4–10). Heffernan suggests that the tale can be read as a 'pictorial threat to the supremacy of the word and the female challenge to male authority': Heffernan (1993), 49, but I would contend that this would be to view 'against the grain' of the traditional rendering of this scene in art.

[114] King (1986), 63.   [115] Esrock (1994), 145.
[116] See Zeitlin (1982), esp. 145 on the apotropaic and prostropaic qualities of *anasurmos*.
[117] Lycophron, *Alexandra* 1.844–5. Very occasionally, women too are petrified. The priestess of Athene Itonia in Boeotia entered the goddess's sanctuary and, on seeing the head of the Gorgon on the statue's tunic, was turned into stone: Paus. 9.34.1.
[118] Cf. Ovid, *Met.* 4.798ff.; Ps.-Apollod. 2.4.3. On Medusa, see Siebers (1983) and Vernant (1991), 143–50.
[119] Doody (1996), 65–6.

genres and disciplines, in the eye and its operations. As Jaś Elsner puts it, imperial Rome was 'a civilization which theorized the visual more intensely than at any time in antiquity'.[120] This survey also puts us in a better position from which to draw some conclusions about the significant similarities and differences between ancient and modern theories of the gaze.

Ancient and modern visualities

There is a radical difference in the way ancient and modern science understands visual processes. Ancient optics typically configures vision as haptic and corporeal; seer and seen, through emanations, actually touch each other. Intromission and extramission are interactive and potentially reciprocal processes; 'there was a certain participatory dimension in the visual process, a potential intertwining of viewer and viewed'.[121] Extramission was the major model until the seventeenth century, when Johannes Kepler's 1604 analogy between the eye and the camera obscura was a factor in its rejection. In the seventeenth century the eye began to be conceived as a passive recipient, not an active agent. This constituted a massive shift, a 'visual turn'. (It should be noted that this move from active to passive seeing did not, as one might think it would have done, mean that the subject abdicated their power in the viewing process, not least because the shift makes the subject, even if it no longer *constructs* the physical world, the centre of that world. However passively, they see from their viewpoint). Moreover, as Theresa Brennan explains, 'perhaps the most significant thing about the dematerialization of the active eye is that it makes us really separate from one another. If the way we see is no longer a way of touching, it makes us truly independent and alone.'[122]

By the beginning of the nineteenth century, emphasis was placed once again on the agency rather than passivity of the viewing subject.[123] This was in relation to the viewer's ability visually to

---

[120] Elsner (1998), 11.   [121] Jay (1993), 30.   [122] Brennan (1996), 225.
[123] Commenting on the diminishing of the Enlightenment trust in sight at the end of the eighteenth century, Jay observes: 'One mark of the change was the replacement of passive sensation by a more active will as the mark of subjectivity in the philosophies dominating the early nineteenth century': Jay (1993), 107, discussed in Brennan (1996), 227.

identify, and thus survey and *control*, their environment. Modern scientific and psychoanalytic theories of vision differ from ancient in their conception of vision as distanced and decorporealised. The body is not implicated in the same way in the objects of its vision. The physical distance between subject and object, and the agency afforded the viewer in the visual process, makes viewing a process of subjectification (of the viewer) and objectification (of the viewed). This leads to mastery, not mutuality.

Subjectification and objectification through vision have been most heavily theorized by feminist and poststructuralist film critics in the 1970s and 1980s, especially in relation to gender and 'the male gaze',[124] but also in relation to race and 'the imperial gaze'.[125] Particularly influential was John Berger's contention that there are 'ways of seeing' built into visual culture that enact and reproduce Western society's gender hierarchy and Laura Mulvey's foundational work of psychoanalytical feminist film criticism. Berger showed, in short, that 'men act and women appear. Men look at women. Women watch themselves being looked at.'[126] Mulvey explains how this works in cinema:

the determining male projects its fantasy on to the female figure which is styled accordingly. In their traditional exhibitionist role women are simultaneously looked at and displayed, with their appearance coded for strong visual and erotic impact so that they can be said to connote *to-be-looked-at-ness*.[127]

Her account has been extended and elaborated by, amongst others, Christian Metz, Kaja Silverman, Mary Ann Doane, Linda Williams and Jean Copjec and much of the emphasis of recent work has been

---

[124] Mulvey (1975) and her second thoughts (1981) both reproduced in Mulvey (1989); Metz (1974); Silverman (1992) and (1996); Stacey (1994); Doane (1987a) and (1991); Williams (1989) and (1995), Copjec (1994); Mayne (1993). For a general overview and further bibliography see Sturken and Cartwright (2001), esp. 72–108.

[125] hooks (1992), esp. 115–32; Kaplan (1997) and Pratt (1992).

[126] Berger (1972), 47.

[127] Mulvey (1975), 19. So strong is the connection between the scopic field and regimes of sexual difference that some have argued that vision excludes female subjectivity altogether. Luce Irigaray contends that vision is an inherently and essentially phallic sense and argues that 'the predominance of the visual . . . is particularly foreign to female eroticism. Woman takes pleasure more from touching than from looking, and her entry into a dominant scopic economy signifies. . . . her consignment to passivity: she is to be the beautiful object of contemplation', Irigaray (1985), 25–6. Cf. Jay on Julia Kristeva, Helene Cixous and Monique Wittig; Jay (1993), 526.

to move away from the model of the gaze as singular and unitary and towards one which is sensitive to the multiple positionalities of the spectator, and the variety of ways in which spectatorial reponses are differentiated. However, it is still clear that the power dynamics of modern visualities are in some ways very different – less reciprocal, more asymmetrical – than those involved in ancient optics.

Optics provides us with important differences between ancient and modern visualities, but it is crucial to recognise that scientific and philosophical theories are not necessary reflected in common culture. It is impossible to ascertain for sure the degree to which optical theories remained specialised areas of knowledge, or how much they became assimilated into everyday thought. Moreover, the reciprocal relations observed in materialist accounts of optics are by no means the only models of visuality. When we come to some symbols and metaphors of vision, we find power structured very differently. Indeed, the *similarities* between ancient and modern Western scopic regimes are even more striking than the differences.[128] Both use the gaze as a technology of ethnicity; a tool of cultural superiority. We can also trace a *longue durée* of gendered visuality, of male gaze and female display. Mulvey's formulation of cinematic woman's 'traditional exhibitionist role', connoting '*to-be-looked-at-ness*', has obvious points of connection with the economy of *epideixis* that I discussed in relation to Xenophon's Theodote and the woman in Philostratus' letter. Part of the gendering of the visual process, then, as now, is to imagine viewing as penetrative.[129] In Greek and Roman art, the eye is often associated with the phallus.[130] Often phalluses (sometimes winged, sometimes not) are depicted as having eyes. Even if (and I am doubtful)

---

[128] It is a major weakness of Fredrick (2002b) that he represents arguments which emphasise that certain concepts or practices (like *scopophilia*) 'persist across time and space' (p. 3) as 'essentialist', despite referring to Richlin (1992a), xviii which takes a more nuanced approach. It is simply not the case that to discern a *longue durée* of a practice or institution necessarily implies an essentialist position, or one that is insensitive to local distinctions. Rather, it is to observe the tenacity of certain patterns, even within very different cultures and contexts, and at the same time as being alert to differences. See further Rose (1993).

[129] See Clover (1992) on 'the assaultive gaze', with Morales (1996).

[130] Cf. Johns (1982), 61–73. Though it was not uncommon for the eye be depicted as phallic; see, e.g. Persius 1.18: *patranti fractus ocello*, 'worn out with his eye attempting to make it', on which Adams comments: 'Here a term strictly appropriate to the *mentula*

these can also be domesticated as good luck charms ('for luck and safety' writes Catherine Johns),[131] these sighted phalluses are graphic images of what the atomists theorised: the eye's ability to penetrate. They flaunt looking (and thus knowing) as a masculine prerogative. As Françoise Frontisi-Ducroux writes, 'The association of the phallus and the eye, which confirms the exclusively male status of the subject (subject of sight and subject of knowledge, the two notions being amalgamated) is deeply anchored in Greek representations.'[132] She even suggests, and I think persuasively, that the psyche's palpitations, swelling and sprouting of feathers when aroused by gazing towards divine beauty in the *Phaedrus* passage discussed above conjure an image of 'a phallus bird, ever so slightly sublimated'.[133]

The 'metaphorics of the gaze', to use Pete de Bolla's formulation, also construct it as male and masterful. By 'metaphorics of the gaze', I mean the repertoire of images used to depict vision, 'the collection of figurative expressions . . . of specific forms of visual experience'.[134] The letter of Philostratus envisages the gaze as consumptive and its object as food. Xenophon's *Memorabilia* does the same. Socrates' encounter with Theodote continues with Socrates encouraging the hetaira to 'play hard to get':

> And you are likely to give them most pleasure if you bestow what you have to give only when they ask for it. You can see that even the most delightful dishes seem disagreeable if they are served before the appetite is ready, and if one is satiated, they actually cause disgust; but even inferior food seems quite attractive if it is served after hunger has been aroused. (3.11.13)

Here Theodote (who is described earlier as 'hunting' men) is like the spoils of the hunt, food on the table, rendered passive and there to satisfy male hunger. She is offered, and indeed offers herself 'on a plate', an eminently edible object. The fetishising of Theodote's

---

has been transferred to the eye, partly because of the belief that the effects of orgasm or sexual desire could be seen in the eye: see Juv. 7.240–1 *non est leve tot puerorum | observare manus oculosque in fine trementis*. Persius was imitated at *Anth. Lat.* 902.3 *sunt lusci oculi atque patrantes*: Adams (1982),143, n. 1. On the eye as phallus, see further Barton (1993), esp. 95–8; Johns (1982), 61–76.

[131] Johns (1982), 66. [132] Frontisi-Ducroux (1996), 94–5.
[133] Frontisi-Ducroux (1996), 95. This would create an interesting dynamic wherein the phallus (bird) is itself penetrated.
[134] De Bolla (1995), 283.

body as food exposes the appetitive nature of the male gaze in its crudest form. The consumptive gaze is one of the most pervasive metaphors of the gaze in ancient literature.[135]

The other dominant set of metaphors, which, like the consumptive gaze, reinforce the male beholder's subjectivity while objectifying the woman who is beheld, involves statues and works of art. The desired woman is frequently likened to famous works of art as the male viewer paints or moulds her in his imagination. Woman is reified as statue, statue lusted after as woman.[136] The now frequent usage of the term 'objectification' should not blind us to the violence inherent in the activity. An anecdote in Athenaeus illustrates this:

Cleiosophus of Selymbria . . . becoming enamoured of the statue in Parian marble at Samos, locked himself up in the temple, thinking he should be able to have intercourse with it; and since he found he wasn't up to it (ὡς ἠδυνάτει) on account of the frigidity and resistance of the stone, he then and there desisted from that desire and placing before him a small piece of flesh, he consorted with that (τηνικαῦτα τῆς ἐπιθυμίας ἀπέστη καὶ προβαλλόμενος τὸ σαρκίον ἐπλησίασεν). (13.605f4–10)

In this account, women, food and statues are interchangeable.[137] All are used to facilitate male desire. Adams, quoting de Lauretis, writes that 'food in general and meat in specific, like the female body, is a "site of visual pleasure or lure of the gaze".'[138] This is also true of statues; display links these two ways of imaging women. The metaphorics of the gaze, then, largely configure visual power differently from ancient optics and can be read as

[135] On which see Henry (1992).
[136] The viewing equation is rarely reversed, and when it is, it is usually the exception which proves – as it breaks – the rule. Livia provides an example of the female gaze (or, more accurately, glance). Cassius Dio reports that one day she met some naked men who were sentenced to death in consequence. She saved their lives: εἰποῦσα ὅτι οὐδὲν ἀνδριάντων ταῖς σωφρονούσαις οἱ τοιοῦτοι διαφέρουσι (*Roman History* 58.4–5). Livia's assurance can either be interpreted as illustrating her modest nature and the difference between male and female ways of seeing (it would make no sense in this visual economy to say that to decent *men* naked women are no whit different from statues), or (less likely) as a disingenuous statement and winking acknowledgement of the desire inherent in viewing statues.
[137] Clement's *Protrepticus* suggests that worshipping statues is a weak version of having sex with statues. On Clement's *Protrepticus*, a brilliant text to analyse beside Achilles, see Goldhill (2001b). Goldhill comments: 'Wrong looking is wrong living': (2001b), 174. See Henry (2000) on Athenaeus as 'the ur-pornographer'.
[138] Adams (1990), 91.

part of a *longue durée* of the gendered gaze. We should not reject the Kappeler/Richlin model of objectification through the gaze because ancient optical theories and philosophical discussions tend to present a less unilinear model of how vision works.[139] Rather, we need to take on board that there is a whole spectrum of ways in which vision is perceived and represented in ancient culture. Some, like the scientific investigations of the mechanics of viewing, may or may not be related to the ideologies of viewing in contemporary practice, and some, more readily than others, will find reflections in modern theories of vision.

The approach in this study is not psychoanalytical, though any work on the gaze must necessarily be indebted to some of the terms and ideas of that discipline. Scopophilia, literally 'love of looking', is usually distinguished from the scopic by its indication of *surplus*, of excessive investment and pleasure in looking. Active scopophilia is commonly known as voyeurism. Passive scopophilia is exhibitionism.[140] However, the Roman Empire is so ocularcentric, and excessive, that surplus – and scopophilia – may be the norm. I use the term 'gaze' in a looser way than psychoanalytic critics do, partly because they have a tendency to make rigid distinctions between *glance* and *gaze* which are not only employed in ways often contradictory to common usage, which can be confusing,[141] but are also hard to map onto ancient descriptions of viewing without distorting or suppressing the rich Greek vocabulary of sight.

The basic Greek verbs for seeing are *horan* (which can also mean, as it does frequently in Achilles Tatius,[142] to perceive something intellectually) and *blepein*, which (followed by preposition and noun) often has more of the sense of 'look at', 'on' or 'towards'.[143] *Theasthai* is used of seeing or beholding (sometimes with connotations of awe) and *he thea* can mean 'a looking at' or

---

[139] Goldhill (1998) is too dismissive of this approach.
[140] Esrock (1994), 145: 'The counterpart to voyeurism, exhibitionism, reflects the pleasure of being seen and, since it is predicated upon a form of identification with the voyeur, thereby shares in the eroticism of sight.'
[141] Cf. Bal's critique of Bryson's use of 'gaze' and 'glance': Bal (1995). Silverman (following but adapting Lacan) distinguishes between, and polarises, the 'glance' which comes from the Self and the 'gaze' which emanates from the Other. Hubbard (2002) applies Silverman's approach to his reading of Pindar's Theoxenus poem.
[142] See O'Sullivan (1980), 302–3 for a list of references to *horan* in *Leucippe and Clitophon*.
[143] See O'Sullivan (1980), 61–2.

'gaze' as well as 'a sight' and 'spectacle'.[144] *Skopein* has both the physical sense of 'keep a look out' and the intellectual sense 'consider' and 'contemplate'.[145] *Theorein* can mean to contemplate something and theorise about it, but also has the sense of 'gaze' or 'gape'. The advantages of working from a linguistics of the gaze, as it were, rather than imposing, for example, a Lacanian schema, are obvious. We can discern immediately that Achilles only once uses the verb *theorein*, and that its singular occurrence, when Clitophon is rooted to the spot gaping at the 'sacrifice' of Leucippe (3.15.5), particularises and characterises that extraordinary scene of viewing. When I am not referring closely to the text and I use the term 'gaze', I use it to denote a way of looking that is intense, focused, and demonstrative of agency. Unlike the look (which is suggestive of a more processual, relational form of communication), the gaze attempts to master and make meaning of the world.

In what follows, I shall attempt to investigate the mastery and construction of meaning through the gazes of the various characters and the two narrators. The next chapter takes as its starting point the beginning(s) of the novel, where three narrative openings inaugurate different points of view and launch specific ways of reading *Leucippe and Clitophon*.

[144] See O'Sullivan (1980), 182. [145] See O'Sullivan (1980), 384.

2

READERS AND READING

Open(ing) readings

In a series of articles, Steve Nimis has laid down an important challenge to the way that we read the Greek novels.[1] He argues that a teleological approach, an approach which tries to identify a novel's 'main idea', dominant reading, or line of interpretation, 'as though the unfolding of a text were the progressive revelation of a predetermined content', does not work well with the ancient novels. Following Godzich and Kittay's Bahktinian 'theory of prosaic composition', Nimis argues that the novels should not be read as if their authors had carefully designed their plots before writing them and that we can, if we get it right, identify what the author was trying to say. Rather, Nimis argues, the novels are best understood as made up as their authors went along; experimental and improvised. Consequently, connections and associations between one episode or image and another are haphazardly generated. This constitutes a very different interpretation from that of Shadi Bartsch, whose foundational work on Achilles Tatius and Heliodorus argues for their being meticulously plotted narratives. Focusing largely on the role of *ekphrasis*, she suggests that the narrative hermeneutics of the two works operate in an intricate and complex way to engage the reader's active skills at 'decoding' the nexuses of prolepsis and hindsight.[2] Nimis sees 'prosaics' as analogous to the Parry–Lord theory of oral composition in Homeric studies, *contra* the 'Unitarian' approach of Bartsch.[3]

With these concerns in mind, the first part of this chapter will turn to the beginning of *Leucippe and Clitophon* and look at

---

[1] Nimis (1994), (1998) and (1999). [2] Bartsch (1989).
[3] Nimis (1998), 100. Sedelmeier (1959) plays the 'Analyst' in this discussion. Her argument that digressions are ornamental and can be discounted is easier to dismiss than Bartsch's approach: see below 96–100.

whether — and, if so, how — it functions programmatically. More precisely, it will consider three 'beginnings' to the novel: the opening episode where we are introduced to the unnamed narrator who describes the picture of Europa (1.1); his subsequent meeting with Clitophon and their conversation, the setting, tone and resonances of which fashion a Platonic frame for the narrative to come (1.2); and the start of Clitophon's narration which (as we never return to the opening frame and the shipwrecked stranger) will comprise the rest of the narrative (1.3).

The shining example of Europa

The novel begins with a description of Sidon and its harbour and the arrival there of a man who has survived a severe storm. He tells us that he made thank-offerings for his survival to the goddess Astarte and, while browsing afterwards among the dedications, he came across a picture: 'a landscape and seascape in one. The picture was of Europa, the sea was the Phoenician, and the land Sidon' (1.1). He proceeds to describe the picture in an *ekphrasis* whose sensuality and vividness, in contrast to the economic and verbless sentences with which the novel begins, provide a powerful opening tableau.[4] It is commonplace in Second Sophistic literature for pictorial descriptions to be used as introductory passages, which anticipate the narrative that follows.[5] Perhaps the most notable example is the *ekphrasis* of the picture in the cave of the nymphs in *Daphnis and Chloe*, the exegesis of which comprises Longus' narrative. Similarly, it is the picture of Europa which inspires Clitophon's narration. As the unnamed narrator is admiring the painting out loud and showing a lover's especial interest in the depiction of Eros leading the bull, Clitophon interrupts his thoughts and introduces

---

[4] Descriptions of Europa riding the bull are common in later literature, e.g. Moschus, *Id.* 2; Horace, *Odes* 3.27; Ovid, *Met.* 2.836–7; *Fasti* 5.605ff.; *Amores* 1.3.23ff.; Lucian, *Dialogues of Fishermen* 15; Nonnus, *Dion.* 1.46ff.

[5] E.g. in the *Pinax* of Cebes and Lucian's *Heracles* and *Slander*. In general see Schissel von Fleschenburg (1913); Harlan (1965); Bartsch (1989), 40–5; on Cebes, see Elsner (1995), 39–46. The body of material on *ekphrasis* is vast. I have found the following useful: Fowler (1991); Leach (1988), 3–24; Billault (1990); Steiner (1988); Heffernan (1993); Goldhill (1994); Elsner (1995), 24–8; Webb (1999).

himself as a living testament to the power of Eros, having suffered many of love's hurts. The narrator presses him for an explanation and Clitophon's story begins. This opening frame and the intricacy of the detail in the description of the painting foster the expectation that the Europa *ekphrasis* will feature prominently in the later narrative.[6]

We shall return to the description's voyeuristic eroticism, and the representation of Europa's complicity in her abduction, in Chapter 4. What concerns me here is that how we make sense of this description – how it fits in to the narrative design; whether or not the author has surrendered that design – is tested a little later, at 1.4.2–3, when Clitophon sees Leucippe for the first time. He describes being struck by her beauty:

παρθένος ἐκφαίνεταί μοι καὶ καταστράπτει μου τοὺς ὀφθαλμοὺς τῷ προσώπῳ.

a maiden suddenly came into my view, and the vision of her face struck my eyes like lightning. (1.4.2)

In a typical novelistic trope, he compares her to a picture that he has seen:[7]

Τοιαύτην εἶδον ἐγώ ποτε ἐπὶ ταύρῳ γεγραμμένην Σελήνην [or Εὐρώπην]· ὄμμα γοργὸν ἐν ἡδονῇ·

She looked like a picture I had once seen of Selene [or Europa] on a bull. She had delightfully striking eyes. (1.4.2–3)

At this climactic moment of love at first sight, there is a textual problem: whether to read 'Selene' or 'Europa'.[8] Readers' ways of dealing with this textual problem, I shall show, are tellingly illustrative of their reading strategies, and the difficulties that these raise.

---

[6] And indeed this expectation is fulfilled. There are thematic parallels between the painting and the subsequent narrative, the opposition between land and sea and the central role of Eros being obvious examples. Leucippe, like Europa, is kidnapped and both women are described in an 'unabashedly voyeuristic' manner; see Bartsch (1989), 49 and 48–51. Anderson's suggestion that *Leucippe and Clitophon* is 'a classical version of the myth of Enlil' and that the proleptic function of the *ekphrasis* is as 'a romantic variant of that same pair's adventures' is not convincing; Anderson (1984), 17.

[7] On comparisons of women in novels with works of art, see Hunter (1994), 1073–6.

[8] See Mignogna (1993), 178–9 for a thorough discussion of the textual problem. Our conclusions are very different; see below: 7–14, 8 n. 27.

Many editors and literary critics choose to read 'Europa',[9] even though this is by far the less well attested reading in the manuscripts.[10] Not all of them explain their rationale, but when they do, it is revelatory. Gaselee translates: 'She was like that picture of Europa on the bull which I saw but just now',[11] and explains: 'The MSS all have Σελήνην (*sic*): but it seems necessary to adopt the reading of the β MSS Εὐρώπην, to give some point to the introduction of the story.' Massimo Fusillo explains: 'proprio per il richiamo all' *ekphrasis* preferisco leggere Εὐρώπην',[12] as does Maurizio Bettini: 'Despite the fact that this second reading appears to have greater support in the manuscripts . . . it nevertheless seems to me that the first reading yields a better text from the point of view of literary consistency.'[13] 'Literary consistency', 'to give some point', betray teleological approaches. These scholars read 'Europa' in order to link Clitophon's simile to the *ekphrasis* of the painting of Europa; to make it *fit*.

Bartsch argues that the *ekphrasis* has a complicated proleptic function, anticipating events in Leucippe's life (and also in Calligone's). When we come to the description of Clitophon's garden in Tyre (1.15.1–8), for example, the numerous similarities between the details of flowers, trees and bubbling spring in the garden (to which Leucippe is explicitly compared at 1.19.1–3) and Europa's meadow operate, in hindsight, to associate Leucippe with Europa. Like Europa, who is portrayed as 'an acquiescent kidnappee',[14] Leucippe happily elopes with Clitophon (2.19.2).[15] Bartsch contends that the *ekphrasis* also foreshadows the abduction

---

[9] '. . . I remembered Europa, sayling upon the backe of the bull', Burton (1597), 5; '. . . [Leucippe] on whom I had no sooner cast mine eyes, but I straightway thought on Europa', Hodges (1638), 8; '. . . she resembled the Europa, whom, in the picture I had seen sitting upon the bull', Smith (1889), 354; 'she was such a one as the painted Europa on the bull I saw just now', Bartsch (1989), 165. See also Billault (1991), 246–60; Fusillo (1989), 165, n. 78.

[10] No papyri are known for this section of the text. Garnaud selects seven manuscripts which broadly fall into three families: W, M and D (often referred to as family α), V, G and E (β) and the lone manuscript F. Two of the three families (α and F) have 'Selene', one (group β) reads 'Europa'. On the papyri and manuscript tradition of *Leucippe and Clitophon* see Conca (1969); Reeve (1981); Laplace (1983b) and especially Vilborg (1955), xv–lxxxiv reviewed by Rattenbury (1956). Plepelits (1996), 391–4 provides a useful summary of the history of the text.

[11] Gaselee (1984), 15.   [12] Fusillo (1989), 165 n. 78.   [13] Bettini (1999), 289.
[14] Bartsch (1989), 54.   [15] Bartsch (1989), 63.

of Clitophon's half-sister Calligone by Callisthenes (2.15), which makes the reader do a double-take and revise his or her initial interpretation:

> the single picture portends two disparate events; this is accomplished in a way that ... satisfies our expectation that what is foreshadowed will be fulfilled, only to undermine that complacency in the course of the narrative's events. Again, not only hindsight (in confirming what seems to be the correct interpretation) but also post-hindsight (in destroying it) come into play.

It is clear that for her, as for the other critics cited, it matters that Clitophon's simile links Leucippe to the opening *ekphrasis* of Europa. Moreover, those who read 'Europa' strengthen the association they are assuming by mistranslating the particle ποτε, the temporal inexactitude of which distances Clitophon from the Europa painting.[16] Winkler and Whitmarsh's translations are more accurate: 'Such was the beauty on a bull I had seen once before, and that was in a painting of Selene on a bull', and 'She looked like a picture I had once seen of Selene on a bull'. Rather than ποτε one would expect a word like ἄρτι, 'just now', if the connection with the Europa painting were to be made clear.

It looks as if 'Selene' is the correct textual reading.[17] It has the greatest manuscript support and 'Selene' is the *lectio difficilior*. We can see why a reader might change the text from 'Selene' to 'Europa', but not from 'Europa' to 'Selene'. (We might conjecture that the scribes who penned the manuscript family β were the first readers to emend Achilles Tatius in order to give the introductory *ekphrasis* 'some point' and 'literary consistency'.) What are we to make of the simile likening Leucippe to Selene (on a bull in a picture), when a comparison between Leucippe and Europa (on a bull in a picture) has been so carefully anticipated? Should we, rejecting a teleological reading, see this as part of the novel's surrender of its own design? An approach which views the novel as a 'prosaic composition' might argue (and I should make it clear that Nimis does not, nor does he refer at all to the simile) that we should

---

[16] Bettini ignores the particle completely: 'She was like the painting I had seen of Europa on the bull', Bettini (1999), 182.
[17] Jacobs (1821), Vilborg (1955), Plepelits (1980), Winkler (1989) and Garnaud (1991) read Selene, in the latter case with no explanation or discussion.

read the inconsistency as part of the narrative's randomness and not seek to make connections in hindsight which assume a grand design. There are two problems with this.

The first is a suspicion that to view open-endness and disunity could be (in this case at least) a more generous and fashionable way of couching that old criticism of authorial ineptitude. If Achilles Tatius describes the picture of Europa on a bull without forward planning ('our author has a general idea for a story, is casting around for a good way to get underway, and that the details he introduces at this point become, as the story unfolds, generative or determinative of events that follow in ways that were not clearly foreseen when they were introduced'[18]) and then only a short while later describes another girl on a bull without intending that the reader make an association between them, then that sounds like poor writing to me. Is it really just 'our own standards for a well-made up story'[19] which prompt a search for unity and meaning? We have enough evidence from ancient readers and critics (if not from novel readers) to indicate that reading organically is not an anachronistic project, even if ancient notions of unity were more inclusive of digression from the main topic and *poikilia* ("richness", "variety", "mottling") than ours.[20]

Second, even with our lack of knowledge about the composition and production of the novels, the proposal that they were not planned and revised is unconvincing. Of course, design and plottedness are properties of a text which are only recuperable to us through the reader's actualisation of them.[21] However, the use of book divisions and descriptions at the beginnings and ends of books for rhetorical impact, and the intricate constructions of subplots, vignettes and imagistic motifs strongly suggest deliberation and design. Moreover, it is all the more likely that Achilles had thought about how his novel would end before he began it, because he has placed the end of the story at the beginning of the narrative.[22] So, while I find much of

---

[18] Nimis (1998), 103.   [19] Nimis (1998), 100.   [20] Heath (1989); Sharrock (2000).
[21] See Sharrock and Morales (2000), especially Sharrock (2000).
[22] Lowe reads *Leucippe and Clitophon* as expertly plotted ('Achilles' fifth book alone offers a combinatorics of couples and a shifting network of dissonant secondary story-models as intricate as anything in Menander'): Lowe (2000), 228, n. 8; 246–9.

Nimis' characterisation of the aleatory and uncanny aspects of *Leucippe and Clitophon* to be acutely observed, my point of disagreement with his approach is that whereas he would see these aspects as indicative of Achilles' lack of predetermination, I, following Bartsch, see them as the opposite: sophisticated design.

Achilles' use of imagery and analogy is designed to court confusion over identification, likeness and referral. The expectation that the narrative will unfold in an orderly progression is thwarted in a way which may be unsettling for the first-time reader. It seems that what we have is one painting (the one among the temple-offerings to the great goddess) and two viewings of it. One viewer, the unnamed narrator, reads it as a depiction of Europa and (despite the fact that the ποτε withholds certainty) there is an obvious temptation to think that the other viewer, Clitophon, reads it as a depiction of Selene. It follows, then – and this is the crucial point – that the painting is bivalent: it can be viewed two ways, both as an image of Europa and as an image of Selene. Viewing is established as a subjective activity, contingent upon the spectator's cultural frame of reference. This is anticipated by the introduction of the great goddess as both Aphrodite and Astarte, depending on the worshipper's perspective, Greek or Phoenician (1.12).[23] Moreover, although Astarte, one of the major deities in the Sidonian

---

[23] Here I accept James Diggle's textual emendation:

> Restore Aphrodite to the first clause and both sense and style are satisfied: either <τῇ Ἀφροδίτῃ > τῇ τῶν Φοινίκων (the article is optional) or τῇ τῶν Φοινίκων <Ἀφροδίτῃ>.

Thus the sense of the passage is restored: 'I went to make my votive offerings for my safe arrival to Aphrodite, the Phoenicians' goddess; the people of Sidon call her Astarte', Diggle (1972). Diggle's emendation is attractive for a number of reasons. Of all the Greek goddesses it is Aphrodite who is the most commonly equated with the Phoenician Astarte. The implied readership of *Leucippe and Clitophon* are not necessarily acquainted with Phoenicia; there are several instances where its customs and history are explained as if to a foreign audience. Therefore, it would make sense to have the goddess's Greek name, followed by an explanation of her other, less well known Sidonian and Phoenician title. A reference to Zeus, later in the novel, provides a parallel:

> [The great god] ὃν Δία μὲν Ἕλληνες, Σέραπιν δὲ καλοῦσιν Αἰγύπτιοι. (5.2.1)

Moreover, it is surely apposite that an erotic novel should begin with a votive offering to Aphrodite, the goddess of love. Longus' *Daphnis and Chloe* itself constitutes an 'offering to Eros' (ἀνάθημα... Ἔρωτι).

pantheon,[24] was most commonly associated with Aphrodite,[25] she is also known, though it is less well attested, to have an affinity with Selene.[26] The dual perspective is also thematically suggested in the motif of doubleness which recurs with striking frequency during the narrative.[27] For example, in the opening *ekphrasis*, the sea is painted with a 'double hue', ἡ χροιὰ διπλῆ (1.1.8); in being betrothed to someone who is not only a woman, but an ugly woman, Charicles is struck by a 'double misfortune', διπλῷ . . . τῷ κακῷ . . . τὸ κακὸν διπλοῦν (1.7.4 and cf. 1.8.8); the pictures of Andromeda and Prometheus comprise a 'double image', εἰκόνα διπλῆν (3.6.3); Perseus' weapon is described as having a 'double form', διφυεῖ σιδήρῳ (3.7.8); the Egyptian clod inflicts a 'double wound', διπλοῦν . . . τὸ τραῦμα (3.13.3) and Leucippe experiences a 'double death', θάνατον διπλοῦν (5.7.8), and so on.[28]

The conclusion that the painting is bivalent largely concurs with that of Daniel Selden.[29] He argues that the painting's duality is an example of syllepsis, which, he contends, is the 'master trope' of the fiction of late antiquity.[30] In his view, the syllepsis of the

---

[24] She was worshipped with the gods Baal and Eshmun. On Astarte and other Phoenician gods see Harden (1962), 82–90; Moscati (1968), 31–8. Just inland of the city of Sidon a major temple was built to Eshmun during the time of the Persian Empire by the kings of Sidon; Grainger (1991), 16–17. One of the titles of the king of Sidon was 'priest of Astarte'; Aubet (1987), 122.

[25] Religious syncretism, the fusion of different religions, was 'along with the flourishing mystery cults the most typical phenomenon of religious life in Hellenistic times': Hägg (1983), 87. See also Moscati (1965), 37ff. Astarte is also known as Ashtoreth (notably in the Hebrew Bible: 1 Kings 2:5, 33 and 2 Kings 23:13), or Tanit and was equated *inter alia* with Ishtar and Aphrodite, and Hera and Cybele; see Harden (1962), 87–9; *LIMC* 1077–86; Selden (1994), 60, n. 116; Lightfoot (2003), 297–8. Visual representations of Astarte often depict her with palm-trees and pomegranates, both of which are featured in *Leucippe and Clitophon* (palm-tree: 1.17.3–5, 2.14.1–2; pomegranate: 3.6.1).

[26] In Greek mythology, Selene is the goddess of the moon, sister of the Sun god Helios. Like her brother, Selene drives a chariot across the sky, sometimes with horses, sometimes oxen. There is an astrological connection between moon-goddess and bull: the exaltation – *hupsoma* – of the moon is the constellation Taurus, sign of the bull: Rose (1928), 34–5. Astarte was said to wear a bull mask as a symbol of her sovereignty (Philo, *FGrH* 3C 2.790 F2.31) and she also has associations with Artemis Tauropolis and Pasiphae, a descendant of Europa who continued the family tradition of bovine liaisons resulting in the birth of the Minotaur. Pausanias 3.26.1 describes a temple at Thalamae with statues of Helios and Pasiphae. Pasiphae, he says, 'is a title of Selene'. This temple is also referred to as dedicated to Pasiphae, the moon-goddess, in Plutarch, *Agis* 9.

[27] On doubling as a recurrent theme, see Mignogna (1995), 27.

[28] See also 1.13.4 (θάνατον διπλοῦν); 1.15.6 (τὸ ἄλσος . . . διπλοῦν); 2.23.3 (τρόμον διπλοῦν); 4.4.4 (κέρας . . . διπλοῦν); 7.5.3 (θάνατον διπλοῦν).

[29] Selden (1994). [30] Ibid., 51.

painting in *Leucippe and Clitophon* conforms to an established practice.³¹ Selden comments:

> The textual problem at 1.4.3 is ultimately a red herring, for the Syro-Phoenician iconography is established by the narrative independent of any reference to Selene. The initial description of the painting is already set up to evoke ambivalent responses in readers competent in one system of representation or the other.³²

However, the dual potential of the painting is not made clear from the outset. We must be careful not to elide our imaginative reconstruction of the painting with the interpretations of the painting presented by the two viewers in the narrative. Neither the unnamed narrator who describes the picture at length, nor Clitophon, who looks at the picture and refers to it later, view it sylleptically. They each grasp only one of the potential interpretations. First, the image of a beautiful woman on a bull is designated, without equivocation, as being that of Europa and it is only later, with Clitophon's enigmatic reference to a painting of Selene on a bull, that we are presented with an alternative reading. Only then is the reader prompted to reassess his or her initial understanding of the painting and to re-evaluate its detail as appropriate to the Selene myth as well as the Europa myth. For example, the unnamed narrator describes the throng of women watching Europa's departure with mixed emotions of joy and fright, their faces distorted as if about to scream in fear. This detail is consistent with an interpretation of the painting as the abduction of Europa. Selden suggests that the picture accommodates a double reading where the girls represent Europa's companions on the one hand, and Selene/Astarte's temple prostitutes on the other.³³ This is possible if the reader imaginatively reconstructs the painting as bivalent, but is not attested in the *ekphrasis*. Far from being a 'red herring', then, the explicit reference to the painting of Selene at 1.4.3 is significant because it constitutes an opposing view of the painting and, in doing so, prompts the reader to 'see through' the partial rendering of the ekphrasist. The initial

---

³¹ This is an overstatement. Selden applies the term 'syllepsis' to refer to smutty innuendo (in Apuleius, *Golden Ass*), transvestism and the scenes of *Scheintod* (following Molinié), class and race (e.g. Charicleia is both white and of black parentage). To employ the term 'syllepsis' to cover all of these different forms of duality dilutes the meaning of the word and elides the differences between these examples of 'doubleness'.

³² Selden (1994), 63, n. 128.   ³³ Ibid., 62, n. 126.

description of the painting is not set up to evoke ambivalent responses; it is only in hindsight that the reader might attempt to reconcile Clitophon's viewing with that of the narrator.[34]

It may be that Achilles Tatius has purposefully selected a location for his image that was renowned for its polysemy and resistance to identification. It is possible that 'temple at Sidon' was shorthand for playing 'guess the goddess'. Lucian tells of a controversy surrounding the identification of the ruling deity of the temple of Sidon in his *De Dea Syria* (*On the Syrian Goddess*), an account of a pilgrimage to Hierapolis in Syria written in the second or third centuries CE:

> There is another large temple in Phoenicia, one belonging to the Sidonians. As they themselves say, it is Astarte's – I myself think Astarte is Selene – but one of the priests told me, it belongs to Europa the sister of Cadmus. She was the daughter of King Agenor; and when she disappeared, the Phoenicians honoured her with the temple and told a sacred tale about her, how Zeus had desired her for her beauty and, changing his form into a bull, seized her and carried her away to Crete. I heard this from the other Phoenicians as well, and the coinage the Sidonians use shows Europa astride Zeus in the form of a bull. Nonetheless, they do not allow that the temple is Europa's. (4)[35]

---

[34] A similar confusion occurs in the description of a real bull, or more accurately, an Egyptian ox, which is one of the sacrificial victims offered to Hercules at Tyre in response to the oracle of the Byzantines (2.15.3–4) The detailed description of the bull's horns concludes with an explicit association between the bull and the moon: 'This sight is the very image of the crescent moon', καὶ τὸ θέαμα κυκλουμένης σελήνης ἐστὶν εἰκών. Horns are often described with lunar imagery (e.g. Horace, *Odes* 4.2.54–60; Moschus, *Europa* 87–8 and Mignogna (1993) on Moschus and this passage of Achilles Tatius). Here the association between bull and moon is more than a literary *topos*. The description continues with another likeness: 'Their colour is that praised by Homer in the horses of Thrace' (2.15.3–4). This is a reference to *Iliad* 10.436–7, where the horses of Rhesus are said to be 'whiter than snow', *leukoteroi chionos*. The image of white horses sketches a further connection between Leucippe, White Horse, and the moon-goddess, possibly strengthened by the iconographic tradition of Selene riding a white horse (cf. *Enciclopedia dell'Arte Antica*, vol. 7, 169; Leclant (1960)). The description of the ox concludes with the statement: 'If there is any truth in the myth of Europa, it must have been an Egyptian bull that Zeus imitated' (2.15.4). First, the description encourages the reader to envisage Selene with moon imagery and allusions to Leucippe, with whom the goddess is previously compared at 1.4.3, but then the explicit reference is not to the moon-goddess, but to Europa. The description of the Egyptian ox uses the same ploy as the opening *ekphrasis* and the first description of Leucippe; it sets up certain expectations only to undermine them, but here the images are reversed. In the former passages, we are led to expect a comparison of Leucippe with Europa, only to have her likened to Selene. In this passage, it is Selene who is evoked, but Europa whom Clitophon explicitly mentions.

[35] The translation is J. L. Lightfoot's: Lightfoot (2003), 249.

Lucian's narrative, whose tonality and purpose is notoriously difficult to read,[36] is concerned throughout with issues of cultural identity.[37] In this passage there is an interrelation between the figures of Astarte, Selene and Europa and a confusion about how to identify them, which provides a parallel (and possible antecedent) for the shifting referent in *Leucippe and Clitophon*.[38] Whereas the introductory *ekphrasis* in *Daphnis and Chloe* focalises the viewer to map the events described there onto the subsequent narrative, the one in Achilles Tatius is a programme for ambiguity, contrariety and illusion.

The second interpretation of the painting, Clitophon's simile, is introduced at 1.4.3 with disconcerting abruptness and is never fully explicated as a reading of the image (the ποτε remains enigmatic). Until the reader makes the connection between Selene and Europa and realises the syllepsis, he or she experiences an aporetic moment. The double meaning is unfolded in such a way as to make the reader do a double-take. It is what could be called a narrative *trompe-l'œil*.[39] This pattern of occlusion and subsequent revelation might be characterised as 'uncanny', Freud's term for describing something which has been hidden (through repression) but then becomes visible.[40] It refers to the experience of happening upon something familiar (*heimlich*) that has become alienated (*unheimlich*) because it has hitherto been repressed. Paul Coates

---

[36] 'The text treads along a knife-edge line between sincerity and irony', Elsner (2001), 149.

[37] See Elsner (2001), esp. 130 on this passage; Goldhill (2002), 78–81.

[38] Lucian's account might prompt us to consider an alternative emendation at 1.1.2, inserting 'Selene' instead of 'Aphrodite'. This reading would have the merit of anticipating Clitophon's reference to Selene at 1.4.3, but I think that 'Aphrodite' remains the stronger reading, for the reasons which I have outlined above. Hodges' translation complicates the picture further, as he refers to the deity as Venus and Selene, with no mention of Astarte: 'I sacrificed to the Goddesse Venus, whom the Sydonians call Selene', Hodges (1638), 2.

[39] On metaphor and *trompe-l'œil* in Achilles Tatius, see Mignogna (1995).

[40] Freud (1919). On uncanniness in literature see Freedman (1991), 78–113; Kofman (1991), 119ff. Steve Nimis discusses the novels as 'uncanny' works: Nimis (1998). His approach is more psychoanalytical than mine. He pays particular attention to the *ekphrasis* of the story of Philomela, 'perhaps the "uncanniest" moment in this very uncanny novel, for it combines many elements Freud enumerates as provoking this sensation: dismemberment with its obvious overtones of castration, but also revenants, repetition, and the envoicing of silent objects'. There is scope for a more profound reading of *Leucippe and Clitophon* as an uncanny text than either Nimis or I have undertaken, which might link the desire to uncover female genitalia (see below, Ch. 4) with Freud's theory and Weber's interpretation of Freud, on which see Doane (1987b), 289–90.

writes that 'the world becomes uncanny when it is perceived as no longer simple substance, but also as shadow, a sign of the existence of a world beyond itself, which it is nevertheless unable fully to disclose'.[41] Viewed in these terms, the representation of the painting at the beginning of *Leucippe and Clitophon* is uncanny, because the reader first perceives it to be simple substance – depicting the myth of Europa's abduction – and then encounters its 'shadow' – the suggestion of an alternative meaning which is hinted at, but never fully disclosed.

This has ramifications for how we understand the novel's female characters. *Who's That Girl* (like)? Like Europa who is like Selene who is like Astarte who is like Aphrodite... According to Bartsch, the function of the description of the Europa painting is to set the tone for the novel's eroticism and to prefigure the character of Leucippe as 'an acquiescent kidnappee'.[42] In so far as the *ekphrasis* foreshadows Leucippe's character honestly, suggests Bartsch, it is 'less deceptive' than the other *ekphraseis* in the novel.[43] However, it is hard to sustain this interpretation if we agree that Leucippe is prefigured by Europa and then compared to Selene. If her likeness to Europa prefigures Leucippe's laxness with her chastity, then what does her likeness to Selene signify? Selene/Astarte is associated with sexual pleasure. Astarte is another aspect of Aphrodite and her cult was notorious for temple-prostitution.[44] If we are prompted to associate Leucippe with Aphrodite, she becomes closer to Melite than is often contended, disrupting the paraded complementarity between the two women.[45] However, the moon-goddess is also commonly linked with the chaste Artemis, with whom Leucippe is paralleled at several points throughout the narrative. (... like Selene like Artemis . . .). Selene/Artemis's motivation for riding a bull, astrological rather than sexual, constrasts sharply with Europa's behaviour and anticipates a very different side to Leucippe's character. I shall return to the contradictory representation of Leucippe in my fourth chapter; suffice it to note here that her character and

---

[41] Coates (1991), 1. [42] Bartsch (1989), 54. [43] Ibid., 78.
[44] See Briquel-Chatonnet (1992), 192–3. Invariably, studies of Phoenicia mention its temple-prostitution, but without adducing much tangible evidence: see Beard and Henderson (1998).
[45] For the association of Melite with Aphrodite and Leucippe with Artemis, see Segal (1984).

its prefiguration by the opening *ekphrasis* is far from one-sided, as Bartsch's analysis implies. The uncanniness of Achilles' text will come up again in a discussion of the description of Alexandria in Chapter 3 and in a look at animals as uncanny figures in Chapter 4.

The painting of Europa/Selene is programmatic in its foregrounding of visual appearance as a site of error. Neither Clitophon nor the narrator sees the painting fully; the reader, too, risks only seeing one aspect of the work if he or she fails to consolidate the perspectives and see the whole syllepsis. Reading is thus staged as erring, or, more specifically, monoscopic reading is staged as erring, as misreading. The mode of reading mobilised here is characterised by excess. One image generates not just one narrative but two. Instead of operating as a site of convergence, like the painting described in the preface of *Daphnis and Chloe*, the Europa/Selene painting is effective as a site of divergence. It is and is not an image of Europa. It makes manifest the multiple narrative possibilities of the sign.

Phoenician tales

The start of Clitophon's narration can be read as a second beginning to the novel. The translations and adaptations of Achilles Tatius discussed in the introduction, which start their works from Clitophon's narration and excise everything which precedes it, literally read this as the beginning of the novel. Readings which downplay the impact of the opening scene implicitly do the same.[46] This beginning opens with the words: Ἐμοὶ Φοινίκη γένος 'I am a Phoenician' (1.3).[47] Casting Clitophon as a Phoenician, and fashioning his story, therefore, as a Phoenician tale, creates particular expectations of both narrator and novel. 'Phoenician' has many associations. Phoenicians are stereotyped variously as sea-loving, skilled craftsmen, avaricious and deceitful as well as being

---

[46] As Fusillo does when he claims that 'le préambule sert . . . seulement à authentifier le recit': Fusillo (1991), 66.

[47] Phoenicians were a people, rather than a race or nation, which makes *genos* hard to render in translation.

associated, in some narratives, with human sacrifice and temple prostitution.[48] Announcing himself to be 'of Phoenician stock', Clitophon suggests a literary as well as a familial genealogy. Being Phoenician marks him as a hero from comedy rather than epic. In contrast with Theagenes' association with the world of myth through his Thessalian origins, this is a more bourgeois affiliation.

Moreover, it stamps his narratives (and the rest of the novel) as 'Phoenician tales'. Indeed, the novel's two main protagonists are Phoenician, their adventures begin and end in Phoenicia, and Phoenician customs and curiosities are a recurrent thematic interest. In this and other Greek novels, Phoenicians are represented as speaking Greek, having Greek names and demonstrating Greek *paideia*.[49] However, geographic and ethnographic descriptions often operate to construct a contrary picture, fashioning Phoenicia as alien and interesting, as an object of curiosity. Phoenicia is configured through objects which are associated with it, both etymologically and culturally. The story of the primacy of Tyrian wine (2.2) and the frequent occurrence of the word *phoinix* with its multiple meanings as the colour purple-red, the phoenix bird, and the date-palm, are some examples of this characterisation.[50] Phoenicia, and Tyre in particular, was famous for its purple-dye industry and, after informing us that Calligone's dress was purple (*porphura* 2.11.4), Clitophon relates the story of the discovery of purple, which led to the invention of dye (2.11.4–8). Here Phoenicia is associated with luxury and the exotic, As Françoise Briquel-Chattonet writes: 'L'image des Phéniciens qui ressort des romans grecs est donc double. Ils sont totalement hellénisés mais, en même temps leur nom continue a être associé a de nombreux clichés.'[51] Like the picture of Europa/Selene on a bull, Phoenicia both is and is not Greek; it is familiar, yet strange. Of course, the first 'beginning' of the novel initiates this characterisation, as

---

[48] Briquel-Chattonet (1992), Winter (1995).   [49] See Briquel-Chattonet (1992).
[50] The phoenix bird is described at the end of book 3 (see below 190–7). The oracle (2.14.1) says that people who live on this island city are 'named from trees', which, Sostratus explains, is because the tree is the *phoinix*, the 'palm-tree'. See Bowie (1998) on the imagery of φοῖνιξ and its cognates in Heliodorus. More generally on the significance of the colour purple in antiquity, see the forthcoming work of Mark Bradley.
[51] Briquel-Chattonet (1992), 194. See also Winter (1995).

the myth of Europa was itself a Phoenician tale: a Greek myth in which Cadmus travelled from Tyre or Sidon in his search for his abducted sister before becoming founder of the city of Thebes; a myth which was 'subsequently integrated and internalised by Phoenicia itself'[52] as it became Hellenised. In the second book of *Leucippe and Clitophon*, during a discussion of the festival of Dionysus, it is mentioned that 'the story of Cadmus is a Tyrian myth' (2.2) and we have external evidence for this in the Hellenistic and Imperial coins from Tyre (and Sidon) which depict Cadmus and Europa.

'Phoenician tales' appear to have been recognisable as a type: there were several works of the first or second centuries CE called *Phoenikika*.[53] Only one, the novel by Lollianus, partially survives.[54] The fragments tell of a loss of virginity, cannibalism and group sex. If *Phoenikika* typically had common features, contents which played on the more salacious stereotypes of Phoenicians, then Clitophon's narration, which stamps this new 'beginning' to the novel as *Phoenikika*, would create a very particular set of expectations. The reader would not be disappointed in these expectations, as some of Achilles' more lurid episodes of murder and cannibalism confirm. If, as has been suggested, the novel originally circulated under the title *Phoenikika*, this would obviously strengthen the directive to read it as a series of 'Phoenician Tales'.[55] This beginning to the novel, then, is a programme for ostentatious salaciousness.

A swarm of narratives

Clitophon's tale is preceded by a conversation between the two men and a description of the physical environment in which they sit to converse. This provides an important framing to the narration and one which parades other perspectives from which to

---

[52] Millar (1983), 67. Millar is uncertain whether or not we might see *Leucippe and Clitophon* as evidence of this integration and internalisation.
[53] Klaudios Iolaus (= *FGrHist* 788, 1–3), Herennios Philon (= *FGrHist* 790 F5) and Moschos (= *FGrHist* 784 F3–5); Henrichs (1972), 11.
[54] Holzberg (1995), 88. On the title of Lollianus' novel, see Stephens and Winkler (1995), 318–19.
[55] On the importance of paratextual elements see Genette (1987).

read the narrative which follows. The first narrator comments that Clitophon appears experienced in love (οὐ μακρὰν τῆς τοῦ θεοῦ τελετῆς 1.2.2) and urges him to relate what he has suffered. Clitophon replies: Σμῆνος ἀνεγείρεις... λόγων· τὰ γὰρ ἐμὰ μύθοις ἔοικε, 'That is a swarm of stories you are stirring up . . . my tale is like a fictional adventure', a ringingly Platonic formulation, which echoes Plato, *Republic* 5 450b: οὐκ ἴστε ὅσον ἑσμὸν λόγων ἐπεγείρετε, 'you don't know what a hornet's nest of stories you are stirring up'. Clitophon leads his companion to a nearby grove, densely populated with thick plane trees (ἔνθα πλάτανοι μὲν ἐπεφύκεσαν πολλαὶ καὶ πυκναί 1.2.3) and with a stream of clear water as cool as if it had come from freshly melted snow (παρέρρει δὲ ὕδωρ ψυχρόν τε καὶ διαυγές, οἷον ἀπὸ χιόνος ἄρτι λυθείσης ἔρχεται 1.2.3). This description recalls the setting of Plato's *Phaedrus*, one of the most elaborate of Plato's topographies, which begins with Socrates and Phaedrus settling themselves in a similar place, with plane trees and ice-cold water, before they too embark on a discussion of *eros*.[56] The narrator's comment: πάντως δὲ ὁ τοιοῦτος τόπος ἡδὺς καὶ μύθων ἄξιος ἐρωτικῶν, 'A setting such as this is delightful, and just right for erotic fiction' (1.2.3), is a wry acknowledgement of the novel's homage to this famous discussion of *eros*. Both the preceding verbal exchange and the location of Clitophon's narration are evocative of Platonic works and thus raise the possibility of this being, in some sense, a philosophical novel.

Critical opinions differ as to the extent and purpose of Achilles Tatius' adoption and adaptation of philosophical *topoi* and ideas. On the one hand, Trapp views the relationship as superficial: 'The *Phaedrus* is being used to infuse either a modicum of philosophy, or a little of the stylistic sweetness for which it was so admired by the rhetors. The total debt, however, is not enormous.'[57] On the other, Anderson contends (without sufficient explanation) that 'Achilles clearly sees himself as a Plato eroticus and much of the first two books as an anti-*Phaedrus*'.[58] For Laplace it is Plato's *Symposium* which is the major intertext. She argues that

[56] *Phaedrus* 229a–259b. On the setting of Socrates' dialogue with Phaedrus see Ferrari (1987), 1–36.
[57] Trapp (1990), 155 [58] Anderson (1982), 25.

Leucippe and Clitophon is an allegorical rendition of Aristophanes' speech in Plato's *Symposium*: 'La fable de l'androgyne informe la totalité des aventures romanesques du récit de Clitophon . . . cette fable est le modèle de l'histoire d'amour entre Leucippe et Clitophon.'[59]

Plato's *Phaedrus* and *Symposium* are the two most influential discussions of *eros* in ancient Greek literature and it is no surprise that Achilles Tatius' *muthoi erotikoi* (1.2.3) draw upon the concerns and ideas expressed in these works.[60] However, I think that we can safely say that the importance of the *Phaedrus* and *Symposium* for *Leucippe and Clitophon* is not limited to introducing 'a modicum of philosophy' or 'a little stylistic sweetness'. The *Symposium*, and in particular Aristophanes' speech on *eros*, with its themes of separation, search for, and reunion of lovers, has clearly influenced the narrative patterns of Achilles Tatius and, to varying degrees, the other Greek novels.[61] Certain episodes in *Leucippe and Clitophon* highlight its relationship with the *Symposium* more strikingly than others; for example the *sunkrisis* on sexuality at the end of Book 2, which quite obviously draws upon the discussion at *Symposium* 180d–182a. Towards the beginning of his narration, Clitophon relates a dream that he had when he was nineteen and his family were preparing for his marriage to his half-sister Calligone (1.3.4–5). In the dream he appears to have merged into one body with Calligone from the navel downwards. A viraginous woman brandishing a sickle slices through where the bodies are joined, separating Clitophon from the maiden.[62] The separation

---

[59] Laplace (1988), 34–35.

[60] For Aristophanes, speech in the *Symposium* as a model for the love, separation and reunion of the central protagonists in the Greek novels, see Fusillo (1989), 189; Winkler (1994), 23–38; Hunter (1996) 139–205. On the *Symposium* and Xenophon of Ephesus, see Laplace (1994) and Laplace (1992).

[61] On the novels and Plato see Fusillo (1989), 187; Winkler (1994), 37–8 and Hunter (1997) on Longus and Plato; MacQueen (1990) on Longus and Plato's *Phaedrus*. On the comic appropriation of a passage of Plato's *Laws* (12 961a–b) by *Leucippe and Clitophon* 8.9.9, see Liviabella Furiani (1985a).

[62] A terrifying figure: φοβερὰ καὶ μεγάλη, τὸ πρόσωπον ἀγρία· ὀφθαλμὸς ἐν αἵματι, βλοσυραὶ παρειαί, ὄφεις αἱ κόμαι, 'A huge terrifying figure with a savage countenance: her eyes were bloodshot, her cheeks rugged, and her hair made of snakes' (1.3.4). This creature is in the tradition of hybrids and monstrosities like the *mixoparthenos*, Herodotus, *Hist.* 4.9; the Echidna, Hesiod, *Theog.* 295–305 and the Sphinx, Eur. *Phoen.* 1023.

of the enjoined bodies into two separate entities by slicing them through the navel is clearly reminiscent, albeit with a nightmarish twist, of the fable of the original androgyne told by Aristophanes. Clitophon interprets the dream as prophetic, warning him of what he is to experience in the future (1.3.2–3). Therefore, at the outset of Clitophon's narration the expectation is established that the events in his story will, in an imaginative way, correspond to those in the myth of the androgyne.

The major concerns of the *Phaedrus* – rhetoric, the nature of *eros*, and the form, unity, and status of written communication – are dramatised and explored in *Leucippe and Clitophon* and, by signposting an intertextual relationship with the *Phaedrus* at the beginning of the novel, Achilles invites the reader to import his or her knowledge and understanding of the Platonic text when engaging with Achilles' treatment of these issues. Of particular significance is the *Phaedrus*' preoccupation with the nature of truth and fiction. In the opening scene of the dialogue (229b–e) Phaedrus mentions the myth (τὸ μυθολόγημα) of the rape of the nymph Oreithyia by Boreas and asks Socrates if he believes in such stories. Socrates rejects rationalisations of myths ('They belong in my view to an over-clever and laborious person who is not altogether fortunate', . . . λίαν δὲ δεινοῦ καὶ ἐπιπόνου καὶ οὐ πάνυ εὐτυχοῦς ἀνδρός 229d) and believes 'what is commonly thought about them' (πειθόμενος δὲ τῷ νομιζομένῳ περὶ αὐτῶν 230a). *Leucippe and Clitophon* also begins with an account of the rape of a maiden by a god and the similarity recalls the discussion in the *Phaedrus* and its concern with the credibility of myths.[63]

The question of the credibility of the narrative is highlighted in Clitophon's characterisation of his narration as a σμῆνος . . . λόγων . . . μύθοις ἔοικε. A 'swarm of narratives' is a splendid image with which to conjure the disorientating confusion of styles and genres that constitute the dialogism of Achilles' discourse. But what does it mean to say a *logos* is like a *muthos*? (Once again the moment of likeness is foregrounded. Leucippe is *like* Selene, the *logos* is *like* a *muthos*.) Echoing Plato's distinction between *logos*

---

[63] See also Maeder (1991), 14 n. 53: 'ils . . . . invitent à une comparaison sémantique générale entre les deux textes'.

and *muthos*,⁶⁴ it seems that what Clitophon is suggesting is that his accounts are true, but like stories.⁶⁵ This is the force of the distinction between *logos* and *muthos* made later in the narrative at 1.17.3 when Clitophon relates the account of the 'vegetable marriage' of palm-trees. He is quite specific about the origins and status of the story:

Περὶ δὲ φυτῶν λέγουσι παῖδες σοφῶν· καὶ μῦθον ἔλεγον ἂν τὸν λόγον εἶναι, εἰ μὴ καὶ παῖδες ἔλεγον γεωργῶν.

Wise men tell a story about plants, a story that would be called a myth if the countryfolk did not tell the story too.

This narrative, like Clitophon's narrative as a whole, is defined as a true story, but an incredible one. Thus Clitophon's qualification that his *logoi* are like *muthoi* can be understood as a realistic detail which acknowledges the far-fetched character of his tale, and so fashions Clitophon as a trustworthy narrator. Clitophon is not expecting his audience not to be surprised by what has happened to him, runs the logic; rather (a neat irony), truth is stranger than fiction.

This reading bears out Reardon's contention that 'one of the effects of ego-narrative ... is to induce credibility: the actor in events is telling you what happened, and he ought to know'.⁶⁶ This could be the case, but the opposite might equally be true. Just as Clitophon is about to embark upon his ego-narrative, his life-story, he undermines his credibility by emphasising the incredibility of his material. This aligns his storytelling with a very different tradition of ego-narration in which first-person narrators are renowned, not for their credibility, but just the opposite, for their

---

⁶⁴ At 1.1.2, Achilles reworks Plato, *Rep.* 5.450b. For the contrast of *muthos* and *logos* see Plato, *Gorg.* 523a, *Prot.* 324d, *Phaedo* 61b, Plutarch, *Mor.* 348a and Theon 2.73.25–30 (ed. Spengel). For other references and discussion of *muthos* and *logos* in Longus, see Hunter (1983), 114 nn. 98–100 and Hunter (1997).

⁶⁵ Compare Longus (2.7.1): Daphnis and Chloe react to Philetas' account of Eros 'as if they had heard a *muthos* not a *logos*', ὥσπερ μῦθον οὐ λόγον ἀκούοντες. See Hunter (1983), 47; 114 nn. 98–100 and Morgan's comment: 'Longus here picks up the terminology of Plato's distinction between fictional and true narrative, and in doing so raises serious questions about what truth really is', Morgan (1994), 76 and 78, n. 8.

⁶⁶ Reardon (1994), 89.

mendacity.⁶⁷ Thus Danielle Maeder suggests that insistent ego-narration in Achilles Tatius (one ego-narrator followed by another) 'fonctionne comme signal avertisseur: ce qui va suivre n'est qu' inventions'.⁶⁸ This is perhaps an overstatement. It is not clear that this approach is sufficiently paraded to suggest that Achilles is playing a sustained Lucianic-style joke upon his reader, whereby we are encouraged to infer that everything the narrator says is a lie. However, this line of interpretation is strengthened if we give more weight to the very first words of Clitophon's tale: 'I am a Phoenician.'

Phoenicians acquired a reputation for dishonesty, or to be more precise, for exaggeration of the truth.⁶⁹ The term 'Phoenician lie' was proverbial.⁷⁰ In Plato's discussion of truth and falsehood in the *Republic*, he explains his theory of the 'noble lie' (*gennaion pseudos*, 414bff.), a lie which would be admitted into the ideal state, because, unlike most lies, it would benefit society. He calls this lie 'a Phoenician affair' (*phoenikikon ti*), a phrase whose exact meaning is uncertain,⁷¹ but which assumes some sort of connection between Phoenicians and telling lies. It is difficult to ascertain how widely the stereotype of Phoenicians as liars was held. However, it is possible that the emphasis on Clitophon's nationality at the opening

---

⁶⁷ Maeder (1991) lists the important examples of ego-narratives in an appendix to her article. The uncertainty surrounding the fictive status of Clitophon's first-person narrative recalls Odysseus, 'a tale-teller who manipulates different levels of fictional (self-) representation': Goldhill (1991), 47, especially in the contentious 'Cretan lies' and his first-person narrative to the Phaeacians, on which see Goldhill (1991), 37–47 and 37 n. 67, 47 n. 85 for further bibliography.

⁶⁸ Maeder (1991), 13.

⁶⁹ See Romm (1992), 18: ' . . . Phoenician naval operations, designed to protect the rich silver trade on the Atlantic coast of Spain, closed them [the Pillars of Heracles] to all non-Punic ships from the late sixth century to around 300 BC. Furthermore, there is speculation that the Phoenicians deliberately exaggerated reports of dire perils beyond the Straits [of Gibraltar] in order to scare away competitors (the legend behind the proverbial expression "Phoenician lie").'

⁷⁰ Romm (1992), 18. How and Wells, commenting on Hdt. 3.104.2–7 assert: 'Φοινικικὸν ψεῦδος was proverbial' and refer the reader to an episode in Pausanias (9.28.2) where a Phoenician appears to exaggerate the venomous properties of a snake; How and Wells (1912), 290.

⁷¹ It has been argued that Plato was wanting to suggest the Phoenicians' association with trade and moneymaking (Page (1991), 21–6) or perhaps to allude to the myth of Cadmus which, like Plato's 'Myths of Metals', is a tale of autochthonous brotherhood (Adam (1963), 195; Guthrie (1975), 462 and Bloom (1991)). Hesk gives the fullest discussion of this issue and the 'noble lie' more generally: Hesk (2000), 151–63.

of his account might invoke a suspicion that *as a Phoenician*, he is not to be trusted. Indeed, we do know that during his adventures as a young man, Clitophon is economical with the truth. When he relates their misfortunes to Leucippe's father, he does not lie about events, but gives a very partial account and omits any mention of his infidelity: 'When I came to the part about Melite, I omitted my performance of the act, reshaping the story into one of chaste self-control, although I told no actual lies' (8.5.2–3). If we suspect the older Clitophon of being as untrustworthy as his younger self, then we might read his entire narrative as a 'Phoenician lie'.

At very least, Achilles is flirting with the possibility that Clitophon has fabricated his account. Questioning the truth of *muthoi* is a repeated motif. As we have seen, at 2.15.4 Clitophon comments: 'If there is any truth in the myth of Europa, it must have been an Egyptian bull that Zeus imitated', thus leaving open the possibility that the myth might not be true. At 3.15.6 he says . .τάχα ὁ τῆς Νιόβης μῦθος οὐκ ἦν ψευδής . . . 'perhaps the myth of Niobe is no lie', which equally suggests that it might be a lie.[72] These asides press the reader to reflect upon the truth not only of the myths referred to but also of Clitophon's narration and the novel itself. The introductory scenes of *Leucippe and Clitophon* manifest a self-conscious awareness, not only of the artifice of Achilles' creation, but also of the tradition of debate on the status and reception of narratives that informs it.

A reading of the novel as Platonic is elicited by the marked allusions to *Phaedrus* and *Republic* which frame Clitophon's narration, and by a narrative patterning which evokes Aristophanes' tale of the androgyne in *Symposium*. The names of the characters are another element which might reinforce this approach. Most are 'motivated' names: names that gesture towards a particular interpretation. 'Conops' – 'Nat' – is an irritant; 'Satyrus' a cunning meddler. 'Clitophon', 'Gorgias' and 'Charmides' are the names of Platonic dialogues. Once prompted in this direction, other resonances suggest themselves. Perhaps 'Leucippe' is the 'white horse' in the myth of the chariot of the soul in *Phaedrus*.

---

[72] On the difficulty of interpreting expressions of scepticism and disbelief, see Stinton (1976).

Perhaps Clitophon, who is sentenced to death and almost offered hemlock (8.8.5–6), is a Socrates figure. It is this kind of association which leads Laplace to read *Leucippe and Clitophon* as a Platonic allegory, a panegyric to eros which rejects an impious model of the androgyne, but celebrates a new model of the androgyne in the marriage of Leucippe and Clitophon. The narrative certainly accommodates Platonic readings; ideas and concerns explored in Plato are incorporated intertextually and prompt reflection upon a range of philoscphical matters. It is a different matter, however, to argue that there is *sustained* philosophical inquiry. The basic pattern and richness of allusion to Plato are undeniable, but Laplace's proves too totalising a reading. In this novel, it is hard to discern a coherent Platonic agenda without distorting the text; it is hard, in other words, *to make it fit*.

Moreover, it is worth considering how philosophising is thematised in the narrative and asking how this frames a philosophical reading of the novel. On several occasions characters are described as philosophising or being philosophers. Sometimes it is used to signify abstinence from sexual activity. Thus Clitophon remonstrates with the ardent Melite not to pressure him into sex while they are travelling over Leucippe's final resting-place (the sea): Φιλοσοφήσωμεν, εἶπον, ὦ γύναι, μέχρι λαβώμεθα γῆς. '"Let us remain philosophical about the matter, my dear wife," I said, "until we reach dry land"' (5.16.7). Thersander, disbelieving Leucippe's claim that she is still a virgin, sneers: Εὐνοῦχοί σοι γεγόνασιν οἱ λῃσταί; φιλοσόφων ἦν τὸ πειρατήριον; 'Were these pirates of yours eunuchs? Or was it a sect of piratical philosophers?' (6.21.3) and Clitophon boasts to Leucippe's father that he and Leucippe did not consummate their relationship, but were philosophers: ἐφιλοσοφήσαμεν, πάτερ, τὴν ἀποδημίαν, 'Our peregrination bespoke philosophical moderation' (8.5.7).

Judith Perkins reads these characterisations of doing philosophy as support for her contention that certain of the romance novels (*Callirhoe*, *Ephesian Tales*, and *Leucippe and Clitophon*) promote Stoic ideology.[73] There is considerable substance to this interpretation; unsurprising, perhaps, given the prominence of

[73] Perkins (1995), 77–103.

Stoicism in the ethical *Zeitgeist* of the early empire. The teachings of writers such as Seneca (4 BCE–65 CE) and Epictetus (c. 55–135 CE) were hugely influential. One of their major values was the importance of withstanding hardships and deprivations, no matter how painful and extreme, with dignity. Surviving 'bereavement', attempted rape, imprisonment and torture with noble forbearance, as Clitophon and Leucippe are shown doing, is to be Stoic. The writings of the Stoic Epictetus, observes Perkins, 'all fabricate a particular cultural subject – a subject for whom pain essentially does not matter. The romances' heroes and heroines embodied this subject.'[74] When Clitophon refuses Melite's wealth, it can be read as an adherence to the Stoic principle that one should reject temptation. The novels' emphases on conjugality and fidelity, and their implicit analogy between marriage and the city,[75] reflect Stoic values.[76] So, when characters in *Leucippe and Clitophon* refer to 'doing philosophy', Achilles is 'articulat[ing] the similarity between the romance hero and the philosophic [i.e Stoic] rendition of the same subject'.[77]

This should give us pause to reflect on two counts. The first is to acknowledge that Platonism is not the only, or even the most important, school of philosophy with which Achilles engages, something that reading *Leucippe and Clitophon* as a Platonic allegory threatens to occlude. The second is that it provides a persuasive challenge to one common criticism of Achilles Tatius: that Clitophon (like Chaereas and Habrocomes) is characterised as passive. Rather than being feeble, a Stoic reading suggests, he is showing admirable forbearance. The most explicit example of this comes at 5.23.7, when Clitophon is savagely assaulted by Thersander, Melite's husband, who has unexpectedly returned home. Thersander strikes Clitophon on the forehead, seizes him by the hair, knocks him to the ground and repeatedly punches him. Clitophon does not defend himself, although, he is quick to add, 'I could have done so.' The fight ends when they both get tired: Thersander of hitting, and

---

[74] Perkins (1995), 89.
[75] Leucippe's father, away fighting for the city of Byzantium, is said to be 'fighting for other men's marriages' (2.42).
[76] See Perkins (1995), 78; Swain (1996), 118–21 and Schofield (1991).
[77] Perkins (1995), 90.

Clitophon of *being a philosopher*: ἐπεὶ δὲ ἔκαμεν, ὁ μὲν τύπτων, ἐγὼ δὲ φιλοσοφῶν, λέγω πρὸς αὐτὸν ἀναστάς... (5.23.7). 'By describing his lack of action with the word *philosophon*,' explains Perkins, 'Clitophon related his "passivity" to a philosophic context where his refusal to become angry and retaliate made perfect sense. Clitophon's passivity in this episode ought to be interpreted as simply a narrative display of the behavior constructed and valorized in philosophic exhortations of this period.'[78]

However, other examples where *philosophein* is used make a reading of this novel as systematically 'Stoic' just as difficult as a reading of it as 'Platonic'. At 1.10–11, Clitophon and Clinias have a protracted discussion about *eros*, with Clinias proffering advice on seduction techniques and Clitophon bewailing his dilemma that desire impels him to take one course of action while duty to his father urges another. Clitophon then comments: Ἡμεῖς μὲν οὖν ταῦτα ἐφιλοσοφοῦμεν περὶ τοῦ θεοῦ, 'We were philosophising about Eros in this vein' (1.12.1). A short while after Clitophon's encounter with her angry and suspicious husband, Melite delivers a powerful speech persuading Clitophon to make love to her. Ταῦτα φιλοσοφήσασα (διδάσκει γὰρ ὁ Ἔρως καὶ λόγους) ἔλυε τὰ δεσμὰ ... 'With this philosophical exposition done (Eros even teaches eloquence) she started loosening my bonds', remarks Clitophon as he succumbs to her persuasive wiles (5.27.1). In what way is *this* a 'narrative display of the behavior constructed and valorized in philosophic exhortations of this period'? 'Philosophising' in this instance indicates not Stoic self-mastery, but seducing a lover and

---

[78] Perkins (1995), 91. It is possible that it is specifically Socrates (a Stoicised Socrates?) who is the philosopher implicated here. This episode is similar to a tale about Socrates related by St Basil. In his treatise *To Young Men on Reading Greek Literature*, St Basil displays Socrates as a model of virtue. He relates how Socrates reacted when he was attacked:

> A certain man kept striking Socrates, son of Sophroniscus, full in the face, falling upon him without mercy; yet he did not fight back, but permitted the drunken man to exhaust his rage, so that his face was presently swollen and bruised by the blows. Now when the man stopped hitting him, Socrates, it is said, did nothing, except inscribe on his own forehead, like the signature of a sculptor on a statue, 'He did these terrible things.' And only to that extent did he get his revenge. (7. 5–7)

St Basil is writing a couple of centuries later than Achilles Tatius, but a similar account in Plutarch suggests that such stories about Socrates might not be uncommon and that Achilles is drawing upon his reputation for passive forbearance; cf. Plutarch, *De. lib. educ.* 10c.

committing adultery. Nor do Clitophon's actions live up to Stoic ideals. It is hard to read his string of excuses – 'I felt a natural human reaction. I was also genuinely scared of Eros, that he might visit his wrath upon me; and, what was more, I considered how I had regained Leucippe, how I was about to be rid of Melite, how the act to be performed was a matter not of marriage but of the remedy for a kind of illness of the soul' – as anything other than specious (and comic) rationalisations. Indeed, although Perkins' specific contention, that both Stoic writings and the novels construct a similar subject, 'a self that is exempt from the experience of pain and suffering', is sound, the broader suggestion that *Leucippe and Clitophon* conforms to a Stoic agenda, clearly is not. To read the Stoic tenet 'endure and refrain' as 'captur[ing] the very essence ... of Achilles Tatius' necessitates some extraordinary editing. There is not much refraining in Clitophon's enthusiasm and Leucippe's willingness to have sex in Book 2 and no refraining whatsoever in his 'therapeutic' tryst with Melite. Reading *Leucippe and Clitophon* as straightforwardly Stoic or Platonic involves distortions and omissions and, crucially, misses much of its humour. Alongside Achilles' representations of Stoic endurance, we have comic episodes of blatant intemperance. Moreover, it can be an easy move to call something 'ironic', but when Achilles uses *philosophein* as a synonym for abstinence, his irreverence elsewhere casts this not – or not only – as philosophical restraint, but (also) as a joke playing upon the *reputation* of philosophers for sexual temperance.[79] Stoic and Platonic ideas form an important part of the fabric of this novel, but in a pastiche, a '*swarm* of narratives', not coherent and exclusive ideologies.

Theatricality and reading

Achilles on Scyros

Book 6 opens with jail-break, Toad of Toad Hall style. Melite helps Clitophon escape by dressing him in her clothes. She finds

---

[79] See also Chariton 1.10.4; Lucian, *Dialogues of the Courtesans* 10; Philostratus, *Letter* 44; Alciphron, *Letters* 4.7 and the fundamental discussion of Goldhill (1995), 94–100 on the novel's 'ironization of the philosophy of chastity'.

his transformation becoming ('How much more handsome you have become with this clothing!' she said') and, in a formula reminiscent of that previously used to liken Leucippe to the picture of Europa/Selene, compares the disguised Clitophon to an image of Achilles: 'He was like Achilles I once saw in a painting': τοιοῦτον Ἀχιλλέα ποτὲ ἐθεασάμην ἐν γραφῇ (6.1.3). The simile refers to the myth where the young Achilles was dressed as a girl and hidden among the daughters of King Lycomedes on the island of Scyros by his mother Thetis, who was anxious to protect him from being drafted to fight in the Trojan War. The Greeks, knowing that Achilles' participation in the war was necessary if they were to win it, sent Odysseus to find him out. Odysseus placed gifts before the king's daughters: jewellery, trinkets, and armour, and scrutinised the group's reactions. Achilles revealed himself by ignoring the feminine finery and seizing the armour. This particular moment was one of heightened spectacle; indeed, Achilles' unveiling was a popular subject in Roman art. The painting of Achilles to which Melite likens Clitophon brings to mind several paintings and mosaics that survive from the Roman Empire.[80] However, in *this* novel, any mention of *Achilles* cannot fail also to evoke the author and, by metonym, his novel (reinforced by the ambiguity inherent in *graphe*, which can mean 'writing' as well as 'painting'). The image of Achilles in drag, in this wry metaliterary moment, also functions as a textual hieroglyph of the novel itself.

It symbolises the marked theatricality of *Leucippe and Clitophon*. The novel stages a series of extraordinary spectacles that fashion the reader, as well as the spectators within the story, as audiences of the drama.[81] It emphatically tropes its world as

---

[80] E.g. the paintings from the *tablinum* of the House of the Dioscuri and the peristyle of the House of Achilles in Pompeii, and the mosaic in the House of Apollo, Pompeii, which are reproduced and discussed in Beard and Henderson (2001), 26–9. The artist Polignotos was also reputed to have painted Achilles on Scyros: *Paus.* 1.22.6. See also Sharrock (2002), 266.

[81] See Bartsch (1989), 109–43 on descriptions of spectacles in Achilles Tatius and Heliodorus and below 167–9 on the 'sacrifice' of Leucippe and 193 on the virginity test. Achilles' style of writing is sometimes elaborate and highly rhetorical; another facet of his theatricality, as the Byzantine rhetor Michael Psellus noted: 'his diction is vulgar and theatrical in the highest degree', δημοτικωτάτην οὖσαν καὶ θεατρικωτάτην παντάπασιν (71), Dyck (1986), 96–7.

a play and its characters as assuming roles and donning disguises.[82] At 2.28.1, Pantheia urges Leucippe to reveal 'the plot of her drama': τὴν συσκευὴν τοῦ δράματος. Later in the novel, Leucippe assumes the identity of a slave girl and calls herself Lacaena.[83] She debates whether or not to keep up her disguise: Ἆρα ἀποκαλύψασα τοῦ δράματος τὴν ὑπόκρισιν διηγήσομαι τὴν ἀλήθειαν; . . . Φέρε πάλιν ἐνδύσωμαί μου τὸ δρᾶμα· φέρε πάλιν περίθωμαι τὴν Λάκαιναν, 'Shall I cast aside the role I have acted and tell him the true story? . . . Come, it is best to reassume my dramatic role, to wear once again the costume of Lacaena' (6.16.4–6).[84] Callisthenes eventually confesses to Calligone: 'love made me act the part of a pirate and weave this plot against you', Ἔρως δέ με λῃστείας ὑποκριτὴν πεποίηκε καὶ ταύτας ἐπὶ σοὶ πλέξαι τὰς τέχνας (8.17.3). The youths who assist Callisthenes to kidnap Calligone disguise themselves in women's clothing (2.18.3–4). Even the peacock has a theatre in his feathers: τὸ θέατρον . . . τῶν πτερῶν (1.16.2).[85]

Moreover, the motifs of theatricality in the novel are crucially bound up with how its narrative design (or lack of it) is presented to the reader. For Leucippe, Callisthenes, and others may play roles, but it is Tyche who scripts the drama and Clitophon who stage-manages (at least part of) it. Clinias counsels Clitophon early on in the novel: ἐὰν δὲ μαλθακώτερον ἤδη θέλῃ, χορήγησον τὴν ὑπόκρισιν, μὴ ἀπολέσῃς σου τὸ δρᾶμα, 'If she now softens, assume the directorial role, in case you ruin the entire play' (1.10.7). *Drama* here might be taken as referring to the plot to win over Leucippe, but as it takes the rest of the narrative for

---

[82] On Heliodorus' even more frequent use of theatrical metaphors, see Walden (1894) and Bartsch (1989), 109–43.
[83] 'The Spartan': a name sometimes assigned to Helen of Sparta.
[84] Disguise suggests ephebic initiation ritual too: in ritual, cross-dressing may form part of an ephebic *rite de passage* which marks incipient adulthood. It is thus a particularly apposite practice for the adolescents Leucippe and Clitophon. See Laplace (1991). Leucippe does not take on the identity of a man, but looks like a man in her garb as Lacaena the slave. Satyrus comments that it was no wonder that Clitophon had failed to recognise Leucippe as 'she had become so much the young ephebe. The mere cropping of her hair transformed her utterly': . . . ἔφηβον οὕτω γενομένην· τοῦτο γὰρ ἡ τῶν τριχῶν αὐτῆς κουρὰ μόνον ἐνήλλαξεν (5.19.2).
[85] Cf. Horace, *Satires* 2.2.26 *picta pandat spectacula cauda* and Dio Chrysostom, *Olympic Discourse* 2 ὅταν ἁβρύνηται πρὸς τὴν θήλειαν, ἀνακλάσας τὴν οὐρὰν καὶ περιστήσας αὑτῷ πανταχόθεν ὥσπερ εὐειδὲς θέατρον.

Clitophon really to get his girl, it also provides a gloss on the rest of the novel. Clitophon is portrayed as the *khoregos*: the director, producer, casting manager, and general impresario of the show.[86] Theatrical metaphors were very common in antiquity, particularly during the time of the greatest show on earth: the Roman Empire. The Stoic Epictetus frequently compares human beings to actors playing roles.[87] However, the image of Clitophon as a *khoregos* is quite a specific one. He is not an actor playing a part, as Stoic philosophy would have it, but the organiser of the drama. The *khoregos* has control; a more fitting image, perhaps, for the knowing narrator who controls the narrative perspective than for the younger, rather inept Clitophon.

The image of Tyche 'scripting' the drama (6.3.1) is important. Tyche, 'Chance', is an abstract deity who began to be anthropomorphised and worshipped widely in the Hellenistic world. She was adopted by cities as their protecting goddess, notably at Antioch, where Eutychides' impressive statue of Tyche was imitated on the coins and iconography of forty-four eastern cities.[88] When Tyche is presented as 'scripting a new drama' (6.3.1), she appears as the divine playwright of the action. However, there are contradictory representations of determination in *Leucippe and Clitophon*. In the first book of the novel, Clitophon, narrating, comments:

Providence (τὸ δαιμόνιον) often shows the future to men in dreams, not so they might avoid what will happen to them – for they can never beat destiny (εἱμαρμένη) – but so that they might endure it with more patience (κουφότερον). (1.3.2)

---

[86] This is a term taken from the Athenian institution of the *khoregia*. *Khoregoi* were elected to recruit, fund and train the choruses for dramatic festivals, an honour and a burden involving 'massive expenditures, multiple toil and long periods of devoted practice', Xen. *Hiero* 9.11. See Wilson (2000).

[87] 'Remember that you are an actor in a play; the sort of play is whatever the playwright [god] wishes: short, if he wants it short, long if he wants it long. If he wants you to play a beggar, play even this part skilfully, or a cripple, or a civic leader, or a private citizen. For this is your business, to play the given role well. To choose the role is another's' (*Handbook* 17), quoted and discussed in Perkins (1995), 84. The point of Epictetus' analogy is to stress that what is important is not the role we are assigned, but how well we play it; to accept our lot in life, not try and escape from it. Achilles Tatius presents a different theatrical paradigm. In his novel, assuming a role is usually associated with deception or seduction, as Bartsch (1989), 127 notes.

[88] Stewart (1997), 201–2.

This is a very Stoic sentiment and Heimarmene is a marked term from that school of philosophy. The Stoic concept of 'Destiny' or 'Fate', Heimarmene suggests a world order that is, in many ways, opposite to that ruled over by Tyche.[89] The tension on the metaphysical level between Tyche and Heimarmene reflects, or might even be held responsible for, the tension on the narrative level between improvisation and plottedness. If the narrative's vicissitudes illustrate the randomness of life, the ending, with the puzzles explained and the loose ends tied up, might suggest a more deterministic view of the world, a world ruled by Heimarmene. This depends on reading the ending of the novel as a resolution, which is by no means unproblematic, as will be discussed in the next chapter. However, if we do see marriage and resolution at the close of the novel, the ending can be read as a victory for Stoicism: Tyche may write the plot, but it is Heimarmene who stages the grand finale.

Within the general vocabulary of acting and drama are references to individual theatrical works that operate to flag particular intertextual relations and frame interpretation accordingly. Two are especially memorable: Homer and Aristophanes. We meet an actor who recites Homer in the theatre, and his prop, a trick knife with a retractable blade which will prove useful in faking the sacrifice of Leucippe, is lovingly described (3.20.4–7). In addition, Homer is frequently quoted.[90] The reference to Aristophanes' plays comes in the final book of the novel, when Nicostratus, the priest of Artemis,

---

[89] On the Stoics, fate, and determinism, see Bobzien (1998); Frede (2003). On Stoic fate and its relation to providence, see Veyne (1990). The Stoics Chrysippus, Boethus, Posidonius and Philopator all wrote works on determinism and fate but none of them survive.

[90] At the beginning of the second book, Leucippe plays the harp, singing of 'Homer's fight between the boar and the lion', alluding to *Iliad* 16.823. The *Iliad* is also evoked at 2.15.3, when Clitophon compares the colour of the Egyptian ox 'to that for which Homer so greatly commends the horses of the Thracian' (referring to *Iliad* 10.435) and the character Menelaus (whose name is itself an obvious Homeric focaliser) quotes the *Iliad* on the abduction of Ganymede as support for his argument that boys are more desirable than women:

> If we must also cite a poet as witness to beauty's ascent to heaven, listen to the words of Homer: 'Him the gods took up to pour wine for Zeus, | thanks to his beauty, so he might be with immortals' (2.36.3, quoting *Iliad* 20.234–5).

Clinias quotes from the *Works and Days* and the *Iliad* to give rhetorical punch to his diatribe against women: at 1.8.2 he quotes *Works and Days* 57–8 and at 1.8.7 quotes *Iliad* 2.478.

speaks in a style explicitly said to emulate that of Aristophanic comedy:

ἦν δὲ εἰπεῖν οὐκ ἀδύνατος, μάλιστα δὲ τὴν Ἀριστοφάνους ἐζηλώκει κωμῳδίαν – ἤρξατο αὐτὸς λέγειν πάνυ ἀστείως καὶ κωμῳδικῶς εἰς πορνείαν αὐτοῦ καθαπτόμενος. (8.9.1)[91]

He was a speaker of no slight ability, and in particular emulated the style of Aristophanic comedy. He delivered his own speech, opening with an extremely suave exordium in the style of the comic poets, accusing Thersander of renting his body.

These episodes, together with other references, quotations and allusions,[92] create a marked awareness of the characters' status as literary constructs, written against a cast of characters from a long tradition of poetry and drama and, more pointedly and politically, from *Greek* poetry and drama. This is part of the novel's flamboyant display of *paideia* and construction of certain characters and ideal readers as *pepaideumenoi*. But it is more than that: references and allusions to other literature direct different ways of reading through and against those works. In sum, the value of the novel is repeatedly being established *relationally*, by comparison with the previous texts and authors it names, quotes and alludes to.

It is perhaps significant that all of the citations from Homer are from the *Iliad* (there are none from the *Odyssey*, though the Cyclops episode is alluded to at 2.23.3). It is not simply that this novel is establishing itself in relation to epic, but more pointedly that it is engaged with the *Iliad*, the epic of *Achilles*. The abduction of a beautiful woman, encounters with conflict, and endurance of loss: the novel's situations, characterisations, and values evoke, yet are set against, those of the *Iliad*. The image of Achilles in a woman's clothes symbolises *Leucippe and Clitophon*'s homage to, but differences from, the epic. Representations of gender are an important example of this relationship. It is significant that the simile depicts not the warrior Achilles, throbbing with masculinity, but the young, effeminate Achilles. It is in comic contrast to a simile used to represent Heliodorus' hero, Theagenes, who is also

---

[91] Cataudella (1954) argues, with tenuous reasoning, that the portrayal of the bishop is really intended to allude to John Chrysostom.
[92] E.g. at 2.9.3, 3.22.3, 7.11.1, 8.10.8, 8.15.4.

(repeatedly) compared to Achilles, but in his case to emphasise his heroic prowess, for example:

he was an impressive sight and admired by all, just the way Homer portrays Achilles contending during the battle along the Scamander. (4.3.1)[93]

Both Heliodorus and Achilles Tatius use Homer as a means for defining their own works. But in Achilles the comparison with the Homeric hero serves to highlight Clitophon's difference from, rather than emulation of, his bold action and masculinity.

The fabrication of the priest of Artemis as an Aristophanic character, and the acknowledgement of this theatrical debt, directs another line of interpretation. It is one episode among several which confirm the general agreement that *Leucippe and Clitophon* is a comic novel. The overt reference to Aristophanes alerts the reader all the more forcefully to the comic possibilities of the narrative. Characters' names are another of the features that flag a comic reading. Gorgias, Chaereas and Clitophon are names which can be read as indices of a Platonic reading, but, together with Sostratos and Clinias, they are also names of characters from plays of Menander, which highlights a different approach: the novel as comedy. It is not hard to appreciate *Leucippe and Clitophon*'s obvious comic features: slapstick, irreverence, parody and jokes, but, as always with this novel, it is hard to know how much to privilege any one line of interpretation; or, if we wish to read this as one element in the pastiche, how the different, and sometimes potentially dissonant elements are to be accommodated.

For example, the name 'Leucippe' can have a Platonic resonance (as the 'white horse' of the *Phaedrus* she would represent 'good' desire) which the evocation of the *Phaedrus* at the beginning of the novel foregrounds. However, it can also be a slang word for penis.[94] This is almost certainly the suggestion in Aristophanes' *Lysistrata* when Kalonike and Lysistrata discuss swearing

---

[93] A reference to *Iliad* 21.203–384. Achilles is even presented as Theagenes' mythical ancestor: *Aeth.* 2.35.1. Chariton's Chaereas is also compared to Achilles: 'surpassingly handsome, like Achilles and Nireus and Hippolytus and Alcibiades as sculptors and painters portray them' (*Callirhoe* 1.1.3). The comparison both serves to suggest Chaereas' gorgeousness (Achilles and Nireus are described as the handsomest of the Greeks at Troy: *Iliad* 2.673–4) and, with the number of comparanda, also makes his desirability less individualised and more generic.

[94] Henderson (1991), 127.

an oath by a 'white stallion', *leukon hippon* (191–3), giving this common sacrificial victim a sexual *double entendre*. The image of the woman who 'rides', like the Amazon, connotes the dominatrix, the 'woman on top'.[95] Names which incorporate equestrian imagery of this kind were commonly used by prostitutes.[96] The speech of Nicostratus is a blueprint for smutty reading, maximising every possible *double entendre* and sexualising the world.[97] If we read the novel as this character reads the world, then 'Leucippe' would most certainly invoke sexual humour. Furthermore, these connotations of Leucippe as a 'phallic woman' and a prostitute colour her character differently from those raised by a Platonic reading. This leads me to qualify the observations I made earlier about motivated names. Characters' names in this novel do not always function as indices of their identities. Rather, they are like 'vacant signs' onto which a number of readings may be mapped. Lack of narrative hierarchy makes it unclear which reading or readings are designed to dominate, so possibilities proliferate.[98] Of course, the possibilities are not necessarily mutually exclusive, but it is hard for their presence not to qualify and modify any reading which tries to pin it down as 'Platonic', 'Stoic', 'comic', 'mythological'. This overdetermination results in indeterminacy. It is part of what creates that sense of reading a work which is experimental and improvisatory (as Nimis has it), rather than designed with one overall interpretation in mind. Achilles dons many disguises.

Choreographing the reader

The repeated motif of *hupokrisis* in *Leucippe and Clitophon* is part of its affinity with certain other genres in which *hupokrisis* is privileged. Lucian discusses *hupokrisis* in his *De Saltatione*,

---

[95] As the scholia on *Lysistrata* 191–2 comment: see Sommerstein (1990), 165.
[96] E.g. Hippe (Mare), Hippaphesis (Starting Post of a Race Course), and Synoris (Pair of Horses), all prostitutes in Athenaeus, *Deipn.* book 13.
[97] On the wordplay here see Goldhill (1995), 99–100.
[98] Another line of interpretation – mythological – which reads the novel as an imaginative version of the myth of Io, lays weight on the fact that the name 'Leucippe' is the name of one of the daughters of Proteus and features in the festival of the Agrionia: cf. Laplace (1983a).

an encomiastic treatise on the pantomime that takes the form of a defence mounted by the character Lycinus against the harsh criticisms of the entertainment by his companion, Crato.[99] Some of his discussion might prove useful for extending our understanding of theatricality in Achilles Tatius. According to the character Lycinus, 'the chief occupation and aim of dancing is impersonation': Ἡ δὲ πλείστη διατριβὴ καὶ ὁ σκοπὸς τῆς ὀρχηστικῆς ἡ ὑπόκρισίς ἐστιν (65). *Hupokrisis*, he continues, is also cultivated by rhetoricians, when they recite their exercises 'for in their case also there is nothing which we commend more highly than their accommodating themselves to the roles which they assume': οὐδὲν γοῦν καὶ ἐν ἐκείνοις μᾶλλον ἐπαινοῦμεν ἢ τὸ ἐοικέναι τοῖς ὑποκειμένοις προσώποις (65). A brief look at Achilles Tatius' relationships with the pantomime (and the related genre of the mime), and with the rhetorical exercises known as *controversiae* might help us better appreciate the novel, especially in relation to three areas: narrative design, gender dynamics, and reception or reader-response.

The *controversiae*, practice-exercises for trainee orators in the Roman *scholae*, such as those recorded (in piecemeal, 'greatest hits', fashion) by Seneca the Elder, present juicy moral dilemmas through frequently sensationalist scenarios. Similarities in subject matter between the novels and these rhetorical exercises (pirates, prostitutes, abductions, mistaken identities) have long been observed, as has their common use of rhetorical devices such as *ethopoieia*, the delineation of character.[100] 'A *parthenos* is abducted by pirates, escapes and claims sanctuary in the temple of Artemis. She claims to have remained a virgin. Her master wants her back'; 'A man falls in love with a girl through hearing a report of her and abducts the wrong girl. He should be punished by marriage' would be quite at home in Seneca, and Melite's avoidance of penalty in her chastity test through a technicality in the

---

[99] For analysis of which, see Kokolakis (1959); Branham (1989), 18–19. Swain (1996), 314 n. 59 has further bibliography. Lucian's work may be in response to a diatribe against pantomime by Aelius Aristides (now lost, but with quotations preserved in Libanius' *Against Aristides On the Dance*; cf. Kokolakis (1959), 9–10).

[100] On ethopoieia in ancient writings, see the material collected in Lausberg (1960) s.v. *ethopoieia*.

wording is the type of clever distinction celebrated by the orators. The ancient novels can be read as a *controversia* or series of *controversiae* come to life: fleshed out and narrativised.

Whether, as has been proposed, these affinities are due to a common source or not is hard to determine.[101] Similarities in design have not been noted, but they might be as telling as the similarities in content. Amy Richlin describes the process of debate: 'The theme was given, and then each speaker played a riff on it, as it were; the plotline was developed as a group project, as in some forms of hypertext. *Controversiae* were fluid, within certain (disputed) boundaries; they were never finished; they could be performed, or created, any number of times by any number of players.'[102] This process of riffing, a creation of a kind of hypertext, strongly recalls Nimis' image of a novel being 'improvised', like a student starting an essay from one point without knowing quite where it is going to go (his image).[103] While I have some reservations about this model overall in relation to Achilles, if we accept that *Leucippe and Clitophon* sometimes has an improvisatory feel to it, then it might be attractive to extend Nimis' model and give this quality, if not a source, then at least a cultural and literary frame.

There is something more at stake in what I have referred to as the 'fleshing out' and 'narrativising' of the cases such as are found in the rhetorical exercises, something with radical potential, which might be couched in terms of a move towards a casuistical ethic. Casuistry, a theological method which was a factor in the emergence of the realistic novel in the early modern period, seeks to expose the reductivism of general principles by investigating particular cases which might challenge, or at the very least qualify, those rules. It insists that 'a case is not to be judged in the abstract, but always relative to its particular circumstances'.[104] The potential for casuistry is built into the *controversiae*, which

---

[101] Richlin (1996) proposes a common source for the *controversiae*, ancient novels and apocryphal Acts, but does not suggest what this might be.
[102] Richlin (1996), 20.
[103] Marrou suggests that the closest modern counterpart to ancient rhetorical performances is jazz; both combine technical skill, knowledge of structure, and imaginative improvisation: Marrou (1956), 200. See also Kaster (2001), 321.
[104] Donovan (1999), xi.

involve probing a law's grey areas by teasing out individual cases. However, this is only realised in a very limited way: the individual cases are not particularised with any detail. Protagonists are only sometimes given names, and events are sketched, in part to allow the orators to supply the particulars in the stories that they then build, but even so brevity and selectiveness are admired.[105] The Greek novels take a step further towards creating particularised narratives and characters. Individuals are given more focus than cities; moral dilemmas are given fuller contexts, and characters, though remaining to a large extent stereotyped, are named and assigned different attributes. It is not the case that Anthia is interchangeable with Chloe or Charicleia: to this degree the narratives are particularised. To be sure, we are still a long way from the individualism of the realist novel. This genre, argues Bakhtin, is subversive precisely because it is casuistical: it challenges theoretism (generalising thinking) by insisting on the importance of the particulars of experience.[106] It is certainly true that in comparison to the realist novel, the ancient Greek novels do not emphasise the singularity of events. They do not particularise story-world, events or characters with nearly enough detail for them fully to operate casuistically. However, taking the realist novel as the point of comparison has served to underplay the ancient novel's interrogatory potential. If we positively stress its relationship with the *controversiae* (be that one of sharing a 'common source' or simply one of being a privileged intertext), then the Greek novel can be viewed as having debate and provocation built into it. To a degree at least, *Leucippe and Clitophon* is inherently contestatory.

A further crucial difference created by couching moral dilemmas in narrative form relates to gender. As Richlin has noted, the *controversiae* 'are marked by an almost complete absence of a female subject'.[107] Despite the fact that women feature prominently in the cases (Richlin calculates that forty-two of the cases (well over half) involve female characters),[108] it was convention for declaimers not

---

[105] So Seneca criticises Albucius' development of a number of themes, when one should have sufficed: 'You may ask: shouldn't every question be developed in all its detail? Of course, but as an adjunct, not as the whole', *Quid ergo? Non omnis quaestio per numeros suos implenda est? Quidni? Sed tamquam accessio, non tamquam summa* (Preface to Book 7 (2)).
[106] Bakhtin (1973).   [107] Richlin (1996), 24.   [108] Richlin (1996), 21.

to impersonate them, but only to pretend to act as the character's advocate (*patronus*). With male characters, in contrast, the speakers could choose whether to act as the *patronus* or to impersonate the character themselves. The novels' gendered theatricality is radically different; in the narratives, the women are given speaking roles and are afforded the subjectivities that the rhetorical exercises deny them. The novels, if you like, give the women in the *controversiae* a voice.

The importance of the pantomime and mime as significant intertexts for *Leucippe and Clitophon* has been well established in a series of articles by Elisa Mignogna.[109] Both pantomime (which involved performing mythological stories through dance and physical theatre) and mime (which took more realistic, everyday scenarios and enacted them with dialogue as well as song and dance) were popular in the early Empire. By the first century CE the mime had become the most prominent theatrical entertainment in the Graeco-Roman world.[110] It is no surprise, then, that these dramatic forms are significant contexts within which to situate the ancient novel. There may have been a direct connection with *Leucippe and Clitophon* in the form of a 'Leucippe' mime. Papyrus PBerol inv. 13927 appears to contain snippets of a mime in which a woman called Leucippe finds herself in a barber's shop. Unfortunately, the very fragmentary state of the papyrus makes it impossible to reconstruct a narrative.[111] What is clear is that mime, pantomime

---

[109] Mignogna (1996a), (1996b), (1997). Although there were important differences between mime and pantomime, for the purposes of her argument, Mignogna elides the two genres.

[110] Lucian (67) says that Italian Greeks call the dancer a *pantomimus* because he imitates characters and emotions. On the mime in antiquity, see Reich (1974); Beacham (1991); Fantham (1989), with further, annotated bibliography; Wiseman (1985), 187–94; Reardon (1991), 163, n. 50; Barton (1993), esp. 165–75; Konstan (1994), 162–67; Gianotti (1996) and Edwards (1993). The fragments of Roman mimes are collected in Bonaria (1965). On the influence of mime on Augustan elegy see McKeown (1979), 71–84 and on the mime, martyrology and novel, see Musurillo (1954), 247–58. On the difficulties of defining mime, see Fantham (1989), 154–5 and on distinctions between the different types of Greek and Roman mimes, mimic terminology, and a review of the scholarship on the mime, see the introduction of Panayotakis (1995). The influence of mime and pantomime on Petronius' *Satyrica* has been well documented, most recently and thoroughly by Panayotakis (1995).

[111] Mignogna (1996b) is not swayed by the editor of the fragment's assertion that it is 'nothing to do with Achilles Tatius' (Cunningham 1987). She even conjectures from the word <ε>ἴσοπτρον the possibility of a scene in which Leucippe is looking into a mirror and bemoaning the absence of Clitophon, as Callirhoe does with Chaereas and Ninus does (in Mignogna's reading) in the Antioch mosaic discussed in Chapter 1.

and ancient novel exhibit strong affinities in tone and content.[112] They appear to share a particularly extreme form of *hupokrisis*: illusionism carried to excess, or, as Lucian's Crato puts it, 'exceeding the due limit of mimicry' (ὑπερβαινόντων τὸ μέτρον τῆς μιμήσεως 82), something he deems κακοζηλία, an uncommon word suggesting 'bad taste'. The 'false deaths' of Leucippe (and similar scenes in Lollianus, Lucian's *Ass*, Apuleius and Petronius) are in this vein and akin to the 'snuff' mime of Laureolus[113] and the excessive 'method' acting of the dancer who played mad Ajax and *really* went insane.[114]

Mignogna has argued that the first *Scheintod* is structured to create a 'mimic-pantomimic' frame based on a parodic version of Euripides' *Iphigenia in Tauris*, which would give the scene a possible parallel with the Charition mime.[115] At the very least, the inclusion in Book 3 of the Homeristae, mime-actors who performed scenes from Homer, functions to flag the mime as a significant intertext for Achilles Tatius. The use of the mime artist's weapon with which to 'disembowel' Leucippe frames the *Scheintod* as a mimic spectacle. Mignogna also makes the case for reading the second half of the novel as an 'adultery mime', a type of drama whose nudity and sexual licence had occasioned offence.[116] The pantomime, too, it seems, provoked strong reactions, in much the same terms as some of the response to Achilles Tatius. Lucian's Crato lambasts the dance as *aischra kai kataptusta*, 'shameful and disgusting' (literally, 'worth spitting on') (4); much as, centuries later, Photius uses the same vocabulary. He deems reading Achilles

---

[112] *Inter alia* sea voyages and shipwrecks, cf. the Charition mime (POxy. 413), Seneca, *De Ira* 2.2.5; viewing pictures in a temple, cf. Zeitlin (1994), 148, Panayotakis (1995), 119; physical punishment, cf. the branding and beatings in Herodas' fifth mime (27–8, 32–4); frequent use of proverbs and gnomic statements (see below pp. 96–151).

[113] Martial, *De Spect.* 7, on which see Coleman (1990). Elagabalus ordered that sex scenes should actually be performed on stage, not simulated; cf. Beacham (1991), 137.

[114] Lucian, *De Salt.* 83–4.   [115] Mignogna (1997).

[116] Mignogna (1996a); (1996b). For adultery see e.g. Athenaeus, *Deipn.* 14 621C; Reynolds (1946); Konstan (1994), 167: '[The Roman mime] went beyond the conventional limits of both New Comedy and elegy in depicting sexual passion and conjugal infidelity among citizen women.' On nudity and sexual licence, see the complaints of Cicero: *In Cat.* 2.23.26, *In Pis.* 2, *In Verr.* 2.3.23; Valerius Maximus 2.10.8; Fantham (1989), 153–4. Female pantomimes were commonly associated with prostitutes: cf. Leppin (1992), 137. Not surprisingly, the mime was hated by the Christian church; cf. Beacham (1991), 138.

Tatius *kataptuston*[117] and calls it *aischros, anaidos*, and an example of *aischrologia*.[118] One aspect of the pantomime's 'shameful' character was the staging of transvestite myths, one of which, tellingly, was 'Achilles on Scyros'.[119] Perhaps Melite's description of Clitophon can thus be read as having a more pointed allusion: it does not just symbolise Achilles Tatius' theatricality and self-positioning *vis-à-vis* epic, but more specifically operates as a metonym for the novel's relationship with *mimic* theatre.

In mapping these similarities, I am not so much interested in tracing a formal generic relationship, such as the mime or pantomime being a source for the novel; suffice it to note that the evident similarities between the forms in part at least suggest their mutual influence and common cultural milieux. Nor I am implying that the novel is simply a narrative version of the drama. It is too sophisticated and richly textured a form for that. Rather, I am suggesting that our understanding of the reception of the novel can perhaps be furthered through reference to the reception of mime and pantomime. By association, the approaches to and reputation of the mime and pantomime can illuminate how *Leucippe and Clitophon*, and novels like it, might have been regarded. Two notes of caution should be sounded. First, mimic theatre is one of a multitude of intertexts and I do not wish to privilege it *per se* over and above the other genres consumed by *Leucippe and Clitophon*. Second, my main source for how the mime and pantomime were interpreted and evaluated is Lucian's essay. There is no way of knowing to what extent the opinions expressed by the protagonists in Lucian's dialogue are representative of critical responses to the pantomime; indeed, the evidence we have about the dramas and their reception is all too insufficient. The argument is necessarily speculative and conjectural. I am suggesting that the relation between novel, mime and pantomime may illuminate just one of the many possible conditions for reception.

---

[117] He also criticises 'the excessive baseness and dirtiness of its thoughts', which 'defile the author's integrity and enthusiasm in everything': ἀλλὰ τό γε λίαν ὑπέπαισχρον καὶ ἀκάθαρτον τῶν ἐννοιῶν καὶ τὴν τοῦ γεγραφότος φαυλίζει γνώμην ἐν πᾶσι καὶ σπουδήν, Photius, *Bibliotheca* cod. 87 (ed. Bekker, t.I, p. 66).
[118] *Bibliotheca*, cod. 94 (ed. Bekker, t.I, p. 73).
[119] Luc. *Salt.* 46; Lib *Or.* 64, 68 Cf. also POxy. 53, 3700 (Heracles – Omphale), a myth mentioned at Achilles Tatius 2.6.2 and possibly PKöln VI 245 (Odysseus).

Crato voices many objections to the pantomime, but he is particularly offended by its eroticism and attendant effeminacy. Going to the pantomime involves watching a man poncing about (ἐναβρυνόμενον), singing licentious songs (ᾄσμασιν ἀκολάστοις) and imitating women in love (μιμούμενον ἐρωτικὰ γύναια). These women are the lewdest in antiquity (τῶν πάλαι τὰς μαχλοτάτας), Phaedras, Parthenopes and Rhodopes. Parthenope's love story was also the subject of a novel, no longer extant.[120] It is this novel, known as *Metiochus and Parthenope*, that the Antioch mosaic is thought to illustrate. Crato emphasises the effeminacy of the performer; he is a womanly man (θηλυδρίαν ἄνθρωπον) with soft clothing (ἐσθῆσι μαλακαῖς). However, what is particularly interesting is that the effeminacy does not just reside with the actor. The dance itself is effeminised. Crato calls it φαύλῳ καὶ γυναικείῳ 'base and womanly' (1). This in turn affects the audience. Crato expresses his worry, albeit tongue in cheek, that Lycinus will turn from being the man he once was to a Lydian or a Bacchant (3). He describes the audience as τοῖς γυναίοις καὶ τοῖς μεμηνόσιν ἐκείνοις θεαταῖς 'girlies and manic spectators' (5) and he refuses to sit among them 'as long as [his] legs are hairy and beard unplucked' (5). This jibe insinuates that most of the audience depilate their body hair, a practice indicative of *kinaidoi*, figures of revulsion and ridicule, by which 'real' men contrast and define themselves. The dance and its readership are gendered and denigrated.

Another branch of 'shame' literature, the erotic handbook, or *ars amatoria*, is similarly characterised. Again, the paucity of evidence is frustrating, but we do know that these handbooks detailing sexual positions and advice on seduction were, like the dance, considered 'shameless', *anaiskhuntos*,[121] and were criticised for their licentiousness, *aselgeia* and *akolasia*.[122] Holt Parker comments that 'the genre [w]as a symbol of immoderation and overindulgence'.[123] Like the pantomime, the works themselves were effeminised. An

---

[120] Text of the fragments, with translation and commentary, in Stephens and Winkler (1995), 72–99.
[121] Timaeus of Tauromenium in Polybius 12.13.1; Dioscorides, *A.P.* 7.450; Clement of Alexandria, *Protreptikos* 53P; cited in Parker (1992), 98.
[122] Suda, s.v. Astyanassa; Pseudo-Lucian, *Erotes* 28; Chrysippus in Athenaeus, *Deipn.* 8 335D-E; cited in Parker (1992), 98.
[123] Parker (1992), 98.

epigram of Martial refers to the works of Elephantis, a renowned writer of erotic handbooks, as *molles . . . libelli*, 'soft' or 'feminine' little books.[124] Like the dance, the gender of the readers of erotic handbooks reflects or is affected by the dubious status of the works themselves. Lucian's 'mistaken critic' is represented as debauched and sexually profligate, known for ἀκολασία . . καὶ ἡ αἰσχρουργία, 'extravagance and obscenity'.[125] It is no surprise, therefore, that he dances in the theatre (19) and keeps to hand the Tablets of Philaenis (24), the most notorious author of sex manuals.[126] *Leucippe and Clitophon* is itself a kind of *ars amatoria*. The extended description of a woman's pleasure in orgasm at 2.37.5–10 would not be out of place in Ovid's *Ars Amatoria*, or, one suspects, in the works of Elephantis or Philaenis. It is often didactic, as when Clinias offers advice on how to seduce a girl, and in Clitophon and Satyrus' tales of erotic unions between plants, rivers and snakes. As we have seen, it has been accused of shamelessness and the charge of *akolasia* would not be hard to sustain.

If, then, *Leucippe and Clitophon* shares marked affinities with the pantomime and with the erotic handbook, it may also share affinities with the way in which the dance and handbook are characterised generically, and with the way their audience is constructed. This implies that Achilles Tatius may not only be viewed as 'shame' literature, and considered excessive (*akolastos*), but would also, therefore, be stamped as effeminate. It follows, given that effeminate works effeminise their audience, that one subject position offered to the reader by the text is that of an effeminate male.

I stress that this is *one* subject position, but it is one which is worth considering not least because it complicates two (related) tendencies which have been of some influence in criticism on the ancient Greek novel. First is the tendency to view the novel as 'feminine', and second, to characterise the novels as appealing to readers along the lines of gender. The idea that the novels are essentially 'feminine' is a tenacious one, from the outmoded view that their poor quality renders them feminine,[127] through approaches that emphasise their similarities to today's Harlequin romances,[128]

---

[124] Martial, *Epigrams* XLIII, line 4.   [125] *Pseudologista* 21.
[126] See Parker (1992), 92–6.   [127] See above p. 2, n. 9.   [128] Montague (1992).

to Margaret Anne Doody's proposal (in part a revival of the mystery-text approach, in part New Age fantasy) that (ancient and modern) novels incarnate the Goddess:

> But of all arts, the Novel offers us the fullest power of the Feminine. In the Novel, at the deepest level, the Feminine fascinates . . . we as readers experience – whether we are male or female – a yielding of ourselves to the body and rhythms of the Mother.[129]

This has led, though not in Doody's case, to assumptions being made about readership which work with fairly crude models of gender. For example, the idea that the novels are female-centred, like twentieth-century romances, and therefore likely to appeal to women,[130] or, conversely, that they, and in particular Achilles Tatius, are 'male' texts, akin in many ways to modern-day pornography and eliciting similar responses of subjectification and empowerment of the male reader.[131] The receptions of the mime, pantomime and erotic handbook put a different slant on the question of to what extent this novel is 'gynocentric' or 'androcentric'.[132] These genres postulate a male audience but one which is (through their immoderation and pleasure in eroticism) feminised. The subject position offered to the reader is that of effeminate male. Through this frame, *Leucippe and Clitophon* is not so much 'feminine' (or 'masculine') but effeminate, like the Graeco-Roman erotic mimes and handbooks. Perhaps this might be a factor in explaining the lack of critical discussion of such novels (real men, even if they read these books, do not announce it). Moreover, the gendering of its audience places its reader in a paradigmatic relationship to the younger Clitophon; both are effeminised. When Thersander accuses Clitophon of being 'a lover who imitates men when among women and women when among men' (8.10.9), this is more than just a slur. It casts him self-consciously as a character in a mime, one who, in a continuation of the Achilles on Scyros image, plays the transvestite. The (titillation and) threat to the reader/spectator, suggest the reader-responses I have tried to reconstruct, is that we too might be effeminised.

---

[129] Doody (1996), 461.
[130] On Harlequin romances, pornography and the ancient novel, see Montague (1992).
[131] Elsom (1992). [132] The terms used in Egger (1990).

Finally, Lucian's Lycinus disagrees with the consensus opinion on the dance. He proffers an alternative and more positive approach to the drama. This, too, is applicable to the novel, though it is most probably an idiosyncratic view:

> In fact, the praise that he gets from the spectators will be the highest when each of those who see him recognises his own traits, or rather as if in a mirror, in the dancer he sees himself and his everyday concerns. Then the people cannot contain themselves with pleasure and as one they burst into applause, each seeing the reflection of his own soul and recognising themselves. In short, that Delphic maxim 'Know Thyself' realises itself in them from the spectacle, and when they go away from the theatre they have learned what they should choose and what avoid, and have been taught what they did not know before. (*De Saltatione* 81)

Those who enjoy going to see the pantomime may for that time eschew formal philosophy, but in a looser sense, the dance's heuristic function, to 'Know Thyself' is unarguably compatible with philosophical aims. In Lycinus' image, looking at oneself in a mirror is a route to self-knowledge. As has been discussed in Chapter 1, this idea has a long tradition. Seeing oneself reflected in the mirror of the dance is a self-conscious mode of viewing and fundamentally theatrical. We might protest that it is a fast leap from seeing a dancer imitate feelings and actions well to realising self-knowledge. However, Lycinus is not stretching credibility when he argues, using the standard vocabulary of philosophical and moral choice, that the dance teaches people 'what they should choose and what avoid' and 'what they did not know before'. This view sees the pantomime as a regulatory fiction. It throws up the possibility that, for all its uncanniness and strategies of indeterminacy and destabilisation, *Leucippe and Clitophon* is a didactic work. It is to a further examination of this didacticism that I shall turn in the following section.

Characterisation and viewing

Readers *of* the novel are guided by readers *in* the novel. The dramatisation of ways of reading within the text serves a metafictive function of raising the awareness of, and prompting reflection on, the reading styles adopted by the reader of the text. I mean this with reference both to literal reading, such as the reading of a book, and figurative reading; how a character approaches, interprets and reacts to the narrative that she or he inhabits. Which characters in the novel we read like and how that might characterise and frame our approaches are questions which inform my analysis in this final section of the chapter. I hope to demonstrate that certain characters in the novel embody and represent particular social roles, and that they employ different and distinctive ways of viewing. Certain characters are more complex than others; Leucippe (as I argue in Chapter 4) becomes less individualised and more abstracted as the narrative progresses and Clitophon is constructed with a constant tension between his older narrating self and his younger less experienced self. So I do not wish to imply that this is wholly systematic. My first two examples of characters reading, Clitophon with a book at 1.6 and Thersander's reactions to Leucippe at 6.20, are of particular moments, privileged moments to be sure, but none the less episodes, rather than sustained elements of characterisation. A second pair of examples examine ways of seeing ascribed to two characters, Conops and Callisthenes, who are both given more minor, and hence more condensed, and strongly characterised, roles. My discussions of these two characters look more broadly at how they are depicted and the roles they play in the narrative. I argue that social roles and stereotypes are constructed, at least in part, through their ways of viewing the world. In turn, the assignation of certain ways of reading to particular stereotypes imprints them with all the attributes and behaviours commonly associated with those types and stigmatises or lionises them accordingly. Thus ways of seeing are not represented as neutral and arbitrary, but social and ideological.

Clitophon: the erastes

Clitophon is the first character we see reading (if we can call it reading) and the only character who is presented reading a book:

Ἀναστὰς οὖν ἐβάδιζον ἐξεπίτηδες εἴσω τῆς οἰκίας κατὰ πρόσωπον τῆς κόρης, βιβλίον ἅμα κρατῶν, καὶ ἐγκεκυφὼς ἀνεγίνωσκον· τὸν δὲ ὀφθαλμόν, εἰ κατὰ τὰς θύρας γενοίμην, ὑπείλιττον κάτωθεν, καί τινας ἐμπεριπατήσας διαύλους καὶ ἐποχετευσάμενος ἐκ τῆς θέας ἔρωτα σαφῶς ἀπῄειν ἔχων τὴν ψυχὴν κακῶς.

When I arose, I deliberately began to amble around the inner parts of the house in full view of the girl. All the while I held a book, and hunched over it to read; but whenever I reached her door, I peeked up surreptiously. After several circuits of the course I had drenched myself with desire thus inspired by the sight of her, and I left with a sickness in my soul. (1.6.6)

This is an extraordinary passage of literary mirroring.[133] It functions intratextually as an interior mirror to the rest of the narrative, both reinforcing and inverting dynamics of reading in the work as a whole. Furthermore, the dramatisation of a reading of a book within a book produces a moment of heightened self-reflexivity, prompting us to compare and contrast our own mode of reading with that of Clitophon.[134] Reading is associated with sight and seeing in a particularly active way, reflecting the ocularcentrism of interpretation throughout the narrative. It is portrayed as a fundamentally erotic activity; the book is a stratagem for seduction and perusing it a pretext for the release of sexual desire. We are not told what sort of book Clitophon is reading (Herodotus? Plato? Chariton?[135]) but he uses it as a means to an end – indulgence of his desire.[136] Reading is presented as a covert activity and the reader's gaze as voyeuristic.

Finally, and most importantly, Clitophon shows that reading is not a stable activity. His reading is distracted by the appearance of his beloved and his perspective is dislocated. He reads the book, reads around the book and reads over the book; his reading is by no means unified or consistent. Clitophon's reading mirrors Thersander's storytelling (or Clitophon's judgement of it) at 6.18.2–3. Thersander, enflamed with desire for Leucippe, controls himself and takes the following approach:

---

[133] The seminal analysis on literary mirroring is Dallenbach (1989). For sensitive discussions, see Chambers (1984), 28–35; Nolan (1990).
[134] See also Goldhill (1995), 70ff.
[135] Stephens observes that 'the novelists.... unlike their eighteenth- and nineteenth-century counterparts, do not show their own characters reading novels', Stephens (1994), 415. This is largely true, but the very lack of specificity about Clitophon's reading matter suggests the possibility that he is reading an *erotikos logos* is toyed with here.
[136] Like Achilles Tatius? A doctor, Theodorus Priscianus, writing in the early fifth century CE, advocates reading love stories as a cure for sexual impotence (*Euporista* 2.11.34). In this (oft quoted) prescription, looking at attractive adolescents and reading erotic *logoi* are analogous in that both inflame and release sexual desire.

Καρτερήσας δ'οὖν καὶ παρακαθίσας διελέγετο, ἄλλοτε ἄλλα ῥήματα συνάπτων οὐκ ἔχοντα νοῦν. Τοιοῦτοι γὰρ οἱ ἐρῶντες, ὅταν πρὸς τὰς ἐρωμένας ζητήσωσι λαλεῖν· οὐ γὰρ ἐπιστήσαντες τὸν λογισμὸν τοῖς λόγοις, ἀλλὰ τὴν ψυχὴν εἰς τὸ ἐρώμενον ἔχοντες, τῇ γλώττῃ μόνον χωρὶς ἡνιόχου τοῦ λογισμοῦ λαλοῦσιν.

He controlled himself, sat down next to her, and struck up a conversation, stringing together various nonsensical themes. This is what lovers are like, whenever they seek to chat with their beloveds. Reason has no authority over their language, and their entire soul is instead focused upon the beloved: they blather with the tongue alone, without reason at the reins. (6.18.2–3)

Thersander's verbal concentration, like Clitophon's visual focus, is haphazard and fragmented. Their aim is to seduce Leucippe and this diverts them from reading and storytelling. So, it may be that *logoi erotikoi* encourage desire, but it is also evident that desire disrupts reading and storytelling. Thus the eclectic and digressive reading and narrating of these lovers mirrors the eclectic and digressive framing narrative. All of the above militates against a stable position of readership and a focused position of spectatorship.

The model of reading displayed by Clitophon reinforces the connection made between love stories and the actualisation of desire in an episode that takes place the evening before his walkabout with the book. After the families' first meal together, during which Clitophon feeds his infatuation rather than his body, a slave sings accompanied by his lyre. The song tells of the love of Apollo for Daphne, her flight from him and subsequent metamorphosis into a laurel tree from which the god made a garland. Clitophon's reaction is as follows:

Τοῦτό μου μᾶλλον ἀσθὲν τὴν ψυχὴν ἐξέκαυσεν· ὑπέκκαυμα γὰρ ἐπιθυμίας λόγος ἐρωτικός. Κἂν εἰς σωφροσύνην τις ἑαυτὸν νουθετῇ, τῷ παραδείγματι πρὸς τὴν μίμησιν ἐρεθίζεται, μάλισθ' ὅταν ἐκ τοῦ κρείττονος ᾖ τὸ παράδειγμα· ἡ γὰρ ὧν ἁμαρτάνει τις αἰδὼς τῷ τοῦ βελτίονος ἀξιώματι παρρησία γίνεται· καὶ ταῦτα πρὸς ἐμαυτὸν ἔλεγον "Ἰδοὺ καὶ Ἀπόλλων ἐρᾷ, κἀκεῖνος παρθένου, καὶ ἐρῶν οὐκ αἰσχύνεται, ἀλλὰ διώκει τὴν παρθένον· σὺ δὲ ὀκνεῖς καὶ αἰδῇ καὶ ἀκαίρως σωφρονεῖς· μὴ κρείττων εἶ τοῦ θεοῦ;"

This song inflamed my soul all the more, for erotic stories fuel the appetite. Even if you school yourself into self-control, an example incites you to imitate it, especially when that example is a divine one; in which case, any shame that you feel at your moral errors becomes an outspoken affront to the station of a higher being. This is how I counselled myself: 'You see, Apollo too desires, and he too desires a maiden. *He* feels no shame at his lust, but hunts the maiden; whereas *you*, you are hesitant and embarrassed, and you practice an untimely self-control (*sophrosune*). Do you think yourself superior to a god?' (1.5.5–7)

Here we have an explicit statement of the incitement to desire of a love story – *logos erotikos*. By the force of example – *paradeigmati* – we are stimulated to imitation – *mimesis*. This statement is mirrored not only in Clitophon's use of a book to further his relationship with Leucippe, but in several episodes in the novel where stories are told to facilitate passion. In one instance, whilst walking in the garden in earshot of Leucippe, Clitophon, assisted by the slave Satyrus, recounts a series of bizarre pseudo-scientific, paradoxographical and mythological tales of love and union. He does this, 'since I was keen to break the girl in to the ways of desire' (Εουλόμενος οὖν . . . εὐάγωγον τὴν κόρην εἰς ἔρωτα παρασκευάσαι 1.16.1), and during his storytelling, 'was eyeing the girl to see how she reacted to hearing about desire' (Ταῦτα λέγων ἔβλεπον ἅμα τὴν κόρην, πῶς ἔχει πρὸς τὴν ἀκρόασιν τὴν ἐρωτικήν, 1.19.1). Clitophon's machinations are successful, both because Leucippe begins to succumb to the seduction (she listened 'not without pleasure' – οὐκ ἀηδῶς) and because of the opportunity seized to gaze at her (1.19.2–3).

Using the gods as justification for men's sexual activities stung St Augustine into apoplexy. In his *Confessions*, he rails against the corruptions of literature and its misuse by teachers. His comments provide an interesting insight into one (Christian) reader's opinions about morally correct and incorrect ways of reading. Firstly, Augustine attacks Greek poets (especially Homer) for dishonesty in their portrayals of the gods as sexually active and the harm caused by this precedent:[137]

Have I not read in you of Jupiter, at once both thunderer and adulterer? Of course the two activities cannot be combined, but he was so described as to give an example of real adultery defended by the authority of a fictitious thunderclap acting as a go-between. What master of oratory can hear with equanimity a person of his own profession saying out loud, 'Homer invented these fictions and attributed human powers to the gods; I wish he had attributed divine powers to

[137] The translation is that of H. Chadwick (1991), *Saint Augustine. Confessions.* Oxford.

us'? It would be truer to say that Homer indeed invented these fictions, but he attributed divine sanction to vicious acts, which had the result that immorality was no longer counted immorality and anyone who so acted would seem to follow the example not of abandoned men but of the gods in heaven. (1.16)

He rejects the argument of schoolteachers that literature like Terence's *Eunuch* is a useful tool for enriching vocabulary and learning rhetorical skills:

> It is as if we would not know words such as 'golden shower' and 'bosom' and 'deceit' and 'temples of heaven' and other phrases occurring in the passage in question, had not Terence brought on to the stage a worthless young man citing Jupiter as a model for his own fornication. He is looking up at a mural painting: 'there was this picture representing how Jupiter, they say, sent a shower of gold into Danaë's lap and deceived a woman'. Notice how he encourages himself to lust as if enjoying celestial authority:
>
> > 'But what a god (he says)! He strikes the temples of heaven with his immense sound. And am I, poor little fellow, not to do the same as he? Yes indeed, I have done it with pleasure.' (1.16)[138]

Augustine's criticisms of Terence are equally applicable to Achilles Tatius. Through his eyes, this sort of writing is an incitement to misdemeanour. Like Clitophon, Terence's Chaerea takes an interest in a representation of a mythological seduction. Like Clitophon, he takes it as a paradigm for his own sexual exploits. Augustine stresses the irresponsible role of the teachers in using this material and the role of such writing in miseducating the young. *Leucippe and Clitophon* presents itself as a didactic text, both portraying the *paideia* of ephebic youth and educating its readership. Applied to Achilles, Augustine's criticisms expose an irony central to the novel; the knowledge that it proffers, be it couched in a philosophical, religious, scientific or paradoxographical frame, is a knowledge of erotics. Like generations of readers before and since, readers of Achilles Tatius, Clitophon and Augustine both imply, do not read for moral edification. No 'untimely *sophrosune*' here, then.

---

[138] The passage he is referring to is *Eunuch* 585ff. The story of Danaë is mentioned at *Leucippe and Clitophon* 2.36.4.

Thersander: the beast

My second example of a moment of reading comes in the scene where Thersander is attempting to assault Leucippe at 6.20.1ff. Thersander, 'Beast-man', is the stereotypical jealous husband and bully.[139] He beats up Clitophon (5.23.5-7), is repeatedly called a 'tyrant' by Leucippe (6.20) and is portrayed as a typically violent Thracian (8.2.1-3). Leucippe has just given her virtuoso 'Whip me .... I am defenceless and alone and a woman' speech, to which I shall return in Chapter 4. She rebukes Thersander in increasingly vehement tones:

Οὐδὲ τὴν Ἄρτεμιν, εἰπέ μοι, τὴν σὴν φοβῇ, ἀλλὰ βιάζῃ παρθένον ἐν πόλει παρθένου; Δέσποινα, ποῦ σου τὰ τόξα;

Tell me, do you not fear that Artemis of yours? Do you rape a virgin in the virgin's city? Lady goddess, where are your arrows? (6.21.2-3)

Thersander is having none of this:

"Παρθένος", εἶπεν ὁ Θέρσανδρος, "ὢ τόλμης καὶ γέλωτος· παρθένος τοσούτοις συννυκτερεύσασα πειραταῖς; Εὐνοῦχοί σοι γεγόνασιν οἱ λῃσταί; Φιλοσόφων ἦν τὸ πειρατήριον; Οὐδεὶς ἐν αὐτοῖς εἶχεν ὀφθαλμούς;"

'A virgin'!' cried Thersander. 'What audacity! How amusing! You, a virgin, after passing so many nights with pirates? Were these pirates of yours eunuchs? Or was it a sect of piratical philosophers? Or did none of them have eyes?' (6.21.3)

This is a wonderful expression of sneering disbelief, puncturing Leucippe's piety with bathetic scepticism. Thersander's reading of the world is a *realistic* one, hinging on what is reasonable and likely and rejecting the improbable and fantastic. His contemptuous 'pull-the-other-one' dismissal, unparalleled anywhere else in the novel, mirrors readings of *Leucippe and Clitophon* that take realism as their criterion for judgement and find the novel lacking. Emile Zola speaks for many when he writes that the Greek novelists '[ont] conté la même histoire banale et invraisemblable ... tiré quelques pantins ridicules de leur imagination et les ont promenés dans une nature fausse'.[140] Zola and Thersander sneer together at novelistic conventions and fail to suspend disbelief.

---

[139] The bandit chief in *Callirhoe* is called 'Theron', 'Beast'.
[140] Zola (1928), 337, also quoted in Billault (1991), 23.

Thersander's heretical cynicism lays bare the unrealistic assumptions of the novel and suggests a parodic reading of the tropes, like 'virginity against all odds', that constitute the idealism of the 'ideal' novel. An extreme result of giving a Thersandrian reading free rein would be something like Petronius' *Satyricon*, whose cruel satire shows the romanticist fancifulness of the 'ideal' novel little mercy.[141] Thersander's reading of the world is thus dangerous, striking at the very heart of the genre which contains him. However, in putting these words in the mouth of the 'baddy', Achilles ensures that they are not (fully) validated, rather coopted and (to some degree) neutralized. The realist is a bully; to read with expectations of realism is to do violence to the text.

Conops: the polupragmon

Conops is introduced as follows:

Ἦν δέ τις αὐτῶν οἰκέτης πολυπράγμων καὶ λάλος καὶ λίχνος καὶ πᾶν ὅ τι ἂν εἴποι τις, ὄνομα Κώνωψ.

Among their slaves was a man who was interfering, garrulous, gluttonous, and anything else you might want to call him, by the name of Conops. (2.20.1)

Like Longus' character Gnathon, Conops' name is an index to his character. Gnathon means 'Jaws', Conops 'Mosquito', or, to capture the pun in English (following Winkler), 'Nat'. Both Gnathon and Conops are characterised by their large appetites. Longus writes of Gnathon:

ὁ δὲ Γνάθων, οἷα μαθὼν ἐσθίειν ἄνθρωπος καὶ πίνειν εἰς μέθην καὶ λαγνεύειν μετὰ τὴν μέθην καὶ οὐδὲν ἄλλο ὢν ἢ γνάθος καὶ γαστὴρ καὶ τὰ ὑπὸ γαστέρα.

But all Gnathon knew how to do was to eat and to drink till he was drunk and to have sex when he was drunk. He was nothing but a mouth and a stomach and what lies underneath the stomach.[142] (4.11.2)

Similarly, Conops is 'slave to his stomach' (γαστρὸς ἡττώμενον, 2.23.1) and is conned into ingesting a sleeping draught, despite suspecting a trick, because he was 'under compulsion of that excellent

---

[141] Cf. Heinze (1899). For a reading of *Leucippe and Clitophon* as another *Satyrica*, orchestrated by the character Satyrus, see Anderson (1988).
[142] The translation is that of C. Gill in Reardon ed. (1989).

stomach of his' (ἡ βελτίστη γαστὴρ κατηνάγκασε, 2.23.1). However, unlike Gnathon, Conops' appetite is not confined to physical greed (food and sex), but is also manifested in visual greed: *polupragmosune*. *Polupragmosune*, a political term in fifth-century discourse,[143] has become a broader, social term by the second century CE and is usually translated as 'busybodiness' or 'curiosity'. Plutarch, writing a century or so earlier than Achilles Tatius, wrote a tract called *Peri Polupragmosunes* (*About Curiosity*) in which he discusses what he considers to be the vice of *polupragmosune* and urges those who are busybodies to change their ways. Plutarch defines *polupragmosune* as φιλομάθειά τίς ἐστιν ἀλλοτρίων κακῶν (515D) and φιλοπευστία τῶν ἐν ἀποκρύψει καὶ λανθανόντων 'a passion for finding out whatever is hidden and concealed' (518C). The *polupragmon* will ignore events that happen in plain view, preferring to spy upon those acting covertly.

This is how Conops behaves. Clitophon relates how Conops scrutinised him and Satyrus in the hope of catching them attempting to visit Leucippe by night:

Οὗτός μοι ἐδόκει πόρρωθεν ἐπιτηρεῖν τὰ πραττόμενα ἡμῖν· μάλιστα δέ, ὅπερ ἦν, ὑποπτεύσας μή τι νύκτωρ ἡμῖν πραχθῇ, διενυκτέρευε μέχρι πόρρω τῆς ἑσπέρας, ἀναπετάσας τοῦ δωματίου τὰς θύρας, ὥστε ἔργον ἦν αὐτὸν λαθεῖν.

It seemed to me that he was observing our actions from afar. He particularly suspected that we might be up to some nocturnal intrigue (which was in fact the case); and so he stayed awake well into the evening with the doors of his room wide open, and as a result it was difficult to avoid his attention. (2.20.1)

Thus Conops shows himself to be a true servant of Pantheia (or Panthea), Leucippe's mother and 'She who sees all'.[144] Conops' intrusive gaze is part of a household that surveys and polices the young. After her night of love with Clitophon is thwarted and he

---

[143] The *polupragmon* was a favourite target in comedy; cf. Timocles, Testimonium 1 and frg. 29 K–A; Diphilus, frg. 67 K–A; Heniochus, Testimonium 1 and frg. 3 K–A; Aristophanes, *Wasps*, *passim*. See also Chariton 1.11.6 Μονοὶ γὰρ ὑμεῖς οὐκ ἀκούετε τὴν πολυπραγμοσύνην τῶν Ἀθηναίων; Δῆμός ἐστι λάλος καὶ φιλόδικος, ἐν δὲ τῷ λιμένι μυρίοι συκοφάνται τεύσονται τίνες ἐσμὲν καὶ πόθεν ταῦτα φέρομεν τὰ φορτία, '"Are you the only ones," he asked, "who have not heard what busybodies the Athenians are? They are a talkative people and fond of litigation, and in the harbour scores of troublemakers will ask who we are and where we got this cargo."'

[144] The MSS read Πάνθεια, 'All Divine', but I agree with Laplace that a pun is intended with Πανθέα, 'all seeing': Laplace (1983a), 316, n. 1.

and Satyrus plan their escape, Leucippe begs to join them, giving as her reason that she needs to get out of her mother's sight: "Δέομαι", ἔφη, "πρὸς θεῶν ξένων καὶ ἐγχωρίων, ἐξαρπάσατέ με τῶν τῆς μητρὸς ὀφθαλμῶν . . .", '"I beg you", she cried, "by the gods, whether foreign or local! Snatch me away from my mother's eyes . . ."' (2.30.1) and threatens suicide if they refuse to agree. Satyrus eventually outmanoeuvres Conops by drugging him and on victory proclaims: Κεῖταί σοι καθεύδων ὁ Κύκλωψ· σὺ δὲ ὅπως Ὀδυσσεὺς ἀγαθὸς γένῃ, 'The Cyclops is lying fast asleep: over to you! See to it that you play the part of Odysseus well!' (2.23.3).[145] This is, of course, a joke at Clitophon's expense. Like Petronius' Encolpius who is also compared to the great hero,[146] Clitophon is far from being an epic lover.[147] However, the pun on Conops/Cyclops invites us to activate the etymology of κύκλωψ, and thus to see Conops as all-eye, emphasising his role as an overseer.[148]

The way of reading the world embodied by Conops is undoubtedly voyeuristic, but it goes further than the lover's voyeuristic gaze because it does not just take pleasure in sights which are on display (like Leucippe, strolling in the garden), but actively strives to glimpse what is hidden, and to uncover what should be private. Plutarch likens *polupragmosune* to adultery in as much as adultery is a curiosity about another man's pleasure and a searching out and examination of what is closely guarded, and *polupragmosune* is: παράδυσίς . . . καὶ φθορὰ καὶ ἀπογύμνωσις τῶν ἀπορρήτων,

---

[145] I follow Vilborg, Plepelits, Gaselee and Winkler in accepting Gottling's emendation of Κώνωψ to Κύκλωψ, which makes much better sense, cf. Plepelits (1980), 232 n. 64. Garnaud and Whitmarsh keep Κώνωψ.

[146] E.g. *Satyrica* 105.10.1.

[147] Fusillo (1988), 24: 'This passage of Achilles Tatius can therefore be considered an epic parody, since it shows a decided incongruity between the Homeric pattern and the romantic rewriting: the Odyssean device to get rid of Polyphemus is here degraded to a comic artifice to get into a girl's bed, in a way that recalls the Freudian conception of comicality.'

[148] Anderson (1993) reads Satyrus' injunction as a sexual metaphor, with Clitophon cast as Odysseus and Leucippe (not Conops) cast as the Cyclops: 'the learnedly lascivious Achilles Tatius delicately implies that the young hero has a sharpened stake for erotic purposes', Anderson (1993), 76. This image would invite the reader to construct sexual intercourse as blinding and the vagina as an eye; violent and 'phallocularcentric' metaphors, which engender and sexualise vision. See Lucian's *False Critic* (27) for similar innuendo.

'an encroaching, a debauching and denuding of secret things' (519c).[149]

To read the novel with *polupragmosune* would be to root out hidden meanings and be alert for subtexts, stripping away at the layers of the narrative. Indeed, this is the way of reading encouraged by Conops' narrative at 2.21.1–4. Irked by Satyrus' jibes about his name, Conops retaliates by telling him a *muthos* about the gnat.[150] In his tale, the gnat terrorises the lion and the elephant: ... ὁρᾷς, ὅσον ἰσχύος ὁ κώνωψ ἔχει, ὡς καὶ ἐλέφαντα φοβεῖν, 'So you see how much power a gnat has: it even terrifies an elephant' (2.21.4). There is no overt moral, no *epimuthion* to the fable, but the allegory is comprehensible. Satyrus well understands 'the innuendo that lies beneath the story', τὸ ὕπουλον αὐτοῦ τῶν λόγων (2.21.5), and replies with a fable of his own in which the gnat becomes trapped in a spider's web. Many readers of Achilles Tatius look for 'the innuendo that lies beneath the story' and search out and uncover symbols and hidden meanings. The Isis *Mysterientexte* theories of Kérenyi and Merkelbach are predicated upon this way of reading, as is Laplace's interpretation of the novel as an allegory of Aristophanes' speech on *eros* in Plato's *Symposium*.[151] If we view the internal model of reading exemplified by Conops as a guide to the text's own conditions of interpretation, then we should recognise that to read like Merkelbach, Kérenyi and Laplace is to read like a *polupragmon*. The reader who pries into symbols and is ever vigilant for subtexts is a Conops, a *polupragmon* and an irritant. However, he or she is placed in a double-bind, for the strategies of concealment and revelation mobilised by the narrative encourage him or her to be vigilant and curious. The sexualised descriptions of Europa, Andromeda and Leucippe are designed to solicit a voyeuristic engagement from the reader.

---

[149] By these criteria the Egyptian priest is also a *polupragmon*, when he scrutinises all parts of the phoenix, even τὰ ἀπόρρητα (3.25.7). See below pp. 190–1.

[150] On the fables told by Conops and Satyrus see Delhay (1990), who suggests Aesop as a possible source. On the form and function of fables in ancient literature see Blackham (1985), esp. ch. 1.

[151] Kérenyi (1927); Merkelbach (1962); Laplace (1988).

Callisthenes: the akolastos

Bryan Reardon writes: 'Callisthenes and Calligone, we may note, are in no way necessary to the plot; they simply serve as a backdrop of normality in a story which throughout distorts the romantic norms.'[152] It is true that Callisthenes' adventures are presented as a kind of sub-plot, mirroring Clitophon's own exploits. Callisthenes and Clitophon are paralleled in their mutual desire for Leucippe, their flight from parental disapproval and subsequent acceptance. However, it can hardly be said that Callisthenes represents 'normality'. Indeed, his introduction paints him in a markedly negative light:

Νεανίσκος ἦν Βυζάντιος, ὄνομα Καλλισθένης, ὀρφανὸς καὶ πλούσιος, ἄσωτος δὲ καὶ πολυτελής. Οὗτος ἀκούων τὴν Σωστράτου θυγατέρα εἶναι καλήν, ἰδὼν δὲ οὐδέποτε, ἤθελεν αὐτῷ ταύτην γενέσθαι γυναῖκα. Καὶ ἦν ἐξ ἀκοῆς ἐραστής· τοσαύτη γὰρ τοῖς ἀκολάστοις ὕβρις, ὡς καὶ τοῖς ὠσὶν εἰς ἔρωτα τρυφᾶν καὶ ταῦτα πάσχειν ἀπὸ ῥημάτων, ἃ τῇ ψυχῇ διακονοῦσι τρωθέντες ὀφθαλμοί.

There was a young man of Byzantium called Callisthenes, a wealthy orphan, but prodigal and extravagant. When he heard that the daughter of Sostratus was beautiful, although he had never seen her, he wanted to make her his wife. His desire was based on hearsay: the wantonness of the licentious is so great that even with their ears they wallow in erotic pleasure, and they suffer through mere words the effects that wounded eyes usually administer to the soul. (2.13.1)

This description of how Callisthenes fell in love with Leucippe could not contrast more strongly with Clitophon's experience. Clitophon falls in love at first *sight*, in a lightning flash that ensnares and conquers his eyes. It is emphasised that Callisthenes does not see Leucippe, but is a lover by hearing, *ex akoes*.

Callisthenes is characterised as an *akolastos*, a profligate; he is typically spendthrift and impulsive. The *akolastos* is a stereotypical character in the New Comedy and in the novel, Longus' Gnathon being a memorable example. But Achilles introduces a new twist into his portrayal of the *akolastos*; whereas Gnathon, 'Jaws', is characterised by his appetite, for both food and sex, Callisthenes' intemperance lies in his privileging of the wrong sensory organ and his denial of the eye as primary instrument of desire. Callisthenes

[152] Reardon (1994), 91.

is lured towards love by the ears – *tois osin* – in pointed contrast to the behaviour of others, who are influenced by their eyes – *ophthalmoi*. In presenting the *akolastos* as a man who does not respect the normal hierarchy of the senses, the narrative conforms to and reinforces the ocularcentrism of Graeco-Roman culture. As Justina Gregory writes, and François Hartog has amply demonstrated, 'it is a commonplace of Greek thought that autopsy is a far better means than hearsay of gaining information'.[153] Callisthenes is painted in the tradition of the notorious profligate Alcibiades, who was reputed to have desired the prostitute Medontis whom he had never seen but had heard a report of her beauty.[154] Like Callisthenes, Alcibiades is a 'hearsay lover', ἐξ ἀκοῆς ἐρασθείς, a sign of his *akolasia*.[155] Unlike Callisthenes, whose sudden change of character ensures that Calligone remains inviolate, Alcibiades satisfies his desire, sharing Medontis with his companion Axiochus.

No wonder that Leucippe's father, Sostratus, loathes such a character and refuses to hand over his daughter to him in marriage: ὁ δὲ βδελυττόμενος τοῦ βίου τὴν ἀκολασίαν ἠρνήσατο, 'he refused out of disgust at his uncontrolled lifestyle' (2.13.2). Callisthenes is enraged by this snub, not just because of Sostratus' disrespect, but because of the strength of his desire. This is how Callisthenes' desire is presented:

ἀναπλάττων γὰρ ἑαυτῷ τῆς παιδὸς τὸ κάλλος καὶ φανταζόμενος τὰ ἀόρατα ἔλαθε σφόδρα κακῶς διακείμενος.

before he knew it he had worked himself into a dreadful state, picturing the girl's beauty to himself and envisaging the invisible. (2.13.2)

It is couched in terms which are normally used to describe a particular aspect of sense-perception, that of *phantasia*. Like the artist who is praised for his use of *phantasia*,[156] Callisthenes moulds an image of Leucippe's beauty inside his head and conjures up that

---

[153] Gregory (1985), 27; Hartog (1988), 260–309, "The Eye and the Ear".
[154] According to an anecdote in Athenaeus, *Deipn.* 13 574E and further examples at 9 375A–376B. The narrator, Myrtilus, comments: 'We need not wonder that people have fallen in love with others on mere report (ἐξ ἀκοῆς), seeing that Chares of Mytilene in the tenth book of his *Histories of Alexander* asserts that many, having seen in a dream certain persons whom they had never seen before, fell in love with them', 13.375A. He gives further examples at 375A–376B.
[155] Athenaeus, *Deipn.* 13 574E.
[156] E.g. Phidias in Plotinus, *Enneads* 5.8.1 and Cicero, *Orator* 9.

which he has never seen. *Phantasia* is a slippery term; its application ranges widely from the general to the specific.[157] Longinus writes: 'the term *phantasia* is applied in general to an idea which enters the mind from any source and engenders speech, but the word has now come to be used predominantly of passages where, inspired by strong emotion, you seem to see what you describe and bring it vividly before the eyes of the audience'.[158] Towards the second century CE, it comes to mean 'imagination' or, in Pollitt's phrase, 'intuitive insight', since, he reasons, 'the word implies not simply fabricating something in the mind but actually "seeing" something that is not perceptible to the senses'.[159] It is connected with a series of ideas like *enargeia*, the quality of creating a vivid, visual image through words and, of course, *ekphrasis*, 'a descriptive account bringing what is illustrated vividly before one's eyes' (λόγος περιηγηματικὸς ἐναργῶς ὑπ' ὄψιν ἄγων τὸ δηλούμενον).[160] All three terms intersect, encompassing the fundamental concept of a 'vision' that is communicated by language. Callisthenes' desire exemplifies what we are told earlier, that he is a lover by hearsay rather than by sight.

Callisthenes decides to act upon his desire and resolves to kidnap Leucippe and rape her, the penalty for which, under Byzantine law, was marriage; his initial request. However, Leucippe is not there when Callisthenes inveigles his way into the party of sacrificers at Tyre and seeks her out among the crowd. What happens next is a classic case of mistaken identity:

Ὁ δὲ Καλλισθένης τὴν μὲν Λευκίππην οὐχ ἑωρακώς ποτε, τὴν δὲ Καλλιγόνην ἰδὼν τὴν ἀδελφὴν τὴν ἐμήν, νομίσας Λευκίππην εἶναι.

'Callisthenes had never seen Leucippe, and so on seeing my sister Calligone he took her for Leucippe. (2.16.2)

---

[157] The bibliography on *phantasia* is vast. I have found helpful: Imbert (1980); Watson (1988); Ioppolo (1990); Vasaly (1993), 92–7; Onians (1980); Zanker (1981) and Long (1996), 266–75.
[158] καλεῖται μὲν γὰρ κοινῶς φαντασία πᾶν τὸ ὁπωσοῦν ἐννόημα γεννητικὸν λόγου παριστάμενον· ἤδη δ' ἐπὶ τούτων κεκράτηκε τοὔνομα ὅταν ἃ λέγεις ὑπ' ἐνθουσιασμοῦ καὶ πάθους βλέπειν δοκῇς καὶ ὑπ' ὄψιν τιθῇς τοῖς ἀκούουσιν (*On the Sublime* 15.1–2).
[159] Pollitt (1974), 53.
[160] Theon ed. Spengel (1885), 2.118. On ancient and modern definitions of *ekphrasis*, see Webb (1999).

Once again, Callisthenes' failure to *see* his beloved is emphasised. In an aside, Clitophon tells us that Callisthenes' mistake was precipitated by his recognition of Sostratus' wife (who is Leucippe's mother). He continues:

πυθόμενος οὐδέν – ἦν γὰρ ἑαλωκὼς ἐκ τῆς θέας – δείκνυσιν ἑνὶ τῶν οἰκετῶν τὴν κόρην, ὃς ἦν αὐτῷ πιστότατος, καὶ κελεύει λῃστὰς ἐπ' αὐτὴν συγκροτῆσαι, καταλέξας τὸν τρόπον τῆς ἁρπαγῆς.

He made no enquiries, for he had been snared by the sight of her, but pointed the girl out to his most trusted servant and bade him assemble a band of robbers to kidnap her in the way he detailed. (2.16.2)

This is a quite remarkable chain of events. *Phantasia*, remember, is supposed to communicate a vivid visual image through language and Callisthenes has imagined such an image of Leucippe. However, he identifies the girl not using this image as a crucial point of reference, not in fact by referring to *her* at all, but by recognising *her mother*. Identification should involve looking at the object in question and making an epistemological connection based on a correct reading of signs. Callisthenes not only does not look at the object of his desire, but looks at someone else, misreads the signs, by inferring that the girl beside Leucippe's mother is indeed her daughter, makes the wrong connection and *misidentifies* the girl. The inadequacy of the senses, including vision, accurately to convey knowledge, is the subject of Plato's *Theaetetus*, and Callisthenes' misidentification of Calligone as Leucippe can be read as a vignette which dramatises some of the concerns of that dialogue. A variety of scenarios, too complicated to detail here, are imagined where false perceptions lead to misidentifications. One envisages 'a man who knows neither Theaetetus nor Socrates' conceiving 'the idea that Socrates is Theaetetus or Theaetetus Socrates' (188b). In another, Theaetetus imagines seeing someone he does not know from a distance and mistaking him for Socrates, even though he knows Socrates (191b). At another stage, Socrates illustrates the point that even when we already have knowledge of something, perceiving (or not perceiving) it still controls our actions:

If Socrates knows Theodorus and Theaetetus, but sees neither of them and does not perceive them in any other way, he could never be of the opinion that Theaetetus is Theodorus. (193a)

None of these scenarios anticipates Callisthenes' error in every detail, but the similarities are striking. Callisthenes' mistake is an effective caution that the senses lead to false perception.

When Callisthenes does look at Calligone he is given no chance to read any signs or make the right connections because he is carried away by Calligone's *thea*. *Thea* is difficult to translate without losing the potency of the word. It can mean 'spectacle' or 'appearance', which for us often have passive connotations of things look*ed* at, or 'gaze' in the more active sense of look*ing* at.[161] This ambiguity conveys the moment of tension when Callisthenes beholds the girl and his active gaze is wrested from him as he in turn is made powerless. Ironically, the man who was inspired by the image of a woman to abduct her is himself abducted (ἑαλωκώς) by a woman's image. Callisthenes may control the image that he sculpts in his imagination, but the (wrongly identified) model for that image controls him. The beauty of *Calli*gone overpowers the strength of Calli*sthenes*. Thus he kidnaps the wrong girl.

The episode illustrates the failure of *ekphrasis*. It is a specific failure: the failure to function mimetically. The relationship between *phantasia* and *mimesis* is a varied one. In Stoic theory, *phantasia* is one of the major criteria for truth,[162] in contrast to the Platonic ideas linking vision, particularly *mimesis*, with deception.[163] According to the Stoics, *phantasia* is seen as a radical departure from *mimesis*. A clear example of this is found in Philostratus, writing in the late second to early third century CE. He envisages a conversation between the wandering Apollonius and an Egyptian sage called Thespesion about the relative merits of theiromorphic and anthropomorphic representations of gods:

'Your artists, then, like Phidias', said Thespesion, 'and like Praxiteles, went up, I suppose, to heaven and took a copy of the forms of the gods, and then reproduced these by their art, or was there any influence which presided over and guided their moulding?' 'There was', said Apollonius, 'and an influence pregnant with wisdom and genius.' 'What was that?' said the other, 'for I do not think you can adduce any except imitation (οὐ γὰρ ἄν τι παρὰ τὴν μίμησιν εἴποις).' 'Imagination

---

[161] For the former, see 3.25.3, 6.18.1, 1.15.8, 2.16.2, 4.3.1, 6.6.3, 6.18.2 and 8.14.3. With more active connotations, 1.5.3, 1.6.6, 4.2.1, 5.1.5 and 5.13.4.
[162] See Diogenes Laertius, *Lives of Eminent Philosophers* 7.49; Rist (1969), 133–51; Watson (1988), 44–58.
[163] See von Staden (1978).

(φαντασία)', said Apollonius, 'wrought these works, a wiser and far subtler artist by far than imitation; for imitation can only create as its handiwork what it has seen, but imagination equally what it has not seen (μίμησις μὲν γὰρ δημιουργήσει, ὃ εἶδεν, φαντασία δὲ καὶ ὃ μὴ εἶδεν); for it will conceive of its ideal with reference to the reality . . . (ὑποθήσεται γὰρ αὐτὸ πρὸς τὴν ἀναφορὰν τοῦ ὄντος . . .). . .'
(*The Life of Apollonius of Tyre* 6.19)

This discussion uses very similar terms to those employed by Clitophon to describe Callisthenes' desire. Apollonius contrasts *mimesis* with *phantasia*, but his last remark belies any simple demarcation between the two. *Phantasia* differs from *mimesis* in that it 'hypothesises', creates an image in the mind, but in doing so 'with reference to the reality' is, at least partly, mimetic. This is like the version of *phantasia* called *kataleptike phantasia* recognised by Zeno and other Stoics who wanted to avoid the sceptical relativism of writers like Gorgias. *Kataleptike phantasia* is '"comprehensive representation", an impression that came from a real source, accurately reproduced that source, and could not have come from anything else'.[164]

This is, is it not, the *phantasia* indulged in by Callisthenes? The *phantasia* prompted by verbal reports of Leucippe was 'an impression that came from a real source', Leucippe herself. In his expectation that his phantasy of Leucippe will be a true likeness of the real woman, will *imitate* her, Callisthenes imbues *phantasia* with the quality of *mimesis*. However, as we know, his *phantasia* did not accurately reproduce its source – Leucippe – and could quite easily have come from someone else, namely Calligone. Thus Callisthenes' *phantasia* fails to function as *phantasia* and his misrecognition of Calligone exemplifies the deceptive role of *ekphrasis* in this book. Just as the painting of the female figure on the bull can be read as depicting Europa and Selene, so the *phantasia* of Callisthenes can be interpreted sylleptically as both Leucippe and Calligone. Once again, ekphrastic vision is turned on itself and visual appearance precipitates misrecognition and error.[165]

---

[164] Pollitt (1974), 54. It is sometimes translated as 'cognitive representation'. See also L & S (1987), 241–53; Sandbach (1971); Long (1974), 126–31; von Staden (1978), 97–99.
[165] Terms related to *phantasia* are used to describe the dreams of Pantheia (2.24.4.) and Leucippe (4.10.6.). Sosthenes inflames Thersander with a *phantasia* of Leucippe (6.11.4.). The association of *phantasia* with the wicked Thersander and Sosthenes emphasises its negative aspect.

Can a reader of Achilles Tatius help viewing as Callisthenes does? Reading necessarily involves *phantasia* and to enjoy a work of erotic literature is, according to some, an act of *akolasia*.[166] We are unable to condemn Callisthenes' excess without acknowledging that, in some way, we also follow his example. It is, perhaps, a matter of degree. Callisthenes' example warns us to enjoy, but not invest too much desire in, a mere report. If we conceive a passion, it should be for someone we have seen, not for a girl in a story.

One of the reasons that critics were, and often still are, quick to disparage the ancient novels is because of what is perceived to be their poor characterisation. The characters are thought two-dimensional and 'cardboard',[167] largely because of their lack of psychological complexity. Characters are not drawn with much interior depth, as a modern reader, coming from the tradition of the realistic novel, might expect or an ancient reader, having witnessed the interior psychological conflicts of characters in, say, Greek tragedy, might hope for. A character's emotions in the Greek novel tend not to be interiorised, but exteriorised in generalised *sententiae* and speechifying. Thus Margaret Williamson writes:

The unsatisfactory thinness of the Greek romances arises partly from the fact that their intense contraction of focus on to individual experience – to the extent that even the lovers' relations normally play a very small part in their lives – is not matched by any development of a sense of interiority...[168]

If we read the Greek novels with an expectation of psychological realism, then it is indeed hard not to feel disappointed by their 'unsatisfactory thinness'. However, if we set aside this expectation, then we might be open to seeing the characters not as 'personalities' but as embodiments of social and moral values and as representatives of different ways of viewing and reading the world.[169] Through the characters we see an acting-out of visual and social relations, made all the clearer with Conops and Callisthenes through the condensation and hyperbole afforded by the stereotype. The narrative thus constitutes a site where visual, social

---

[166] See below 74–5.   [167] Williamson (1986), 23.   [168] Ibid, 35.
[169] See Morgan (1997) and the response of Hunter (1997) on 'personality' and character development in the Greek novel. Brooks' analysis of character in melodrama has been useful here: Brooks (1976).

and moral choices are displayed for debate. It operates to heighten the reader's awareness of what is at stake in his or her own way of reading. Thersander and Conops are unsympathetic characters (we might think of them as 'baddies'), and accordingly their ways of reading the world are stigmatised. To a certain extent, then, characters in *Leucippe and Clitophon* are constructed to function as regulatory fictions,[170] directing the reader against particular ways of reading. However, Achilles' moral universe is not sharply polarised and no one character or way of reading is stamped with a clear seal of approval. There is no internal 'ideal reader' who serves as a metafictive model of reading, but by dramatising the various ways of reading, the narrative pre-empts, reflects and positions its own readers.

[170] A formulation prompted by Lennard Davis' analysis of the modern realistic novel: Davis (1987).

3

DESCRIPTION, DIGRESSION AND FORM

One of the most striking features of Achilles' narrative, and to a greater or lesser extent of all the Greek novels,[1] is what Bartsch calls its 'proclivity for the parenthetic',[2] the frequency with which the action is suspended and descriptions and sententious passages foregrounded over the story. One reader claims to have counted 'well over one hundred digressions' or 'irrelevancies'.[3] There have been few critics of Achilles who would agree with the character in *Tristram Shandy* that 'Digressions, incontestably, are the sunshine – they are the life, the soul of reading.'[4] Instead, they are often thought 'extremely tiresome'[5], and the cause of 'such frustration', at least for modern readers.[6] Scholarly analyses of the digressions vary, but they tend to downplay or ignore intratextual dynamics: how the 'digressions' function relationally *within* the narrative. Some have argued that the digressions were the very motivation for and the main substance of the novels, with the narrative as almost incidental. Ben Perry writes that Achilles Tatius, Heliodorus and Iamblichus were 'almost ashamed' of the love story element:

They tolerate it because they know that it is popular and will bring them readers, but they try to improve upon it as much as they can by the injection of a more respectable kind of subject-matter and artistic display. They do not tell the love story for its own sake ... but rather use it as a framework within which to display their sophistical wares.[7]

This is a view still held over twenty years later:

---

[1] So-called digressions occur frequently in *Leucippe and Clitophon* and in Heliodorus' *Ethiopian Tales*, and to a lesser degree in Longus' *Daphnis and Chloe* and Chariton's *Callirhoe*.
[2] Bartsch (1989), 3.   [3] McDermott (1989), 33.   [4] Quoted in Orr (1991), 53.
[5] Gaselee (1984), 341.   [6] McDermott (1989), 33.   [7] Perry (1967), 119.

Achilles Tatius' ineptitude can possibly be explained by the author's own attitude towards the romance. It seems very likely that he was not interested in the story qua story but in the enormous readership the romance would bring him: he could then use the story to display his many and varied sophistical wares.[8]

It is at least true from the time of Hermagoras (c. 150 BCE), that descriptions such as *ekphrasis*, generalisation (*gnome*), commonplace (*koinos topos*) and comparison (*sunkrisis*) were stock elements of the *progumnasmata*, handbooks of preliminary exercises in composition which were part of an orator's training.[9] The novelists' 'sophistical wares' it is suggested, are rhetorical displays symptomatic of those widely enjoyed during Hellenistic and Roman times. The story is merely a lure for the lazy, who, once engaged by it, will then be faced by the more edifying material in the rhetorical showpieces.

Bryan Reardon also sees a hierarchy of different levels of writing, but in the opposite order. The story is paramount and the digressions disposable:

> The sophistic novel can absorb [digressions] without strain; but for all that they are subordinate, in the design of the novel, to the story.[10]

Bartsch's study pays greater tribute to Achilles' and Heliodorus' sophistication. She argues that the descriptions of pictures and dreams 'are no mere rhetorical showpieces but forge playful and intricate connections with the narrative and its events'.[11] *Ekphraseis* and dreams function proleptically, encouraging anticipation and reinterpretation of important events in the story. This is persuasive as far as certain descriptions are concerned, but it by no means helps us understand all of them. We are left with the question: 'Why

---

[8] McDermott (1989), 33. Sedelmeier (1959) discounts digressive and descriptive passages as extraneous. Rattenbury comments: 'He sometimes gives the impression that he had used erotic romance as a framework in which he might conveniently display his erudition': (1933), 255. Garson (1978) writes that *ekphrasis* in Achilles Tatius is 'a dispensable appendage to his novel' in which 'he attained absolute mastery', 83.

[9] Webb (2001) is the best study of *progumnasmata* and lists all the sources. The handbooks themselves are conveniently all translated in Kennedy (1999). Theon, who wrote the earliest surviving handbook, stresses that this training was also useful to 'poets, prose writers, or anyone wishing to exploit the power of words' (2.24–8); see Webb (2001), 291.

[10] Reardon (1991), 161.   [11] Bartsch (1989), 6–7.

did the authors themselves wish their work to include digressions that neither explained nor made plausible a particular character's actions?' Bartsch's answer, 'Perhaps simply because their readers found them interesting and of genuine educational worth. The *topoi* in question are largely culled from the works of historians, geographers, and natural scientists ... and these same *topoi* were treated in the schools of rhetoric',[12] is inadequate. It contradicts her main thesis and fits ill with her vision of *Leucippe and Clitophon* as an inexorably intratextual work, all parts of which convey and revise meaning. Nor does it address why the descriptions might be interesting or in what way educational. What 'educational worth' is to be found in, for example, the description of dazzling Alexandria, or that of the exhibitionist phoenix?[13] These novels' representations of *paideia* are far from simple.

These criticisms raise important questions about how we evaluate narrative. First, what do we mean by 'digression'? As Alison Sharrock points out, it is a loaded word: 'With its implications of a hierarchy of textual elements, the term "digression" itself suggests the criticism of self-indulgence and irrelevance.'[14] *To what* is an irrelevance deemed irrelevant? These terms are too often employed indiscriminately, referring to a wide range of passages in Achilles. Such passages differ in form – descriptions, descriptions told as stories, fables, sententious propositions – and in theme – descriptions of places and objects, and discourses on sense-perception, women, animals and kissing, to name but a few. It is not sufficient to lump them all together under the label 'digression'. They engage the reader in a variety of different ways, with differing functions and pleasures.

Second, how does the framing of the so-called digressions determine our reading of them, and in turn, how do they affect our reading of the story? The contextualisation of these passages is extremely important. Perry, McDermott, and, in some cases, Bartsch focus on external factors to explain the digressions. That the novelists were influenced by their literary and cultural milieux is not in question, but a genetic explanation of the digressions – that they are *topoi* cut and pasted from rhetorical, historical, and

---

[12] Ibid., 155.   [13] See below 190–7.   [14] Sharrock (1994), 89.

geographical handbooks – is insufficient and distorting. If Achilles had simply wanted 'to display his . . . sophistical wares', then he could have written a work like Philostratus' *Imagines* or Seneca's *Controversiae*, both of which, in their different ways, contain rhetorical set-pieces, but in a collection, not in continuous narrative form. Unlike the disengaged descriptions in these collections and in the *progumnasmata*, the descriptions in the novels are bound by the narratives to be read in a particular order and in a specific context.[15] Achilles Tatius, like his Eros, is a 'clever *bricoleur*' (Winkler's gloss on αὐτοσχέδιος σοφιστής at 5.27.4) and, as with all bricolage, of particular interest in this novel are the relations between the different parts, rather than the relations between text and 'reality'. As Celia Britton puts it, 'In a system of relations between interdependent parts, meaning is necessarily *differential*, as opposed to the *referential* conception of meaning that underpins traditional realism in literature.'[16]

This chapter is concerned to investigate how one particular form of 'digression', the sententious statement, and the narrative that frames and is framed by it, interact with and impact on each other. Its aim is to contribute to a narratology of *sententiae*. It seeks a greater understanding of what Mary Ann Caws calls the 'architexture' of the text, 'the building of the text as it is seen and is formed with the reader's collaboration, special attention being given to the surface of the building material, its texturality'.[17] A text may be said to become textural when its structure and texture are illuminated and the surface of the narrative is drawn attention to, defamiliarised. The focus will be those privileged moments of narrative in Achilles which seize the gaze and so throw into relief the coarseness of the text's fabric, revealing its texturality. This involves consideration of the pleasure, or lack of pleasure, involved in reading literature that might be called digressive. As Kenneth Burke writes: '*Form* in literature is an arousing and fulfilling of desires. A work has form in so far as one part of it leads a reader to anticipate another

---

[15] Of course, the works of Philostratus and Seneca have very different agendas and structures. The descriptions and rhetorical set-pieces contained within them are not totally disengaged – they are framed by the prologues and authorial comments. However, they do not demand a linear reading in the same way as novelistic narrative does.
[16] Britton (1992), 59–60.   [17] Caws (1981), 10.

part, and so to be gratified by the sequence.'[18] Part of the project will be to explore how Achilles uses form to manipulate desires. What is it about the disruption of a narrative's temporal and thematic flow that so disturbs some readers? It will not be looking just at the form, but also at the content of sententious digressions. The subjects chosen to be pronounced upon sententiously are significant and whether we subordinate or parade particular chunks of text affects our understanding of the ideology of *Leucippe and Clitophon*. Whether, and how, to read intratextually, are decisions that necessarily have political ramifications.

Sightseeing in Alexandria

Anderson, who is one of the few scholars to pay much attention to the description of Alexandria which begins Book 5, does so with a caveat: 'the context in Achilles' plot must . . . be taken into account. This is only a brief breathing space between the mishaps of Leucippe.'[19] Only a brief breathing space – merely a digression, then. Still, it is a pretty spectacular breathing space:

Τριῶν δὲ πλεύσαντες ἡμερῶν εἰς Ἀλεξάνδρειαν ἤλθομεν. Ἀνιόντι δέ μοι κατὰ τὰς Ἡλίου καλουμένας πύλας συνηντᾶτο εὐθὺς τῆς πόλεως ἀστράπτον τὸ κάλλος καί μου τοὺς ὀφθαλμοὺς ἐγέμισεν ἡδονῆς. Στάθμη μὲν κιόνων ὄρθιος ἑκατέρωθεν ἐκ τῶν Ἡλίου πυλῶν ἐς τὰς Σελήνης πύλας· οὗτοι γὰρ τῆς πόλεως οἱ πυλωροί. Ἐν μέσῳ δὴ τῶν κιόνων τῆς πόλεως τὸ πεδίον. Ὁδὸς δὲ διὰ τοῦ πεδίου πολλὴ καὶ ἔνδημος ἀποδημία. Ὀλίγους δὲ τῆς πόλεως σταδίους προελθών, ἦλθον εἰς τὸν ἐπώνυμον Ἀλεξάνδρου τόπον. Εἶδον δὲ ἐντεῦθεν ἄλλην πόλιν καὶ σχιζόμενον ταύτῃ τὸ κάλλος. Ὅσος γὰρ κιόνων ὄρχατος ἐς τὴν εὐθυωρίαν, τοσοῦτος ἕτερος εἰς τὰ ἐγκάρσια. Ἐγὼ δὲ μερίζων τοὺς ὀφθαλμοὺς ἐς πάσας τὰς ἀγυιὰς θεατὴς ἀκόρεστος ἤμην καὶ τὸ κάλλος ὅλον οὐκ ἐξήρκουν ἰδεῖν. Τὰ μὲν ἔβλεπον, τὰ δὲ ἔμελλον, τὰ δὲ ἠπειγόμην ἰδεῖν, τὰ δὲ οὐκ ἤθελον παρελθεῖν· ἐκράτει τὴν θέαν τὰ ὁρώμενα, εἷλκε τὰ προσδοκώμενα. Περιάγων οὖν ἐμαυτὸν εἰς πάσας τὰς ἀγυιὰς καὶ πρὸς τὴν ὄψιν δυσερωτιῶν εἶπον καμών "Ὀφθαλμοί, νενικήμεθα."

After three days sailing we reached Alexandria. As I entered through the so-called 'gates of the Sun', I was immediately confronted with the brilliant beauty of the city, and my eyes were filled with pleasure. Two opposing rows of columns ran in straight lines from the gates of the Sun to the gates of the Moon (these two deities are the city's gatekeepers). Between the columns extended the open part of the city. Many a road criss-crossed this part: you could be a tourist at home. When I

---

[18] Burke (1953), 147, quoted in Orr (1991), 54. [19] Anderson (1984), 99.

had advanced a few stades into the city, I reached the place named after Alexander, where I saw another city altogether. Its beauty was dissected as follows: a row of columns ran in a straight line, traversed by another of equal length. I divided my eyes between all the streets, an insatiable spectator incapable of taking in such beauty in its entirety. There were sights I saw, sights I aimed to see, sights I ached to see, sights I could not bear to miss . . . my gaze was overpowered by what I could see before me, but dragged away by what I anticipated. As I was guiding my own tour around all these streets, love-sick with the sight of it, I said to myself wearily: 'We are beaten, my eyes.' (5.1.1–5)

Clitophon speaks of the dimensions of the city in terms commonly used to describe paradoxographical *thaumata*; he found them καινὰ καὶ παράλογα, 'extraordinary novelties' (5.1.6). Of crucial importance to descriptions of foreign lands is autopsy, where 'the eye is used as an indicator as to who is speaking, the "I have seen" as an intervention in his narrative on the part of the narrator, as a way of providing truth'.[20] For writers like Herodotus, Strabo and Polybius, autopsy validates their information and makes their reports credible. Metrology is a fundamental component of autopsy, as Hartog explains:

The joys of surveying are also the sign of a certain power. What better way of making people believe that one knows a building or a country, especially if it is far away, than showing oneself capable of giving its measurements?

It is interesting to compare Clitophon's account of Alexandria with that of Strabo. Both are examples of autopsy, but in very different ways. Strabo's description of Alexandria is full of metrological information:

the coast from Pelusium as one sails towards the west as far as the Canobic mouth is about 1,300 stades long . . . from there to the island of Pharos is a further 150 stades . . . the long sides of [the city] . . . have a diameter of about 30 stades while the isthmuses form the short sides, each of them seven or eight stades wide . . . (17. 1. 6–10)[21]

Alexandria was divided into five *klimata* which would in turn have been subdivided into blocks, thought to be rectangular strips, by

---

[20] Hartog (1988), 261.
[21] Given the lack of archaeological evidence that survives, our most important sources on ancient Alexandria are Strabo (17.1.6ff.) and Diodorus (17.52). Cf. Tomlinson (1992), ch. 7, and Owens (1991), 68–9 who gives details of the city's foundation, layout and buildings, but says nothing about how the city was viewed.

DESCRIPTION, DIGRESSION AND FORM

the grid of the street plan.²² In contrast to Strabo, Clitophon could not be less precise with his information:

Εἶδον δὲ δύο καινὰ καὶ παράλογα, μεγέθους πρὸς κάλλος ἅμιλλαν καὶ δήμου πρὸς πόλιν φιλονεικίαν καὶ ἀμφότερα νικῶντα· ἡ μὲν γὰρ ἠπείρου μείζων ἦν, ὁ δὲ πλείων ἔθνους. Καὶ εἰ μὲν εἰς τὴν πόλιν ἀπεῖδον, ἠπίστουν εἰ πληρώσειέ τις δῆμος αὐτὴν ἀνδρῶν, εἰ δὲ εἰς τὸν δῆμον ἐθεασάμην, ἐθαύμαζον εἰ χωρήσειέ τις αὐτὸν πόλις. Τοιαύτη τις ἦν ἰσότητος τρυτάνη.

I saw two extraordinary novelties, grandeur competing with splendour and the populace striving to exceed their city. Both sides won: the city was bigger than a continent and the people more numerous than an entire race. When I considered the city, I could not believe that it could be filled with people; when I beheld the people, I was amazed that a city could hold them. The scales were that finely balanced. (5.1.6)

Unlike the cold, particularizing gaze of Strabo and its technically accurate description, Clitophon's account is impressionistic. As Saïd remarks: 'What is depicted by Achilles Tatius is the idea of the city, not its concrete, individualised form.'²³ We are left in no doubt as to Clitophon's presence in Alexandria or that he describes the city from first-hand experience. We expect a description of the city, but the emphasis is on the very process of describing, or rather, of failing to describe. Clitophon conveys every possible permutation of *viewing* the city, but we are none the wiser as to *what* he viewed. 'To describe is to see and make seen.'²⁴ Clitophon's description collapses as a description because he cannot see, let alone make seen. He has an excess of points of view. The scopic goes into overdrive, a sort of optical psychosis. It is a paradox that Alexandria is so visible, so eye-intense that it cannot be seen, but can only dazzle the seer. Clitophon's eye is glutted by the surface of the city, it cannot get a grip on and detail its contents. Colonnaded streets pull Clitophon's gaze from every direction.²⁵ The streets and columns blur and merge together. Unlike Strabo, Clitophon exercises no mastery over the city with his surveying

---

[22] Ps.-Call. 1.32.9; Phil. *In Flacc.* 55. Tomlinson (1992), 99–100; 228 n.12 gives examples of the known dimensions of blocks in Macedonian or Macedonian-planned cities.
[23] Saïd (1994), 231. See also Orlandini (1993) on ekphrastic descriptions of places in the Greek novels.
[24] Hartog (1988), 248.
[25] On the likelihood of there being colonnades in Alexandria at the time when Achilles wrote, see Saïd (1994), 231.

eye. Clitophon's Alexandria is a city derealised and resistant to sense.[26] In contrast to the *flâneur*, the modernist urban viewer, who is a self-possessed, leisurely consumer and commodifier of city sights, Clitophon is awed and overwhelmed by his surroundings.[27] The *flâneur* 'moves through space and among the people with a viscosity that both enables and privileges vision'.[28] Clitophon is an anti-*flâneur*, keenly gorging himself on sights, and with a velocity and intemperance which privilege vision, but do not enable it. His viewing is a parody of autopsy, an inversion of sight as credibility. Like Henry James' Mr Brooke on arriving in Italy en route for Venice, what Clitophon is spellbound by is not *what* he observes, but the very experience of observing: 'Imagination, panting and exhausted, withdrew from the game; and Observation stepped into her place, trembling and glowing with open-eyed Desire'.[29]

Modern theorists have remarked upon the metaliterary function of the images of the city and its institutions. Wendy Faris focuses on the motif of the labyrinth and argues that it serves a metaliterary purpose, as a commentary on the activity of writing itself.[30] Novels like Joyce's *Ulysses*, Butor's *Passing Time*, and Robbe-Grillet's *In the Labyrinth* 'duplicate the form of the labyrinth in the structural design of their prose, so that in them besides the labyrinths *in* the texts, we experience the labyrinths *of* the texts. The labyrinthine structure of error and backtracking, of dead-ends and repetitions is most clearly developed in the structure of *In the Labyrinth*.'[31] Viewing Alexandria similarly reflects the experience of reading Achilles Tatius in that both experiences are eye-intense and enigmatic, forcing the reader to turn this way and that and to retrace his steps. Furthermore, traversing Alexandria, says Clitophon, is like being ἔνδημος ἀποδημία (5.1.3). There is no verb in this sentence. Independent of time it has a certain 'floating' authority. Translators often supply the optative: 'you would fancy yourself abroad while still at home' (Gaselee) 'you would

---

[26] Like Renée's Paris in Zola's *La Curée*, discussed by Prendergast (1991), 192.
[27] On the *flâneur*, see Baudelaire (1964), 7–9; Herbert (1988), 33–4 and Jenks (1995b).
[28] Jenks (1995c), 146.
[29] *Complete Tales of Henry James*, ed. Leon Edel, 12 vols. (London, 1962), vol. 2, 162, quoted by Tony Tanner, who comments, 'Passion has all run into the eye and the eye is trembling to be taken': Tanner (1992), 2.
[30] Faris (1991), 34.   [31] Ibid., 35.

think you were going abroad, though staying at home' (Winkler). This phrase articulates what has been identified as a characteristic dynamic of Achilles' narrative; the uncanny. The curious sensation when reading of encountering something familiar that has been defamiliarised is deftly encapsulated in this one phrase, ἔνδημος ἀποδημία.³² Clitophon's description of touring Alexandria thus offers the reader various opportunities to read it as a metaliterary evocation of his or her tour around the novel.³³

The subjective impressionism of Clitophon's account bears closer analysis. Anderson is critical of the description:

> He has idealised Alexandria as he has sensationalised the romantic plot, and he has gone over the top again. He has said nothing about the civic and racial tensions for which the city had long been notorious, and one catches not a whiff of the stench of an ancient metropolis.³⁴

So, what Anderson misses is realism! However, he deems the description apposite for a man of Clitophon's social standing:

> Yet from Clitophon's point of view, the description is valid. A wealthy young man of student age in the early Empire could well have reacted in this way... In a world where aristocratic values so unquestionably predominated, one would not expect Clitophon to look behind any facade.

Anderson misses the point: it is not Clitophon's aristocratic status that informs his outlook, but his status as a *lover*. On entering the gates of the city, Clitophon is struck by the beauty of the place, as if hit by lightning (ἀστράπτον τὸ κάλλος). It is a fine comic touch that Clitophon is dazzled when he walks through the gate of the Sun, but it is also the typical response of lovers on first sight of their beloved. When Clitophon first sees Leucippe he is struck, as if by lightning (καταστράπτει μου, 1.4.2), and, in a passage which

---

³² See also Nimis (1997) who takes a more psychoanalytic approach. He reads this episode as representing 'the workings of the imagination and the unconscious, and more particularly of a kind of surrender to those workings, an inability of the symbolic order, represented by the grid of streets, to master the effects of the unconscious, represented by the swarming population surging forward at every turn'. He also makes the excellent linguistic point: 'Freud cites the Greek word ξενικός as an equivalent, but the pair ἔνδημος ἀποδημία is a remarkable parallel to the pair of German terms based on *heim*.'
³³ See also Doody (1996), 10: 'The experience of reading a novel may be a bit like Kleitophon's experience of his first visit to Alexandria. You cannot take it all in at one go, it requires a deal of noticing, eyes always on the stretch.'
³⁴ Anderson (1984), 99.

will be analysed in some depth below (135–40) and in the next chapter, Leucippe stuns Thersander in the same way (τὸ κάλλος ἐκ παραδρομῆς ὡς ἁρπαζομένης ἀστραπῆς, 6.6.3). The city actively fills his eyes with delight, as heroines do in romances. (Unlike heroines, however, the city cannot express delight or dismay at its effect on its viewers.) Clitophon becomes a lover of the city, not as in Pericles' politically motivated exhortation that the people should be 'lovers' of Athens,[35] but in a more literal sense; he reacts to Alexandria as he would to his girlfriend.[36]

Clitophon calls himself 'an unsatisfied spectator', θεατὴς ἀκόρεστος, a phrase which brilliantly captures the young man's 'leer lust'. It is normally used not of sightseers, but of would-be lovers, spying on beautiful maidens. Unsatisfaction and insatiability in particular animate scopophiliac desire, or to put it another way, *eros* is inherently voyeuristic. To be ἀκόρεστος or ἀκόρητος is the common experience of most voyeurs. We remember Socrates, in Xenophon's *Memorabilia*, complaining that admirers of beautiful women get shortchanged because they leave titillated, but unsatisfied. A work that (relentlessly) provides good illustrations of the insatiability of desire is Nonnus' *Dionysiaca*, a poem very much concerned with protocols of viewing. It is a fitting text to choose, because it appropriates and develops elements in *Leucippe and Clitophon*.[37] At 11.101–2 we learn that 'loving eyes are never sated with viewing' (καὶ γὰρ ὀπωπαὶ οὔ ποτε δερκομένοισι κόρον τίκτουσιν ἐρώτων). Poseidon catches sight of Beroe and repeatedly runs his 'love-maddened eye' (ἐρωτομανὲς ὄμμα, 42.454) over her face, all the while 'staring unsatisfied at her whole body'

---

[35] 'You should judge the benefits [of defeating the enemy] not from discussion alone, but more from watching the actual power of the city every day and becoming her lovers', μὴ λόγῳ μόνῳ τὴν ὠφελίαν ... ἀλλὰ μᾶλλον τὴν τῆς πόλεως δύναμιν καθ' ἡμέραν ἔργῳ θεωμένους καὶ ἐραστὰς γιγνομένους αὐτῆς (*Thuc.* 2.43.1).

[36] Zeno the Stoic sees *eros* as a crucial factor in the harmony of the city. Exactly how he conceived this relationship to be is not clear, as we have only a fragment of his thought on the subject mentioned in Athenaeus: 'Zeno of Citium took Eros to be a God who brings friendship and freedom and concord, but nothing else. That is why in his Republic he said that Love is a god, and there as a helper in furthering the safety of the city' (*Deipn.* 13 561e). On the sense of this passage see Schofield (1991), 2–56.

[37] The date is uncertain; see Hopkinson (1994), 4. On the *Dionysiaca*, see Winkler (1974), esp. ch. 1 on voyeurism; Hopkinson (1994); Shorrock (2001). Heath (1992) discusses Nonnus' version of the tale of Actaeon (6.301–11) and identifies over sixty direct references in this one episode to 'direct and indirect vision': Heath (1992), 142.

(παπταίνων ἀκόρητος ὅλον δέμας 42.455). Beroe is beset by another peeping Tom, Dionysus: 'He could not have enough of his gazing; for the more he beheld the maiden standing there, the more he wanted to watch' (οὐδέ οἱ εἰσορόωντι κόρος πέλεν· ἱσταμένην γὰρ | παρθένον ὅσσον ὄπωπε, τόσον πλέον ἤθελε λεύσσειν, 42.47–8).[38] Typhon imagines gazing upon a girl in his mind's eye: 'he delights to let his eye run over and over her body never satisfied' (ἀκόρητον ὀπωπήν 1.531–2). These are just a few of the many sybaritic stagings of voyeurism in the *Dionysiaca*,[39] all of which articulate and parade the eye-intensity and insatiability of desire. As Winkler comments, 'looking brings satiety when you have seen all there is to see, voyeuristic looking does not bring κόρος ἐρώτων'. And it is voyeuristic looking which Clitophon indulges in when sightseeing in Alexandria. Clitophon bemoans this sorry state when he calls himself πρὸς τὴν ὄψιν δυσερωτιῶν, 'sick with love' or 'passionately loving' the spectacle of the city (6.1.5). Alexandria is feminised and sexualised. Luring his gaze to ever more enticing sights, the city seduces Clitophon. Like Leucippe, she conquers his eyes. So 'drenched with desire' is Clitophon that even sightseeing is ineluctably imbued with erotic yearning and a city tour becomes a romantic encounter.

Sententiousness and the arrested eye

Παῖς γὰρ καὶ παρθένος ὅμοιοι μέν εἰσιν εἰς αἰδῶ· πρὸς δὲ τὴν τῆς Ἀφροδίτης χάριν κἂν γνώμης ἔχωσιν, ἃ πάσχουσιν ἀκούειν οὐ θέλουσι· τὴν γὰρ αἰσχύνην κεῖσθαι νομίζουσιν ἐν τοῖς ῥήμασι.

Boys and girls are equally shy: even if they are inclined towards the pleasures of Aphrodite, they do not want to hear about what they are undergoing. They think that the shame lies in talking about it. (1.10.3)

There are numerous statements in *Leucippe and Clitophon* like those quoted above. Usually, they stand alone, without an introductory gloss, but in this case the statements comprise part of

---

[38] He is again described as ἀκόρητος at line 60.
[39] Zeus spies upon Semele at 7.210–18 and on Persephone at 5.587–621. The latter scene is a wonderful nexus of scopic activities, with a protracted description of Persephone studying herself in the mirror, as well as Zeus gazing upon her as she loosens her clothing in the heat and then when she is naked and bathing. Once again the emphasis is on the insatiable male gaze (5.587–9). See Winkler (1974), 61.

SENTENTIOUSNESS AND THE ARRESTED EYE

Clinias' advice to Clitophon on how to seduce Leucippe and he prefaces them with the following words:

Ὅσα δέ ἐστι κοινὰ καὶ μὴ τῆς εὐκαίρου τύχης δεόμενα, ταῦτα ἀκούσας μάθε.

But you should also hear and learn all the general rules, which do not depend on lucky breaks. (1.10.2)

Clinias' annotation not only applies to the advice that he is about to offer on boys and girls' behaviour, but also characterises numerous other passages of similar kind throughout the novel. *Koina*, 'common maxims', 'les conseils d'ordre général' or 'allgemeingültige Grundsätze',[40] are statements which claim to be universal and eternal, 'applicable at any time',[41] by appearing independent of any specific context. They might be considered as sententious or gnomic statements. The terms *gnome* and *sententia* basically meant 'opinion' or 'way of feeling',[42] but ancient writers define and categorise them in a number of ways.[43] There was a long tradition of advice-giving – *gnomologia* – and philosophical debate about the nature and applicability of *gnomai* and *sententiae*.[44] I use the terms loosely and inclusively to refer to statements or descriptions which generalise or universalise.[45] Usually written in the present tense, sometimes referred to as the 'gnomic present'[46] (like the examples above at 1.10.3), sententious propositions appear formally to be detached from the narrative, disengaged from their diegetical context. They thus appear to present universal truths, relevant beyond

[40] The translations of Gaselee, Garnaud and Plepelits respectively.
[41] Gaselee's translation.   [42] Quintilian, *Institutio Oratoria* 8.5.1.
[43] Quintilian comments on the broad semantic range of *sententia* (8.5.3). *Institutio Oratoria* 8.5 is the most extensive discussion in ancient texts. Aphthonius and Theon give interesting accounts of *gnomai*, with Aphthonius dividing them into protreptic, apotreptic, declarative, simple, compound, persuasive, true and hyperbolic: Matsen, Rollinson and Scusa (1990), 268–70. Some of what I might call *gnomai*, Aristotle would class as enthymemes because of the inclusion of syllogisms. Some proverbs are also *gnomai*: Aristotle, *Rhetoric* 2.21.12.
[44] Seneca, *Epistles* 94 – Aristo the Stoic contends that general advice does not have as much impact as advice that is tailored to specific circumstances. Aristo says: 'He who has made a careful decision as to what should be sought and what should be avoided knows what he ought to do, without a single word from you' (12). For further background see Billault (1991), 293ff.
[45] So e.g. by Aristotle's criteria, I would also be including enthymemes etc. For Quintilian, the difference between a *sententia* and a *chria* (a moral essay) can be as little as the prefix 'he said'. But not all *chriae* share the same qualities as *sententiae*: 1.9.4. See also Webb (2001).
[46] Cf. Hartog (1988), 255.

the world of the novel in which they appear. *Sententia universalis est vox*, as Quintilian puts it.[47]

How are we to interpret the *sententiae* in *Leucippe and Clitophon*?[48] Morgan suggests that:

> Their function is to illustrate that the behaviour of the fictional characters and their world conforms to normative statements acceptable as descriptions of the real world. They thus define a plausibility which is relevant to the narrative.[49]

Clearly, this is right, up to a point. As Roland Barthes has argued, the inclusion of information extrinsic to the propulsion of the plot – *unnecessary* detail – is the essence of realism.[50] Moreover, the incorporation of objects and *dicta* which are familiar, or at least comprehensible, to the readers from their own environment, persuades them that 'they have a referent beyond themselves, in a supposedly objective world'.[51] They thus enable the reader to 'concretise' the fictional world, to accept it and engage with it as 'real'.

Sententious passages are overtly prescriptive (they do not just reflect but '*define* a plausibility' . . .). In Geoffrey Bennington's study of sententiousness in eighteenth-century French fiction, he shows how '[s]ententious formulations imply a value-judgement grounded in social norms; they transmit a cultural heritage and are inherently conservative.'[52] In doing so, they 'lay down the law'.[53] Indeed, Quintilian suggests that the terms *gnome* and *sententia* have their origins in 'laying down the law' because 'these sayings are like proposals or decrees' (*similes sunt consiliis aut decretis*, 8.5.3). So it is worth asking what laws are laid down by the sententious formulations in *Leucippe and Clitophon*. In other words, what are the values and norms in the society of the novel and thus *what sort* of plausibility is relevant to Achilles Tatius?

Sententious statements in *Leucippe and Clitophon* can be classified as follows:

---

[47] *Institutio Oratoria* 1.9.3 (he is making the comparison here with *ethologiae*, which are concerned with persons).
[48] I briefly discuss sententiousness in the other novels in Morales (2000).
[49] Morgan (1993), 202.   [50] Barthes (1986). See also Bryson (1990).
[51] Jordanova (1989), 47.
[52] Bennington (1985), 9. Cf. Scarcella (1987), 270.   [53] Ibid., xi.

On lovers, lovemaking and emotions

(1.5.5–6)	Clitophon as narrator (N)	how love stories enflame desire
(1.6.2–4)	Clit. (N)	lovers' emotions
(1.10.1–7)	Clinias to Clit.	courtship, women's feigned modesty, lovers as actors.
(2.8.1–3)	Clit. (N)	kissing
(2.13.1–2)	Clit. (N)	*akolasia*, love and hearsay
(2.29.1–5)	Clit. (N)	shame, grief and lust (*thumos*)
(2.36.1–2)	Men. to Clit.	satisfaction and desire
(4.8.1–4)	Clit. to Men.	kisses
(4.8.4–6)	Men. to Clit.	nature of lovers' desire
(5.22.8)	Clit. (N)	joy and hope
(5.27.1)	Clit. (N)	nature of *eros*
(5.27.4)	Clit. (N)	Eros as *autoskhedios*
(6.13.4)	Sosthenes to Leucippe	amiability
(6.18.3–4)	Clit. (N)	lovers' discourse
(6.19.1–7)	Clit. (N)	desire and love

On vision

(1.4.4)	Clit. (N)	beauty and the eye
(1.9.4–5)	Clinias to Clit.	mutual gazing as a sexual activity
(2.3.3)	Clit. (N)	Cupid, Dionysus and vision
(3.4.4–5)	Clit. (N)	slow death and the eye
(3.11.1–2)	Clit. (N)	eye and tears in grief
(5.13.4)	Clit. (N)	pleasure, vision and beauty
(6.6.2–3)	Clit. (N)	face as mirror, joy and eyes
(6.6.3)	Clit. (N)	beauty and eyes
(6.7.1–3)	Clit. (N)	tears, beauty and eyes
(6.7.4–8)	Clit. (N)	tears, beauty and eyes
(7.4.4–8)	Clit. (N)	grief, tears and eyes

On women

(1.7.4–5)	Charicles to Clinias	marriage, women and beauty
(1.8.1–9)	Clinias to Charicles	women and marriage
(1.9.3–7)	Clinias to Clitophon	courtship and taming women
[(2.35.3–5)	Men. to Clit. and Clinias	youths' superiority to women
(2.37)	Clit. to Men and Clinias	superiority of women, how women kiss
(2.38)	Men. to Clit. and Clinias	superiority of boys, vileness of women]
(5.4.2)	Clit. (N)	women and stories

(5.5.7–8)	Clit. to Leuc. *et al.*	nature of women who have been wronged sexually
(6.17.4)	Sosthenes to Thersander	fickleness of women

On the way the world works

(1.3.2–3)	Clit. (N)	Providence
(6.10.4–6)	Melite to Thersander	Rumour and Slander

Slaves

(7.10.5)	Clit. (N)	the cowardice of slaves

Barbarians

(4.14.9)	Clit. (N)	Egyptians' extreme emotions
(5.5.2)	Clit. to Leuc. *et al.*	the sexual appetite of barbarian men

Of course, my acts of selecting, collating and labelling the *sententiae* are open to the charge of being somewhat arbitrary and subjective.[54] They have been grouped thematically, but many categories cover a range of topics under their umbrella title and there are other ways in which they could have been ordered. None the less, it is a useful exercise because it shows quite clearly what subjects are chosen and pronounced upon sententiously. The largest class of *sententiae* pronounces upon lovers, lovemaking and emotions: the physical, psychological and emotional processes of desire. A large number concern vision: the mechanisms and appearances of viewing and being viewed. A significant proportion is on women. I have included but bracketed those that appear in the long *sunkrisis* on sexual preferences in the latter part of the second book. They are included because they are sententious in so far as they are generalising statements, but bracketed because they are spoken in the specific, contestatory context of a debate and thus do not so much

---

[54] Scarcella's survey counts (but does not list) fifty-eight *gnomai* in *Leucippe and Clitophon*, which he divides into those concerning *eros*, those on the problems of society and those which comment on social manners and attitudes: Scarcella (1987), 270. Hedrick uses the following categories: anecdotes and digressions where 'generally there is no transition into and out of the digressions'; digressions which are 'accommodated by inclusion in the speeches of the personae in the novel'; digressions which are digressions 'only in the sense that they wander from the topic'; anecdotes and digressions where the narrator moralises and 'shorter anecdotes and asides': cf. Hedrick (1998), 179–80. Billault (1991) distinguishes between 'scientific' disgressions and 'moral' digressions.

lay down the law as argue the law. To a much lesser degree, abstract forces, slaves and barbarians are also talked about sententiously.

It is not strange that a work which announces itself as a love story (μύθων . . . ἐρωτικῶν, 1.2.3) contains material on love. Nor is it unusual that a love story should be interested in vision. Sexual desire, as I discussed in the introductory chapter, was primarily a visual impetus. No surprise, either, that attention is paid to familiar objects of desire: women. The point is that although the *sententiae* are structurally digressive, in no way can they be called thematically digressive. Whilst their form is detached, their content is utterly relevant. The sententious passages lay down laws about desire – its theory and practice – all of which create a plausibility that is relevant to a love story.

The *sententiae* are digressions in so far as they are nonsequential: they break up the linear flow of the narrative. This happens to a much greater degree with the longer sententious passages in Achilles Tatius and Heliodorus, than with the shorter *sententiae* in Chariton, Longus and Xenophon. As Leonard Orr notes, 'to give too much detail in description, [or] to go on for too long . . . foregrounds the description over the story and halts the temporal insistence of the narrative'.[55] The reason why *sententiae* tend to irritate readers is that nobody likes to be put on hold. This is one of the ways that sententious writing insists on its own importance, as retarding the temporal flow of the narrative makes the *sententia* 'stand out'.[56] Texturally, *sententiae* are knots in the 'rough weave of the textual surface',[57] or patches on the textual cloth.[58] Sententious patches arrest the reader and catch the eye.[59] In one old English translation of *Leucippe and Clitophon*, they do this not only on a temporal and textural level, but on a typographical one also. Printed in 1638, Hodges' *The Loves of Clitophon and Leucippe* is introduced as 'A most elegant History, written in Greeke by Achilles Tatius and now Englished'. The edition italicises

---

[55] Orr (1991), 86. [56] See Bennington (1985), 45. [57] Caws (1981), 9.
[58] Bennington (1985) discusses *sententiae* as patches: 49–50. Quintilian compares *sententiae* to purple stripes on a robe: one is becoming, but several are not (8.5.28). Seneca: 'wherever you direct your gaze, you will meet with something that might stand out from the rest, if the context in which you read it were not equally notable': *Epistles* 33.4. See also Cicero, *De Or.* 3.26.101 on *sententiae* as flashes against a shady background.
[59] They are sometimes thought to block vision: cf. Seneca, *Epistles* 94.

sententious passages throughout, which visually stresses the detachment of the passages from the surrounding text. The italics seize the reader's gaze and indicate iconically the powers of arrest of the *sententiae*.[60]

The italicisation, like other characteristics of sententious writing (present tense, self-aggrandisement and universality), may well serve to underline the passages' importance. All these trumpet the *sententiae* as essential reading, demanding attention and special regard. This was particularly important for English translators and adaptors of the Greek novels in the sixteenth and seventeenth centuries like Hodges, who, as Laurence Plazenet has shown, felt the need to maximise the didacticism of Achilles Tatius and Heliodorus in order to palliate the hostility that the novel aroused.[61] Moreover, these characteristics invite the reader to detach the *sententiae* from the narrative. This way of reading was taken to a literal extreme when *sententiae* were collected in anthologies, where they were literally detached from any narrative contexts. Numerous *sententiae* from the mimes of Publilius Syrus, for example, were selected and listed in alphabetical order in collections for schoolboys to memorise.[62] Alternatively, their paraded extractability from the narrative makes it easier for the reader to skip over them. As Barthes argues, much of the enjoyment of reading a novel comes from skipping some stretches of writing and grasping others:

> our very avidity for knowledge impels us to skim or to skip certain passages (anticipated as 'boring') in order to get more quickly to the warmer parts of the anecdote (which are always its articulations: whatever furthers the solutions of the riddle, the revelation of fate): we boldly skip (no one is watching) descriptions, explanations, analyses, conversations [and *sententiae*] . . . it is the very rhythm

---

[60] On the paratext, see Genette (1987). Vessey (1991–3), 145–6 stresses the importance of paratextual features of novels.
[61] Plazenet (1997), 152.
[62] Some thought his aphorisms more morally edifying than those expressed by characters in more serious dramatic genres: Seneca, *Controv.* 7.3.8; Seneca, *Epistles* 8.9–10. Fourteen *sententiae* attributed to Publilius Syrus are quoted in Aulus Gellius, *NA* 17.14. In Petronius' *Satyrica* the pseudo-intellectual Trimalchio misquotes a maxim from Publilius (*Sat.* 55). Two Byzantine collections, the *Gnomologion* of Ioannes Georgides Monazon and the *Melissa* of Antonius include *sententiae* plucked from *Ethiopian Tales*: cf. Morgan (1996), 423. In 1615 in Spain, an anthology of *sententiae* was published which was also culled from Heliodorus: *Una tabla de sentencias, y cosas notable*; cf. Plazenet (1997), 62 n. 117; Crane (1937), 173–4.

of what is read that creates the pleasure of the great narratives: has anyone ever read Proust, Balzac, *War and Peace* word for word?[63]

Or Achilles Tatius? The self-advertisement of the *sententiae* may well afford the reader, anxious to avoid a lecture and eager to find out what happens next in the story, the pleasure of skipping over them.

It is not coincidental that women, slaves, and barbarians are pronounced upon sententiously. To lay down the law about something is predicated upon having a position of mastery over that object. It assumes a superior and arrogant stance. For Quintilian, it is therefore important that universalising pronouncements are spoken by those with the *auctoritas* appropriate for assuming a position of mastery: 'Such reflections are best suited to those speakers whose authority is such that their character will lend weight to their words. For who would tolerate a boy, or a youth, or even a man of low birth who presumed to speak with all the authority of a judge and to thrust his precepts down our throats?'[64]

It is significant that, with one exception,[65] all the *sententiae* are spoken by male characters and only male characters pronounce on desire and its objects. Leucippe never utters a sententious statement and is rarely present to hear them uttered. Yet all of the sententious pronouncements outside the *sunkrisis* are about women, not boys, as objects of desire. *Sententiae* on men as love objects do not feature once in the course of the novel. Despite the fact that Melite and Leucippe are given a lot to say and some powerful speeches, women in Achilles Tatius do not 'lay down the law'; instead, laws are laid down about them. This is just one aspect of the narrative that should qualify Egger's evaluation of the novel as 'emotionally gynocentric'.[66] Reading generalising statements as detachable

---

[63] Barthes (1975), 11.
[64] *Institutio Oratoria* (8.5.8), echoing Aristotle *Rhetoric* 2.21.9: 'the use of maxims is suitable for one who is advanced in age, and in regard to things in which one has experience; since the use of maxims before such an age is unseemly, as also is storytelling; and to speak of things of which one has no experience shows foolishness and lack of education'. Seneca (*Epistles* 33) contrasts the Epicureans, who ascribe their sayings to one single authority, with the Stoics, who are more eclectic in their collections of *sententiae*. He criticises *sententiae* and *chriae* for being derivative and not generated from one's own experience.
[65] Melite advises Thersander about Rumour and Slander at 6.10.4–6.
[66] Egger (1990), 365.

chunks, as if they were rhetorical displays in the *progumnasmata*, threatens both to ignore important aspects of focalisation and to elide significant differences between the novels.

In pointed contrast to Leucippe, the heroines in Chariton and Heliodorus do speak sententiously. Callirhoe comments on a woman's vulnerability: 'A woman, all alone and a foreigner, is easy prey for contemptuous treatment' (3.2.4), which, of course, reflects her own worries about how Dionysius will treat her. Other women also speak sententiously. Plangon advises Callirhoe that 'big enterprises can only be brought off by big ideas' (2.10.3) and the Persian Queen Statira generalises scornfully about Greeks: 'Greeks are boastful, impoverished creatures. That is why they are so easily impressed' (5.3.2). Longus' Chloe is not given *sententiae* to utter, but neither is Daphnis. Charikleia, however, lays down the law about men and desire on more than one occasion:

immovable resistance only aggravates the force of irresistible passion, whereas a meek answer and swift submission can curb the first eruption of desire and soothe away the pangs of lust with the sweet taste of a promise given. Lovers of a coarser grain, it seems to me, consider a declaration of intent as the first act of love: a promise makes them think that they own you, and thenceforth secure in the haven of their hopes, they act with more composure. (1.26.6; cf. also 5.29.4)[67]

I suggest that the gendering of *sententiae* in the novels broadly supports other aspects of their representations of gender. Arguably, the novels of Chariton and Heliodorus include more powerful and empowering representations of their heroines than Achilles Tatius presents with Leucippe. Together with factors like the male ego-narration and sexualised descriptions of her 'murder', the gendered inequalities between who speaks and is spoken about sententiously plays a role in making *Leucippe and Clitophon* perhaps the *least* 'emotionally gynocentric' of all the Greek novels.

Barbarians are other objects of generalising pronouncements; once again mastery is asserted through sententiousness. In the fourth chapter of the novel, the general Charmides and his men are ambushed by Egyptian *boukoloi* ('herdsmen', or 'desperadoes') who terrorise the Nile Delta. The attack is successful and the outlaws exult in triumph because, comments Clitophon, they put

---

[67] The translation is that of J. R. Morgan in Reardon (1989).

victory down to their courage, rather than a deceitful stratagem. This precipitates a sententious statement from Clitophon on the nature of the Egyptian:

Ἀνὴρ γὰρ Αἰγύπτιος καὶ τὸ δειλόν, ὅπου φοβεῖται, δεδούλωται, καὶ τὸ μάχιμον, ἐν οἷς θαρρεῖ, παρώξυνται· ἀμφότερα δὲ οὐ κατὰ μέτρον, ἀλλὰ τὸ μὲν ἀσθενέστερον δυστυχεῖ, τὸ δὲ προπετέστερον κρατεῖ.

Thus it is with an Egyptian: in times of fear, cowardice leads him to servility, whereas his bellicosity is exacerbated in positive situations. Both reactions are immoderate: in the former instance he is too weak in the face of of misfortune, and in the latter too headstrong in victory. (4.14.9).

In this respect Egyptians are like slaves, who are also the subject of Clitophon's pronouncements (after Sosthenes, Thersander's slave, has fled in fright):

Μάλιστα γὰρ τὸ τῶν δούλων γένος ἐν οἷς ἂν φοβηθῇ σφόδρα δειλόν ἐστιν.

For the class of slaves is really vile in times of fear. (7.10.5)

On occasion, the sententiousness serves to reveal the hypocrisy of the speechifying narrator. At 5.5.2 Clitophon begins his narration of the tale of Tereus' rape of Philomela with a short *sententia* on the behaviour of barbarians:

βαρβάροις δέ, ὡς ἔοικεν, οὐχ ἱκανὴ πρὸς Ἀφροδίτην μία γυνή, μάλισθ' ὅταν αὐτῷ καιρὸς διδῷ πρὸς ὕβριν τρυφᾶν.

It seems that with barbarians one wife will not satisfy Aphrodite's needs, especially when the opportunity to indulge in rape presents itself. (5.5.2)

This judgement not only applies to Tereus, but is also relevant to Thersander: both are adulterous and both Thracian. It is, however, a reflection cast as a generalisation, condemning all barbarians. Scarcella conflates Clitophon in his capacity as narrator with Achilles Tatius the author and thus argues that the *sententiae* narrated by Clitophon 'riflettano esperienze e convinzioni, esplicite o profonde, dell'A'.[68] This suggests that the *sententiae* stand out as providing direct access to the author's own philosophy, akin perhaps to the function that some ascribe to the parabasis in Old Comedy.[69] There are, however, no indications in the text which direct

---

[68] Scarcella (1987), 270. [69] Not without difficulties; cf. Hesk (2000), 237–248.

us to read Clitophon as a cypher for the novelist, and the characterisation of him as cowardly, effeminate and self-serving makes this conflation even less credible. Moreover, reading the *sententia* in the light of the rest of the narrative promotes a very different reading of it. For, as we find out in the episode at the end of Book 5, it is Clitophon who is the adulterer and Clitophon for whom one woman is not sufficient. On re-reading the novel, or on reflecting back to 5.5.2, the *sententia* is a joke, an ironic jibe at Clitophon's hypocrisy, which undermines, rather than underpins, his authority in laying down the law about other people. Clitophon is revealed as an unreliable judge and the didacticism of his sententiousness exposed to ridicule as absurdly pompous. Indeed, we might also question Clitophon's right to criticise anyone else for being 'too weak in the face of misfortune', and 'really vile in times of fear', given what might be construed as his own cowardice. However, these ironies inflect, rather than undermine absolutely, the discourse of mastery.

We should note once again that it is not a coincidence that the subjects pronounced upon are women, slaves and barbarians. To lay down the law about something assumes a position of mastery (even if that mastery is ridiculed) and arrogance (even if that arrogance is ill-founded). Leucippe, Clitophon and Clinias are all Phoenician, as Leucippe proudly proclaims at 6.16.5–6. There are no generalising statements made about Phoenicians. The implication is that Egypt, unlike Phoenicia, needs surveying, evaluating and explaining. It is 'Other' to Greek-speaking Phoenicians, and *sententiae* are one means of codifying and controlling its strangeness. They are only one part of the discourse of ethnocentrism in *Leucippe and Clitophon* and should be considered together with the ethnographic descriptions (several of which are also commonly referred to as 'digressions') which reinforce their message.

In *Callirhoe*, *sententiae* are delivered on both foreigners and Greeks. Both Greeks and Persians are subject to generalisation and disparagement. Thus we learn that 'Barbarians are naturally passionately fond of women' (5.5.6), but also that 'Greeks find fault over trifles and they gossip' (6.6.7) and that 'Greeks are boastful, impoverished creatures. That is why they are so easily impressed' (5.3.2). But even here, authority is not invested equally.

SENTENTIOUSNESS AND THE ARRESTED EYE

The sententious statements on Greeks are spoken by Persians (Statira at 5.3.2 and Artaxerxes at 6.6.7), whereas the generalisations about barbarians (with the exception of Dionysius' comment at 5.2.8) are all pronounced by the narrator, who announces himself at the opening of the novel as Chariton. The comments on the Greeks are thus portrayed as partial accounts, in contrast to those on barbarians, which are delivered with all of the authority invested in the authorial narrative voice. Thus the *sententiae* play a role in constructing a discourse of ethnocentrism which, however nuanced and open to negotiation, maintains Greek superiority.

Desire and frustration

Some of the passages classed in this section, those that tell how love stories work, have already been discussed in the previous chapter. It concluded that we are encouraged to read these embedded statements as models of the text's own power and that they testify that the digressive is a central strategy in the lover's discourse. This section will consider *sententiae* that concern lovers' emotions, and takes as its first example a dissertation on *eros* (desire) and *thumos* (rage) at 6.19.1–19. In so far as this comprises a generalising pronouncement with the narrator assuming an authoritative tone, it can be classified as a sententious statement, even though its length would typically prevent it being classed as a *sententia*.[70] It is also an allegorical treatment of desire and anger and one which portrays Thersander as the personification of the tyranny of desire, using and distorting the vocabulary in Plato's discussion of desire in *Republic* 9 586c-e.[71] Let me put the passage into context. The sexually predatory Thersander is persisting with his pursuit of Leucippe, while she assiduously and inventively avoids his advances. There is much slapstick in this scene, as Clitophon narrates in detail the physical manoeuvres of the couple. The precision with which this 'wrestling match' (τῇ τῆς χειρὸς πάλῃ, 6.18.5) is choreographed conveys the struggle in a slow-motion replay. Finally Thersander stops trying to force Leucippe, 'whether because he had won, or because

---

[70] Quintilian complains about the extravagant use of *sententiae* and mentions orators who utter everything as if it were a *sententia* (*IO* 8.5.25–34).
[71] Laplace (1988), 433.

he had failed', or as Clitophon narrates with characteristic bathos 'because he was exhausted' (ἢ τυχών, ἢ μὴ τυχών, ἢ καμών, 6.18.6). Leucippe seizes the opportunity to rebuke him soundly for acting like his slave, not an *eugenes*, and to state clearly that he will not make headway with her 'unless you become Clitophon'. This prompts an emotional reaction from Thersander:

Ταῦτα ἀκούσας ὁ Θέρσανδρος οὐκ εἶχεν ὅστις γένηται· καὶ γὰρ ἤρα καὶ ὠργίζετο.

When Thersander heard this, he did not know which way to turn, consumed as he was with desire and anger. (6.19.1)

A long pronouncement follows, an exhaustive (and exhausting) exegesis on *thumos* and *eros* (6.19.1–5).

It begins with a metaphor; *thumos* and *eros* are given physical form as fires. Note the precision of the terms of comparison of the two fires; rage has 'a fundamentally opposed nature (although it has a similar force)', τὴν μὲν φύσιν ἐναντιωτάτην, τὴν δὲ βίαν ὁμοίαν. There follows a neat antithesis: 'for the one provokes hatred, the other love', Ὁ μὲν γὰρ παροξύνει μισεῖν, ὁ δὲ ἀναγκάζει φιλεῖν. The register then shifts to physiology and we are informed about the physical locations of the emotions. We are treated to another metaphor – the soul is envisioned as a pair of scales (τρυτάνη) which, impractically, weighs the fires. Mixed metaphors pile up and complicate the scene as *thumos* and *eros* fight (μάχονται) to tip the scales. The now personified emotions befriend one another (anger rallies to *eros*'s support 'like a neighbour') and fight each other (anger enslaves love, ὡς δοῦλον). Like a human being, anger falls asleep and wakes up again. Another change of metaphor sees *eros* 'swamped by' anger (βεβαπτισμένος) and it sinks down into it (καταδύεται). It is compelled to hate the beloved (ἀλλὰ μισεῖν ἀναγκάζεται τὸ φιλούμενον). *Eros*, itself an emotion or drive, is not only endowed with the ability to feel emotion, but also – a nice oxymoronic touch, this – feels hate. Anger bubbles up; another metaphor, with the onomatopoeic καχλάζων, then tires and subsides. *Eros* takes up arms (ὁπλίζει), feels remorse and tries to patch things up with the beloved. If it fails, then the chain of events begins anew. Then we switch back once again to Thersander and are told of the outcome of these emotions: 'when he failed to get what he had hoped for, he abandoned the reins of his soul to anger'. He then beat Leucippe around the side of her head while shouting abuse and threats at her (6.20.1–2).

There are three immediate points to make. First, the description endows emotions – *thumos* and *eros* – with agency, working, as if independently, inside their host. At one stage, *eros* seems to cut out the middleman and liaises directly with the object of his desire. The person who experiences these emotions – and although the *sententia* generalises, we think of Thersander – is portrayed as incidental to the machinations of his instinctual drives. This renders him passive, invisible, even; cipher for, rather than subject of, his emotions.

Second, as so often happens in the novel, this passage manipulates the categories of the natural and the cultural. *Thumos* is, we are told, 'by nature', φύσει, implacable, yet this implacability is described in overtly cultural and social terms – it 'enslaves' *eros*. The whole account 'lays down the law' for emotions and prescribes social norms for what are considered natural impulses. It is with knowing irony that Achilles expends not inconsiderable time and effort teaching his reader about what happens naturally.

Third, it can hardly escape notice that the description is a remarkable pastiche of erotic *topoi*. *Eros* as a lamp or flame is a common image,[72] as is the slavery of love[73] and *militia amoris*.[74] With baroque excess, *topoi* pile on, one after another, as if the narrator were anxious to include the whole metaphorical range for portraying *eros*. The humour of the exaggeration is underscored by the inversion of a standard trope. Typically, the seat of love was placed in the liver and the seat of anger in the heart.[75] Achilles' physiology inverts the organs – love resides in the heart and anger in the liver – and comically subverts the erotic tradition.

In the description the repeated antitheses (τὴν μὲν φύσιν ... τὴν δὲ βίαν and Ὁ μὲν παροξύνει ... ὁ δὲ ἀναγκάζει (6.19.1–2)) and hypothesising (Ἢν δὲ αὐτὸν ἀτιμάσῃ τὸ ἐρώμενον (6.19.3) ...

---

[72] Usually located in the eyes, which are also commonly compared to lamps, e.g. Heliod. *Aeth.* 3.4. For other references, see the aptly named Ogle (1913), 133–5.
[73] See Létoublon (1993), 70–74 on 'La prison d'amour' in the novel.
[74] On which see e.g. Kennedy (1993), 46–63.
[75] For the former, see Aristaenetus 2.5.3 and for the latter, Homer, *Il.* 9.642, Aesch. *Choeph.* 181.

Τυχὼν μὲν ... ἀτιμούμενος δέ (6.19.7)) are typical of rhetorical exercises of the *progumnasmata*.[76] In addition, there is a similarity between passages like this one in Achilles and rhetorical descriptions of painted and sculpted figures' emotions of the sort found in the *ekphraseis* of Philostratus, Callistratus and Lucian.[77] However, as I stressed earlier, merely acknowledging the debt to rhetorical theorists and a tradition of ekphrastic writing does not help us fully appreciate *how* Achilles has appropriated these genres and the manner in which they operate within their novelistic context.

The sententious description and the framing narrative relate intratextually in a variety of ways. The pronouncement on *thumos* and *eros* not only stands out because of its form, the change from past to present tense and universalising tone, but also because of the change in register, from romantic diegesis to physiological and psychological exegesis. The description is packaged as a scientific discourse and thus gains a specific kind of epistemological status and value. It has the trappings of straightforward, serious teaching. However, there is a tension between the didacticising form of the sententious declaration and the hackneyed lessons which it conveys, the ridiculousness of which is heightened by the sabotage of the erotic tradition upon which the account draws. The sententious lesson's authoritative stance is exposed as a laughable pretension. This is underscored by the juxtaposition of the pseudo-scientific information with events that take place in the narrative. After the statement on *thumos* and *eros*, we see the result of these emotions working in Thersander; he hits Leucippe and shouts at her. There is bathos in the disjunction between the self-authorising, self-important pronouncing of the pseudo-science and the predictable ordinariness of the jealous lover flying into a rage. In this extreme case (not every case is as clear as this), the romantic narrative renders the pseudo-scientific sententiousness absurd and defuses its significance.

The sententious passages also operate as instruments of deferral, postponing the fulfilment of the reader's desires. This is because, during his narration, Clitophon has been seduced into making long pronouncements. He is led astray from the thread of his story. My

---

[76] See Bartsch (1989), 125–6. [77] Ibid., 125.

terminology of desire here is not just contemporary critical idiom. The same metaphor is used by Seneca when he is commenting on some orators' behaviour in one of his *suasoriae*:

> The sweetness of making an epigram (*sententiae dulcendo*) overcame some – they couldn't resist it. The dry (*aridi*) declaimers keep the *colores* they have proposed more faithfully; for nothing disturbs them – no ornament, no epigram. In the same way, women who have ugly faces are more often chaste; it's not the willingness they lack, but a seducer.[78]

In this simile, as confusing as it is sexist, 'the declaimer is in the place of the woman, his personal style is like a woman's beauty, and the seductive *sententia* is like the seducer of the woman, carrying him/her off into narrative'.[79] Sententiousness has seduced Clitophon, and in so doing, teases his audience. The dissertation on *thumos* and *eros* substitutes for what the reader is led to expect, a description of Thersander's emotions. The detailed and measured build-up to the moment (the couple's wrestling) fosters the anticipation of further insight into Thersander's feelings. But instead of elaborating upon Thersander's experience of anger and desire, we are treated to a long *sententia* upon how anger and desire work *in general*. We are given an objective commentary on what typically might be experienced. There is an abrupt transition from the specific (what a particular character is doing) to the universal (how all men desire, how *thumos* typically operates), marked by the change from past to present tense. As Hägg writes, 'the "timeless" pieces of commentary serve as a kind of substitute for the description of the actual process in the individual concerned'.[80] When Leucippe rebuffs Thersander and he becomes enraged, we want to know what that rage is like, how he feels. However, Achilles exploits the reader's emotional engagement with the narrative and denies us further insight into the protagonists' feelings. The digression on *thumos* and *eros* short-circuits the report of Thersander's expressions of desire and supplants them with a commentary on how those emotions operate.

Deferral of desire is the basic resource of the novelistic genre. A scene from *Chaereas and Callirhoe* illustrates the deferral of

---

[78] *Suasoriae* 1.7. [79] Richlin (1996), 25. [80] Hägg (1971), 107.

(a more explicitly sexual) desire. The Persian king is fantasising about gazing upon Callirhoe, with increasingly agitated eroticism:

> He only saw Callirhoe, though she was not there; he heard only her, though she was not speaking. In fact love had accompanied him to the hunt, and being a god who likes to win and seeing that the king was opposing him with well-laid plans, as he thought, Love turned his own strategy against him, and used the very cure to set his heart on fire. Love entered his mind and said, 'How wonderful it would be to see Callirhoe here, with her dress tucked up to her knees and her arms bared, with flushed face and heaving bosom. Truly
>
>> even so roves the archer Artemis over the mountains,
>> along the ridges of Taygetus or Erymanthus,
>> as she delights in the hunt of boar or speedy deer.'
>
> As the king so pictured and imagined her, his passion flared up. (6.4.5).

Eros conjures up for the king Callirhoe as a set of parts, with a mounting lust that ends not in a climactic sexual visualisation, but with a Homeric quotation. *Odyssey* 6.102–4, a simile used to describe the maiden Nausicaa, is quoted, unfairly recalling an episode not without sexual tension, but altogether more chaste. The quotation acts as a veil to the king's mental striptease, exposing but not indulging his voyeuristic longing. Such are the games of *eros*. Unfulfilment and dissatisfaction are inherent in desire.[81] The novelists' games ensure that the reader is kept in a delicious, yet excruciating, state of anticipation, as he or she repeatedly lacks yet desires that which is missing. However, while both novelists tease their readers, Chariton's punchline is mercifully quick, whereas Achilles revels in his joke, prolonging (the *sententia* and) the agony. Perhaps this is why he, above all, has provoked so much resentment from some of his readers.

The discussion so far has argued that *sententiae* in *Leucippe and Clitophon* function to tease and frustrate the reader, keeping him or her in a state of longing and anticipatory desire. I want now to show how the reader's experience parallels that of Clitophon. Throughout his many adventures, despite numerous attempts to fulfil his desires, Clitophon remains insatiate. On the night of Leucippe's arrival, Clitophon retires to bed stimulated by his 'undiluted gazing' (ἀκράτῳ θεάματι) at Leucippe during the

[81] See Tanner (1979), 87; Carson (1986), 10.

evening meal (1.6.1). Theomnestus, a character in Pseudo-Lucian's *Erotes*, relates how frustrating it is not to achieve more than seeing one's beloved:

For it's not enough to look at the loved one (οὐ γὰρ ἀπόχρη τὸ θεωρεῖν ἐρώμενον) or to listen to his voice as he sits facing you, but love has, as it were, made itself a ladder of pleasure (ἡδονῆς κλίμακα) and has for the first step that of sight, so that it may see the beloved, and, once it beholds, it wishes to approach and to touch (πρῶτον ἔχει βαθμὸν ὄψεως, ἵνα ἴδῃ, κἂν θεάσηται, ποθεῖ προσάγων ἐφάψασθαι). (53)

Thus far, Clitophon has not yet climbed further up the ladder of desire than the first rung. However, that night when he is asleep, he fantasises about Leucippe:

πάντα δὲ ἦν μοι Λευκίππη τὰ ἐνύπνια· διελεγόμην αὐτῇ, συνέπαιζον, συνεδείπνουν, ἡπτόμην, πλείονα εἶχον ἀγαθὰ τῆς ἡμέρας· καὶ γὰρ κατεφίλησα, καὶ ἦν τὸ φίλημα ἀληθινόν·

All my dreams were of Leucippe. I was talking with her, frolicking with her, eating with her, touching her, and having more successes than I did by day: for I even kissed her, and this kiss was real. (1.6.5)

Clitophon's fantasies enable him to make headway with Leucippe; he courts her and kisses her, as he will do for real later in the novel. For the dreamer this is no fantasy, but the real thing – his kiss is ἀληθινόν. The breathless asyndeton – συνέπαιζον, συνεδείπνουν, ἡπτόμην – progressing to the kiss, makes it clear that these activities are leading somewhere. However, he has no such luck:

...ὥστ' ἐπειδή με ἤγειρεν ὁ οἰκέτης, ἐλοιδορούμην αὐτῷ τῆς ἀκαιρίας, ἀπολέσας ὄνειρον οὕτω γλυκύν.

so that I set about abusing the slave for his ill-timed attempts to wake me and for having spoiled so sweet a dream. (1.6.5)

His servant's ἀκαιρία results in *somnus interruptus* for Clitophon and no 'true' climax.

Later in the novel Clitophon has indeed spoken, played and eaten with Leucippe and has also touched and kissed her. At 2.8.1 he kisses her, but they are forced to desist by the approach of Leucippe's servant. That evening another opportunity presents itself. Alone – he thinks – with Leucippe and emboldened by wine,

DESCRIPTION, DIGRESSION AND FORM

Clitophon embraces and kisses her. Once again, he tries to go further, but is obstructed:

Ὡς δὲ καὶ ἐπεχείρουν τι προὔργου ποιεῖν, ψόφος τις ἡμῶν κατόπιν γίγνεται· καὶ ταραχθέντες ἀνεπηδήσαμεν. Καὶ ἡ μὲν ἐπέκεινα τρέπεται τὴν ἐπὶ τὸ δωμάτιον αὐτῆς, ἐγὼ δὲ ἐπὶ θάτερα, σφόδρα ἀνιώμενος, ἔργον οὕτω καλὸν ἀπολέσας, καὶ τὸν ψόφον λοιδορῶν. Ἐν τούτῳ δὲ καὶ ὁ Σάτυρος ὑπαντιάζει με φαιδρῷ τῷ προσώπῳ· καθορᾶν γάρ μοι ἐδόκει ὅσα ἐπράττομεν, ὑπό τινι τῶν δένδρων λοχῶν μή τις ἡμῖν ἐπέλθῃ· καὶ αὐτὸς ἦν ὁ ποιήσας τὸν ψόφον, προσιόντα θεασάμενός τινα.

But just as my attempts were beginning to pay off, there was a sudden noise behind us, and we leapt up in a panic. She headed off in one direction towards her room and I in the other, deeply aggrieved at having missed the opportunity for so excellent an achievement, and cursing the noise. Thereupon Satyrus waylaid me, grinning broadly: apparently he had been watching all our actions whilst hiding behind a tree in case anyone should come upon us. It was he who had made the noise, because he had seen someone approaching. (2.10.4–5)

Satyrus' voyeurism parallels but then laughingly interrupts our own. Spying upon the lovers he is our double, our specular reflection. Performing the identical action to Satyrus, we are made aware that our own viewing is intrusive. However, it is Satyrus who thwarts our desire and that of Clitophon. He does so, he says, because he saw someone coming. We are not told who this person was, but Satyrus' grin suggests we do not take this excuse too seriously. Indeed Clitophon himself seems uncertain (μοι ἐδόκει). His pretext for spying upon the lovers seems not only disingenuous, but heavily ironic; he himself is the intrusive presence. Yet it was Satyrus who set up the liaison and taught Clitophon rudimentary seduction skills. He is a teacher, overseeing his student at work. Having primed his pupil to 'become a man', he covertly watches him put the lesson into practice and, as he nears fulfilment, happily sabotages his attempts. He encourages and thwarts desire, leaving his pupil in a state of dissatisfaction, of yearning, of wanting to learn more.

Undeterred, our enthusiastic lover tries again and successfully makes it into Leucippe's bedroom in a state of nervous apprehension: τρέμων τρόμον διπλοῦν, χαρᾶς ἅμα καὶ φόβου, I felt a double tremor, of simultaneous pleasure and fear' (2.23.3).

SENTENTIOUSNESS AND THE ARRESTED EYE

However, just as Clitophon enters Leucippe's room, Pantheia is disturbed by a dream in which Leucippe is attacked by a bandit and sliced from her groin to her stomach with a sword (2.23.4–5). Awakening in fright, she races to her daughter's room and enters, just as Clitophon had lain down (ἄρτι μου κατακλιθέντος, 2.23.5). Foiled once again, Clitophon makes a hasty exit.

When the couple are alone at the beginning of Book 4, Clitophon embraces Leucippe and essays yet another time 'to become a man' or 'to become her husband' – ἀνδρίζεσθαι (4.1.2). Leucippe prevents him – οὐκ ἐπέτρεπε – much to Clitophon's consternation:

"Μέχρι πότε," εἶπον, "χηρεύομεν τῶν τῆς Ἀφροδίτης ὀργίων; Οὐχ ὁρᾷς οἷα ἐκ παραλόγου γίνεται, ναυάγια καὶ λῃσταὶ καὶ θυσίαι καὶ σφαγαί; Ἀλλ' ἕως ἐν γαλήνῃ τῆς Τύχης ἐσμέν, ἀποχρησώμεθα τῷ καιρῷ πρὶν ἢ χαλεπώτερον ἡμᾶς ἐπισχεῖν."

'How long will we go without Aphrodite's rites?' I cried. 'Think of all the extraordinary events that have occurred, the shipwreck, bandits, sacrifices, and deaths! Let us take the opportunity while Fortune's seas are calm, before some crueller fate prevents us!' (4.1.2–3)

Clitophon recalls the events that have prevented the couple from having sex and thus presents a summary of the novel so far, highlighting the stunts and special effects and their incredibility (ἐκ παραλόγου). His contemplation, almost an afterthought, that worse things might yet befall them is a generic indicator that worse things most certainly will befall them: an acknowledgement of novelistic conventions. Clitophon articulates his, and our, frustration. However, on this occasion, it is Leucippe who insists on postponing their union. She has had a dream in which the goddess Artemis appeared and demanded that she remain a virgin until she herself gives her away. 'I was certainly irritated by the delay' adds Leucippe, 'but equally titillated by my expectations for the future,' Ἐγὼ δὲ τὴν μὲν ἀναβολὴν ἠχθόμην ταῖς δὲ τοῦ μέλλοντος ἐλπίσιν ἡδόμην (4.1.5). This prompts Clitophon to remember that he too has had a dream, in which he tried to enter a temple of Aphrodite, where he could see a statue of the goddess, but the doors slammed shut, denying him access. A woman who strongly resembled the statue appeared and said:

DESCRIPTION, DIGRESSION AND FORM

Νῦν . . . οὐκ ἔξεστί σοι παρελθεῖν εἴσω τοῦ νεώ· ἢν δὲ ὀλίγον ἀναμείνῃς χρόνον, οὐκ ἀνοίξω σοι μόνον, ἀλλὰ καὶ ἱερέα σε ποιήσω τῆς θεοῦ.

It is not permitted for you to enter the temple for the time being. If you wait a brief period, though, I shall not only open up for you, but even make you a priest of the goddess. (4.1.7).

Clitophon correctly interprets the dream as a message that he is not to have sexual intercourse now (although when he is allowed, it will be worth the wait).[82] He presses Leucippe no further, but is 'more than a little upset' (οὐ μετρίως ἐταραττόμην, 4.1.8).

The thwarting of desire may well be a commonplace of romantic literature, but in Achilles it becomes an architectural principle around which the plot is structured and the reader knowingly manipulated. It is also a recurring theme in the *sententiae* themselves. At 2.36.1, Menelaus expounds upon τὸ κεφάλαιον τῆς ἡδονῆς, 'the crucial point about pleasure':

Ποθεινὸν γὰρ ἀεὶ τὸ ἀκόρεστον. Τὸ μὲν γὰρ εἰς χρῆσιν χρονιώτερον τῷ κόρῳ μαραίνει τὸ τερπνόν· τὸ δὲ ἁρπαζόμενον καινόν ἐστιν ἀεὶ καὶ μᾶλλον ἀνθεῖ· οὐ γὰρ γεγηρακυῖαν ἔχει τὴν ἡδονήν.

That which is unfulfilled always generates longing. The delights of something that is experienced over a period wilt through satiety; whereas something snatched is ever fresh and blooms all the more, since the pleasure it provides is unaged.

This is in response to Clitophon's complaint that a youth's beauty, unlike a woman's, is ephemeral (2.35.4). The debate is reminiscent of Socrates' comments on spiritual and carnal desires in chapter 8 of Xenophon's *Symposium*.[83] In both Xenophon and Achilles the discussions on κόρος ἐρώτων form part of a larger debate about whether boys or women are better objects of love (and most probably both are written with Aristophanes' speech in Plato's *Symposium* in mind).[84] Achilles returns to the theme of satisfaction at 4.8.1–2. The general Charmides has accepted

---

[82] Although he incorrectly interprets to whom the goddess's statue refers. He will have sex not with Leucippe, but Melite.
[83] 8.15–16. Socrates argues that *eros* of the soul is far superior to *eros* of the body, one reason being that it is less easily satisfied.
[84] Menelaus goes on to discuss the two types of beauty, one heavenly, one vulgar, which correspond to the two goddesses who represent them (2.36.2). Socrates refers to the goddesses by name (Aphrodite Ourania and Aphrodite Pandemos) and conjectures that carnal love is the province of the common Aphrodite and spiritual love inspired by her heavenly counterpart (Xen. *Symp.* 8.9–10). Both appear to be written against the famous

126

SENTENTIOUSNESS AND THE ARRESTED EYE

Menelaus' nifty excuse for why Leucippe will not sleep with him (that she has her 'monthly'), but has insisted that she kiss him. Clitophon is appalled at this news, saying he would rather die than see Leucippe kiss another:

Οὗ τί γάρ . . . ἐστὶ γλυκύτερον; Τὸ μὲν γὰρ ἔργον τῆς Ἀφροδίτης καὶ ὅρον ἔχει καὶ κόρον, καὶ οὐδέν ἐστιν, ἐὰν ἐξέλῃς αὐτοῦ τὰ φιλήματα· φίλημα δὲ καὶ ἀόριστόν ἐστι καὶ ἀκόρεστον καὶ καινὸν ἀεί.

What is sweeter than a kiss? With Aphrodite's act comes satiation and culmination – but it is all reduced to nothing if you take away the kisses from it. A kiss, on the other hand, neither satiates nor culminates, but is ever renewed. (4.8.1–2)

Kissing, declares Clitophon, is better than sex itself, because it has no end and thus promises infinite pleasure. The terms used in this *sententia* recall those used in the *sunkrisis*, and the message is the same: to be in a state of yearning is far preferable to reaching a climax. *Sententiae*, with their claim to be universal truths, demand that their message exceed their immediate context. Like other forms of 'digressive' writing such as embedded narratives and *mises en abîme*, *sententiae* promote themselves as models (or anti-models) of the text's own power. There is therefore an invitation to read in the *sententiae* on κόρος ἐρώτων an articulation of the narrative's own dynamics of deferral and desire.

Desire is not only a force that governs the text, it is also itself presented as an object, or, more precisely, a process upon which the novel reflects. Consequently, the novel shows desire from a particular analytical and critical angle. Meta-desirous statements make the reader conscious of his or her participation in the erotic flux of the narrative and thus distance the reader, promoting observation of desire over engagement with desire, reflection over empathy. The novel incorporates its own criticism, thereby functioning as a

---

argument in Plato's *Symposium* (180d–182a) that those who are inspired by the heavenly Aphrodite love boys, while those inspired by the vulgar Aphrodite love men and women indiscriminately. Unlike the Platonic model, Xenophon's is positive about the merits of marriage. Achilles Tatius is less explicit; no-one wins the debate, but the novel overall can be understood as a celebration of marriage and heterosexuality. As Hunter suggests, the debate in Achilles can be read as a 'subversive reversal' of Xenophon's chapter 8; Hunter (1993), 202. Socrates is concerned with evaluating the relative merits of physical and spiritual desire. Clitophon and Menelaus are concerned with whether boys or women are better in bed. Whether or not Plato's *Symposium* was written before Xenophon's is a matter for debate; cf. Dover (1965).

commentary on itself.[85] This erases any clear distinction between a book and its criticism.[86]

Often, the 'sense of detail' is quite remarkably developed. In the *sententia* on *thumos* and *eros*, there is an extravagance of detail that appears contrary to the expected hierarchy of description. Some detail helps construct a realistic story-world, but too much detail has quite a different effect, promoting not realism, but hyperrealism. As we have seen, veiling or withholding something from view is seductive, soliciting the desire to uncover and learn more. Conversely, exposing or exhibiting something in full view is not seductive; it lacks the requisite mystery. Moreover, viewing in close-up and removing the eye's distance from the object viewed actually prevents the viewer from grasping the overall picture. Jean Baudrillard calls this overly close scrutiny the 'voyeurism of exactitude'. He writes: 'by giving you a *little too much* one takes everything'.[87] For example, when a viewer looks so closely at a newspaper image that he or she can see the dots, the image itself is lost. Analogously, when a reader looks too closely at the components of anger and desire, the emotions themselves are lost.

Also important are the details chosen for enlargement. We expect to focus more on significant events, images or emotions and less upon aspects that do not seem to be as major. When these expectations are overturned, the effect for the reader may be one of alienation. This is a common tactic of the *nouveaux romanciers*, as Susan Stewart explains:

> To describe more than is socially adequate or to describe in a way which interrupts the everyday hierarchical organisation of detail is to increase not realism but *the unreal effect of the real*. If such writing as that of the 'nouveau roman' seems inhuman, unmotivated, it is because the surface of detail has been leveled to significance without hierarchy; it does not tell us enough and yet it tells us too much.[88]

In another example, Clitophon has just heard that Melite has had Leucippe killed. Unlike in the description of the first *Scheintod*,

---

[85] On the prominence of incorporation of criticism in the self-conscious novel and film, see Stam (1992), 154–9.
[86] Cf. Stewart's discussion of the narrative technique of the Marquis de Sade, who also incorporates criticism into his narrative: Stewart (1991), 239.
[87] Baudrillard (1990), 31 and 30.   [88] Stewart (1984), 26–7.

the narrator Clitophon tells the reader this time that it was a ruse and Leucippe was not really dead. At the time, however, he did not suspect this and felt grief:

Ὡς δὲ ἤκουσά μου τὸν μῦθον τῶν κακῶν, οὔτε ἀνῴμωξα οὔτε ἔκλαυσα· οὔτε γὰρ φωνὴν εἶχον οὔτε δάκρυα· ἀλλὰ τρόμος μὲν εὐθὺς περιεχύθη μου τῷ σώματι καὶ ἡ καρδία μου ἐλέλυτο, ὀλίγον δέ τί μοι τῆς ψυχῆς ὑπελέλειπτο.

When I heard this fiction, which spelled disaster for me, I neither wailed nor wept: I had neither voice nor tears. A sudden trembling enveloped my body and my heart dissolved; only a tiny fragment of my soul remained intact. (7.4.1)

This is recognisable as an expression of distress and the reader can relate to it and engage with it. A short while later, Clitophon does cry, but as he continues to convey how he felt, in the long description from 7.4.4–5, he does so in overdetailed, hyperrealistic terms, shifting once again from the emotional to the physical and physiological. Characteristically, this passage evinces a proliferation of (mixed) metaphors and slippage from one register to another. A wealth of detail is provided, but the emphasis is not upon the emotion of grief so much as the disparate images that go to make up the depiction of that emotion. The comparison of grief with a bodily wound is detailed and protracted, but so much so that we are prevented from grasping an overall impression of the emotion. The density of detail proclaims the significance of the description, but because the focus is not on what the reader deems most important, it is significance without hierarchy and alienates the reader.

This prompts us to revise our earlier discussion about Achilles' pedagogy. It is not so much that the reader is denied knowledge about emotions and desire, but that we are given too much knowledge or, more precisely, too much of the wrong sort of knowledge. The desire for depth, an insight into the ineffable realm of emotions, is swamped by the superfluity of surface. Furthermore, the changes in intensity of description operate elliptically. In an ellipsis, the part which is most revealed hides that which is not shown but, by implication, it also reveals what there is to be shown, the potential of the hidden part.[89] In such a way the hyperrealistic patches in the narrative not only hide descriptions of emotions and

---

[89] Caws (1989), 48.

desire (how it *felt*) but also make us aware of what they deny us, the depth of description which it would take to reveal what is hidden. This is a perverse practice, parasitic upon the desire of the 'student' for enlightenment that is generated by the narrative. Thus the reader, whilst stimulated into interpretive proactivity, may also feel conned, as if the dupe of a practical joke.

Vision and the eye

It is striking that, with the exception of that told to Clitophon by Clinias, all the *sententiae* concerning vision are spoken by Clitophon in his capacity as narrator. This increases his subjectivity and enhances his panoramic, omniscient persona. Also, unlike some of the generalisations about lovers and lovemaking, those about vision are never told as part of a debate or in a context which would make one question their reliability. Over and above anything else in this novel, what is claimed about vision and the eye is presented as an immutable, natural law. We have already noted the importance of vision in the erotic experience, and the popularity of the trope that love is engendered by the eyes. However, the extent to which vision is privileged in *Leucippe and Clitophon*, making the narrative pervasively and emphatically ocularcentric, is quite remarkable.

On the mechanics of vision

This section will consider two extraordinary descriptions detailing the processes involved in viewing one's beloved. The first comprises part of Clinias' advice to Clitophon. He reminds Clitophon of his good fortune in being able to see Leucippe every day, while some lovers have to be content with snatched glimpses of their beloved. He continues as follows:

Οὐκ οἶδας οἷόν ἐστιν ἐρωμένη βλεπομένη· μείζονα τῶν ἔργων ἔχει τὴν ἡδονήν. Ὀφθαλμοὶ γὰρ ἀλλήλοις ἀντανακλώμενοι ἀπομάττουσιν ὡς ἐν κατόπτρῳ τῶν σωμάτων τὰ εἴδωλα· ἡ δὲ τοῦ κάλλους ἀπορροή, δι' αὐτῶν εἰς τὴν ψυχὴν καταρρέουσα, ἔχει τινὰ μίξιν ἐν ἀποστάσει· καὶ ὀλίγον ἐστὶ τῆς τῶν σωμάτων μίξεως· καινὴ γάρ ἐστι σωμάτων συμπλοκή.

You do not understand the value of the sight of the beloved: it yields more pleasure than the act itself. You see, when two pairs of eyes reflect in each other, they forge images of each other's body, as in a mirror. The effluxion of beauty floods down through the eyes to the soul, and effects a kind of union without contact. It is a bodily union in miniature, a new kind of bodily fusion. (1.9.4–5)[90]

The second is a *sententia* in a similar vein, told by the narrator Clitophon after he has described how Melite gazed at him lustfully:

Ἡ δὲ τῆς θέας ἡδονὴ διὰ τῶν ὀμμάτων εἰσρέουσα τοῖς στέρνοις ἐγκάθηται· ἕλκουσα δὲ τοῦ ἐρωμένου τὸ εἴδωλον ἀεί, ἐναπομάσσεται τῷ τῆς ψυχῆς κατόπτρῳ καὶ ἀναπλάττει τὴν μορφήν· ἡ δὲ τοῦ κάλλους ἀπορροὴ δι' ἀφανῶν ἀκτίνων ἐπὶ τὴν ἐρωτικὴν ἑλκομένη καρδίαν ἐναποσφραγίζει κάτω τὴν σκιάν.

The pleasure of the spectacle floods in through the eyes and settles in the breast, ever drawing with it the image of the beloved. This pleasure is impressed upon the soul's mirror, leaving its form there; then the beauty floods out again, drawn towards the desirous heart by invisible beams, and imprints the shadowy image deep down inside. (5.13.4)

Both of these descriptions are extended explanations of the statement at 1.4.4–5:

κάλλος γὰρ ὀξύτερον τιτρώσκει βέλους καὶ διὰ τῶν ὀφθαλμῶν εἰς τὴν ψυχὴν καταρρεῖ· ὀφθαλμὸς γὰρ ὁδὸς ἐρωτικῷ τραύματι.[91]

Beauty pricks sharper than darts, and floods down through the eyes to the soul: for the eye is the channel of the wounds of desire.

The first description is a stunning synaesthetic account of viewing. Optical processes are endowed with haptic qualities to the extent that gazing upon the beloved can be described as a kind of bodily copulation. Vision is coextensive with the lover's body.[92] There can be few theories that eroticise the gaze to the extent of that proposed by Clinias.[93]

Both *sententiae* aspire to an epistemological status; they are pseudo-scientific. Commentators usually content themselves with

---

[90] Musaeus 92–7 imitates this passage.
[91] *Eros* wounds in Apoll. *Argonautica* 3.280–4. The image of *eros* assaulting or invading the lover through the eyes is also common; cf. Philostratus, *Epistles* 12 on which see Walker (1992), 133.
[92] Eyes are corporealised less dramatically at 7.16.4 when Leucippe and Clitophon embrace each other only with their eyes: ἀλλήλους ἠσπαζόμεθα τοῖς ὄμμασιν.
[93] But see here Goldhill's discussion of the eroticised gaze in Clement and Philo as like, but more extreme than, that in Achilles Tatius: Goldhill (2001b).

cataloguing the use of Plato's *Phaedrus*, for example at 250d: ὄψις γὰρ ἡμῖν ὀξυτάτη τῶν διὰ τοῦ σώματος ἔρχεται αἰσθήσεων. Achilles' phrases ἡ δὲ τοῦ κάλλους ἀπορροή (1.9.5) and διὰ τῶν ὀμμάτων (5.13.4) echo *Phaedrus* 251b: δεξάμενος γὰρ τοῦ κάλλους τὴν ἀπορροὴν διὰ τῶν ὀμμάτων.[94] There is also mention in *Phaedrus* of the eyes acting like mirrors. The lover finds himself in a state of *aporia*, being in love but not knowing what with: 'like a man who has caught an eye-disease (ὀφθαλμίας) from someone he can give no account of it, and is unaware that he is seeing himself in his lover as if in a mirror (ὥσπερ δὲ ἐν κατόπτρῳ, 255d).

However, mention of beauty's effluence (ἀπορροή) is common in discussions of vision, and we should not jump too readily to the conclusion that Plato is the primary source. In fact, the theory of vision proposed in *Phaedrus* is quite different from that outlined in Achilles, despite their common terminology.[95] Plato is concerned with earthly beauty in so far as it reminds the lover of the spiritual beauty that he once encountered in a previous existence. The lover sees his image reflected in the pupils of his beloved's eyes (unlike the mirrors in the passages from Achilles that grasp the image of the beloved, and do not reflect the self). The idea of effluences is also found in *Meno* 76c–d, in a discussion about vision occurring through intramission and extramission (effluences emanating from objects and flowing into the eye through pores) attributed to Empedocles and Gorgias.[96] Plato's own account of vision in the *Timaeus* develops the theory of effluences, but he argues that sight flowing from the eye joins with the colour from the object; again, a very different direction from that taken by Achilles.[97]

Another approach has been to read Achilles' descriptions of sense-perception as indicating a 'specific and pointed allusivity' to Stoicism.[98] Certainly the verb *enapomatto*, 'impress on', is a central term in the Stoic writer Zeno's definition of *phantasia*

---

[94] διὰ τῶν ὀμμάτων is also used at *Phaedrus* 255c.
[95] Morales (1997) and Bychkov (1999).
[96] KRS 309. On Empedocles' theory see Long (1966) and O' Brien (1970). Krier (1990) traces the use of theories of intromission and extramission in later literature.
[97] *Timaeus* 45b, 67c, 156–7. See also *Republic* 507d–e, 508d and *Cratylus* 420a. Plutarch draws on Platonic theories of vision in his *Moralia* 390b, 433d, 436d, 921d–e. On Plato's theories of vision, see Jonas (1954); Havelock (1963); Fox Keller and Grontkowski (1983) and Jay (1993), 26–30.
[98] Goldhill (2001b),177.

kataleptike.⁹⁹ When Achilles' descriptions of vision are discussed side by side with those of other writers of the period who more explicitly draw upon Stoic models, as in Simon Goldhill's comparison of Achilles and Clement, they gain a more Stoic flavour by association. However, it is only by positively stressing *enapomatto* and by playing down other allusions that we can say that he '*quote*[*s*] Zeno the Stoic'.¹⁰⁰ The other terms used by Achilles, such as *apomatto*, 'impress', and *antakluo*, 'reflect', are standard technical terms which typically occur in discussions of materialist optics be they from Platonic, Stoic, or, say, Epicurean perspectives. Indeed, if we look at the theory in play in Achilles' descriptions – that of intromission – as well as at the vocabulary, it most closely resembles that of the atomists.

As mentioned in Chapter 1, the atomists were among the first philosophers to devise a systematic theory of vision.¹⁰¹ Vision occurs when an emanation of corpuscles is emitted in a continuous stream from the object being seen to the eye. This effluence is called an ἀπορροή, the word used at *Leucippe and Clitophon* 1.9.5 and 5.13.4. Ἀπορροή first appears in Empedocles, in his assertion that effluences are given off by everything and are capable of entering the pores of the eye where symmetrical: πάντων εἰσιν ἀπορροαὶ ὅσοι ἐγένοντο (frg. 89). According to Theophrastus, writing on Empedocles, a μίξις (mingling or fusion) results: ὅλως γὰρ ποιεῖ τὴν μίξιν τῇ συμμετρίᾳ τῶν πόρων (*De Sensu* 12).¹⁰² In Clinias' account the very same term is emphasised: ἔχει τινὰ μίξιν ἐν ἀποστάσει καὶ ὀλίγον ἐστὶ τῆς τῶν σωμάτων μίξεως (1.9.5). Another technical term used in both *sententiae* is εἴδωλα, meaning 'images', a word which features strongly in the atomists' theories of sense-perception. Leucippus (like Democritus and Epicurus) proposed that εἴδωλα are given off by objects and affect the eyes:

εἴδωλα τινα ἀπορρέοντα ὁμοιόμορφα τοῖς ἀφ' ὧν ἀπορρεῖ (ταῦτα δέ ἐστι τὰ ὁρατά) ἐμπίπτειν τοῖς τῶν ὁρώντων ὀφθαλμοῖς καὶ οὕτως τὸ ὁρᾶν γίνεσθαι.

---

⁹⁹ See above 93 and Goldhill (2001b), 175.   ¹⁰⁰ Goldhill (2001b), 179 (my emphasis).
¹⁰¹ See Lindberg (1976), 1–3.
¹⁰² Though Long (1966) and O'Brien (1970) both reconstruct Empedocles' theory of vision as being one primarily of intromission, rather than a combination of intromission and extramission.

images flowing from <bodies> and having similar shapes to the <bodies> from which they flow (and these are visibles) fall on the eyes of the people seeing and that seeing comes about in this way.' Alexander, *De Sensu* 24.14 (DK 67A29)[103]

As in the account in Achilles, atomists are interested in mirroring; they discuss mirror reflections that occur κατ' εἰδώλων ἐνστάσεις, which come from us and are 'set' on the mirror's surface in reverse.[104] Συμπλοκή is another technical term used by Clinias that also features in Leucippus and Democritus. Aristotle remarks (critically) that Leucippus and Democritus say that 'generation ... consists entirely in the combination and entanglement of these atoms (τῇ τούτων συμπλοκῇ)' (*De Caelo* 303a6). Furthermore, the extreme synaesthesia of Clinias' description that transforms viewing into a haptic, somatic experience, also has its roots in atomism. Aristotle criticised the atomists precisely for reducing all sensation to touch:

> Democritus and the majority of natural philosophers who discuss perception are guilty of a great absurdity (ἀτοπώτατόν τι) for they represent all perception as being by touch (πάντα γὰρ τὰ αἰσθητὰ ἁπτὰ ποιοῦσιν). (*De Sensu* 4 442a29)[105]

I am by no means suggesting that the *sententiae* on vision in Achilles are *coherent* accounts of atomism, but it does seem clear that they contain numerous allusions to the ideas and terminology of the atomists. If we discern a point of reference here, rather than just eclectic allusion, it is primarily these philosophers whom we are encouraged to remember, rather than Plato. Atomic theory offers accounts of *sumploke* and *mixis* that are entirely physical

---

[103] The translation is that of Towey: A. Towey (2000), *Alexander of Aphrodisias On Aristotle On Sense Perception*, London. See also Alexander, *De Sensu* 56.12, Aetius 4.8.10: 'Leucippus, Democritus and Epicurus say that perception and thought arise when images (εἰδώλων) enter from outside; neither occurs to anybody without an image impinging', and Theophrastus, *De Sensu* 50 (DK 68A 135), who enlarges upon this theory, but only mentions Democritus. *Aisthesis* is said to occur εἰδώλων ἔξωθεν προσιόντων (Aristotle, *De Sensu* 30). For corpuscular effluences flowing off bodies and objects, see Epicurus, 'Letter to Herodotus', in Diogenes Laertius, *Lives of Eminent Philosophers* 10.48–9. On Epicurus and sense-perception, see further Long (1974), 21–9, 52–7; L & S 72–90. Lucretius' theory of *simulacra* or *rerum effigias tenuesque figuras* (4.26ff.) is similar, *De Rerum Natura* 4.54–61. Bychkov draws our attention to the important Epicurean inscription of Diogenes of Oenoanda, quite possibly a contemporary of Achilles (c. 120–200 CE) whose theory of vision is close to that of Epicurus: Bychkov (1999), 342.

[104] For Aristotle's criticisms of the Democritean theory of mirroring, see *De Sensu* 2 438a5–12.

[105] Text and translation in KRS.

and have no sense of emotion. The application of this to a narrative like Achilles' effects a juxtaposition of the sensual (eye contact with a beloved) and the theoretical (the language of the atomists), itself a parodic *mixis*.

Furthermore, this might be a deliberate, if subtle, joke. More often than not, it is Empedocles whom we think of when we think of atomism. More anecdotes about Empedocles survive, giving him a higher profile than others in his field. However, it is Leucippus who is generally considered to have invented atomism.[106] Might it not be Leucippus who has infiltrated *Leucippe*? Not the best joke in the world, but none the less a pun that is quite consistent with Achilles' humour and intertextual play. Moreover, the linguistic abuse that energises the pun highlights the generic abuse of the *sententiae*, which incorporate pseudo-science into a romance story.

Eyeing eyes: a discussion of 6.6.2–3

This discussion will now focus on sententious descriptions of the appearance of the eye and its operations, and how these interact with the characters who view and are viewed. First let me outline the episode. At 6.6.2 Thersander goes to see Leucippe, enflamed by Sosthenes' reports of her beauty. Anticipating his attentions, Leucippe is afraid, and her face, we are told, displays 'grief mixed with fear'. The narrator then glosses this statement with an exegesis on the mind and appearances:

Ὁ γὰρ νοῦς οὔ μοι δοκεῖ λελέχθαι καλῶς ἀόρατος εἶναι τὸ παράπαν· φαίνεται γὰρ ἀκριβῶς ὡς ἐν κατόπτρῳ τῷ προσώπῳ. Ἡσθείς τε γὰρ ἐξέλαμψε τοῖς ὀφθαλμοῖς εἰκόνα χαρᾶς καὶ ἀνιαθεὶς συνέστειλε τὸ πρόσωπον εἰς τὴν ὄψιν τῆς συμφορᾶς.

It is my opinion that the saying that 'the processes of the mind are completely invisible'[107] is not sound: they are visible in the face as if in a mirror. If the mind is pleased, it beams forth the image of joy through the eyes; if it is saddened, it contorts the face into a vision of calamity. (6.6.2)

After this we are returned to the action, where Leucippe, when she heard the doors of the hut opening, 'raised her head for a

---

[106] See KRS 403–4.
[107] A common sentiment: see e.g. Eur. *Hipp.* 925–7; *Medea* 516–19.

moment and then cast her eyes down again'. Then Thersander looks at Leucippe and tries to make eye contact with her. Leucippe attempts to discourage Thersander and averts her eyes, but even so, beauty flashes from them like a lightning bolt:

Ἰδὼν δὲ Θέρσανδρος τὸ κάλλος ἐκ παραδρομῆς ὡς ἁρπαζομένης ἀστραπῆς – μάλιστα γὰρ ἐν τοῖς ὀφθαλμοῖς κάθηται τὸ κάλλος – ἀφῆκε τὴν ψυχὴν ἐπ' αὐτὴν καὶ εἱστήκει τῇ θέᾳ δεδεμένος, ἐπιτηρῶν πότε αὖθις ἀναβλέψει πρὸς αὐτόν. Ὡς δὲ ἔνευσεν εἰς τὴν γῆν, λέγει· "Τί κάτω βλέπεις, γύναι; Τί δέ σου τὸ κάλλος τῶν ὀφθαλμῶν εἰς γῆν καταρρεῖ; Ἐπὶ τοὺς ὀφθαλμοὺς μᾶλλον ῥεέτω τοὺς ἐμούς."

When Thersander caught a glimpse of her beauty (for beauty resides most of all in the eyes), illuminated as if by a sudden flash of lightning, he abandoned his soul to her and stood there, bound by the spectacle, waiting for the time when she would raise her eyes towards him again. But since she hung her head towards the ground, he asked: 'Why so downcast, woman? Why is the beauty of your eyes flowing away onto the ground? Let it flow into my eyes, instead.' (6.6.3-4)

This makes Leucippe cry – Ἡ δὲ ὡς ἤκουσεν, ἐπλήσθη δακρύων – but instead of telling us about how Leucippe felt, Clitophon comments on her appearance or, more precisely, the pleasure afforded him by her appearance: καὶ εἶχεν αὐτῆς ἴδιον κάλλος καὶ τὰ δάκρυα, 'even her tears had their own distinctive beauty' (6.7.1). There then follows a *sententia* on how a tear enhances the eye:

Δάκρυον γὰρ ὀφθαλμὸν ἀνίστησι καὶ ποιεῖ προπετέστερον. Κἂν μὲν ἄμορφος ᾖ καὶ ἄγροικος, προστίθησιν εἰς δυσμορφίαν· ἐὰν δὲ ἡδὺς καὶ τοῦ μέλανος ἔχων τὴν βαφὴν ἡρέμα τῷ λευκῷ στεφανούμενος, ὅταν τοῖς δάκρυσιν ὑγρανθῇ, ἔοικε πηγῆς ἐγκύμονι μαζῷ. Χεομένης δὲ τῆς τῶν δακρύων ἄλμης περὶ τὸν κύκλον, τὸ μὲν πιαίνεται, τὸ δὲ μέλαν πορφύρεται, καὶ ἔστιν ὅμοιον τὸ μὲν ἴῳ, τὸ δὲ ναρκίσσῳ· τὰ δὲ δάκρυα τῶν ὀφθαλμῶν ἔνδον εἰλούμενα γελᾷ.

For a tear swells in the eye and makes it more prominent. If the eye is vulgar and unattractive, it contributes to the ugliness; but if it is sweet, the black dye of the pupil garlanded with white, it resembles a fountain's generous breast whenever moistened by tears. When the salt water of tears floods around the eye, the outer part shines, while the black part turns deep crimson: the latter is like the violet, the former the narcissus. The tears laugh as they spin around the eyes. (6.7.1-2).

We are brought back to the drama with the comment: Τοιαῦτα Λευκίππης ἦν τὰ δάκρυα, τὴν λύπην εἰς κάλλος νενικηκότα, 'Such were Leucippe's tears: they overmastered her grief, and turned it into beauty' (6.7.3) and the wonderful image: εἰ δὲ ἠδύνατο παγῆναι πεσόντα, καινὸν ἂν εἶχεν ἤλεκτρον ἡ γῆ, 'If they could have congealed as they fell, the earth would have had a novel kind of amber.' Thersander, we are told, also begins to cry, struck by Leucippe's beauty and stung by her grief. But, once again, we are denied any elaboration on Thersander's feelings, and are given instead a long *sententia* concerning how tears elicit emotions from those who see them (6.7.4–6) before returning to the story: Τοιοῦτό τι τῷ Θερσάνδρῳ συμβεβήκει, 'Of this sort was Thersander's reaction' (6.7.7). There are three levels of scopic activity at work here. Characters look at each other; the reader (and the reminiscing Clitophon) observes them looking; and, through the *sententiae* proposed by the narrator Clitophon, the reader also scrutinises the site and dynamics of the look, the eye and its workings, viewing, crying and desiring. This episode involves a complex choreography of gazes, the gender dynamics of which will be discussed in more depth in the next chapter.

The description at 6.7.1–3 is an *ekphrasis* of a beautiful eye. The *ekphrasis* generalises but it is preceded by Leucippe crying, and followed by a comparison with Leucippe's tears. In terms of gaze, or narrative eye, we go from specific focus and limited trajectory to panoramic gaze and back again. Once again, appearance ousts emotion when Leucippe's beauty hijacks her grief: Τοιαῦτα Λευκίππης ἦν τὰ δάκρυα, τὴν λύπην εἰς κάλλος νενικηκότα, 'Such were Leucippe's tears: they overmastered her grief and turned it into beauty' (6.7.3). The tears swimming in her eyes are even depicted as laughing (6.7.2). The *ekphrasis* is framed by comments on the attractiveness of tears and their appeal to the onlooker, and these comments are gendered:

Ἔστι μὲν γὰρ φύσει δάκρυον ἐπαγωγότατον ἐλέου τοῖς ὁρῶσι· τὸ δὲ τῶν γυναικῶν μᾶλλον, ὅσῳ θαλερώτερον, τοσούτῳ; καὶ γοητότερον. Ἐὰν δὲ ἡ δακρύουσα ᾖ καὶ καλὴ καὶ ὁ θεατὴς ἐραστής, οὐδ᾽ ὀφθαλμὸς ἀτρεμεῖ, ἀλλὰ τὸ δάκρυον ἐμιμήσατο.

It is a fact of nature that a tear is most likely to attract pity in its beholders. All the more so in a woman's: in that it is more luxuriant, it has more power to bewitch. If the weeper is a woman of beauty and the spectator her lover, then not even the eye is unmoved, but it imitates the tears. (6.7.4)

This statement elucidates what is repeatedly dramatised in this novel: that fear and distress in a woman precipitate desire in a man.

DESCRIPTION, DIGRESSION AND FORM

The terms in which it is described and the form of the *ekphrasis* reinforce this message. The eye welling with tears is compared to a spring (πηγή) bubbling with water. With chromatic vividness, we are told of the colours of the eye (6.7.1–2). The comparisons with the spring and narcissus evoke the description of Clitophon's garden at 1.15.1–8, itself a sexual image.[108] The narcissus is not only one of the flowers growing there, but is also depicted growing in the meadow in the painting of Europa (1.1.3). The garden contains a spring (πηγή) which bubbles up (ἀνέβλυζε) (1.15.1). Fountains are there to be drunk from (as we have already seen in a similar image in Philostratus' Epistle 26, discussed in the introduction). Both similes sexualise the eye and emphasise its desirability and passivity.

The *ekphrasis* of the eye might be seen as a form of *blason*, a poem that praises a particular body part. The *blason* was a poetic form that reached its nadir in sixteenth-century poetry, most notably in the (1543) French collection *Blasons anatomiques du corps féminin*.[109] Like the *blason*, the *ekphrasis* glorifies a body part that is detached from its corporeal context. It thus necessitates a fragmentation of the body, demarcating it into separate parts, which can be inventoried and itemised. This is a mechanism of subjugation, 'the taking control of a woman's body rhetorically through its division into parts'.[110] The body part is further objectified by what Pacteau calls the 'disjunctive moment', its fragmentation into various disparate images and the iconisation of the part which is to be glorified.[111] In Clitophon's description the eye is fragmented first of all because it is decorporealised, and secondly because it is scattered into images of a bubbling spring, violet and narcissus. This poetic practice generates a particularising, objectifying gaze, which metonymises the eye, rather than granting it coherence.

It is this narrowness of focus and selection of particular parts to the detriment of the whole that Seneca finds problematic about *sententiae*. He argues against skimming off nuggets of advice: 'Look into [philosophers'] wisdom as a whole; study it as a whole.

---

[108] On meadows as symbols of virgin bodies, see Littlewood (1977); Bartsch (1989).
[109] On the *blason anatomique*, see Vickers (1986); Parker (1987), 126–54 and Pacteau (1994), 57–72.
[110] Parker (1987), 126.   [111] Pacteau (1994), 56.

They are working out a plan and weaving together, line upon line, a masterpiece, from which nothing can be taken away without injury to the whole' (*Epistles* 33.5). Tellingly, he compares this practice to singling out a particular body part for praise: 'Examine the separate parts [of wisdom] if you like, provided you examine them as parts of the man himself. She is not a beautiful woman whose ankle or arm is praised, but she whose general appearance makes you forget to admire her single attributes' (33.5). This metaphor makes clear the essential similarity of *sententia* and *blason*. In a narrative, *sententiae*, *ekphraseis* and *blasons* all halt the temporal flow, insisting that we pause to inspect what is on display. This arrests the eye, as Pacteau remarks: 'the close poetic scrutiny of the body-part in the anatomical *blason* suggests a gaze which has come to rest – *arrested*, a close-up'.[112] There is an irony in it being the eye that Clitophon chooses for his *blason*. The eye is arrested to scrutinise the eye. The organ that enables a subject to see is transformed into an object that is seen, a picture.

At 6.6.1–3 there is another metavisual *sententia*, which advises that the face, and in particular the eyes, acts as a mirror of the soul and reveals their subject's inner feelings. In effect, we are given a physiognomics lecture, a longer version of which is found in Philostratus:

For in many cases a man's eyes reveal the secrets of his character, and in many cases there is material for forming a judgement, and appraising his value in his eyebrows and his cheeks, for from these features the dispositions of people can be detected by wise and scientific men, as images are seen in a mirror. (*Apoll. Tyan.* 2.30).

Achilles' description conforms to the rules of gesture in oratory laid down by Quintilian:

In the face itself, the most important feature is the eyes. The mind shines through especially in these. Even unmoved they can sparkle with happiness or be clouded over with grief. Nature has given them tears as well, as an indicator of feelings; and these either burst out in grief or flow for joy. And when the eyes do move, they become intent, relaxed, proud, fierce, gentle, or harsh; these qualities should be assumed as the pleading demands. They must never be fixed, popping out, languishing, sleepy, stupefied, lascivious, shifty, swimming, voluptuous, looking

---

[112] Pacteau (1994), 69.

askance, or (if I may say so) sexy, or, finally, asking or promising favours. Of course, no one but a boor or a fool would keep his eyes closed or half closed as he speaks. (*I.O.* 11.3.75–7)

The physiognomical *sententia*, like the other passages of pseudo-science or rhetorical theory, interrupts the scopic communication of the characters. The theory intrudes upon the practice. We firstly observe vision as contingent, dependent upon individual characters and their particular relations in concrete situations, and then we focus on vision as universal, the laws on vision laid down by the sententious descriptions. The process of viewing, which is dramatised in Leucippe's sparring with Thersander, is dismantled and rendered pictorial and static.

Thus the narrative performs a running commentary on itself and its own visual trajectories. The text attempts an 'omnivoyance', a totalised visual consciousness. Self-reflexive texts are always aware of their own ontology, always see themselves seeing, but this text goes a step further and sees itself seeing seeing. This dizzying multiocular construct could be termed baroque. The French philosopher Christine Buci-Glucksmann, rejecting the rigid subject/object dualism of Cartesian Perspectivalism, celebrates a baroque model of vision called 'la folie du voir',[113] which enjoys what we might call polyscopy, 'the dazzling, disorienting, ecstatic surplus of images in baroque visual experience'.[114] For Buci-Glucksmann, 'the baroque self-consciously revels in the contradictions between surface and depth, disparaging as a result any attempt to reduce the multiplicity of visual spaces into any one coherent essence'.[115] In Achilles, the excessive play with the gaze and about the gaze, the change from limited trajectory to panoramic eye, and from density to surface, celebrates this model of vision, the 'folie du voir'.

The eye as icon

The eye is not only iconicised in the *ekphrasis* already discussed, but also appears as a recurring image throughout the narrative.

---

[113] Buci-Glucksmann (1986), discussed in Foster (1988), 16–19.
[114] Foster (1988), 16. [115] Ibid., 17.

VISION AND THE EYE

In Clitophon's garden (1.16.3) a peacock displays its 'theatre of feathers': 'gold grows naturally on its plumes, and a ring of sea blue surrounds the gold in the form of an eye – ἔστιν ὀφθαλμὸς ἐν τῷ πτερῷ'. Legend has it that the eyes on the peacock are those of the herdsman Argos Panoptes, so called because he had eyes all over his body.[116] Hera set him to watch over Io, Zeus's then favourite, but Hermes killed him and Hera plucked out his myriad eyes and placed them on the tail of her bird, the peacock. Such was the persistence of the Argos myth that he became the archetype of the watchful seer. Lucian writes of those readers of history who pay scrupulous attention, hoping to criticise:

Nothing will escape their scrutiny: their eyes are sharper than Argos's and all over their bodies. (*How to Write History* 10)

Laplace, developing a suggestion of Merkelbach, argues that the legend of Io informs all of Leucippe's adventures. Her thesis is that the three episodes of the wakefulness of Conops, the attack of the *boukoloi* and Leucippe's 'madness' are influenced by the events in Aeschylus' *Prometheus Bound*, where the gadfly is identified with Argos' ghost (566–9) as well as Io's dementia. Conops (2.20.1ff.) and the *boukolos* (3.9.2) are incarnations of Argos, 'the herdsman who sees all' (πανόπτην οἰοβουκόλον).[117] She writes that 'Les malheurs de Leucippé sont, comme ceux d'Io, l'histoire des réapparitions successives d'Argos.'[118] This thesis depends on positively stressed intertextuality to the exclusion of the many other invocations and allusions in the narrative. However, it does give us a sense of the mythological viewer Argos who uncannily casts his eyes onto the world of Leucippe and Clitophon through the peacock's feathers.

One of the most intricate and vivid descriptions in *Leucippe and Clitophon* is the *ekphrasis* of Calligone's necklace at 2.11.2ff. This spectacular piece of jewellery seems almost to come to life in its disparate images:

Ἥριζον δὲ πρὸς ἀλλήλους οἱ λίθοι. Ὑάκινθος μὲν ῥόδον ἦν ἐν λίθῳ, ἀμέθυσος δὲ ἐπορφύρετο τοῦ χρυσοῦ πλησίον.

---

[116] See Burkert (1983), ch 2.   [117] Aesch. *Supp.* 304.   [118] Laplace (1983a), 318.

The stones vied with each other: the ruby was a rose in a stone. The amethyst's purple flushed next to the gold. (2.11.2–3)

The *pièce de résistance* is the pendant:

Ἐν μέσῳ δὲ τρεῖς ἦσαν λίθοι, τὴν χροιὰν ἐπάλληλοι· συγκείμενοι δὲ ἦσαν οἱ τρεῖς· μέλαινα μὲν ἡ κρηπὶς τοῦ λίθου, τὸ δὲ μέσον σῶμα λευκὸν τῷ μέλανι συνεφαίνετο, ἑξῆς δὲ τῷ λευκῷ τὸ λοιπὸν ἐπυρρία κορυφούμενον· ὁ λίθος δὲ τῷ χρυσῷ στεφανούμενος ὀφθαλμὸν ἐμιμεῖτο χρυσοῦν.

In the centre were three stones, their colours shading into one another. The three stones had been fused together, so that the base of this single stone was black, the middle part was white but interpenetrating the black, and, next to the white, the remainder of the stone at the peak was a blazing red. Around the stone ran a chaplet of gold, the very image of a golden eye. (2.11.3)

Once again the eye becomes an icon, detached from the body. Once again, it is aestheticised and becomes the focus of visual attention, here crystallised as a gem around Calligone's neck.

Finally, the rose is described as the eye of all flowers. Leucippe plays music on the harp in praise of the rose, and this is part of her eulogy:

Γῆς ἐστι κόσμος, φυτῶν ἀγλάϊσμα, ὀφθαλμὸς ἀνθέων . . .
[The rose is] the embellishment of the earth, the adornment of the plants, the eye of the flowers . . . (2.1.2)

To refer to something as 'the eye of . . .' indicates its superiority and splendour. Pindar writes that the ancestors of Theron of Acragas 'were the eye of Sicily' – Σικελίας τ' ἔσαν ὀφθαλμός.[119] However, in *Leucippe and Clitophon* this traditional metaphor is animated by the relentless eye-intensity of the narrative. This encourages the reader to 'unpick' the metaphor and envisage the image literally; to see the rose *as an eye*.

Eyes in various media float through the pages of Achilles' novel. When a bodily part is decontextualised and appropriated for other uses, it becomes a fetish.[120] This novel repeatedly constructs vision as a fetish. This gives it a surreal quality. One thinks of the eyes painted by Magritte which hang suspended against a backdrop of

---

[119] *Olympian Odes* 2.9–10. Cf. Pindar, *Pyth.* 5.18, Aesch. *Pers.* 168.
[120] Liviabella Furiani (2003) 140–2 lists all references to different parts of the body in *Leucippe and Clitophon*.

sky, or Salvador Dali's *Architecture of the Eyes*, in which rows of eyes stare unblinkingly from the wall into which they are set. The fetishising of the eye is a metavisual ploy that prompts us to be aware of vision and to reconsider its functions. As Caws writes in her discussion of disincarnated eyes in Redon: 'the very separation of the eye from the context of the body makes of it an icon and puts its own relevance into question'.[121] Once again it is vision which comes under scrutiny.

A passage from Quintilian links the two central concerns of this section, *sententiae* and the eye:

> For what is the crime in a good *sententia*? Does it not help one's cause? Does it not affect the judge? . . . Personally, I think these highlights are in a sense the eyes of eloquence. But I do not want there to be eyes all over the body, lest the other organs lose their function. (*IO* 8.5.32, 34).

Many of the *sententiae* in Achilles Tatius concern eyes. In Quintilian's simile, *sententiae* are like eyes. Quintilian's plea is for a text to have proportion. A disproportionate text is like a body with too many eyes. This chapter so far has discussed the many ways in which Achilles' novel is disproportionate. To continue with Quintilian's somatic simile, it has an excess of *lumina . . . velut oculos*. Readers' apprehensions of Achilles' 'digressions' are analogous to Quintilian's fear of the body being crippled.

The ending of the novel

The previous section has shown that the soliciting and thwarting of desire is a recurrent theme in *Leucippe and Clitophon* and that the reader's frustration is reflected in Clitophon's experiences. This leads me to a consideration of what is perhaps the ultimate frustration in this novel: its ending. The novel closes with Clitophon informing us that he and Leucippe sailed to Byzantium, where they celebrated their 'long prayed-for wedding' (πολυεύκτους . . . γάμους, 8.19.2) and then (in the same sentence) that they set off for Tyre. He relates that there they attended the wedding of his sister and Callisthenes and that prayers were said for the good fortune of both marriages. The final sentence speaks of future plans:

[121] Caws (1981), 101.

Καὶ διεγνώκαμεν ἐν τῇ Τύρῳ παραχειμάσαντες ἐπανελθεῖν εἰς τὸ Βυζάντιον.

Then we decided to spend the winter in Tyre before returning to Byzantium. (8.19.3).

The ending is viewed as problematic because it leaves so much unexplained, actively generating questions, rather than tying up loose ends. There appear to be various inconsistencies between the close of the novel and its beginning, prompting a re-evaluation of the introductory scene. At the beginning of the novel, Clitophon is in Sidon, but we are given no indication of why Leucippe is not with him or of how he came to be there and not in Byzantium, where he is heading at the end of the narrative. The novel begins with the word Sidon and ends with the word Byzantium, emphasising the discrepancy and suggesting that it is designedly inconsistent. We do not return to the opening frame and the unnamed narrator, who might be expected to comment on the story and show his appreciation.

There is no evidence that the original ending has been lost in the manuscript tradition, which would be a convenient, if unimaginative, solution to the difficulty. Similarly, there is no textual evidence that the opening of the novel is inauthentic and should be cut, as the later translations and adaptations of Achilles which suppress the opening chapters and begin the novel at the start of Clitophon's narration imply. Nor is attributing the discrepancy to authorial amnesia (the 'very lax forgetfulness of the promises made at the beginning'[122]) or the stupidity of his readership ('it is extremely doubtful that his contemporary readers would have noticed any incongruity'[123]) any answer. Besides betraying a patronising attitude to ancient literature, these are impossible claims to sustain given the intricate cross-referencing and meticulous planning of some aspects of the novel's construction and the demands these make on the reader. As Most observes:

So far from having forgotten towards the end of his romance the limited first-person viewpoint, Achilles Tatius painstakingly, even legalistically, provides narrative justifications for apparent breaches of the perspective from which the story has been told. His scrupulous care in explaining how Cleitophon came by the

---

[122] Boorsch (1967), 85. See also Bowie (1985), 694 and Vilborg (1962), 10.
[123] McDermott (1989), 36, see also Vilborg (1962), 140.

knowledge of what he had reported as many as six books earlier is practically unparalleled in ancient fiction; it testifies to a degree of sophisticated reflection about the exigencies of first-person narrative we are more familiar with from modern novels.[124]

Perhaps we are overestimating the problem. Winkler suggests that Achilles is following the precedent of Plato's *Symposium*, a work which, as has been mentioned previously, he does appropriate extensively.[125] The narrative of the *Symposium* does not return to its opening frame and it is possible that Achilles is deliberately reflecting this structure in his work. This theory encourages us to play down the discrepancies in geographical setting. However, it leaves one major incongruity unexplained. The end of the narration sees Leucippe and Clitophon newly wedded and embarking and setting off to live happily ever after. However, the Clitophon at the beginning of the novel seems far from contented, complaining that 'Eros has dealt me enough blows', τοσαύτας ὕβρεις ἐξ ἔρωτος παθών (1.2.1). Ὕβρις and πάσχω are not always heavily charged words, but they are elsewhere in Achilles.[126] Most argues that 'we would have expected [these words] to be spoken not by a victor who has gained his love, but by a victim who has lost it, not by a happily married husband, but by a man bitter and alone'.[127] This is perhaps an overstatement; Clitophon did indeed suffer many outrages before his marriage, disasters and conflicts that provide much of the enjoyment of his narration, so his prefatory remarks are not untrue, merely selective. However, it is odd that he makes no mention at all of the happy outcome, and this makes Leucippe's unexplained absence appear all the more curious. Nimis writes, 'it is my view that one of the things that makes the ancient novels important is that they are experimental and heuristic: the end is not fully contained in the beginning.'[128] But this is simply not true for Achilles: the final actions of the narrative, chronologically speaking, are Clitophon's encounter with the unnamed narrator to whom he tells his story. Plot-wise, the end *is* fully contained in the beginning. It is hard to believe, given, for example, the care with

---

[124] Most (1989), 116.   [125] Winkler (1989), 284 n. 72.
[126] Ὕβρις refers to chains at 6.5.4, pirates at 6.16.5 and physical violence at 7.14.3, 8.1.4, 8.3.2, and 8.5.5. Cf. Most (1989), 117 n. 16.
[127] Most (1989), 117.   [128] Nimis (1999), 217.

which the author has taken to provide narrative justifications for Clitophon's knowledge of certain events, that not completing the circle of narrative can be put down to improvisation rather than design.[129]

Fusillo agrees that the ending is deliberately 'anticlosural', but sees this as typical of Achilles' general strangeness.[130] Most's discussion of the problem suggests that the answer lies in Achilles' choice of first-person narration, unique among the extant Greek romances. He examines first-person narratives embedded within third-person narratives in the Greek novels[131] and concludes that they are all tales of woe and misfortune, which often reduce their audiences to tears.[132] Significantly, all of these tales are told to strangers. A survey of fictional first-person accounts addressed to strangers in the corpus of Greek literature reveals that they are all tales of hardship and suffering, never of happiness and success.[133] Most attributes this to the Greek ideal of αὐτάρκεια, 'self-sufficiency', which created a 'taboo against excessive self-disclosure'.[134] In other words, it went against the ethos of αὐτάρκεια to give a stranger an account of personal good fortune, and even to portray a fictional character doing this would be to flout convention. According to Most, this convention coerced Achilles Tatius to make Clitophon appear to tell the unnamed narrator, a stranger, a tale of woe, even though this is in conflict with the generic expectation that romance novels have a happy ending:

> These, then, were the constraints within which Achilles Tatius was operating: and we may see one measure of just how strong they were in the fact that, despite his evident originality and sophistication, he was in the end unable to escape them. Speaking before friends and relatives, Cleitophon would likely have praised himself or recounted his good fortune, without doing more than boring or irritating those nearest and dearest to him. But speaking before others, he adopted

---

[129] It is telling that Nimis (1999) does not discuss the ending of Achilles Tatius, or that of Longus, which also seems less experimental and more deliberately plotted.
[130] Fusillo (1997), 220.
[131] E.g. Xen. Eph. 3.3.1–3, Chariton 4.3–5, Achilles Tatius 2.34.1 (Menelaus' narrative).
[132] The tale told in Xenophon of Ephesus (5.1.2–3) is the only one that does not conform to this pattern. It is the exception which proves the rule, being told to an acquaintance and not a stranger.
[133] E.g. in the *Odyssey*, Odysseus tells tales of misfortune only to strangers. Those with happy outcomes are reserved for friends and family.
[134] Most (1989), 131.

the stranger's stratagem: the transformation of a situation of need into a narrative of loss adapted rhetorically to a specific audience and designed to gain power, discursive and/or real, over that audience.[135]

So, are we to imagine a Clitophon who really had a great time and is distorting it in order to conform to the social rules about autobiography, or to assume that Achilles would have portrayed Clitophon in a state of wedded bliss were it not for generic constraints? I think these are highly unlikely for two reasons. First, it is debatable how strong the limitations on autobiographical discourse actually were. As Most himself admits, the Archaic and Classical constraints were 'somewhat less coercive in reality' in the Hellenistic age and under the Empire and so 'this is evidently a generic, and presumably an archaizing, feature of these romances'.[136] Secondly, it is an implausible conjecture that Achilles Tatius would have felt constrained by generic expectations into including in his work jarring inconsistencies that he would otherwise have avoided. Indeed, it is much more characteristic of this author to confound generic expectation and break with tradition. If there were an expectation that autobiographical stories told to strangers must be tales of woe, then it seems quite in character for Achilles to have chosen for his romance the form of first-person narration precisely in order to exploit and parade the dislocations that would ensue.

However, it might be more fruitful to seek illumination of the problem not in external forces, but in the paraded hermeneutic patterns of the narrative itself. This leads me to reconsider a (tentative) suggestion made by Bartsch. She notes that many of the descriptions in *Leucippe and Clitophon* arise smoothly out of the narrative, but end abruptly with no attempt to reintegrate them into the narrative. She considers the ending of the novel in this context:

Perhaps we should consider this [lack of closure] an intentional omission, a hint that we are to view the work itself as we view the (often unintegrated) descriptive passages that it contains . . .[137]

We can take Bartsch's thesis further. The failure at the end of the novel to return to the opening frame not only reflects the disengagement of the descriptive passages, but also conforms to a recurring

---

[135] Ibid., 133.   [136] Ibid., 133, n. 99.   [137] Bartsch (1989), 170.

narrative pattern of lack of closure. In the *sunkrisis* between paederasty and love of women there is no judgement or conclusion. The debate ends with the close of the book, but there are no concluding remarks made and no formal closure. This is in marked contrast to a similar debate in Pseudo-Lucian's *Amores*, where the paederasts are judged the winners and the *synkrisis* is drawn to a close.[138]

Similarly, in the fables told by Satyrus and Conops there is no explicit moral. Conops' tale ends with the gnat terrorising a huge elephant, and we assume that this is a veiled threat by Conops to be aware of his power. Satyrus responds in kind with a story of how the gnat conquers a lion, but gets caught in a spider's web. Ὥρα τοίνυν . . καὶ σὲ τὰς ἀράχνας φοβεῖσθαι, concludes Satyrus with a smile (2.21.7). We are probably meant to infer that Satyrus is the spider and Conops the gnat and that the fable is a warning to Conops that Satyrus is more than a match for him.[139] However, the message is left implicit, with no clear *epimuthion*, in contrast to the majority of the fables of Phaedrus and Babrius. Let us take the example of Phaedrus' wonderful fable of careerist she-goats, *De Capris Barbatis*:

When the she-goats had obtained, by application to Jupiter, the favour of a beard, the male goats were very unhappy about it and began to express their indignation that women had attained a dignity equal to their own. 'Let them,' said Jupiter, 'enjoy their empty glory and usurp your medals of office, so long as they are not your peers in toughness.' (4.17.1–6)

The fable leaves the reader in no doubt as to its moral: 'This example teaches you to endure it with patience when those who are

---

[138] For a useful collection of the texts that debate love of boys and love of women see Cantarella (1992). For analysis of these see Goldhill (1995).
[139] Satyrus is not consequently connected with spiders in any way that might reinforce this reading of the fable. However, at 3.7.5 there is a striking simile involving a spider's web. In the *ekphrasis* of the painting of Andromeda, Andromeda's robe is lavishly described; it is like a bridal gown, reaching the ground, white in colour and delicately woven 'like a spider's web' (ἀραχνίων ἐοικὸς πλοκῇ). As we are primed to be alert and to 'look out for spiders', this connection is puzzling. It is even more so, if we read Andromeda as a cipher for Leucippe (both are bound and await death as propitiatory sacrifices, both are rescued by men with imposing weapons; cf. 174–7). If we map the ostensible logic of the fable onto this association, are we to understand that Leucippe is the spider and a potential danger? Or that Satyrus has her caught in his web? Lack of closure with an overt message leaves the fable open to doubt and reinterpretation.

inferior to you in merit wear the same uniform as yourself' (4.17.7–8).[140] (So much for power-dressing.)

Form is that which mobilises desire, and the *sententiae* function to defer fulfilment of desire. Lack of closure in the *synkrisis* and fable comprises another facet of the narrative's strategies of postponement. Perhaps we should consider the ending of the novel with these strategies in mind. The reader holds certain expectations of the ending of a romance novel. Not only should loose ends be tied up (such as showing how Clitophon gets to Sidon) but we also anticipate some focus upon, maybe even description of, the couple's wedding night. In *Daphnis and Chloe* we are given considerable information about their wedding night, even if it is not sexually very explicit and slides into tantalising euphemism. We are also told that Daphnis and Chloe had children, a boy and a girl, and how they named and reared them. However, this information comes before the account of the wedding night, a rhetorical manoeuvre to ensure that it is the couple's sexual union, whatever and however we imagine that to be, that brings the novel to a close. The *Aethiopika* describes at length the wedding vows and procession of Theagenes and Charicleia and the narrative concludes with our seeing the couple drive off to celebrate their wedding night, before the final sentence, with a decisive authorial signing-off:

So concludes the Aithiopika, the story of Theagenes and Charikleia, the work of a Phoenician from the city of Emesa, one of the clan of Descendants of the Sun, Theodosius' son, Heliodorus. (10.41.4)[141]

The reader of *Leucippe and Clitophon* is encouraged to anticipate an even greater, and more revelatory, finale. The expectation is fostered by the novel's interest in virginity and when is the right time to lose it, by Clitophon's medicinal tryst with Melite and most of all by the extraordinary description of a woman having sex at 2.37.6–10. This forms part of Clitophon's praise of women in the

---

[140] Similarly, Babrius' Fable 116 ends with an explicit directive on how to interpret it: 'So it happened.' And the meaning of the fable (ἔμφασις δὲ τοῦ μύθου): 'it's bad for anyone to let himself be imposed upon, when it lies within his power to avenge himself' (15–16).

[141] In Xenophon of Ephesus, we are not offered a prolonged description of nuptials, but we are told that 'they themselves lived happily ever after; the rest of their life together was one long festival', αὐτοὶ τοῦ λοιποῦ διῆγον ἑορτὴν ἄγοντες τὸν μετ' ἀλλήλων β.ον (5.15.3).

debate with Menelaus. He details why a woman makes a good sexual partner and unsparingly describes her reactions during sex, until she reaches orgasm, τὸ τέρμα ... τῆς Ἀφροδίτης (2.37.9).[142] This description gives us an insight, unparalleled in ancient literature, not only into a woman's pleasure in the sexual act but also into what is normally obscured by euphemism in the closing scenes of novels, when the couple finally make love. This passage is a sneak preview of what we expect Leucippe to experience when she finally gets it together with Clitophon. It is a promise of what is to occur at the end of the novel.[143]

It proves to be an empty promise. The wedding is mentioned in passing, once it has already happened, with a dismissive gloss on events. There is no focus on the emotional or sexual experiences of the couple whatsoever. What happens instead is that our desire to see the scene which is denied us is designated and exposed and the reader feels cheated. We want to know what happened to Leucippe and Clitophon — was kissing more exciting than sex itself? Was the wedding night an anticlimax? Did Leucippe reach τὸ τέρμα ... τῆς Ἀφροδίτης, or was the experience more like being ripped apart with a bandit's knife?

We have seen that want or lack is inherent in *eros* and drives narrative. As Elizabeth Cowie writes of adventure stories: 'The pleasure is in how to bring about the consummation, is in the happening and the continuing to happen; in how it will come about, and *not* in the moment of *having happened*, when it will fall back into loss, the past.'[144] The reader of a good novel does not want it to end, but finds he or she cannot stop reading to prolong the pleasure. However, novels do end and there is a tacit, contractual agreement with the reader that they do so satisfactorily; that they give us the knowledge we long for. Achilles Tatius breaks this agreement *as we know he will do* if we are sensitive to the narrative's hermeneutic code. We have already been let into the secret of 'the height of pleasure', that 'to be unsatisfied is always a desirable state.' Achilles keeps his reader unsatisfied and thus suspended

---

[142] Τέρμα literally means 'end' or 'goal'. It can be used of both sexual desire and narrative closure, having similar semantic range to our word 'climax'.
[143] As Hunter (1993), 202 also observes.
[144] Cowie (1984), 80, quoted in Pacteau (1994), 174–5.

in desire. It is a sting in his swarm of stories, but consistent with the repeated pattern of deferral of desire and the lessons on that strategy broadcast by certain *sententiae*.

The 'want' or 'gap' in narrative and desire is also crucial to teaching. In a brilliant article, Angela Moger explains the interrelation:

> Teaching and telling exist, endure, function, by means of perpetually renewed postponement of fulfillment. . . . Stories work by going through the motions of imparting information which they only promise but never really deliver. A story is a question to be pursued; if there is no enigma, no space to be traversed, there is no story.
>
> Teaching is another such 'optical illusion'; it functions by a similar sleight of hand, the pedagogical stance is a pretext that there is something substantive to be deciphered and appropriated. But wisdom, like love and the story, is not found in nature, it has no empirical status. Like the beloved, or the narrative, it exists only in the eye of the beholder . . . to teach is only to continue to generate the desire for wisdom . . . pedagogy and narrative are subject to the same double bind which immobilizes desire – they must not perform the closure which it is definitionally their function to perform.[145]

Achilles Tatius exposes this double bind. He is a teacher like Satyrus, encouraging but thwarting desire. The lack of effective closure exposes the reader's (possibly) prurient longing to see the lovers' consummation. However, it does more than that: it exposes the inadequacy of teaching and the student's delusion that *eros* could ever be taught rather than experienced.

---

[145] Moger (1982), 135–6.

4

GENDER, GAZE AND SPEECH

This chapter, which aims to examine in more detail how male and female characters in *Leucippe and Clitophon* look and are looked at, takes as its point of departure an episode of teaching, and a particularly inadequate one at that. In the first book, Clitophon, frantic for advice about how to get his girl, turns to his friend Clinias, who delivers an *ars amatoria* which includes the 'common maxims' about *eros* whose form (but not content) was discussed in the previous chapter. Clinias is Clitophon's cousin, a couple of years older than him and 'an initiate in the cult of eros' (ἔρωτι τετελεσμένος, 1.7.1). However, he is also presented as 'a slave to erotic pleasures' (δοῦλος . . ἐρωτικῆς ἡδονῆς, 1.7.2) who curses womankind and is besotted with a young man called Charicles whom he unwittingly kills when the horse he has given the boy as a love gift throws him off and tramples him to death. The tragedy, luridly related, is a cautionary tale against Clinias' way of loving. It is significant in this regard that the other paederastic friend in the novel, Menelaus, who debates with Clitophon whether loving women or loving boys is the superior choice, is also inadvertently responsible for the death of *his* boyfriend. A raving paederastic misogynist whose affair ends in disaster might seem an inadequate tutor for Clitophon, and the fact that his younger self does not realise it (though his older narrator self does not comment on it either) reveals his *naiveté*.

Moreover, it is not entirely clear why Clitophon needs advice. Unlike his counterparts in other Greek novels, he is sexually knowledgeable and experienced before he meets the girl he falls in love with. He plays down his experience, calling himself 'a novice when it comes to women', πρωτόπειρος . . . εἰς γυναῖκας, and insists that his experience is slight: μετρίως ἔχω πείρας (2.37.5–6). However, his account of the excitement involved in having sex with a woman (2.37.6–10), a description unparalleled in ancient writings for its remarkably detailed and candid observations of the woman's pleasure, betrays his knowledge. He not only informs his audience how a woman envelops the man, how she kisses, how her breasts feel, how she becomes frenzied in orgasm and pants afterwards, but even gives them tips on how to increase their pleasure (2.37.8–9). Menelaus is surely right to contradict Clitophon's protestations of ignorance: 'Well, as far as I can tell, you are no inexperienced youngster but an old hand at Aphrodite's game!', Ἀλλὰ σύ μοι δοκεῖς... μὴ πρωτόπειρος ἀλλὰ γέρων εἰς Ἀφροδίτην τυγχάνειν (2.38.1). Indeed, Clitophon states unambiguously that he has consorted with prostitutes: '... extending only to intimacy with those who put Aphrodite up for sale', ὅσον ὁμιλῆσαι ταῖς εἰς Ἀφροδίτην πωλουμέναις (2.37.5). This leaves little doubt that he is sexually experienced, though 'consorting' is not elaborated upon. It would seem that Clitophon is making some kind of distinction between sex and love; a distinction which is easily blurred by the ancient and modern vocabularies of desire.[1] His sexual knowledge is important when it comes to reflecting upon larger issues relating to the novel's constructions of gender and power. Clitophon and Leucippe may exhibit the 'symmetrical *passion* of the primary couple that is the hallmark of the Greek novel'[2] but it is only by suppressing the fact that Clitophon has kept company with prostitutes that one could claim that this amounts to *sexual* symmetry. From the outset of the narrative there is a crucial asymmetry between Clitophon, the sexually experienced man, and Leucippe, the sexually inexperienced *parthenos*. Despite the fact that Clinias has a beloved (for the time being), whereas Clitophon has never had a beloved, it is still a moot point which youth is better qualified to preach about women.

Despite its negative framing, Clinias' tuition in some ways sets an agenda. The reader is invited to read the narrative that follows as a fulfilment of his advice, and waits in anticipation of Clitophon's success or failure. Moreover, although parts of Clinias' advice are contradictory, it is wisdom which, as this chapter will show, is largely borne out by the characters and events which follow. Clinias' teaching comprises the theory of the practice that is yet to come.

---

[1] He is also making a distinction between prostitutes and other women; see below 216.
[2] Konstan (1994) 68 (my emphasis).

The first part of his discourse concerns the role of the gaze in seduction. Clinias stresses Clitophon's advantage in having constant visual access to his girl, unlike less fortunate lovers:

Ἄλλῳ μὲν γὰρ ἐραστῇ καὶ βλέμμα μόνον ἤρκεσε τηρουμένης παρθένου, καὶ μέγιστον τοῦτο ἀγαθὸν νενόμικεν ἐραστής, ἐὰν καὶ μέχρι τῶν ὀμμάτων εὐτυχῇ . . . Οὐκ οἶδας οἷόν ἐστιν ἐρωμένη βλεπομένη· μείζονα τῶν ἔργων ἔχει τὴν ἡδονήν.

After all, for another lover, the mere glimpse of a girl who is kept under surveillance has to suffice, and that lover considers it the greatest boon if he gets lucky even with his eyes . . . You do not understand what it is to have a sweetheart in sight: it gives more pleasure than the act itself. (1.9.3-4)

Clinias expands on this with the sensational description of viewing as a 'new kind of bodily entanglement' which I discussed in the previous chapter, and further insists upon the centrality of the eye in the seduction of one's girl:

Μέγιστον γάρ ἐστιν ἐφόδιον εἰς πειθὼ συνεχὴς πρὸς ἐρωμένην ὁμιλία. Ὀφθαλμὸς γὰρ φιλίας πρόξενος καὶ τὸ σύνηθες τῆς κοινωνίας εἰς χάριν ἀνυσιμώτερον.

Continual association with your beloved is the best starting-point on the road to seduction, for the eye serves as the go-between of amorous feelings, and mutual familiarity is the most effective route to gratification. (1.9.5)

The effectiveness of persistant visual contact is emphasised with a simile which compares a woman's tractability with that of wild animals who are tamed – the imagination of the homosexual misogynist never fails to impress – a comparison and perspective which are discussed in full in a section below.

At this point, after some further musings on how women need to be thought beautiful, Clitophon interjects with protestations that he still does not know how to proceed; he needs to be given clear information. Clinias' response falls into two parts and deserves some attention. In the first, he explains that *eros* is an αὐτοδίδακτος . . . σοφιστής, 'self-taught sophist' (1.10.1), an image which encapsulates Achilles Tatius' highly rhetoricised narrative of desire. His elaboration of this assertion (1.10.1-2) is worth comment. The lover is compared to a new-born baby whom no one teaches (οὐδεὶς διδάσκει) where to suckle. Of its own accord it intuits and knows where to feed (αὐτόματα δὲ ἐκμανθάνει καὶ οἶδεν ἐν τοῖς μαζοῖς οὖσαν αὐτοῖς τὴν τράπεζαν). Thus it is with a young man:

οὕτω καὶ νεανίσκος ἔρωτος πρωτοκύμων οὐ δεῖται διδασκαλίας πρὸς τὸν τοκετόν. Ἐπὰν γὰρ ἡ ὠδὶς παραγένηται καὶ ἐνστῇ τῆς ἀνάγκης ἡ προσθεσμία, μηδὲν πλανηθείς, κἂν πρωτοκύμων ᾖς, εὑρήσεις τεκεῖν, ὑπ' αὐτοῦ μαιωθεὶς τοῦ θεοῦ.

Likewise, a young man who is pregnant with his first desire also needs no instruction to give birth to it. Whensoever the birth-pangs strike, and fate's appointed time arrives, you will unerringly discover a means of parturition, though it be your first pregnancy. The god himself will be your midwife. (1.10.1–2)

The imagery of pregnancy and childbirth is deployed to depict the birth of desire. The metaphor of labour leading to birth effectively conjures the impetus of sexual stimulation and the release of climax. Both have, suggests Clinias, a 'point of no return'. The term πρωτοκύμων, 'swelling for the first time' is a neologism that strikingly evokes the burgeoning physicality associated with both activities. The point of the comparison seems clear. It is to communicate the natural inception of desire; there are few events that are, at least symbolically, more natural than childbirth. However, it is also reminiscent of a passage in another work that draws on the terminology of midwifery, Plato's famous account of spiritual pregnancy in *Theaetetus*. At 149a–151d, Socrates likens his investigative technique to the method of a midwife, delivering wisdom from men's souls. Clinias' account is perversely Platonic; it invokes an important moment of philosophy, and reclaims the imagery from philosophy, only to describe, with a comic juxtaposition of images and registers, erotic ejaculation.

The second part of his statement blithely, and with some contradiction, undermines the suggestion that *eros* is 'self-taught', as Clinias proffers: κοινὰ . . . μὴ τῆς εὐκαίρου τύχης δεόμενα, 'the general rules, which do not depend on lucky breaks' (1.10.2). The main substance of this sermon concerns protocols of speech; when and how the lover should or should not speak, the differing pleasures in speech enjoyed by girls, boys and women, and how maidens react to verbal approaches. This long and detailed exegesis on seduction is unparalleled in other novels. In *Daphnis and Chloe* the advice of the herdsman Philetas (at 2.7.7) and that of the seductress Lykainion (at 3.19) go further than that of Clinias in that they concern sex, but are much less detailed and skip the protocols of courtship, upon which Clinias dwells.[3] Clinias' instruction is a step-by-step guide to persuading the beloved to accede to commit to the deed (κἂν μὲν προσῇ τις συνθήκη τῆς πράξεως...) but fades into abstraction before tackling the physical details of sex itself. He speaks sententiously about the behaviour of men and women, youths and girls, and the *sententiae* prescribe the behaviour of the characters, encouraging us to view them as types, before we have encountered them as individuals. Moreover, Clinias is quite specific about the differences in behaviour to be expected from these groups. His advice 'lays down the law' about gender. During the course of this chapter these laws, and the degree to which the protagonists uphold or break them, will be looked at in some detail. The focus will be on the two major concerns of the seduction manifesto – viewing and speech – and we shall explore how the practice of each of these conforms to the theory.

Looking at Leucippe

Love at first sight

'To discover the body of La Zambinella', writes Barthes of the character in Balzac's novel, 'is to put an end to the infinity of the codes, to find at last the origin (the original) of the copies.'[4] A major motivating force of Achilles' narrative is to discover the body of Leucippe. A compelling image, her body is discovered and uncovered, dissected and inspected with increasing ferocity as the narrative progresses. However, as much as Leucippe's body is displayed, it remains elusive. Clitophon recalls his first sighting of the girl, stressing the impression her appearance made upon him: 'the vision of her face struck my eyes like lightning' (1.4.2–3). Nevertheless, he does not describe her directly, but through simile: 'She looked like a picture I had once seen of Selene on a bull' (1.4.3). Comparison of Leucippe to a figure in a picture is one of several codes through which she is depicted. She is revealed to (and hidden from) us in a series of comparisons, similes and sublimations. As Pacteau

---

[3] *Daphnis and Chloe* 3.19.   [4] Barthes (1974), 115.

writes, 'Behind the woman there is, always, the image to which the question of her beauty must be referred. *As beautiful as* . . .'[5] Leucippe is as beautiful as Selene (. . . as Europa . . .), with cheeks like the scarlet dye with which Lydian women tint ivory and a mouth like a rose in bud (1.4.3–4). Leucippe is assembled through disparate comparisons, with very little direct description. We are told the following:

ὄμμα γοργὸν ἐν ἡδονῇ· κόμη ξανθή, τὸ ξανθὸν οὖλον· ὀφρὺς μέλαινα, τὸ μέλαν ἄκρατον· λευκὴ παρειά, τὸ λευκὸν εἰς μέσον ἐφοινίσσετο καὶ ἐμιμεῖτο πορφύραν οἵαν εἰς τὸν ἐλέφαντα Λυδίη βάπτει γυνή.

her eyes were delightfully animated; her hair was blonde, curling blonde; her brows were black, unadulterated black; her cheeks were white, a white that blushed towards the middle, a blush like the purple pigment used by a Lydian woman to dye ivory. (1.4.3)

A little later we are told that she has stature (τὸ μέγεθος, 1.4.5). This is a typical, formulaic description of a novelistic heroine.

Clitophon goes on to elaborate upon the sensation of having been 'struck by lightning' at the sight of Leucippe. 'As soon as I saw, I was done for', he says and after pausing to gloss this with a sententious comment on beauty and the eye ('beauty pricks sharper than darts, and floods down through the eyes to the soul (for the eye is the channel of the wounds of desire)') he describes the emotional turmoil into which seeing Leucippe has flung him: 'All kinds of reactions possessed me at once: admiration, awe, terror, shame, shamelessness.' 'I admired her stature', he says, 'I was awestruck by her beauty, I was terrified in my heart, I gazed without shame, I felt ashamed at having been captivated so.' Leucippe's beauty is depicted as a powerful force which transfixes Clitophon's eyes against his will:

Τοὺς δὲ ὀφθαλμοὺς ἀφέλκειν μὲν ἀπὸ τῆς κόρης ἐβιαζόμην· οἱ δὲ οὐκ ἤθελον, ἀλλ' ἀνθεῖλκον ἑαυτοὺς ἐκεῖ τῷ τοῦ κάλλους ἑλκόμενοι πείσματι, καὶ τέλος ἐνίκησαν.

I tried to force myself to tug my eyes away from the girl, but they resisted, tugging themselves back there again, as if towed by the lure of beauty, In the end, my eyes won. (1.4.5)

It has a similar effect on the general Charmides, who is 'ensnared' at 4.3.1–2. Thersander, too, experiences being struck by

[5] Pacteau (1994), 31.

Leucippe's beauty 'like a flash of lightning' and is 'spellbound' by the sight.

These scenes where a man views a woman have important elements in common. They employ a vocabulary of violence: striking, ensnaring, destroying. These are traditional metaphors for depicting what happens during the visual encounter, but ones which fashion the viewer as disempowered and the person viewed as wielding awesome and disabling power. The physical mechanics of this phenomenon operate irrespective of gender: the one who views is captured, the one who is viewed captures. When Hippodamia looks at Pelops in Sophocles' (now fragmentary) tragedy *Oenomaus*, Pelops' glance (anticipating that of Leucippe) is like a lightning flash which instils desire in Hippodamia, burning her and even warming him in the process.[6] However, as discussed in Chapter 1, typically in Greek literature the one who views is a man, the one viewed, a girl; so, whereas the physical mechanics of the phenomenon operate irrespective of gender, the cultural practice of it does not. What kind of visual engagement is this? What kind of 'gaze' is depicted in the descriptions of men looking at Leucippe?

Scopic asymmetry is structured into Achilles' narrative in a way in which it is not in the other ancient Greek novels, through the mode of first person narration. As the narrator, Clitophon is the figure through whom all events are focalised, and through whom Leucippe is scrutinised, often with lavish detail. Thus David Konstan entitles his chapter on Achilles Tatius 'The hero as voyeur'. He characterises the scopic regime in *Leucippe and Clitophon* as follows:

In its indulgence of the voyeuristic moment that both binds and differentiates the viewer and the viewed, Achilles Tatius' novel implicitly casts the relationship between Clitopho and Leucippe as asymmetrical or transitive. In making the heroine an object of display, it subordinates her autonomy to that of the hero.[7]

---

[6] Frg. 474 *TGF*. Fire from the eyes: cf. also Aesch frg. 243 *TGF*. Dioscorides (late third century) describes 'eyes that flash under eyebrows, nets and traps of the heart': *Pal. Anth.* 1.157 (*AP* 5.56). The fiery gaze is a *topos* of the Hellenistic epigram: see Rhianus, *AP* 12.93.9–10; Meleager, *AP* 5.96, 12.63, 12.72, 12.101, 12.109, 12.110, 12.113, 12.122, 12.144; Strato, *AP* 12.196. The wound is often described as a sting, as in Longus 1.17: ὥσπερ οὐ φιληθείς ἀλλὰ δηχθείς. See Pearson (1909) on Pindar, *Pyth.* 4.162ff. and related imagery in other works. In *Phaedrus* 254b the face or sight of the beloved flashes: ὄψιν . . . ἀστράπτουσαν.

[7] Konstan (1994), 64.

This is, broadly speaking, true. However, the 'voyeuristic moment' is more complicated than is sometimes acknowledged, and the descriptions of Leucippe incapacitating her voyeurs with a lightning-flash make 'transitive' a questionable characterisation of these visual relationships. Clearly it will not suffice simply to talk in terms of a 'male gaze' which is controlled by a secure viewing subject, and which commodifies the female object in a one-way process. The descriptions of viewing in the novel complicate the unilinear power differential articulated in most modern theories of the gaze, although, as I hope is clear, this does not mean their critical insights are no longer useful to us. Objectification, as has been discussed and to which we will return in the next section, is a process very much in evidence in *Leucippe and Clitophon*. However, in these scenes of gazing at Leucippe the male viewing subjects are far from secure; indeed Leucippe might be thought to gain the advantage in these encounters. Margaret Anne Doody advances a strong version of this interpretation:

The powerful new women of the novels are Medusas in that they are brazen and overt persons who must be witnessed, whether their spectators like it or not. The heroines of the Greek novels may largely be champions of virtue and chastity, *sophrosune*, but they are also reclamations of Medusa, unconquered.[8]

This bold reading has much to recommend it, not least that it is attractive, on a political level, to recoup the ancient novel as a radical genre when it comes to gender; reading and reinscribing ancient sexism can be tiresome. On the textual level, Doody's image of Leucippe as Medusa (though she does not say so) invites us to revisit and reanimate the initial description of Leucippe at 1.4.3 as possessing ὄμμα γοργὸν ἐν ἡδονῇ. Translating this as 'an eye at once piercing and voluptuous' (Gaselee), or 'her eyes were blissfully brilliant' (Whitmarsh) fails to do justice to the potential mythological connotations of the adjective *gorgon*; 'delightfully animated eyes' (Winkler) is more suggestive.[9]

[8] Doody (1996), 66.
[9] Hence my adaptation of Whitmarsh's translation above, 157. In the passage of Aristides Quintilianus' *De Musica* discussed in Chapter 1 (see above 23) the the adjective *gorgon* is used of the female gaze, in contrast with men, whose look is *hugron*, 'languid'. The rhetoric of the passage, which compares these viewers with beardless men and bearded women, makes it clear that *gorgon* used of a woman's gaze can imply a transgressive way of viewing.

There is a fantasy of female empowerment through exhibitionism on offer in *Leucippe and Clitophon*, especially in the scenes where looking at Leucippe causes men, metaphorically at least, to be stricken, slain and stupefied, and at the end of Book 6 where Leucippe baits Thersander and Sosthenes to witness her suffering ('look.. look.. look...', 6.21.1–2). In Achilles Tatius, Leucippe's power is limited to mesmerising individual men who chance to see her. In Chariton, the fantasy extends from the woman having power over individuals to her exerting power over whole cities. Callirhoe's beauty makes satraps faint at the sight of her, attracts whole populations who flock to gaze on her, and induces crowds to prostrate themselves in awe before her.[10] Brigitte Egger writes, 'Her irresistibility amounts to erotic omnipotence' which threatens to challenge male authority.[11] This is a fantasy of *political* empowerment and it is precisely in political terminology that it is couched.[12] We are told: ἐκείνη μόνη τοὺς ἁπάντων ἐδημαγώγησεν ὀφθαλμούς. Literally, this means 'she alone became a demagogue of everyone's eyes', i.e. she held them in her sway (4.1.10); Callirhoe becomes a demagogue, a leader of the people, through display. The Persian women talk about Callirhoe's beauty as if it constitutes a clear and present danger to their national security:

The wives of the foremost Persians went to the king's consort, Statira, and one of them said, 'Madam, a Greek female is waging a campaign (ἐπιστρατεύεται) against our women, whom the world has long admired for their beauty; there is a danger that in our time the renown of Persian women will be ended. Let us consider how we can avoid humiliation by the foreigner.' (5.3.1)

They select the most beautiful Asian ('what Callirhoe was to Ionia, Rhodogune was to Asia', 4.3.4) with the plan that she will welcome Callirhoe and eclipse her beauty. Despite their expectations ('We have won (νενικήκαμεν)! The Persian will destroy (ἀποσβέσει) the foreigner', 5.3.6), Callirhoe is victorious. This beauty competition re-enacts the Persian Wars. It is couched in terms that make it clear that, in this novel, beauty functions not only as an index of personal

---

[10] Mithridates faints (4.1.9), Callirhoe's beauty attracts crowds in Miletus (3.2) and all of Babylon travels to see her (5.5).
[11] Egger (1994), 39 and 40.
[12] This paragraph is indebted to Elsom (1992) and Hunter (1994), 1071–8.

prestige, but also as a metonym for cultural and political identity. 'Once Callirhoe had resolved upon marriage', we are told, 'she considered that her beauty constituted her country and lineage' (καὶ πατρίδα καὶ γένος τὸ κάλλος ἐνόμισεν, 3.2.16). Implicitly, Leucippe's beauty also functions as an index of her social and cultural superiority, but her power has more modest, and not as overtly politicised, repercussions.

The terms of Leucippe's 'empowerment' need closer attention. Doody writes that Leucippe must be witnessed 'whether her spectators like it or not', but it might be added that she must sometimes be witnessed whether *she* likes it or not. In the scene in Book 6, Thersander rushes to the cottage to see Leucippe and finds her lying on the floor. The sequence of events which follow, which involve the direction of visual play between the characters, are relayed with some precision and nuance:

Ὡς οὖν ἤκουσεν ἡ Λευκίππη ἀνοιγομένων τῶν θυρῶν, ἦν δὲ ἔνδον λύχνος, ἀνανεύσασα μικρὸν αὖθις τοὺς ὀφθαλμοὺς κατέβαλεν. Ἰδὼν δὲ ὁ Θέρσανδρος τὸ κάλλος ἐκ παραδρομῆς ὡς ἁρπαζομένης ἀστραπῆς – μάλιστα γὰρ ἐν τοῖς ὀφθαλμοῖς κάθηται τὸ κάλλος – ἀφῆκε τὴν ψυχὴν ἐπ' αὐτὴν καὶ εἱστήκει τῇ θέᾳ δεδεμένος, ἐπιτηρῶν πότε αὖθις ἀναβλέψει πρὸς αὐτόν. Ὡς δὲ ἔνευσεν εἰς τὴν γῆν, λέγει· "Τί κάτω βλέπεις, γύναι; Τί δέ σου τὸ κάλλος τῶν ὀφθαλμῶν εἰς γῆν καταρρεῖ; Ἐπὶ τοὺς ὀφθαλμοὺς μᾶλλον ῥεέτω τοὺς ἐμούς."

Now, when Leucippe heard the door opening, she raised her head a little (there was a lamp in the hut) and then lowered her eyes again. When Thersander caught a glimpse of her eyes (for beauty resides most of all in the eyes), illuminated as if by a sudden flash of lightning, he abandoned his soul to her and stood there, bound by the spectacle, waiting for the time when she would raise her eyes towards him again. But since she hung her head towards the ground, he asked: Why so downcast, woman? 'Why is the beauty of your eyes flowing away onto the ground? Let it flow into my eyes instead.' (6.6.3–4)

The play of power here is complex. Thersander is described as 'bound' (δεδεμένος) by the sight of Leucippe, a word that suggests powerlessness on his part. However, it is a state that he clearly wishes to prolong rather than stop. He *asks* her to look at him; he *wants* her to let her beauty flow into his eyes.

Leucippe is an entirely *unwilling* participant in this encounter. She averts her eyes from Thersander, thus demonstrating proper *aidos. Aidos* is signified by an averted gaze, a protocol which is wickedly parodied in the 'symposium of *aidos*' at 8.4.1–2, where all the diners are so embarrassed by their previous actions that day that none of them will look at anyone else.[13] Leucippe shows a sense of modesty proper for someone of her sex and status, and seeks to avoid eye contact with Thersander. When Thersander asks her to look at him, she bursts into tears, expressing distress. Thersander certainly reads her crying as a sign of her misery: 'You can see how upset she is' (ὁρᾷς γὰρ ὡς ἔχει λύπης, 6.7.8), he says to Sosthenes, and to Leucippe: 'Cheer up! I shall soon cure you of your tears' (θάρρει· ταχὺ γάρ σου ταῦτα τὰ δάκρυα ἰάσομαι, 6.7.9). However, this is not the spin put on her crying by Clitophon as he narrates the events to his unnamed acquaintance, and to the readers of the novel. His response is to read Leucippe's distress as an enhancement of her beauty: 'her tears had their own distinctive beauty' he comments, and continues with an elaborate *ekphrasis* of the weeping eye which has been discussed in the previous chapter. Leucippe's crying is interpreted as a provocation of Thersander, who responds with increased desire for her: 'Such were Leucippe's tears: they overmastered her grief, and turned it into beauty ... Thersander gaped at her beauty, while her grief drove him wild' (6.7.3). Despite her visible signs of distress and, at the end of the book, a very strong statement that she does not want Thersander's attentions, Clitophon portrays Leucippe as complicit in her unhappy situation.

If Leucippe is empowered by her effect on Thersander, it is a strange kind of empowerment. Power is not just the ability to have an effect on someone, it is the capacity to control that ability, to use it if and when a person wants to, and for its effect to be a desired effect. Leucippe is not given this capacity. Nor is Callirhoe. The target for relentless scopophiliac display, Callirhoe also attracts unwelcome male admirers and the threat of rape.[14] She, like Leucippe, is obviously distressed by the effect she has

---

[13] *Aidos* is a concept which is 'closely related to ideas of seeing and visibility, and particularly associated with the eyes': Cairns (1993), 218. The association of *aidos* with the eyes was proverbial, cf. Euripides frg. 457 *TGF*.
[14] 'Shall I violate an unwilling woman?' considers Dionysius at 2.6.3.

on people.[15] There is a marked discrepancy between what Leucippe is presented as *wanting* to do and what she is presented as doing. Leucippe does not *own* her physical abilities; she exercises impact through the gaze *despite herself*, not because of it. This is true of Callirhoe also. The women wear their beauty as if it were a fetish, something extraneous to themselves. Callirhoe laments of her 'treacherous beauty' that it is 'given to me by nature', as if it were a handicap she would gladly be rid of, if only she had the choice. As it is, Callirhoe, named for her beauty – insult to injury – has an effect on people *despite herself*.

If the 'new women of the Greek novels' are 'Medusas', they are not 'reclamations of Medusa, unconquered', in Doody's celebratory reading. Rather, they resemble aspects of Medusa which are less attractive to rehabilitation by New Age optimists. First, as some versions of the myth have it, Medusa's deadly gaze is inflicted upon her as a punishment, rather than a power she wields willingly. She, like Leucippe and Callirhoe, was 'the most dazzling beauty' (*clarissima forma*) and a 'jealous ambition' (*spes invidiosa*) of many noblemen.[16] Her crime was, variously, the hubristic claim that her beauty rivalled a goddess's (Callirhoe's constant fear),[17] or to have had sex with the god Poseidon.[18] In Book 4 of his *Metamorphoses*, Ovid, with breathtaking misogyny, has Medusa raped by Poseidon because of her supreme beauty (*vitiasse* at line 798 strongly implies violation), and then punished for the rape by Athena. Medusa's ability to petrify is a punishment for being beautiful and being raped, not an enviable skill.

Second, it is not at all clear that Medusa's capacity to kill with her eyes is a skill, as such, at all. She was unable to control this capacity; it continued even after her death: the ultimate surrender of agency. Making eye contact with Medusa brings death; the 'power' is an optical effect, independent of any will on her part. A similar dynamic is at work in Leucippe and Callirhoe's 'power' to enthrall men. In the description of Clitophon's first encounter

---

[15] E.g. 2.3.7 and 5.4.3: 'Oh treacherous beauty' (κάλλος ἐπίβουλον).
[16] Ovid, *Met.* 4.794, 795.
[17] Apollodorus (2.4.3) has Medusa angering Athena. Callirhoe is understandably frightened when she is compared to Aphrodite.
[18] Hesiod, *Theog.* 278.

with Leucippe, he recalls that as he saw Leucippe 'she lightning-flashed my eyes with her face' (1.4.2). The subject of the verb (καταστράπτει) is 'the girl', Leucippe. The syntax of the sentence makes her face (τῷ προσώπῳ) the instrument of *her* action. Likewise, Clitophon 'gazes shamelessly' (ἔβλεπον ἀναιδῶς) at her, a phrase in which he is the subject of his action. It is worth looking more closely at how he describes his gazing:

Τοὺς δὲ ὀφθαλμοὺς ἀφέλκειν μὲν ἀπὸ τῆς κόρης ἐβιαζόμην· οἱ δὲ οὐκ ἤθελον, ἀλλ' ἀνθεῖλκον ἑαυτοὺς ἐκεῖ τῷ τοῦ κάλλους ἑλκόμενοι πείσματι, καὶ τέλος ἐνίκησαν.

Try as I would to drag my eyes away from gazing upon her, they would not obey me, but remained fixed upon her by the force of her beauty, and at length they won the day against my will. (1.4.5)

In this extraordinary description, Clitophon's eyes and Leucippe's beauty are afforded agency of their own, independent of, and in Clitophon's case, actively against the will of, their hosts. Clitophon's pseudo-scientific sententious statement, 'beauty pricks sharper than darts, and floods down through the eyes to the soul (for the eye is the channel of the wounds of desire)' (1.4.4), explains the process and also casts beauty, the eye, and love's wound as active agents, though the image of the eye as a 'channel' is a more passive one than that of Clitophon's rebellious organs a few lines later.

When Thersander is spellbound by Leucippe in Book 6, it is due to the most fleeting eye contact between the pair. The narrator takes pains to stress how fleeting this moment was. Leucippe 'raised her head' or 'glanced up a little' (ἀνανεύσασα μικρόν) and Thersander gets a 'cursory glimpse' of her beauty (ἡ παραδρομή literally means 'a running past'), 'like a flash of lightning'. The sentence continues: 'for beauty resides most of all in the eyes. He abandoned his soul to her and stood there, bound by the spectacle, waiting for the time when she would raise her eyes towards him again.' It is not clear whether it is beauty, the subject of the previous phrase, which is the subject of the verb ἀφῆκε or Thersander himself, and the confusion reflects the ambiguity surrounding agency in the visual process. Sometimes the narrative makes the men active subjects in the viewing process, at other times they surrender agency to their eyes and to external forces. Leucippe is denied control over her potent beauty and her powerful eyes, yet is held responsible for their actions.[19]

Of course, there are other occasions in the narrative when Leucippe is presented as wanting to be desired and as actively looking. At the festival of Dionysus, Clitophon and Leucippe drink wine which has the effect of emboldening Clitophon's gaze: Τοῦ δὲ πότου προϊόντος ἤδη καὶ ἀναισχύντως ἐς αὐτὴν ἑώρων, 'As the drinking progressed, I now began to gaze upon Leucippe, shamelessly even' (2.3.3). Leucippe is similarly encouraged: Ἤδη δὲ καὶ αὐτὴ περιεργότερον εἰς ἐμὲ βλέπειν ἐθρασύνετο, 'Now she too plucked up the courage to gaze upon me more attentively' (2.3.3). Clitophon comments that they carried on like that for ten days, 'but we achieved and dared nothing more than visual stimulation', πλέον τῶν ὀμμάτων ἐκερδαίνομεν ἢ ἐτολμῶμεν οὐδέν (2.3.3). This suggests active participation in viewing by Leucippe. This is the only such description and it is, of course, narrated by Clitophon, who appropriates Leucippe's own narrative. It is significant that the scene where Leucippe looks and takes pleasure in being looked at is not given nearly as much space as those in which she is threatened by the gaze. There is no description, as there is in Chariton, Xenophon of Ephesus, and Heliodorus, of the heroine falling in love at first sight in similar fashion to the hero, and there is no physical description of Clitophon. However, the moments where we do see Leucippe looking give us a glimpse of a different narrative that could have been written were the story to have been told as if through her eyes, or with the more objective perspective of a third person narrator. In Clitophon's account, it is not that Leucippe does not look, but that we are not allowed to focus on her looking. The young female protagonist's 'voyeuristic moment' is only hinted at. It is the male gaze, however insecure and however nuanced, which is paramount.

The consumptive gaze

The most recurrent metaphor of the gaze in *Leucippe and Clitophon* is that of eating. In this respect it participates in the Greek literary

---

[19] In *Callirhoe*, more of the responsibility is laid at Aphrodite's door.

tradition of what has been called the 'consumptive gaze'.[20] Clitophon consumes Leucippe with his eyes. He ignores his dinner: ἑῴκειν γὰρ τοῖς ἐν ὀνείροις ἐσθίουσιν, 'I was like someone eating in a dream', and he gazes instead at his sweetheart. The gazing is his sustenance: τοῦτο γάρ μου ἦν τὸ δεῖπνον, 'and that constituted my dinner' (1.5.3). After the meal is over, Clitophon reiterates and reinforces this image:

οἱ μὲν δὴ ἄλλοι τῇ γαστρὶ μετρήσαντες τὴν ἡδονήν, ἐγὼ δὲ τὴν εὐωχίαν ἐν τοῖς ὀφθαλμοῖς φέρων τῶν τε τῆς κόρης προσώπων γεμισθεὶς καὶ ἀκράτῳ θεάματι καὶ μέχρι κόρου προελθὼν ἀπῆλθον μεθύων ἔρωτι.

The others had measured their bliss by their bellies, but I departed savouring the banquet of my eyes, stuffed with the girl's face, and drunken with desire, having sated myself with undiluted gazing. (1.6.1-2)

In this richly synaesthetic description, the language of consumption is deployed to communicate the process of viewing. In pointed contrast to those who have taken pleasure through their stomachs, Clitophon's banquet is served through his eyes; he has his fill of Leucippe's face, drinks in the sight of her and retires for the night intoxicated with desire. An optical orgiast, Clitophon's satiety is in gazing at his girl, a point underlined by the punning play on κόρης . . . κόρου. Furthermore, propriety dictated that normally revellers at symposia practise moderation and avoid excessive indulgence.[21] The phrase μετρήσαντες τὴν ἡδονήν 'measured their bliss' suggests that Clitophon's fellow diners complied with this standard. Clitophon, however, exceeds it, drinking *undiluted* vision (ἀκράτῳ θεάματι). He drinks his fill of it and so gets drunk. The phrase μεθύων ἔρωτι is an example of characteristic Clitophontic self-consciousness. It appears to be borrowed from a poem of Anacreon, and may have become a cliché, as it is also quoted in one of Philostratus' *Imagines*.[22] In his narration of his desire, Clitophon remains an aesthete.

In this scene Clitophon's consumptive gaze serves up Leucippe as food metaphorically, but in what is the most striking and violent

---

[20] See above 32-4.
[21] It is a common *topos* of sympotic poetry to warn against excess and praise temperance. See e.g. Eubulus frg. 94 and Hunter (1983), 185-9; Bielohlawek (1940).
[22] Anacreon frg. 31, *PMG* 190; Philostratus, *Imagines* 1.15.

display in the novel – that of the *Scheintod* (or 'false death') at 3.15–22 – she is eaten as food quite literally. The episode is a spectacular set-piece, a spot-lit extravaganza. Leucippe is captured by bandits and is doomed to be a propitiatory virgin sacrifice.[23] The episode is relayed through a restricted narrative perspective and we see events unfold as Clitophon does. There are hymns and libations and Leucippe is strapped to the altar, 'just as the artists represent Marsyas tied to a tree'. She is then sacrificed:

Εἶτα λαβὼν ξίφος βάπτει κατὰ τῆς καρδίας καὶ διελκύσας τὸ ξίφος εἰς τὴν κάτω γαστέρα ῥήγνυσι· τὰ σπλάγχνα δὲ εὐθὺς ἐξεπήδησεν, ἃ ταῖς χερσὶν ἐξελκύσαντες ἐπιτιθέασι τῷ βωμῷ, καὶ ἐπεὶ ὠπτήθη, κατατεμόντες ἅπαντες εἰς μοίρας ἔφαγον.

Then he took his sword and plunged it in below her heart; twisting it downwards, he ruptured her belly. Her innards leaped out at once. Tearing them out with his hands he placed them upon the altar. When they were roasted, each man cut off a portion and ate it. (3.15.4–5)

Clitophon, the general and his men are watching all this from the other side of a deep trench and he reports their reactions to the spectacle:

Ταῦτα δὲ ὁρῶντες οἱ στρατιῶται καὶ ὁ στρατηγὸς καθ' ἓν τῶν πραττομένων· ἀνεβόων καὶ τὰς ὄψεις ἀπέστρεφον τῆς θέας, ἐγὼ δὲ ἐκ παραλόγου καθήμενος ἐθεώμην. Τὸ δὲ ἦν ἔκπληξις· μέτρον γὰρ οὐκ ἔχον τὸ κακὸν ἐνεβρόντησέ με. Καὶ τάχα ὁ τῆς Νιόβης μῦθος οὐκ ἦν ψευδής, ἀλλὰ κἀκείνη τοιοῦτόν τι παθοῦσα ἐπὶ τῇ τῶν παίδων ἀπωλείᾳ δόξαν παρέσχεν ἐκ τῆς ἀκινησίας ὡσεὶ λίθος γενομένη.

The general and his army were watching and cried out at each one of these rites, averting their eyes from the spectacle. I, on the other hand, beyond all expectation, simply sat there as a spectator. My reaction was one of pure shock: this unbounded calamity had thunderstruck me. Perhaps the myth of Niobe is no lie: she too may have experienced something like this when she lost her children, and given the impression through her immobility of having turned into stone. (3.15.5)

This scene is catoptric; we watch those watching and mirror their activity. However, of the two ways of seeing which are staged, the reader is compelled to follow only one. We do not have the option to avert our eyes as the soldiers chose to, but instead watch the scene focalised through Clitophon. His transfixedness, his attempts to interpret what is happening by deciphering the Egyptian priest's

---

[23] On the oracle that demands the sacrifice, see Laplace (1988b).

movements and gestures (using language which can have theatrical connotations: τὸ .. σχῆμα τοῦ στόματος, 3.15.3), and the emphasis on viewers' reactions to the scene, all serve to heighten the pantomimic atmosphere of the episode.[24]

The theatricality, and ostentatious grotesquerie, of the episode protect the reader from reacting with the sort of horror that a realistic 'snuff' drama is likely to provoke.[25] Even the first-time reader, in all probability, will realise that the hyperbole, and the unlikelihood of the heroine being killed in the third book, suggests a narrative contrivance. A reader with any knowledge of the other novels, in which coming back to life is a trope,[26] or of the histrionics of Roman rhetorical exercises – 'pirates standing on the beach, dangling manacles, tyrants writing orders for sons to cut off their fathers' heads, oracles advising the sacrifice of three or more virgins during a plague – a mass of cloying verbiage: every word, every move just so much poppycock', complains Encolpius in Petronius' *Satyrica* – will be attuned to the tricks of the melodramatic trade. But it is worth remembering that the frisson of the description of Leucippe's 'death' trades on violent deaths that actually took place,[27] and those which were confabulated as part of a discourse of ethnocentrism. It evokes two practices, for which the Phoenicians, rather than Egyptians, were renowned: the ritual defloration of virgins and human (usually child)

---

[24] See further Mignogna (1997), who argues that the structure of the episode is based on Euripides' *Iphigenia in Tauris*, with Menelaus and Satyrus playing pantomimic versions of Orestes and Pylades. On the theatricality of the scene, see Liviabella Furiani (1985b).

[25] Elsom (1992) likens the episode to a 'snuff movie'. See also Hall (1995), 57 on 'ancient snuff theatre' in the Pseudo-Lucianic *Ass*.

[26] False deaths: Chariton 1.4.12; Xen. of Eph. 3.5.11; 3.7; Iambl. 3–4; 7; 18; Heliod. 2.3.5; 8.7.7. See Létoublon (1993), 74–80. With the theme of death at sea resulting in only partial recovery of the corpse on land, McGill (2000) suggests that Achilles is adapting an epigrammatic motif found in several sepulchral poems in the *Palatine Anthology*.

[27] There has been considerable debate on the relationship of the *Scheintod* to actual religious rites. See Henrichs (1972) for the argument that *Scheintode* in Achilles Tatius and Lollianus represent religious rites, probably those practised by the Egyptian *boukoloi*. Winkler counters that their design is 'fundamentally aesthetic rather than religious': Winkler (1980), 155. Hopwood concurs: 'This act is a bestial parody of an everyday religious act, made more frightening by its generalised similarity to any ritual', and makes some telling parallels between the *Scheintod* and the oath taken by the Catilinarian conspirators: Hopwood (1998), 201. Resurrection after death is 'one of the most conspicuous features of the fiction of the Roman empire': Bowersock (1994), 99. He posits religious, or quasi-religious, reasons for this.

sacrifice.²⁸ 'Enjoying the kitsch'²⁹ should not lead us to downplay the nastiness of cartoon cruelty, nor the gender ideology at work here. Cultures where violence against women is an amusement – in the arena, in mime, and in the novel – are cultures which foster violence against women.

Moreover, the *Scheintod* takes the consumptive gaze to a literal and grotesque extreme. Even though it is not Clitophon who eats Leucippe, he looks on her as she becomes food. Leucippe is seen being butchered and eaten. As he views it, the female body is not merely imagined as food, it *is* food. Metaphor becomes reality. Voyeurism is taken to new depths. Not content with looking *at* the woman, the male gaze now penetrates *into* the woman.

Mutilation as sexual violation is the subject of Leucippe's mother's dream, earlier in the novel at 2.23.4–5:

ἔτυχε γὰρ ὄνειρος αὐτὴν ταράξας. Ἐδόκει τινὰ λῃστὴν μάχαιραν ἔχοντα γυμνὴν ἄγειν ἁρπασάμενον αὐτῆς τὴν θυγατέρα καὶ καταθέμενον ὑπτίαν, μέσην ἀνατεμεῖν τῇ μαχαίρᾳ τὴν γαστέρα, κάτωθεν ἀρξάμενον ἀπὸ τῆς αἰδοῦς.

She was disturbed by a dream, in which a brigand carrying a naked blade kidnapped her daughter and carried her off; then he laid her down on her back and cut open the middle of her belly with the knife, starting down below at her most intimate parts.

The all-seeing Panthe(i)a even sees in her sleep, in so far as dreaming is metaphorical seeing. She rushes to her daughter's room, where she discovers Leucippe and Clitophon about to have sex. She and the reader interpret the dream as proleptic of Leucippe's initiation, but we are now compelled to re-evaluate this interpretation and to understand that the dream also predicts the *Scheintod*. The sequence of connections between episodes, which Achilles' games of prolepsis and hindsight encourage the reader to attempt, forges a fundamental link between sexual intercourse and bloody assault, sacrifice and death. This association colours how we view

---

[28] On the ritual defloration of virgins, usually by a stranger or strangers, see Socrates, *Eccl. Hist.* 18; Augustine, *City of God* 4.10: 'To her [Venus] also the Phoenicians offered a gift by prostituting their daughters before they united them to husbands.' See further Henriques (1962), 21–7 with the caveats of Beard and Henderson (1998). Archaeological evidence, particularly from the Tophet region in Carthage, suggests that Phoenicians sacrificed children from the seventh to as late as the second centuries BCE. See Brown (1991); Briquel-Chatonnet (1992), 192–3 and more generally Hughes (1991).

[29] Reardon (1997), 83: the author is 'expecting his audience to enjoy the kitsch'.

sex in the novel and fashions Clitophon, and all lovers, as violent aggressors, a point to which I shall return later.

In the description of her 'murder', Leucippe and Clitophon are both compared to mythical figures: Leucippe to Marsyas and Clitophon to Niobe. Leucippe is likened to Marsyas presumably to stress her powerlessness and the bloodiness of the assault to follow. More specifically, she is not compared to Marysas, but to the image of Marsyas as represented by statue makers, a simile that creates a static image and further objectifies her. The comparison between Clitophon and Niobe emphasises his paralysis at the sight of the murder and his grief on losing a loved one. However, it is notable that these comparisons reverse the genders of the characters. Elsom suggests that a Freudian reading of the episode might explain this reversal. She argues that Clitophon exhibits castration anxiety, which is enacted symbolically as Leucippe becomes the phallus, hence the comparison between her and a male figure: 'the murder of Leucippe displaces the threat of loss from the male viewer to the female victim'.[30] However, one can put a different slant on the Freudian analysis of petrification, as Brooks explains: 'whereas turning to stone, like the decapitation of Medusa's head, evokes terror of castration, becoming stiff with terror also means "an erection", offering the observer the consolation that "he is still in possession of a penis"'.[31] Petrification denotes both castration and sexual desire, loss and potency.

This certainly seems to be the case in the opening section of Lucian's *Essays in Portraiture*, in which the character Lycinus is effusing to his friend Polystratus about the beauty of a woman he has just seen. Their first exchange is worth quoting at some length:

Ἀλλ' ἦ τοιοῦτόν τι ἔπασχον οἱ τὴν Γοργὼ ἰδόντες οἷον ἐγὼ ἔναγχος ἔπαθον, ὦ Πολύστρατε, παγκάλην τινὰ γυναῖκα ἰδών· αὐτὸ γὰρ τὸ τοῦ μύθου ἐκεῖνο, μικροῦ δέω λίθος ἐξ ἀνθρώπου σοι γεγονέναι πεπηγὼς ὑπὸ τοῦ θαύματος.

---

[30] Elsom (1992), 216. See also Barton (1993), 96: 'The source of identification of the eye with the genitals (especially the phallus) was that the genitals shared with the eyes the excruciating paradox of exceptional vulnerability and power. Fascination, therefore, is associated with immoderate rigidity and flaccidity, with sexual potency both fantastically augmented and (thus) utterly destroyed. As Fenichel observed, 'To be turned into rigid stone symbolizes not only erection but also castration.'

[31] Brooks (1993), 12.

Upon my word, Polystratus, those who saw the Gorgon must have been affected by it very much as I was recently when I saw a perfectly beautiful woman: I was struck stiff with amazement and came within an ace of being turned into stone, my friend, just as it is in the fable!

Polystratus professes astonishment that Lycinus should react like this over a *woman*, when it is usually boys who affect him:

ὥστε θᾶττον ἄν τις ὅλον τὸν Σίπυλον μετακινήσειεν ἢ σὲ τῶν καλῶν ἀπάγοι μὴ οὐχὶ παρεστάναι αὐτοῖς κεχηνότα καὶ ἐπιδακρύοντά γε πολλάκις ὥσπερ ἐκείνην αὐτὴν τὴν τοῦ Ταντάλου.

so that it would be a simpler matter to move all Sipylus [where Niobe was turned to stone] from its base than to drag you away from your pretties and keep you from standing beside them with parted lips, yes, and not infrequently with tears in your eyes, the very image of the daughter of Tantalus [i.e. Niobe].

It is interesting that this discussion of viewing makes an association between Niobe and Medusa; Medusa as a petrifying figure; Niobe as petrified. However, this Medusa is not Doody's 'brazen and overt person[s] who must be witnessed . . . Medusa unconquered', rather, a new object of desire. Much of the humour comes from the disjunction between the elevated mythological exempla and the laddish lusting which they are used to articulate. Medusa and Niobe afford the opportunity for *double entendres* about 'getting hard', innuendo which continues when Polystratus urges Lycinus for more information, so that he can scope this Medusa out:

But tell me about this petrifying Medusa, who she is and where she comes from, so that we, too, may have a look at her. You surely will not begrudge us the sight or be jealous, if we ourselves are going to be struck stiff at your elbow on seeing her!

The image of petrification is an ambiguous one, used both to signify terror and to indicate sexual arousal. In the comparison with Niobe, the same image is used by Polystratus to express what it feels like to view a beautiful body, as is used by Clitophon for what it feels like to view an eviscerated body. The dual possibilities implied by petrification complicate a straightforward reading of Clitophon's reaction and create an undercurrent of eroticism in the audience's reception of the *Scheintod*. We might also detect an erotic frisson in the similarities between the description of how Clitophon reacts when viewing Leucippe's 'murder' and the earlier description of how he reacts when seeing Leucippe for the very first time. In both scenes he is 'astounded': ἔκπληξις (1.4.5); ἔκπληξις (3.15.6); and in both he is striken as if by an external force of weather: ἐνεβρόντησέ με, 'I was thunderstruck', at 3.15.6 recalls καταστράπτει μου τοὺς ὀφθαλμούς, 'struck my eyes like lightning', at 1.4.2. Metaphor relates the experiences of gazing with desire and gazing with horror.

It is an integral part of Leucippe's torture and humiliation, as Clitophon later reconstructs it, that she is cut up while still alive and 'watching the whole carving process', βλέπουσαν ὅλην τὴν ἀνατομήν (3.16.3). Now, Leucippe is, of course, in on the plot, but at no stage in the episode is she given space to describe her feelings or to relate the events from her perspective. Even when she 'comes back to life' the only speech of hers which is reported is when she interjects briefly to urge Menelaus to tell the tale (3.18.5). Clitophon, Menelaus and Satyrus do the narration; Leucippe is the silent star of the show. 'The gendered focalisation of the episode implies that "inside" Leucippe is blood and guts; "inside" Clitophon is a subjective self.'[32] It is Clitophon who speaks and feels. The emphasis is on *his* feelings, not those of Leucippe, and his incongruous musings on the veracity of the Niobe myth further efface her suffering (as it seems then). Once again, the narrative transition from the specific to the general is designed to distance the viewer and dissipates any emotional or empathetic response to the scene.

The display of weapons

We are kept in suspense for three chapters, but later learn that Leucippe's death was a hoax. Menelaus and Satyrus obtained a trick knife belonging to an actor who recites Homer in the theatre (3.20.5). The weapon and its retractable blade are described as follows:

τὴν μὲν κώπην ἔχον παλαιστῶν τεσσάρων, τὸν δὲ σίδηρον ἐπὶ τῇ κώπῃ βραχύτατον, δακτύλων ὅσον οὐ πλείω τριῶν. Ὡς δὲ ἀνελόμενος τὸ ξίφος ὁ Μενέλαος ἔλαθε μεταστρέψας κάτω τὸ τοῦ σιδήρου μέρος, τὸ μικρὸν ἐκεῖνο ξίφος ὥσπερ

---
[32] Elsom (1992), 214.

ἀπὸ χηραμοῦ τῆς κώπης κατατρέχει τοσοῦτον, ὅσον εἶχεν ἡ κώπη τὸ μέγεθος· ὡς δὲ ἀνέστρεψεν εἰς τοὔμπαλιν, αὖθις ὁ σίδηρος εἴσω κατεδύετο.

Its hilt was the length of four palms but the blade attached to the hilt was tiny, no longer than three fingers' length. Menelaus picked up the sword, and when he inattentively lowered the blade-segment, that paltry sword shot out to the same length as the hilt, as if from a compartment in the hilt! When he lifted it up again, the blade once again retracted inside. (3.20.6–7)

Considerable emphasis is placed on the knife; it is described extensively and with precision. Satyrus returns to the knife in his explanation of how the *Scheintod* was staged:

Ὁρᾷς δὲ τουτὶ τὸ ξίφος ὡς ἔχει μηχανῆς. Ἂν γὰρ ἐρείσῃ τις ἐπί τινος σώματος, φεύγει πρὸς τὴν κώπην ὥσπερ εἰς κολεόν· καὶ οἱ μὲν ὁρῶντες δοκοῦσι βαπτίζεσθαι τὸν σίδηρον κατὰ τοῦ σώματος, ὁ δὲ εἰς τὸν χηραμὸν τῆς κώπης ἀνέθορεν, μόνην δὲ καταλείπει τὴν αἰχμήν, ὅσον τὴν πλαστὴν γαστέρα τεμεῖν καὶ τὴν κώπην ἐν χρῷ τοῦ σφαζομένου τυχεῖν· κἂν ἀποσπάσῃ τις τὸν σίδηρον ἐκ τοῦ τραύματος, καταρρεῖ πάλιν ἐκ τοῦ χηραμοῦ τὸ ξίφος ὅσον τῆς κώπης ἀνακουφίζεται τὸ μετέωρον καὶ τὸν αὐτὸν τρόπον τοὺς ὁρῶντας ἀπατᾷ.

You can see how the mechanism in the sword works: if you press it against someone's body, it retreats into the hilt as though it were being sheathed. The audience thinks that the blade is being plunged into the body, but in fact is has shot up into the compartment in the hilt, leaving only the tip; enough to slice through the bastard belly as the hilt reaches the skin of the victim. If you withdraw the blade from the wound, the sword gradually slips back down from the compartment the more that you raise the hilt up high: the audience is similarly taken in. (3.21.3–5)

The length of the description of the knife and the painstaking care with which the mechanism is explained is remarkable. Bartsch reads this as part of Achilles Tatius' concern with narrative credibility.[33] The weapon is a pivotal prop in the *Scheintod* and its mechanism must be carefully described. However, to read this as being the only function of this extended description is to downplay its thematic and symbolic importance.

Hannah Arendt, in her study of violence, emphasises the role that weapons play, not solely in the implementation of violent acts, but by association, as visual symbols of violence, embodying violence.[34] Elaine Scarry agrees: 'What assists the conversion of absolute pain into the fiction of absolute power, is an obsessive, self-conscious display of agency. On the simplest level, the agent

---

[33] Bartsch (1989), 153.   [34] Arendt (1970), 4.

displayed is the weapon.'[35] 'Absolute pain' is not actually suffered by Leucippe, but for a while the reader is under the illusion that she has suffered, and the threat of violence is never very far away. The focus in Menelaus and Satyrus' account of the *Scheintod* is not upon Leucippe, but on the weapon used against her; there is 'an obsessive, self-conscious display of agency'.

This display is strongly reminiscent of a previous description of a weapon, that of Perseus' implement in the *ekphrasis* of the painting of Andromeda at 3.7.8–9. The painting of Andromeda, twinned with one of Prometheus, constitutes a remarkable thematisation of the scopic regime. They are highly performative and constructed with a constant awareness of the interaction of the object of the gaze with the seeing subject. I want briefly to consider its staging of the gaze, including the significance of the description of Perseus' sickle, before making some general points about the representation of Leucippe in the passages discussed so far.

The paintings are unusual, and possibly unprecedented, in that they form and are interpreted as a diptych, εἰκόνα διπλῆν (3.6.3).[36] This invites the viewer to compare the paintings and the figures in them. Clitophon suggests that the reason why the two paintings are put together is because both Andromeda and Prometheus are depicted in chains: διὰ τοῦτο γὰρ αὐτούς, οἶμαι, εἰς ἓν συνήγαγεν ὁ ζωγράφος, 'This was the reason, I suppose, why the artist had combined the two subjects onto one canvas' (3.6.3). He also mentions other similarities; in both the chains are attached to a rock, both characters are hurt by animals and their rescuers belong to the same Argive family. However, hindsight suggests another reason for their parallelism. Both paintings thematise aspects of display and torture which bear uncanny relation to what happens

---

[35] Scarry (1985), 27.
[36] Goldhill notes that they are 'the first example in Western art history of a pair of paintings being analysed precisely as a diptych with significant links'; Goldhill (1995), 72. The paintings are described as 'twinned', ἀδελφαί, which is a word sometimes used to denote eyes; Borthwick (1980). This lends the image of the paintings an uncanny twist; as the viewers look at them, they, as ἀδελφαί, look back. Cf. Gandelman on 'the dialectic of seeing, which always implies a being-seen relationship', (1991), 43. He asserts that all visual works of art declare to their spectators 'I am watching you watching me'; Gandelman (1991), 48. On the Perseus and Andromeda *ekphrasis* and a wall painting of Perseus and Andromeda excavated from the villa rustica at Boscotrecase near Pompeii and a relief in the Capitoline museum, and Philostratus' description and another Pompeian wall-painting, see Elsner (2000), 46–52.

to Leucippe in the first *Scheintod*. Both Andromeda and Leucippe are propitiatory sacrifices, both are tied up, both compared to statues (Andromeda is likened to a 'novel kind of statue', ἀγάλματι καινῷ, at 3.7.2), and both are depicted as 'brides of death'. Andromeda is so described:

Δέδεται μὲν οὖν οὕτω τὸν θάνατον ἐκδεχομένη· ἕστηκε δὲ νυμφικῶς ἐστολισμένη, ὥσπερ Ἀϊδωνεῖ νύμφη κεκοσμημένη.

Thus she was bound, awaiting death. She stood there dressed in bridal clothes, done up as if she were a bride for Hades. (3.7.5)

This detail is all the more striking for its innovation, breaking with the strong pictorial tradition of Andromeda in which she was never portrayed as a bride.[37] It is an image thrown into new relief when Leucippe is described in similar terms by Clitophon immediately prior to the first *Scheintod* (3.10.5). He laments: 'It is a dirge they are singing for you, not a wedding-song', ἀντὶ δὲ ὑμεναίων τίς σοι τὸν θρῆνον ᾄδει (3.10.5). The appearance of a pomegranate (held by the statue of Zeus Casius at 3.6.2) with a 'mystic meaning' (λόγος μυστικός) just before Clitophon's party see the paintings, and the fact that Leucippe 'returns' from Hades, strengthens her connection with Persephone, the mythical bride of Hades.[38]

The fate of Prometheus anticipates that of Leucippe, as both are disembowelled and their innards consumed, and both are described as watching the process, Leucippe at 3.16.3, and Prometheus at 3.8.7:

πῇ μὲν γὰρ εἰς τὸ ἕλκος, πῇ δὲ εἰς τὸν Ἡρακλέα βλέπει, καὶ θέλει μὲν αὐτὸν ὅλοις τοῖς ὀφθαλμοῖς ἰδεῖν, ἕλκει δὲ τὸ ἥμισυ τοῦ βλέμματος ὁ πόνος.

He was gazing both at the wound and at Heracles: he wanted to devote his full attention to the latter, but half of his gaze was distracted by the pain.

Once again, being made to view the violence is an integral part of the torture.

Like Leucippe's fear when encountering Thersander in Book 6, Andromeda's fear is aestheticised and enhances her desirability:

Ἐπὶ δὲ τῶν προσώπων αὐτῆς κάλλος κεκέρασται καὶ δέος· ἐν μὲν γὰρ ταῖς παρειαῖς τὸ δέος κάθηται, ἐκ δὲ τῶν ὀφθαλμῶν ἀνθεῖ τὸ κάλλος. Ἀλλ' οὔτε τῶν

---

[37] Harlan (1965), 117; Bartsch (1989), 57.
[38] On Achilles Tatius 3.6 and the pomegranate see Anderson (1979).

παρειῶν τὸ ὠχρὸν τέλεον ἀφοίνικτον ἦν, ἠρέμα δὲ τῷ ἐρεύθει βέβαπται, οὔτε τὸ τῶν ὀφθαλμῶν ἄνθος ἐστὶν ἀμέριμνον, ἀλλ' ἔοικε τοῖς ἄρτι μαραινομένοις ἴοις.[39]

In her face were combined beauty and fear: the fear resided in her cheeks, while the beauty bloomed from her eyes. Yet her pallid cheeks were not altogether without colour, tinged as they were with a gentle blushing; nor were her florid eyes without anxiety, resembling as they did violets in the first stage of wilting. (3.7.2-3)

Prometheus is fashioned as an object of pity: 'a pitiable spectacle, as though the very painting were suffering', Ἠλέησας ἂν ὡς ἀλγοῦσαν τὴν γραφήν (3.8.4), but Andromeda, like Europa in the *ekphrasis* which opens the novel, is enhanced by 'comely fear' εὐμόρφῳ φόβῳ (3.7.3-4). Unlike Prometheus, who is represented as actively looking, Andromeda's eyes only reveal her beauty. However, as with the description of the *Scheintod*, this scene is potentially hazardous for the viewer, although in the *ekphrasis* it is Medusa who threatens petrification, not the maiden. It reads as follows:

Τῇ λαιᾷ τὴν τῆς Γοργοῦς κεφαλὴν κρατεῖ καὶ προβέβληται δίκην ἀσπίδος. Ἡ δέ ἐστι φοβερὰ καὶ ἐν τοῖς χρώμασι· τοὺς ὀφθαλμοὺς ἐξεπέτασεν, ἔφριξε τὰς τρίχας τῶν κροτάφων, ἐγείρει τοὺς δράκοντας· οὕτως ἀπειλεῖ κἂν τῇ γραφῇ.

In his left hand he wielded the Gorgon's head, which he held out like a shield. Even when represented by pigments, she was terrifying: her eyes were protruding and her hair bristling from her temples, the serpents erect. Even in a painting this was a threatening sight. (3.7.7-8)

In one of Philostratus' *Imagines*, where the same subject is depicted, Perseus is careful to keep the Gorgon's head hidden from the plane of vision of the viewers of the painting (1.29.3). So potent is Medusa's gaze that it cannot be contained in representation, but, unlike Philostratus, Achilles Tatius does not let the spectators avoid the encounter. The word that Achilles uses to describe her eyes is ἐξεπέτασεν, which means 'spread out', 'unfurl', 'stretch out'. It is a gestural term, connoting movement and protrusion (the same verb is used to describe Andromeda stretching out her arms at 3.7.4), and its use here gives the impression that Medusa's eyes are actually penetrating through the painted plane of the picture's surface.

---

[39] Like Andromeda's eyes, Leucippe's eyes are compared to the violet (6.7.2).

Breaking through the two-dimensional structure which houses her, Medusa's gaze ruptures the fundamental boundary that the surface of the picture constitutes and invades the viewer's space.

As has already been mentioned, great emphasis is laid on the weapons in both episodes. Perseus' implement is a fascinating piece and almost lovingly described, inviting the eye to trace its contours and reflect upon its potential:

ὥπλισται δὲ καὶ τὴν δεξιὰν διφυεῖ σιδήρῳ εἰς δρέπανον καὶ ξίφος ἐσχισμένῳ. Ἄρχεται μὲν γὰρ ἡ κώπη κάτωθεν ἀμφοῖν ἐκ μιᾶς, καὶ ἔστιν ἐφ' ἥμισυ τοῦ σιδήρου ξίφος, ἐντεῦθεν δὲ ἀπορραγὲν τὸ μὲν ὀξύνεται, τὸ δὲ ἐπικάμπτεται. Καὶ τὸ μὲν ἀπωξυμμένον μένει ξίφος, ὡς ἤρξατο, τὸ δὲ καμπτόμενον δρέπανον γίνεται, ἵνα μιᾷ πληγῇ τὸ μὲν ἐρείδῃ τὴν σφαγήν, τὸ δὲ κρατῇ τὴν τομήν.

In his right hand he was armed with a double weapon, split between a sickle and a sword. The hilt for each blade shared a common point of origin down below, and up until half way the weapon was a sword; thereupon it diverged into two, the one part sharpening in a line, the other curving. The part that sharpened remained a sword as before, while the part that curved became a sickle, so that with a single blow the one blade could drive home the lethal stab and the other could complete the decapitation. (3.7.8–9)

Like the stage sword, Perseus' weapon is strangely double and its explicit function is to stab and cut, which is the method of disembowelling used in the sham sacrifice. Both implements are markedly phallic, Perseus' weapon in its visual appearance and the actor's weapon in its function; great emphasis is laid on the mechanism which allows it to protude and then retract.

All of the parallels outlined above between the *ekphraseis* and the *Scheintod* suggest, as Bartsch argues, that 'together the paintings of Andromeda and Prometheus are "proleptic similes" respectively for Leucippe's sacrifice and disembowelling'.[40] More generally, they form part of a series of episodes that couch sexual union in images of violence and penetration. In addition to the first *Scheintod*, the *ekphraseis* of Andromeda and Prometheus and Pantheia's dream, there are several passages which reinforce this construction and which represent male sexuality as predatory and aggressive.

[40] Bartsch (1989), 58–9; cf. Harrison (1989).

Visual masks of mythology

In the first book of the novel, a slave sings the story of Apollo's pursuit of Daphne, a pursuit which is thwarted at the last moment when Daphne turns into a tree from which Apollo makes a wreath (1.5.5). As has been discussed in Chapter 2, Clitophon takes this myth as a paradigm for his own amorous pursuit and Apollo as his role model. One interpretation of the myth is that it exemplifies triumph for the woman and frustration for the male, as through her metamorphosis Daphne escapes rape. However, in casting himself as an imitator of Apollo, Clitophon fashions his seduction of Leucippe as one of erotic aggression, with the male as the active pursuer and the female as his unwilling quarry.

In an artist's studio in Alexandria, the couple encounter another painting which also concerns violence and sexual violation; more specifically, in Clitophon's summary, Φιλομήλας γὰρ εἶχε φθορὰν καὶ τὴν βίαν Τηρέως καὶ τῆς γλώττης τὴν τομήν, 'It told of the violent rape of Philomela by Tereus, who cut out her tongue' (5.3.4). We are in fact given an *ekphrasis* within an *ekphrasis*: in the painting Philomela shows and explains through gestures to her sister Procne the tapestry on which she has embroidered Tereus' assault on her. The description of the painting is framed by invitations to read it as an omen, prefiguring disasters about to befall Clitophon, Leucippe and party. Before coming across the painting they are disturbed by an 'evil omen' (οἰωνὸς ... πονηρός, 5.3.4.) when a hawk chasing a swallow clipped Leucippe's head with his wing. Clitophon asks Zeus for another sign to explain this portent and it is then that he sees the painting which, he comments, had a hidden significance (ὑπῃνίττετο, 5.3.4). After the description of the painting Menelaus advises cancelling their journey because of 'the danger implied by the picture' (τῆς εἰκόνος τὴν ἀπειλήν, 5.4.1). He validates his decision by drawing on the authority of soothsayers:

Λέγουσι δὲ οἱ τῶν συμβόλων ἐξηγηταὶ σκοπεῖν τοὺς μύθους τῶν εἰκόνων, ἂν ἐξιοῦσιν ἐπὶ πρᾶξιν ἡμῖν συντύχωσι, καὶ ἐξομοιοῦν τὸ ἀποβησόμενον τῷ τῆς ἱστορίας λόγῳ.

Interpreters of signs say that if we encounter paintings as we set off to do something, we should ponder the myths narrated there, and conclude that the outcome for us will be comparable to the story they tell. (5.4.1–2)

This is the only occasion in *Leucippe and Clitophon* that an *ekphrasis* is accompanied by guidance on its interpretation; this passage, therefore, may have particular importance for understanding the hermeneutics of the narrative. Menelaus then lists what he supposes it presages: ἔρωτος παρανόμου, μοιχείας ἀναισχύντου, γυναικείων ἀτυχημάτων, 'illicit desire, shameless adultery, female misfortunes' (3.4.2). How exactly these themes depicted in the painting of Philomela's rape correspond to what happens to the characters in the main story is a moot point. The readers of, and protagonists in, the narrative anticipate that the painting prefigures Chaereas' abduction of Leucippe, which does indeed happen the following day. This is how Konstan interprets the scene, although he notes that the analogy is an imperfect one, as Tereus' 'shameless adultery' betrayed his own wife, whereas Chaereas' intended liaison threatens to make an adulteress of the wife of another, his friend Clitophon. Konstan contends that, 'As injured parties, Philomela and her sister Procne are in the place of Leucippe and Clitopho',[41] which assists his argument that overall, despite the asymmetry of the ego-narrative form, Achilles' novel conforms to the generic principle of sexual parity between hero and heroine:

In this ecphrasis . . . Clitopho identifies not with the pursuer, as the anonymous narrator seems to have done at the beginning of the book (and as Clitopho himself did during the song about Apollo and Daphne), but with the victim. Whatever Clitopho's pretensions were to the role of active lover, or *erastes*, early in the story . . . erotic aggression is by now securely associated with the behaviour of rivals rather than that of the male protagonist.[42]

However, the identifications do not seem so clear-cut. It is true that Thersander's attempted assault on Leucippe while he is married to Melite provides a closer parallel to Tereus than the actions of any other figure. There are other parallels too; both are Thracian, and both visually intrusive. Tereus, as his name 'Watcher-Over' betrays, is associated with voyeurism. Ovid, in his version of the myth in *Metamorphoses* 6.478, emphasises this aspect of his character: 'Tereus looked at her and in looking prefondled her' (*spectat eam Tereus praecontrectatque videndo*). In Achilles Tatius' version, it is, of course, significant that in struggling to

[41] Konstan (1994), 69. [42] Konstan (1994), 69.

defend herself Philomela aims for Tereus' *eyes* (5.3.6).[43] It is clear that Leucippe is associated with Philomela, as no other named female character is victimised, whereas Leucippe is threatened by the sexual advances of Chaereas and Thersander. Like Philomela, Leucippe is the object of unwanted voyeuristic attentions. Moreover, the comparison between Leucippe and Philomela is encouraged by Leucippe's unexpected keenness to understand what the picture represents. She bombards Clitophon with questions about the image, prompting his comment that 'the female species is rather fond of myths' (5.5.1), which is hard not to read as ironic on more than one level.

It is not easy to see Clitophon cast as a Procne figure. The part of the Philomela myth which might be expected to appeal to womankind is that where she and her sister exact their revenge upon Tereus with their perverted banquet of human flesh (5.3.8, 5.5.6–8). However, far from celebrating their retaliation or presenting it as a fitting response to the savagery of their husband, Clitophon uses it as an opportunity to deliver a homily on women's susceptibility to *zelotupia* (5.5.7). This does not show the empathy towards Leucippe that Procne showed towards Philomela. Moreover, at no stage in the narrative is Clitophon subjected to any violation which parallels that of Leucippe or Philomela. If the *ekphrasis* can in any way be read as proleptic of Clitophon's adventures, the correspondence would be between Tereus' adultery and Clitophon's adulterous tryst with Melite. So, it is not as easy to read the *ekphrasis* of Philomela's rape as evincing parity between the young male and female protagonists as Konstan suggests. Instead Clitophon's commentary maximises the differences between the sexes, and the *ekphrasis* exemplifies, in a general way that is not easily and exclusively mapped onto specific characters, male aggression towards women and the danger to women that male sexuality poses.

Before Leucippe's virginity is tested in the grotto which Pan had dedicated to Artemis, the priest of Artemis regales the assembly with the story behind the test (8.5.9ff.).[44] The pan-pipes originated from a maiden (who is not named by the priest but in other versions

---

[43] On the poking out of eyes as a form of punishment, see Nutting (1922).
[44] On this and other virginity tests, see Rattenbury (1926).

of the story is called Syrinx)⁴⁵ who fled from Pan's sexual advances. Pan loses his quarry in a clump of reeds which he angrily cuts down, thinking that she is hiding in them. When he realises that she has metamorphosed into the reeds and that it is she whom he has mutilated, he creates a new body from the reed-girl, the pan-pipes:

Συμφορήσας οὖν τὰ τετμημένα τῶν καλάμων ὡς μέλη τοῦ σώματος καὶ συνθεὶς εἰς ἓν σῶμα, εἶχε διὰ χειρῶν τὰς τομὰς τῶν καλάμων καταφιλῶν ὡς τῆς κόρης τραύματα.

So he gathered together the fragments of reeds, as though they were the limbs of a body, and recomposed them into a single body. Then he held the cut-up reeds in his hands and kissed them, as though they were the girl's wounds. (8.6.10)

Pan's breath as he kisses the reeds produces sound and gives the pan-pipes their voice. This myth is yet another account of attempted rape and echoes in particular the earlier story of Apollo's pursuit of Daphne; both maidens metamorphose into plants in order to escape being violated by a deity and both are then cut down and fashioned into symbols of the god's creativity. This parallel in turn reminds the reader of when Clitophon first determined actively to pursue Leucippe, seeking validation for this in the paradigm of Apollo. Are we therefore invited to see Clitophon also as playing the role of a Pan, like, but less overt than, Longus' Daphnis, who dances the myth alongside Chloe as Syrinx (2.37)? Such a reading seems unfounded if we focus on Clitophon's concern for Leucippe's safe return from Pan's cave. Imagining the worst, he compares Leucippe to Syrinx, fearing that she might suffer the same fate (δέδοικα μὴ δευτέρα καὶ σὺ Σύριγξ γένῃ) and, being shut inside the cave, with less chance of eluding the god should he strike (8.13.3). However, the description of Pan's kissing the broken reeds 'as though they were the girl's wounds', a feature which is absent in Longus' version of the myth, is, in its grotesque sentimentality, strikingly reminiscent of Clitophon's kissing the truncated body of 'Leucippe' at 5.7.9: καταφιλήσω τὴν σφαγήν. In this uncanny moment, Clitophon both is and is not Pan.

All of the myths discussed above, some emphatically, others less so, by overt comparison or implicit association, cast Leucippe

---

[45] *Daphnis and Chloe* 2.34; Ovid, *Met.* 1.691.

as the one violated. Her body – or mythological analogues of it (Daphne, Andromeda, Philomela and Syrinx) – is displayed for assault repeatedly throughout the narrative. What are we to make of this pattern of images? Bartsch sees the point of Achilles' design as lying in the *making* of connections, not in the connections themselves. The links forged between inset moments – 'theatrical' display, *ekphrasis*, dreams, myth – and narrative events are structured to seduce the reader into a complex game of hermeneutics. This is true, but risks underplaying the importance of the motifs themselves.

Let us take the example of the descriptions of Perseus' weapon and that used in the first *Scheintod*. It does not seem plausible that the parallel between the two implements is an incidental one, as a prosaics approach would have it. The striking similarities of events and images between the *ekphraseis* and the *Scheintod* as a whole and the marked parallels between the two weapons militate against such a reading. However, the association is not as easily mapped as Bartsch suggests. If we read the *ekphrasis* of Andromeda as a proleptic simile of the *Scheintod* then how are we to include the weapons in this reading? Perseus' weapon has caused harm to Medusa to the benefit of Andromeda, whom he rescues. The hero's weapon cannot prefigure the weapon used to disembowel the heroine without sinister implications. Are we to view Perseus, and by implication not only Menelaus and Satyrus, but also Clitophon, as potential violators of maidens? If so, does this hint at the violence suffered by women at the hands of *all* men? And, if so, to what end?

It is significant that in the narrative there is relatively little violence encountered by Leucippe. The violence is largely contained in the *ekphraseis*, dreams and theatrical interludes. These categories are being used loosely, as technically the first *Scheintod* belongs to the main narrative; but, as has already been noted, the physical distance between the scene and its viewers and the nature of the hoax serve to create the frame of a theatrical set piece. It is also true that Leucippe is beheaded, though once again not for real, but the act of beheading is not dwelt upon; the focus is upon Clitophon's reactions to the event. The stressed moments of violence, especially sexual violence, are found in passages of description, which are inset from and temporarily halt the linear progression of the narrative. Central to the question of how to read these 'digressions' is the issue of empathy.

Like the so-called 'digressive' descriptions of the eye and the paradoxographical phenomena discussed in the previous chapter, *ekphraseis*, dreams and *mises-en-scène* are demarcated from the narrative that contains them. It is this differentiation which has allowed so many readers of the novel to overlook them or dismiss them on the grounds of irrelevance. The use of *ekphraseis* and visions through which to frame representations of violence has two, paradoxical, functions. It is a strategy of disavowal, operating to distance the reader from an emotional and empathetic response to the subject. The violence is displaced, set aside, at one step removed from the 'real world' of the narrative action. We can compartmentalise the subject matter and rationalise it away, protected from emotional engagement by the narrative form. (Don't worry, it was all a pretence, only a dream, just a picture . . .) However, the framing and demarcation of these episodes is precisely and paradoxically what makes them stand out and demand attention. They arrest the reader and hold the gaze at the same time as they announce their detachment.

On the other hand, the connections forged between *ekphraseis* and dreams of violence and events and characters in the narrative suggest that these episodes cannot be easily sealed off.[46] There is an excess of signification, a leakage, as it were, from one medium to another. The very transposability of images in Achilles Tatius means that a description, whether or not it prefigures an episode which follows it, leaves a deposit, a residue which alters our perception of that episode. This is the literary equivalent of the optical phenomenon of 'visual masking', the overlapping of one image onto another produced by stereopticon machines and kaleidoscopes in the early nineteenth century.[47] Commenting on this technique in the writings of Charles Darwin, James Krasner describes how 'the

---

[46] See also Heffernan (1993), 58: 'Just as the notes of the syrinx and the final reference to the teachings of Lykainion drop echoes of rape right into the wedding-night chamber of Daphnis and Chloe, the paintings described in Leucippe and Clitophon forge links between rape and marriage that the plot never wholly dissolves.'

[47] Krasner (1992), 60; Crary (1991), esp. ch. 4.

"ghost" or residual image of one form does not have time to clear before the next one is presented'.[48] This is what happens in Achilles Tatius. The world of the narrative is not receptive to a monadic gaze; instead, the characters, and Leucippe most of all, are presented to us through a pattern of sublimations and visual masks. They are haunted by the 'ghosts' of mythic predecessors and superimposed upon by eroticised and violent after-images.

Women and other animals

In the course of his advice, Clinias urges Clitophon to stay in Leucippe's presence:

Μέγιστον γάρ ἐστιν ἐφόδιον εἰς πειθὼ συνεχὴς πρὸς ἐρωμένην ὁμιλία. Ὀφθαλμὸς γὰρ φιλίας πρόξενος καὶ τὸ σύνηθες τῆς κοινωνίας εἰς χάριν ἀνυσιμώτερον.

Continual association with your beloved is the best starting-point on the road to seduction, for the eye serves as the go-between of amorous feelings, and mutual familiarity is the most effective route to gratification. (1.9.5)

He caps this with an explanatory flourish:

Εἰ γὰρ τὰ ἄγρια τῶν θηρίων συνηθείᾳ τιθασσεύεται, πολὺ μᾶλλον ταύτῃ μαλαχθείη καὶ γυνή.

If wild beasts are tamed by familiarity, then woman too will be similarly softened, indeed much more easily. (1.9.6)

This is a telling comparison: women are likened to wild animals and seduction to taming. The constant presence (*sunetheia*) of the male is guaranteed to soften both. Is this an accurate description of how Clitophon perceives and persuades Leucippe? What is the relationship between women and animals in Achilles' menagerie of beautiful creatures?

The first meeting between Leucippe and Clitophon after his consultation with Clinias is in the garden of his house, where birds, tame and wild (a detail which is repeated and echoes Clinias' *sententia*), fly, sing and display their plumage (1.15.7–8). The birds provide a convenient focus with which to turn Leucippe's thoughts

---

[48] Krasner (1992), 61. See also McHale (1987), 99–111 on 'worlds under erasure'.

to desire (1.16.1). In order to impress Leucippe, who is walking with her maid and has stopped, quite fortuitously, opposite the peacock, Clitophon lectures upon the character of the bird. It behaves 'not without design' (οὐκ ἄνευ τέχνης), for it is a lovebird (ἐρωτικός). The peacock displays himself in order to attract his beloved (1.16.2). Clitophon points out the peahen and remarks that it is for her that the peacock exhibits. This is a none too subtle way of Clitophon revealing his designs upon Leucippe, but his display is a verbal one. Ἐπαγαγέσθαι at 1.15.2 echoes εὐάγωγον at 1.16.1, strengthening the association between the two exhibitionists. The peacock's visual display is a metaphor for Clitophon's sophistic display, an image paralleled in the explicit comparison of sophists and peacocks in Dio Chrysostom's *Olympic Discourse*.[49]

Satyrus takes up the theme and leads Clitophon into an extended account of the mating habits of various exotica, magnetic stones, the palm tree, the river Alpheus and spring Arethusa and the land viper and sea eel. This last union (1.18.3–5) is a 'mystery of desire' (ἔρωτος μυστήριον) because it does not merely attract two individuals of the same race together, but a member of one species to a member of another.[50] The tale facilitates what it exemplifies: the union of male and female leading to marriage. Telling the tale is part of Clitophon's strategy for seducing Leucippe, 'keen to break the girl into the ways of desire' (Βουλόμενος οὖν εὐάγωγον τὴν κόρην εἰς ἔρωτα παρασκευάσαι, 1.16.1). Clitophon puts into practice the advice which Ovid gives the would-be lover in the first book of his *Ars Amatoria* (1.219–28), namely to spend time describing foreign marvels (in Ovid's case, those paraded at Caesar's spectacles) in order to prolong enjoying the beloved's presence. It is advice echoed by Menander Rhetor in a treatise probably dating to the late third century CE, part of which discusses the Epithalamium, the 'wedding speech' or λόγος γαμήλιος, and the subsequent 'bedroom speech' or λόγος κατευναστικός, which is quite explicitly 'an exhortation to intercourse' (προτροπὴ πρὸς τὴν

---

[49] Dio likens his own attractiveness as a speaker to that of the owl, at whose cry the birds all flock to him. He writes that one would think that the peacock would be the most popular bird, given his splendour (which is described at 2–3). The large number of sophists resemble multicoloured peacocks (ὡς ταὼς ποικίλους, πολλοὺς σοφιστάς, 5).
[50] For variations on the viper and eel story see Arist. *HA* 504b34; Ael. *DNA* 1.50; 9.66; Pliny, *NH* 9.76; 32.14; Opp. *Cyn.* 1.381; *Hal.* 1.554; Nonn. *Dion.* 40.394.

συμπλοκήν).⁵¹ Menander advises that the wedding speech 'delights in stories of charm and love, for these are germane to the subject' (χαίρει δὲ διηγήμασιν ἐπαφροδίτοις τε καὶ ἐρωτικοῖς· ταῦτα γὰρ οἰκεῖα τῇ ὑποθέσει, 399.15–16). He suggests that the speaker should tell how marriage was created by nature (φύσις) and how the god affects 'even streams and rivers, creatures that swim and those of the land and of the air' (401.27–8). He continues:

> You should incorporate narratives (διηγήματα) in all this: stories of rivers, e.g. how Alpheus the Pisan loves the Sicilian spring Arethusa and goes against his own nature, and, like a passionate bridegroom, goes bubbling through the sea, seething to the island of Sicily, and falls into the lap of his beloved Arethusa and unites with her, and stories of creatures that swim, for it is plain that the beasts of the sea know the rites of passage, like those of the land and all that fly ... As to trees you should point out that they too are not without their part in marriage, for the tendrils on leaves are devices of trees for mating, and these too are inventions of the god. (401.29–402.4, 402.7–10)

All of these exempla are used by Clitophon to woo Leucippe. Moreover, Menander also suggests that an epithalamium should contain descriptions of the young man and woman, emphasising the youth's gaze (404.8–10), a description of Eros and stories of the gods' romances, for example that of Zeus's marriage to Europa (402.10). Achilles' novel performs all of these, not just within Clitophon's narration to Leucippe but throughout the entire narrative, starting with the opening *ekphrasis* of the painting of Europa, told by the unnamed first narrator. Thus, on one level, the whole work is an extravagant epithalamial performance, and the descriptions of animals play a fundamental role in *Achilles'* seduction of *his* audience.

Using animals through which to convey and comment upon human activities was common practice throughout Graeco-Roman culture. As Geoffrey Lloyd has stressed, animals were used as 'vehicles for the expression of fundamental social, moral, religious and cosmological categories',⁵² most obviously in writers

---

⁵¹ The translation is that of Russell and Wilson (1981) whose commentary is also useful.
⁵² Lloyd (1983), 12. See also the recent and substantial work of French (1994); cf. Padel (1992), 147–52 on 'animal semantics' in Greek tragedy and Hughes Fowler (1989), ch. 9.

such as Aristotle, Artemidorus, Philo, Plutarch, Aelian and Pliny.[53] Semonides of Amorgos wrote of women who shared their various unpleasant characteristics with animals, and physiognomic treatises like that of Pseudo-Aristotle explicitly parallel human characters with those of animals.[54] Often animals are portrayed as superior moral beings and are set up for humans, lesser creatures, to emulate.[55] This is best exemplified in the dissertations of Plutarch's Gryllus the pig, one of Odysseus' crew who has been turned into a pig by the sorceress Circe. Gryllus has kept his human faculties through the metamorphosis and – in an ironic twist – uses them to argue for the supremacy of animals over humans. The porcine 'clever sophist' contends that if you acknowledge that animals are taught by nature, 'you are elevating the intelligence of animals to the most sovereign and wisest of first principles' (*De Sollert. Anim.* 991F).

The physiognomists stress the similarities between animals and humans. However, animals are also distanced from humans – we can dissociate ourselves from them, make them 'Other'. In her study of the function of animals in literary texts, Jean Addison Roberts argues that they have:

a built-in duality, a haunting combination of the recognised and the strange. In Freudian terms, they are 'uncanny', both familiar and mysterious, and thus they often serve as links between the known and the unknown.[56]

It is no surprise to find uncanny figures in Achilles Tatius' most uncanny of novels. The uncanny duplicity of animals makes them good 'agents of revelation'[57]: devices for communicating in an oblique way ideas and information which might otherwise prove awkward. It is their recognisability that makes animals useful vehicles for commenting on human life, while their strangeness allows this to operate on an oblique, rather than overt level. Take this example from Aelian:

---

[53] See Winkler (1990) esp. ch. 1. for a discussion of Artemidorus and Philo. I am grateful to Piers Aitman for showing me his unpublished paper *Aelian and Human Nature*.
[54] See also Plato, *Tim.* 91d6ff.
[55] A practice Lovejoy and Boas call 'animalitarianism': Lovejoy and Boas (1935). See also Beagon (1992), 137ff.
[56] Roberts (1991), 75.   [57] Roberts (1991), 75.

The camel would never copulate with its mother. Once a camel-keeper covered up a female (as is done when mating some animals) and led the son to its mother. The randy beasts had sex, but then the son-camel realised what had happened. He killed the keeper then threw himself off a cliff. (*De Nat. Animal.* 3.47)

This is a morality tale about, *inter alia*, the undesirability of incestuous relations between mother and son. The camel is endowed with agency and the ability to make decisions (he *realises* he has mated with his mother and *chooses* to kill the keeper and himself). Aelian underlines the moral and its applicability to human behaviour with the conclusion that 'Oedipus should have done the same' (3.47), but often the analogies are left unstated and it is up to the reader to make the connections, as in the description of the halycon. The bird is similarly described in anthropomorphic terms; she is virtuous, faithful and not wanton, she shows her partner friendship and affection '*as with any lawful wife*'. The didacticism is clear – to be a good wife, you should be virtuous, faithful and not wanton, friendly and affectionate. Cultural values are projected onto natural practices. Moreover, as Rosalind Coward argues in her analysis of natural history programmes on television, more often than not nature is used to 'confirm rather than contradict the assumptions made in this society about male and female behaviour'.[58] It is no coincidence that the camel and the halcyon are favoured paradigms, rather than the praying mantis and the black widow spider.

The anthropomorphising in Clitophon's tale is striking. The viper and eel are endowed with the ability to make decisions, and their union is termed a 'marriage' – τὸν γάμον. The viper is the 'bridegroom', τὸν νυμφίον. Viper and eel gaze at each other – πρὸς ἀλλήλους βλέποντες – the classic symptom of love shown by Leucippe and Clitophon several times during the novel. The viper and eel are explicitly gendered and given typical gender roles: the male is the active lover, ἐραστής, and the female his beloved, ἐρωμένη (the same terms as were used to speak about the peacock and peahen). Finally, the viper is said to give his bride 'kisses' – τὰ φιλήματα. This passage is as prescriptive as it is descriptive, naturalising the 'heterosexual' union (and this union is very 'hetero' – the differences between the viper and eel are paraded) and

---

[58] Coward (1984), 213.

marriage. However, unlike the tale of the lovesick palm trees and the amorous aquatics of Alpheus and Arethusa, the story of the viper and eel sounds a discordant note. If Leucippe and the reader appreciate Clitophon's subtext and understand the viper and eel to be analogues of Clitophon and Leucippe respectively, then what are we to make of the viper's toxicity? Once again, as we have seen so often in this novel, Achilles implies parallels that prove difficult to map. The implicit analogy between the viper and Clitophon suggests that Clitophon might be dangerous and poses a threat to Leucippe. We cannot be too literal, as Clitophon obviously does not have poisonous spittle, although it is interesting that the emphasis on the viper's mouth uncannily prefigures the elaborate description of and commentary on the couple's first kiss.[59] The serpentine bride is afraid of an oral encounter with her groom. When literature represents human brides as afraid, typically their fear is of their first experience of sexual intercourse.[60] The story's image of the male's discharging of fluid is evocative of ejaculation, and the snake can readily be seen as a symbol of the penis.[61] In a similar version of the story told by Oppian, after his encounter with the eel the viper sucks up again the poison that he had spat out. The viper, who is unable to find the fluid, commits suicide, so ashamed is he to be ἄναλκις ὅπλων, 'without the strength of his weapons', a phrase which can also suggest sexual impotence and which reinforces an interpretation of the story as sexualised.[62] Whether or not we feel pressed to read Clitophon's tale as a symbolic harbinger of the fear that a human bride, and in particular Leucippe, will feel on her wedding night, it is undeniable that the account represents male sexuality as potentially dangerous to the female. At the same time as the tale naturalises and celebrates heterosexual desire and marriage, it does so with a jarring, even sinister undertone, which is never adequately explained.

Clitophon's strategy for seduction having proved a success ('She seemed to be signalling that the experience was not without a

---

[59] At 2.7.8. On orality see Goldhill (1995), 18.   [60] E.g. in Theocritus, *Idylls* 2.136–8.
[61] For which there are literary parallels, e.g. Strato's use of ὄφις (*AP* 11.22.2); Adams (1982), 30.
[62] Oppian, *Halieutica* 1.578. Weapons are common metaphors for the penis; Adams (1982), 14–22.

certain pleasure', 1.19.1), he once again reflects upon Leucippe's beauty:

Τὸ δὲ κάλλος ἀστράπτον τοῦ ταὼ ἧττον ἐδόκει μοι τοῦ Λευκίππης εἶναι προσώπου.

The effulgent beauty of the peacock seemed to me a lesser thing than Leucippe's countenance (1.19.1)

With this introduction he embarks upon an encomiastic inventory of Leucippe's lovely features. Clitophon likens himself to the peacock to highlight his amorousness, skill in pursuit and excellence in epideictic oratory. Also, by association, the peacock's appearance, with an eye on every feather (ἔστιν ὀφθαλμὸς ἐν τῷ πτερῷ, 1.16.3), is suggestive of Clitophon's scopophilia.[63] In contrast, the point of comparison with Leucippe is to emphasise her beauty.

In a description later in the novel, almost the same simile is used to evoke the beauty of another — not a human, but a bird, the phoenix. Like Leucippe, the phoenix is said to surpass the peacock in its beauty (3.25.1). This is by no means the only similarity between Leucippe and the phoenix, whose extraordinary description is one of the most remarkable in the novel (3.25). The details of the burial of the parent phoenix in a lump of myrrh broadly concur with Herodotus' account of the bird, and both Herodotus and Philostratus mention the phoenix's golden and sunlike appearance.[64] Achilles has added idiosyncratic touches, such as making the bird an ἐπιτάφιος σοφιστής, 'conductor of the funeral ceremony' or 'graveside sophist' (3.2.7). But what is most striking and quite

---

[63] Cf. Rowland (1978), 128: 'In Christian Rome, on Easter days when the Pope was carried in state into St Peter's, he flourished a fan (flabellum) of ostrich feathers on which were sewn the eye spots from peacocks' plumes, the latter signifying the vigilance of the church.'

[64] Herodotus 2.73 and Philostratus, *Apoll. Tyana* 3.49. Tacitus also discusses the phoenix and how it buries its father. He comments: *Haec incerta et fabulosis aucta* (*Ann.* 6.28). Keitel (1991) discusses the Tacitean phoenix as a figure through which Tacitus highlights the destruction of the nobility and the cruelty of the emperor Tiberius and his heir Gaius. Plepelits uses the description of the phoenix in Achilles as a tool to date the novel. In his view, the description is a documentary account of one of the actual historical appearances of the phoenix. Three appearances are attested during the Roman Empire: 34, 36, and 47 CE. 47 CE would best fit the temporal frame of the last Thracian war, so Plepelits conjectures the strong probability that Achilles Tatius intended 47 CE to be the date of the setting of the novel.

unprecedented is the phoenix's self-exposure, displaying even his 'unmentionables' – τὰ ἀπόρρητα – to the Egyptian priest. The word ἀπόρρητα resists clarity of translation; 'unspoken things' are just that. There is a suggestion of mysteriosophic language here, of the *arrheta* of the mystery religions. Thus Whitmarsh translates that the bird reveals 'the secret mysteries of its body'. However, as Laura McClure has observed, 'the word ἀπόρρητα, although ambiguous ... can be used of the female genitals in both literary and ritual contexts'.[65] This appears to be the meaning in Longinus' discussion of how nature has constructed the body: 'Nature did not place in full view our unmentionable parts (τὰ μέρη τὰ ἀπόρρητα) nor the drains that purge our whole frame.'[66] Moreover, Plutarch tells the tale of poor Helvia, a *parthenos* who was struck by lightning while out horseriding: 'Her horse was found naked of its trappings, and she herself was naked, for her tunic had been pulled up above her unmentionables (ἀπὸ τῶν ἀπορρήτων) as if on purpose.'[67] So, we should allow for *ta aporreta* in the description in *Leucippe and Clitophon* to have a sexually suggestive, as well as mysteriosophic, meaning. Why does Achilles Tatius have the phoenix display its 'unmentionables'?

First, as was noted in the discussion of the crocodile, animals often operate as metonyms for countries that they represent. Although the phoenix is said to come from Ethiopia, it also represents Phoenicia, as its etymological root makes clear.[68] The Phoenicians had a reputation for being lusty, or, more specifically, for enjoying cunnilingus. The verb φοινικίζω, which commonly means 'to speak Phoenician', also has the sense 'to perform cunnilingus'.[69] One might, therefore, expect a phoenix-ian bird to expose its genitalia, but for very different motives than those attributed to the

---

[65] McClure (1999), 127 (discussing Euripides' *Hippolytus* 293).
[66] *On the Sublime* 43.5.
[67] *Moralia* (*The Roman Questions*) 284A. See also Ar. *Eccl.* 12, where the *double entendre* ἀπορρήτους μυχούς also suggests female genitalia.
[68] A poem of Antiphanes preserved in Athenaeus (*Deipn.* 14 655B) plays on this double meaning.
[69] Lucian, *Pseudol.* 1.28; Galen, *De simplicium medicamentorum temperamentis ac facultatibus libri* 12.10–14. Jocelyn (1980); Nicarchus' epigram on cunnilingus (11.329), on which see Richlin (1992a), 49. On the ascription of particular sexual practices to ethnic groups, see Adams (1982), 202.

Egyptian priest. The association of this particular sexual practice with the Phoenicians is an especially unpleasant ethnic stereotype. Performing cunnilingus was deemed disgusting behaviour. Lucian considers it on a par with λεσβιάζειν (to fellate) and Galen considers it more shameful for a decent person to have a reputation for 'Phoenician practices' (τοὺς φοινικίζοντας) than for fellatio or eating excrement, and as disgraceful as being called a drinker of menstrual blood.[70] There is, I suggest, a typically Achillean joke at play here, a visual pun, displaying the phoenix as truly phoenix-ian in its exposure of its sex organs and at the same time snidely alluding to the Phoenicians' famed preoccupation with female genitalia.

Secondly, despite the fact that the phoenix is androgynous, there are a series of images and similes that link the creature to Leucippe. The first of these I have already mentioned; the comparison between the phoenix and peacock recalls the simile of 1.19.1, where it is Leucippe who is compared to the peacock. The parallel is thrown into greater relief because in comparing the phoenix to a peacock Achilles diverges from other literary parallels, notably Herodotus and Apollonius of Tyre, in which it is likened to an eagle.[71] Furthermore, both Leucippe and the phoenix are compared to a rose. The phoenix's halo of feathers is 'deep crimson in colour, like a rose'. Clitophon compares Leucippe's lips to a rose, after listening to her sing a song in praise of the flower (2.1.2–3). The erotic charge of the simile, richly suggestive of labial pleasures, is heightened by Clitophon's reminiscence: ἐγὼ δὲ ἐδόκουν τὸ ῥόδον ἐπὶ τῶν χειλέων αὐτῆς ἰδεῖν, ὡς εἴ τις τῆς κάλυκος τὸ περιφερὲς εἰς τὴν τοῦ στόματος ἔκλεισε μορφήν, 'I thought that I could spy the rose on her lips, as if someone had enclosed the outline of the calyx within the shape of her mouth.'[72]

Moreover the phoenix, like Leucippe, dies and is reborn. Achilles dwells only upon the death of the phoenix, but the myth

---

[70] Lucian, *Pseudol.* 1.28; Galen, *De simplicium medicamentorum temperamentis ac facultatibus libri* 12.10–14.

[71] Hdt. 2.73; Phil. *Apoll.* 3.49. Cf. Hubaux and Leroy (1939).

[72] The description of the calyx of the rose in the garden at 1.15.5–6 focuses on the gradations of colour in the flower, in terms similarly suggestive of labia. There is evidence which links the phoenix to Aphrodite, much as the *benu* bird was associated with Sothis-Isis, for example the fragment of the poem *Pterygion Phoenicis* written by Laevius and preserved in Flavius Sosipater Charisius, for discussion of which see Hefferman (1988), 35.

was so common that the bird came to symbolise resurrection.[73] Leucippe 'dies' and is 'reborn' three times during the novel, twice with graphic theatricality. She first dies when pirates sacrifice her, rip out her innards and consume them. She is reborn when it is later revealed that Menelaus and Satyrus staged the death with the help of an actor's knife and a false stomach. Her second death is by decapitation, but she is reborn to tell how a prostitute was slain in her place. Her third death is reported to Clitophon by a fellow inmate in the prison, but once again this proves to be a ruse and Leucippe is 'reborn'.[74] Furthermore, the phoenix is sacred to the sun-god, Helios,[75] paralleling Leucippe's association with the moon-goddess, Selene.

However, the most striking point of comparison is the test which both phoenix and *parthenos* undergo. The bird's genital examination prefigures Leucippe's virginity test in the final book of the novel (8.6.). The phoenix is tested by a religious man, as is Leucippe; the priest of Artemis oversees her ordeal. The phoenix submits to the test willingly, as does Leucippe, who does not heed the reservations of her father and her fiancé, but eagerly enters Pan's grotto. Garnaud suggests that the phoenix's acceptance of the fact that it may be tested is a reference to the false phoenix, described by Pliny.[76] The story goes that a phoenix flew down into Egypt, was brought to Rome in 47 CE and displayed in the Comitium, 'but no one would doubt that this phoenix was a fabrication' (10.2.5). It is possible that this story was one of the many in circulation and that Achilles drew upon a source or sources also used by Pliny, but this explanation alone ignores the *strangeness* of the test willingly submitted to by the phoenix. All of the bird's body is checked but the only parts specifically referred to – and therefore spotlighted – are his genitals.

---

[73] See Hubaux and Leroy (1939) and e.g. Dionysius' account (*De Avibus* 1.32) which emphasises this aspect of the phoenix myth. Early printed representations of the phoenix bore the legend *ex me ipso renascor* – 'I am reborn from myself'; see Rowland (1978), 134. As a symbol of resurrection, the phoenix was an obvious choice for adaptation by Christian imagery.

[74] On resurrection as a *topos* in imperial fiction see Bowersock (1994), 99–120.

[75] Like its Egyptian counterpart, the *benu* bird; see Hefferman (1988), 21ff. The *benu* bird is a mythical heron-like bird that also has the power to regenerate itself, like the phoenix; Hefferman (1988), Hubaux and Leroy (1939).

[76] Garnaud (1991), 105.

The bird is deemed a true phoenix when his genitalia are verified; he refutes the charge of being a 'false phoenix' by exposing his sexual parts. Leucippe's status is also doubted; Thersander accuses her of being a false virgin, a ψευδοπάρθενος (8.3.3). However, in one significant way, her test could not be further removed from that of the phoenix. The phoenix undergoes an openly physical examination as the priest scrutinises and checks off its various body parts. One might say that the test is too matter-of-fact and clinical to pander to voyeuristic desires. Leucippe's 'virginity test' is markedly abstract and non-physical. It is not clear exactly what determines her virginity, but it is known or decided by Pan or Syrinx rather than any somatic investigation. Even in this novel it seems that it would be pushing the boundaries of acceptability too far to lift up the skirts of a *parthenos* and check her genitalia against the text of a book, but it is possible to do this to an animal. The phoenix is thus doubly an 'agent of revelation', physically revealing himself and symbolically revealing what Leucippe cannot.

The seventeenth-century translation of Anthony Hodges translates, or more accurately adapts, the phoenix's examination as follows:

> ... who straightway comes out of an holy place with a booke in his hand, and comparing the bird with the description which is given of her, he judges whether it be a true phoenix or no; and so curious he is (lest he should be mistaken himselfe) that hee makes anatomie of her as it were, and shows each part to the standers by; after a full triall, adding some short speech in commendation of her, he buries her.[77]

In this version the similarities between the phoenix and Leucippe are pressed more emphatically than in Achilles' original. The translator explicitly genders the bird as female, choosing not to take refuge in the more technically accurate (given the phoenix's androgyny) pronoun 'it'. There is also greater emphasis laid on the visual examination of the phoenix. An additional motivation to scrutinise the phoenix is attributed to the priest; he looks not solely to verify the bird's identity, but also to satisfy his own curiosity. This priest is a consummate *polupragmon*. Moreover, the priest compounds the prurience by inviting passers-by to participate in

---

[77] Hodges (1638), 92.

the scrutiny. This is a conspicuous innovation that transforms the phoenix's exposure into an overtly theatrical event. This gives the spectacle a greater affinity with the first *Scheintod* and allies the phoenix's test more closely to that of Leucippe, whose trial attracts a great audience. The phrase 'makes anatomie of' is commonly used in the seventeenth century to mean 'dissect', or 'vivisect'.[78] The adjoinder 'as it were' acknowledges that the writer is speaking figuratively in this case. The bird is dissected by the priest's examination; she undergoes a visual vivisection. This shows the voyeuristic gaze at its most intrusive and objectifying and further aligns it with the *Scheintod*, where Leucippe is 'made anatomie of'.

The translation develops and foregrounds aspects of the event which Achilles' prototype presents more subtly. However, in doing so it dilutes the strangeness of the phoenix necessary for it to operate as an 'agent of revelation'. There is not sufficient distance in the representation between the bird and the girl for the phoenix to function obliquely as a figure of Leucippe. Indeed, this seems to be acknowledged by the fact that Hodges does not, as Achilles does, use a word that can denote genitals. In the translation, the priest 'shows each part' of the bird and gives it 'a full triall', a much less specific and sexual a description.

That it is unacceptable to scrutinise a girl's genitals is underscored by an episode in the following chapter. While out walking, Leucippe has fallen to the ground and is thrashing about, 'eyes rolling'. Menelaus and Clitophon attempt to help:

Συνέντες οὖν ὅτι μανία εἴη τις [ἐπὶ] τὸ κακόν, βίᾳ συλλαβόντες ἐπειρώμεθα κρατεῖν· ἡ δὲ προσεπάλαιεν ἡμῖν, οὐδὲν φροντίζουσα κρύπτειν ὅσα γυνὴ μὴ ὁρᾶσθαι θέλει.

We realized that the problem was some madness, and so we grabbed her forcibly and tried to get the better of her. She struggled with us, with no thought to conceal the parts that a woman would not wish to be seen.

---

[78] The *OED* cites several examples of this usage, of which these are two: 'Dr. Moulin and myself . . . made our Anatomies together . . . we shew'd to the Royal Society that all Flat-bill'd Birds . . . had three pairs of Nerves' (J. Clayton 1688 in Phil Trans XVII, 990); 'he had formerly cut in pieces a number of living Creatures with his own hands to make Anatomies' (*Life of Father Sarpi* 1676, 16); *The Oxford English Dictionary*, second edition (1989), prepared by J. A. Simpson and E. S. C. Weiner, vol. 1, 441.

(It transpires that an Egyptian soldier named Gorgias was so enamoured of the beautiful maiden that he concocted an aphrodisiac with the aim of seducing her. However, he bungled this plot by administering the potion undiluted and causing Leucippe to go temporarily insane.)[79] The last phrase, 'with no thought to conceal the parts that a woman would not wish to be seen', is a telling comment on the direction of Clitophon's gaze during the crisis. He knows about Leucippe's indiscretion because he has witnessed it, seeing precisely what she wants no one to see and, acting as focaliser, invites the reader to follow his line of sight. It is also a clear statement of the visual intrusion that Leucippe has unwittingly brought upon herself. In Euripides' *Hecuba* Polyxena scrupulously attempts to avoid such an intrusion:

> She, although she was dying,
> still took great care to fall in a becoming fashion to the ground
> hiding from male eyes what should remain hidden (κρύπτουσ'
> ἃ κρύπτειν ὄμματ' ἀρσένων χρεών). (568–70)[80]

If a dying tragic heroine can manage to cover herself modestly, how much more shameful – and comically titillating – that Leucippe cannot.

That no sane woman would permit herself to be exposed is reinforced by the recovered Leucippe's reaction upon learning of her indecency: Ἡ δὲ ᾐσχύνετο ἀκροωμένη καὶ ἠρυθρία καὶ ἐνόμιζε τότε αὐτὰ ποιεῖν, 'She was embarrassed to hear it and blushed as if she had been performing those actions now' (4.17.5–6). Ironically, Leucippe's unwitting self-exposure while under the influence of the drug highlights the impossiblity, the outrageousness, of a similar examination happening under normal circumstances. The reader's voyeuristic desire to see this happen – to see Leucippe exposed and scrutinised – is deferred and mapped onto the figure of the phoenix. The bird operates as an analogic model of the *parthenos*, exposing Leucippe by proxy. Description constructs a second order of narrativity underscoring the main narrative, and

---

[79] McLeod (1969) analyses the symptoms and diagnosis of Leucippe's 'fit' and compares them to cases discussed in Celsus, Erasistratus, Asclepiades and Galen. He concludes that the episode is a comic and hyperbolic representation of Erasistratean dogma.

[80] She does not, of course, avoid the voyeuristic attentions of the Achaean army and the theatre audience. The description of her sacrifice is sexualised and objectifying.

the fantasies teasingly suggested by the narrative are played out in the metanarrative. We can conclude that the description of the bird, far from being a frustrating irrelevancy or merely a 'tone setter', plays a crucial role in the narrative's soliciting and thwarting of desire and the novel's erotic education.

If the phoenix is anthropomorphised, then Leucippe is simultaneously beastified. The implicit analogy between her and the bird encourages the reader to look upon her as an animal. The general Charmides does this at 4.3.1–2. He catches sight of Leucippe and at once desires her.[81] This occurs when the company is assembled to look at a hippopotamus that has just been captured:

Καλεῖ δὴ πρὸς τὴν θέαν ἡμᾶς ὁ στρατηγός· καί ἡ Λευκίππη συμπαρῆν. Ἡμεῖς μὲν οὖν ἐπὶ τὸ θηρίον τοὺς ὀφθαλμοὺς εἴχομεν, ἐπὶ Λευκίππην δὲ ὁ στρατηγός· καὶ εὐθὺς ἑαλώκει. Βουλόμενος οὖν ἡμᾶς παραμένειν ἐπὶ πλεῖστον, ἵν' ἔχῃ τοῖς ὀφθαλμοῖς αὐτοῦ χαρίζεσθαι, περιπλοκὰς ἐζήτει λόγων, πρῶτον μὲν τὴν φύσιν τοῦ θηρίου καταλέγων, εἶτα καὶ τὸν τρόπον τῆς ἄγρας.

The general invited us to behold the spectacle, and Leucippe was also present. While all our eyes were on the beast, the general's were on Leucippe. He was immediately captivated; and so, wishing us to prolong our sojourn with him for as long as possible so that he could gratify his eyes, he sought to weave elaborate pretexts, giving us a catalogue first of the beast's attributes, then of the means of his capture. (4.3.1–2)

Clitophon then gives us one such report, as if quoting what Charmides had said. Expounding upon the lifestyle of the hippo is, we are told, a pretext to gaze upon Leucippe for as long as possible, another example of using animal lore to facilitate desire, as Clitophon did in the episode in the garden. Leucippe is present as a spectator but she is denied the opportunity actively to spectate. The subject function of looking is reserved for the male and instead Leucippe becomes part of the spectacle. Moreover, the general gazes at Leucippe while the crowd gazes at the hippo and the sentence is structured, with the *men . . . de* clause at 4.3.1, so as to highlight the parallel between animal and woman as objects of

[81] This is a reversal of the viewing relations in Plato's *Charmides*, whose dialogue and star Achilles' character evokes. In Plato, it is Charmides who is beautiful and the object of obsessive visual attention. Socrates feels awe (*thauma*) at the sight of him and observes that the men who are gazing at the youth 'like a statue' are astounded (*ekpeplegmenoi*) by him: *Charm*. 154c. On this dialogue and vision, see von Reden and Goldhill (1999).

the gaze. Leucippe is not just compared to an animal (as she was to the peacock at 1.19.1), but instead is placed in paradigmatic relationship to it. 'River horse' and 'white horse' – Leuc-ippe – are specular reflections of each other, parallel objects of scrutiny.

The animalising of woman, first theorised in Clinias' *sententia*, can be seen to be an organising principle in the narrative. Women, in particular Leucippe, are compared to animals (besides the peacock, woman is likened to a lion clawing and scratching at 2.22.1 and the proverbial jackdaw at 2.38.2), revealed through the analogic model of an animal (the phoenix) and looked at with an animalising gaze (the hippopotamus).[82] Apart from the story of the viper and the eel and the creatures in Conops and Satyrus' fables, men are not beastified in these ways. On no occasion does a woman look upon a man as an animal. Susanne Kappeler, adapting John Berger's study of how humans look at animals, argues that such a scopic regime is characteristic of patriarchy:

Woman, in the history of culture, has occupied a place on a par with animals. She has been recognised as similar but different... [the man] does not like being seen, abrogating the subjectivity of his own look and becoming the object of another's look. The subject function of looking must be preserved and reserved for him.[83]

Viewing women as animals empowers the (male) viewer and 'others' the woman. This characterises the dominant scopic order in *Leucippe and Clitophon*, exemplified in the hippopotamus passage, but the dynamic in this episode is more complex than I have so far allowed. First, although it is Leucippe who is gazed at as the hippopotamus is gazed at, it is the gazer, Charmides, who is ensnared (ἑαλώκει), as the hippopotamus is ensnared. Her powers of attraction do not translate to affording her any real or practical power and Charmides' subjectivity is not seriously threatened. Nevertheless, in gazing at Leucippe in a way that animalises her, Charmides simultaneously animalises himself. Beastification implicates both viewer and viewed.

[82] There is an implicit parallel for the animalising gaze in Xenophon's *Ephesiaca*, where Anthia is sold into prostitution (5.7.1ff.). She is forced to exhibit herself in front of the brothel and attracts a crowd of admirers. This episode bears similarities to Antiphon's description of the captivity and exhibition of the peacock in Athens, during the Peloponnesian War (reported in Athenaeus, *Deipn.* 9 397C); cf. Cartledge (1990).
[83] Kappeler (1986), 65 and cf. 63–81; Berger (1980).

Second, the reader, too, is ensnared; he or she is a captive audience to Charmides' lecturing. Charmides' ogling of Leucippe and his desire to keep looking at her for as long as possible lead us to expect a description of Leucippe's physical appearance, her face, body and dress. However, we are not allowed to participate vicariously in Charmides' voyeurism. Instead, we are positioned as Leucippe's double, forced to endure listening to a long description of the hippopotamus. This may have its own intrinsic interest, but is surely no substitute for a closer look at Leucippe. Here description operates as a screen, concealing rather than revealing the real focus of enquiry. The reader, thus blinkered, is once again made aware of his desire, but is unable to satisfy it.

Speech and spectacle

Leucippe's greatest spectacle, where she baits her audience to witness her being tortured, is the speech in defence of her virginity at the end of the sixth book. Angered by Leucippe's continued refusal of his advances, Thersander hits her across the face, calls her a slave and a whore and asserts his authority over her (6.20.3). Leucippe replies that even if she has to be dominated, he will not force himself upon her: Κἂν τυραννεῖν ἐθέλῃς, κἀγὼ τυραννεῖσθαι, πλὴν οὐ βιάσῃ. Sosthenes urges Thersander to use firmer treatment, whips and 'countless tortures' (μυρίαις βασάνοις) but Leucippe invites him to do his worst:

"Πείσθητι τῷ Σωσθένει", φησὶν ἡ Λευκίππη· "συμβουλεύει γὰρ καλῶς· τὰς βασάνους παράστησον. Φερέτω τροχόν· ἰδοὺ χεῖρες, τεινέτω. Φερέτω καὶ μάστιγας· ἰδοὺ νῶτος, τυπτέτω. Κομιζέτω πῦρ· ἰδοὺ σῶμα, καιέτω. Φερέτω καὶ σίδηρον· ἰδοὺ δέρη, σφαζέτω. Ἀγῶνα θεάσασθε καινόν· πρὸς πάσας τὰς βασάνους ἀγωνίζεται μία γυνὴ καὶ πάντα νικᾷ."

'You should do as Sosthenes says,' replied Leucippe, 'it is good counsel. Prepare the tortures! Someone bring in the wheel and stretch my hands: here they are! Someone bring in the whips, too, and beat my back: here it is! Someone bring in fire and burn my body: here it is! Someone bring in a blade and slice up my skin: here it is! You will behold a novel kind of contest: one woman competes against all your tortures, and conquers them all. (6.21.1–2)

She then berates him for assaulting a virgin in the city of the virgin Artemis, to which Thersander replies with scornful scepticism.

Leucippe gives an even more impassioned defence of her virginal status and imagines the praise which people will bestow upon her for remaining a *parthenos*. She renews the call for weapons to be used against her: ὁπλίζου τοίνυν, ἤδη λάμβανε κατ' ἐμοῦ τὰς μάστιγας, τὸν τροχόν, τὸ πῦρ, τὸν σίδηρον, 'So, arm yourself, bring on the whips, the wheel, the fire, the knife, and use them on me!' (6.22.4). She concludes with a *tour de force* which celebrates her transcendence above physical torture:

Ἐγὼ δὲ καὶ γυμνὴ καὶ μόνη καὶ γυνή, καὶ ἓν ὅπλον ἔχω τὴν ἐλευθερίαν, ἢ μήτε πληγαῖς κατακόπτεται μήτε σιδήρῳ κατατέμνεται μήτε πυρὶ κατακαίεται. Οὐκ ἀφήσω ποτὲ ταύτην ἐγώ. Κἂν καταφλέγῃς, οὐχ οὕτως θερμὸν εὑρήσεις τὸ πῦρ.

I am unarmed, alone, and a woman: freedom is my only weapon, but it will not be battered by your blows, nor cut up by your knife, nor scorched by your fire. My freedom I will never renounce – not I! Even if you set it ablaze, you will find the fire is not hot enough. (6.22.4)

This is a magisterial marshalling of parataxis, repetition and metaphor. Her whole oration is marked by the melodramatic grandiosity of the *controversiae* and *suasoriae*.[84] It has all the more impact for coming at the end of the book.[85] If the novel itself finishes with an underwhelming ending, each of its previous seven chapters punches home with a climax. Books 1, 3 and 4 end with spectacle: extravagant descriptions of, respectively, Leucippe's face, the phoenix, and the crocodile (an interesting grouping of *thaumata*). Books 5 and 7 close with moments of high drama important for the plot: Clitophon and Melite making love (Book 5) and the reunion of Clitophon and Leucippe after Clitophon's release from custody (Book 7). Book 2 ends with the *sunkrisis* on sexuality (without an *epimuthion*, as discussed above), and Book 6 culminates in this impassioned aria by Leucippe.

The scene is all the more conspicuous because it comes during the course of a narrative that has repeatedly put constraints

---

[84] An orator reported in Seneca's *Controversiae* 1.7 imagines a wronged father railing against his estranged son in language very similar to that employed by Leucippe: 'Call for whips, tear my wrinkled flesh . . . use fire on me, use flames to finish off this half-dead shape that breathes only to suffer insult – for it cannot be snuffed out. If that is not enough, do what you say that even the pirates did not do – cut off my hands . . . Where is your sword? Draw it! (1.7.9).

[85] On the closural power of book divisions, see Fowler (1997), 88–93.

on Leucippe's speech. She is far from being a mute character: she takes part in dialogue, notably her robust response to her mother's accusations of unchastity, and she narrates events, such as her long speech in the final book, where she relates how the second *Scheintod* happened. However, her range of verbal communications is limited. Most significantly, she alone of the major characters in the novel never speaks sententiously. We are never given the opportunity to hear the law according to Leucippe. She is conspicuously absent from the debate concerning whether boys or girls make the best lovers. Asleep below deck, Leucippe, like Semonides' bee-woman – the only 'good' woman in his misogynist catalogue – refrains from sitting with others 'when they are talking about sex'. When Leucippe experiences emotions (shame, grief and anger at 2.29.1–5) they are pronounced upon sententiously, but it is Clitophon who analyses, not Leucippe. Furthermore, she is physically silenced at 6.4.2 when Sosthenes gags her (τὸ στόμα ἐπισχών), and images of the myth of Philomela which recur through the narrative and culminate in the *ekphrasis* of the story at 5.3.3 adumbrate and reflect her voicelessness. Earlier in the novel (3.11.2), Leucippe and Clitophon are in shock after being captured by bandits and Clitophon asks Leucippe why she is silent. She replies that her voice has died (τέθνηκεν ἡ φωνή) before her soul: a wry and oxymoronic moment which nods self-consciously towards Leucippe's relative voicelessness.

In her one soliloquy Leucippe is compromised. It comes at 6.16.1–6, where she laments her imprisonment by Thersander and Sosthenes and addresses the absent Clitophon with fears for his safety. Her speech shows her to be strong and determined. She asserts herself as the daughter of a Byzantine general and the wife of Clitophon and warns Thersander not to underestimate her: Μή με νομίσῃς ἀνδράποδον εἶναι, Θέρσανδρε, 'Do not think I am a slave, Thersander' (6.16.4–5). However, Leucippe thinks that she is speaking to herself, but we know that Thersander and Sosthenes are listening at the door (6.15.4). This action is important in forwarding the plot, enabling Thersander to learn the truth about Leucippe's identity and her allegiance to Clitophon. However, the scene is also reminiscent of other 'listeners at keyhole' scenes, for example in Petronius, where Quartilla and Encolpius watch Giton and

Pannychis, and in the Apocrypha story where the elders peer at Susanna in her bath.[86] These episodes are more overtly voyeuristic than that in Achilles Tatius and more obviously sexual, but they serve to highlight the intrusion which the men's spying upon Leucippe constitutes. The reader's knowledge of their presence jeopardises the empathetic response to Leucippe which her soliloquy invites. We do not simply observe Leucippe speaking, but observe Thersander and Sosthenes observing Leucippe speaking. Moreover, the reader, who is also listening in to a private monologue, is positioned in a parallel relation to Thersander and Sosthenes. This forges a collusion between them and further distances the reader from Leucippe. Leucippe unwittingly divulges information to her enemies and thus proves not to be in control of her speech. A similar violation occurs with respect to her letter to Clitophon when it falls into the hands of Melite, who reads it and gleans information that was not for her to know. Both acts of communication provide an opportunity for Leucippe's privacy to be invaded, which qualifies, if not totally undermines, the agency afforded her through speech.

Leucippe's letter to Clitophon is forceful, resolute and efficacious in that it has a great impact on Clitophon. The letter is a selective revision of the narrative so far and Clitophon rereads it sentence by sentence, an interesting and pointed internal model of reading. Through her writing Leucippe conjures for herself an almost physical presence and Clitophon *sees her* through her words: ἅμα αὖθις ἐντυγχάνων τοῖς γράμμασιν, ὡς ἐκείνην δι' αὐτῶν βλέπων . . . (5.19.5). She lists the bodily violations which she has undergone, but without detailed description. Clitophon, however, is so moved by her account of being tortured that he sees (with the eyes of his soul, τῆς ψυχῆς τὰ ὄμματα) the tortures as if they are enacted before him (ἐδείκνυε τὰ ὁρώμενα ὡς δρώμενα, 5.19.6), an image obviously evocative of the first *Scheintod*, and which anticipates the spectacle at the end of Book 6. Leucippe's letter affords her agency and the power to influence characters and events from afar. In his reply, Clitophon sums up the paradoxical power of his *phantasia*, through which (in another uncanny moment) she achieves an absent

---

[86] The Book of Susanna in the Apocrypha. On which see Engel (1985); Steussy (1993).

presence: σὲ παρὼν παροῦσαν ὡς ἀποδημοῦσαν ὁρῶ διὰ γραμμάτων, 'I can visualise you in my presence, but I know that you are absent' (5.20.5). However, it is significant that the focus is on Leucippe's body and the abuses which she has endured and it ends with a firm statement of what she has been protecting: her chastity: Ἐγὼ δὲ ἔτι σοι ταῦτα γράφω παρθένος, 'As I write this, I am still a virgin' (5.18.6). Leucippe does act through speech, but the result – as with her speech at the end of Book 6 – is to emblazon her once again as an abused body and as spectacle.

In some respects, Leucippe's speech conforms to good Roman – and Stoic – values, especially in its final flourish that whatever they may do to her body, they cannot take away her freedom. It is a recurrent theme of Epictetus' discourse 'That we ought not to yearn for the things which are not under our control'[87] that when someone is in trouble, it is not a sign that god is displeased with him, but that god is displaying him as a 'witness before the rest of men' (μάρτυρι πρὸς τοὺς ἄλλους) that no external circumstances can cause harm, only the value an individual assigns to his predicament (3.24.114). Leucippe's speech echoes this vocabulary of 'witnessing' and imperviousness to external affliction. Habrocomes in Xenophon's *Ephesian Tales* makes a very similar statement to Leucippe's: 'I am a slave, but I know how to keep my vows. They have power over my body, but I have a free soul' (*Eph.* 2.4). Making a distinction between the violated body and unviolated mind, will or spirit, is a common motif in Latin literature. 'The will, not the body, makes one impure' says a character in a mime,[88] a sentiment echoed by Seneca's Phaedra: 'The mind makes one unchaste, not the circumstance.'[89] But it is Livy's Lucretia who most famously makes the distinction: 'My body has been violated, my mind is innocent';[90] and it is through and against her celebrated model of purity that Leucippe is presented here.

In its obsessive exaltation of virginity, Leucippe's oration also fashions her as a martyr, speaking with the voice of a Thecla or

---

[87] Arrian, *Discourses on Epictetus* 3.24.
[88] *Voluntas impudicum, non corpus facit* (Publilius Syrus 7.10).
[89] *Mens impudicam facere, non casus, solet* (line 735). For other references, see Boyle (1987), 180.
[90] *Corpus est tantum inviolatum, animus insons* (Livy 1.58.9).

an Eulalia. This invites a Christian perspective, or a perspective, at least, which is familiar with Christian literature. The generic similarities between the ancient novels and Christian writings, including martyrologies, are well established.[91] Their precise relations are open to debate, but a fairly symbiotic relationship of influences, in which pagan literature affected Christian and vice versa, is assumed here.[92] Like many female martyrs, Thecla, a heroine whose story is roughly contemporary with that of Leucippe, protects her virginity against all odds, in one version of the story even finding herself able to walk through a rock in order to escape from would-be rapists.[93] Virginity threatened and defended is a recurrent theme in Christian tales, as it is in *Leucippe and Clitophon* and other Greek novels. The martyr Irene is sentenced to stand naked in

[91] In an important study, Frye argues that what became known as romance is in fact 'secular scripture', Frye (1976); Kermode (1979) analyses the Gospels as novelistic fictions. On similarities between the Apocryphal Acts and Greek novels, see von Dobschutz (1902) and Soder (1932), who identifies five main themes in the Apochryphal Acts (travelling, aretalogy, teratology, a philosophical and moral focus and desire) which, she argues, were borrowed from the Hellenistic novel. Clark (1984), ch. 4. compares the *Life of Melania the Younger* with the Hellenistic romance. Haight (1945), 48–80 discusses *The Acts of Paul and Thecla* and *The Acts of Xanthippe and Polyxena* as romances. Richard Pervo and Peter Brown have taken the view that the novels were appropriated by Christian writers. Thus Brown writes, 'The Christian authors of the Apochryphal Acts had only to replace a manifest destiny to the wedding bed, with which every pagan novel had ended, by the Apostle's call to continence': Brown (1988), 156. But even this suggests that there were two distinct genres that contaminated each other, whereas in fact the boundaries between the two are not so clearly demarcated.

[92] See the recent argument of Bowersock (1994), ch. 6. Chronology is not a problem here – the martyrologies were produced contemporaneously with or even before the Greek novels (e.g. the *Acts of Paul and Thecla* is dated to 140 CE and the martyrdom of Saint Perpetua to 200 CE). However, how Christian and pagan literature influenced each other is a matter for careful consideration. Bowersock interprets the episode at 2.2.1–6 describing the feast of Dionysus and the Harvest of Grapes as influenced by the Christian Eucharist. The line τοῦτό ἐστιν ὀπώρας ὕδωρ, τοῦτό ἐστιν αἷμα βότρυος (2.2.5) would appear to evoke the language of the Eucharist and, as Winkler suggests, 'If the resemblance of Dionysus's words and gesture to the Christian eucharistic rite is not accidental, it must surely be interpreted as parody', Winkler (1989), 192 n. 25. Bowersock's contention that 'in the rich texture of Achilles Tatius's novel, parody is an element so hard to find that it would be rash to invoke it here' (1994, 126) is a strangely humourless reading of the novel. If the allusion is deliberate, then at the very least the juxtaposition of Christian religious rite with the story of a drunken Dionysiac celebration, leading to an amorous encounter creates a parodic pastiche. Bowersock is right to reject the literalist reading of Smith (1975), that interprets 2.2.1–6 as a pagan precedent for the eucharist. The Byzantine novels, however, use eucharistic imagery in an overt way, as Burton (1998) discusses.

[93] Hägg (1983), 159. See also Haight (1945), 48–65; Burrus (1987), 47–57: 'Common Tale Types Underlying the Novel and the Thecla story'.

a brothel, like Xenophon's Anthia, but remains inviolate under the protection of the Holy Spirit.[94] Martyrdoms are distinguished for their spectacular displays, with an almost relentless focus on the body and the instruments of torture which defile it.[95] Eulalia suffers her skin being clawed to the bone with a hook. Agnes imagines the sword plunging into her chest, but in fact dies by decapitation. Although Leucippe ultimately escapes torture, the emphasis on body and weapons is suggestive enough. Leucippe calls for the wheel, whips, fire and the sword (6.21.1–2) and she inventories her bodily parts and the injuries appropriate to each in a markedly theatrical way. One might say Leucippe 'makes Anatomie of herself'.

Μαρτύρησον... ἰδοὺ... ἰδοὺ... ἰδοὺ... ἰδοὺ... θεάσασθε – the repeated injunctions to look invite us to visualise her body exposed for assault. She repeatedly enumerates the weapons that will be used to hurt her. Typically, martyrs submit willingly, even eagerly to their punishments. Eulalia is *laeta .. et intrepida*, 'happy and bold', as she faces mutilation.[96] Perpetua guides the sword that will kill her to her throat.[97] Leucippe is similarly defiant, and imagines the public adulation which will follow, as indeed it did for the martyrs. She goads Thersander and Sosthenes into punishing her for the very reason that their shamelessness will bring her 'a more fulsome encomium' (ἐγκώμιόν ... πλεῖον, 6.22.2) and again 'a greater encomium' (τὸ δὲ μεῖζον ἐγκώμιον, 6.22.3) and she imagines, with an indulgence typical of martyrological writings, what these encomia might be and with what words of praise people will remember her. In one sense, of course, Leucippe's fantasy is an ironic, self-referential comment on the book itself, which can be read as an encomium to Leucippe.

---

[94] *The Martyrdom of Saints Agape, Irene, and Chione at Saloniki* 5.10–6.20 in Musurillo (1972). See also the story of Trophima in *The Acts of Andrew the Apostle*, the story of the virgin in Ambrose's *De Virginibus* (2.4.22) and the account of Agnes in Prudentius' *Peristephanon* 14. Cf. Burrus (1987), 65, n. 29. Doody (1996), 58 makes the comparison with St Catherine of Alexandria; cf. Ephesians 6.10–17.
[95] On martyrdom as spectacle see Potter (1993). On the display of weapons as part of the torture process, see Seneca, *Epistles* 14.6: 'the spectacle overcomes those who would have patiently withstood the suffering', *specie enim vincuntur qui patientia restitissent*.
[96] Prudentius, *Peristephanon* 3.131–45. On Eulalia see Malamud (1990), 282–8.
[97] *The Acts of SS Perpetua and Felicity* 21.9–10.

One approach to Leucippe's speech, which gains support from a Christian framing, is that the values espoused by Leucippe are to be viewed in a positive light. Her aria is propaganda for the sanctity of virginity until marriage. There are three factors which, I suggest, modify this interpretation, and which merit some discussion. First, the almost obsessive emphasis on the sanctity of virginity in Leucippe's speech is at odds with the lack of premium placed on virginity elsewhere in the novel. Leucippe herself is only too willing to sleep with Clitophon for the first half of the narrative. Her subsequent refusal to do so is not due to a sincere change of heart or a sudden discovery of moral inhibitions, but because an external force, Artemis, who visits her in a dream, commands it (4.1.3–5). It is clear that it is compliance rather than eagerness on Leucippe's part which presses her to abstain from sexual activity, as she declares herself to be disappointed by the delay (4.1.5).[98] Unlike the heroines in other novels and in martyr tales, Leucippe becomes 'the good virgin' by a formula abruptly imposed upon her halfway through the novel, not through her own desire and adherence to virtue. At the beginning of the novel, Leucippe's reason for leaving home and eloping with Clitophon (to get away from her mother's sight, 2.30.1) delights because, whilst it may very well represent the true feelings of many a young girl, it is far from being a literary cliché.[99] During the course of the narrative, Leucippe goes from being an individual to becoming a mythic abstraction, a stereotype, which is why her defences of her virginity in her diatribe against Thersander, and in the scene where she is tested by Pan, are not entirely convincing.

Moreover, Leucippe's values do not seem to be shared by the other main characters. Melite has no compunction about her adulterous liaison with Clitophon and escapes detection and society's approbation purely on a technicality in the wording of the chastity

---

[98] In some early editions of Achilles Tatius these lines were attributed to Clitophon, and Leucippe's speech ended with Artemis' injunction, presumably because editors deemed it more fitting that the hero should be frustrated by the postponement of the lovers' consummation than the heroine; Gaselee (1984), 190.

[99] Napolitano argues that the portrayal of Leucippe is 'vivo e realistico . . . lontano dal rigido modello tradizionale'; Napolitano (1983–4), 88. This is true of her representation in the first half of the novel, but she is then made to conform to a 'traditional model'.

test. There is no comment from the narrator that frowns upon her acquittal and brazen deceit. The reader is at no stage invited to disapprove of the moral standards here displayed, an omission which encourages us instead to join in the conspiracy (a conspiracy which excludes Leucippe) and appreciate its humour. Moreover, Clitophon does not reciprocate Leucippe's fidelity. There is a parallel for the hero's infidelity in Daphnis' encounter with Lykainion in Longus' novel. However, unlike Daphnis, who wanted to be initiated into sexual experience so that he could consummate his love for Chloe and who did not immediately share his knowledge with Chloe for fear of harming her, Clitophon has no honourable reasons for sleeping with Melite. He tries to justify his disloyalty thus:

ἔπαθόν τι ἀνθρώπινον καὶ ἀληθῶς ἐφοβήθην τὸν Ἔρωτα, μή μοι γένηται μήνιμα ἐκ τοῦ θεοῦ, καὶ ἄλλως ὅτι Λευκίππην ἀπειλήφειν, καὶ ὅτι μετὰ ταῦτα τῆς Μελίτης ἀπαλλάττεσθαι ἔμελλον, καὶ ὅτι οὐδὲ γάμος ἔτι τὸ πραττόμενον ἦν, ἀλλὰ φάρμακον ὥσπερ ψυχῆς νοσούσης.

I felt a natural human reaction. I was also genuinely scared of Eros, that he might visit his wrath upon me; and, what was more, I considered how I had regained Leucippe, how I was about to get rid of Melite, how the act to be performed was a matter not of marriage but of the remedy for a kind of illness of the soul. (5.27.2)

The first in his tricolon of excuses is feeling a human reaction, the second a sincere (ἀληθῶς) fear of the god, the third a rambling and dismissive (καὶ ἄλλως . . .) justification. This last excuse is the one which rings true and with a neat anticlimactic touch exposes the previous reasons as disingenuous. Clitophon freely admits that he did not resist Melite's embraces and that they greatly enjoyed themselves, compounding his offence with a sententious statement on the pleasure in acting spontaneously. Clitophon's blithe infidelity ends the fifth book of the novel and Leucippe's fearsome loyalty ends the sixth book. The structural parallel between the two episodes highlights the contrast between the behaviour of the hero and that of the heroine. All of this operates to isolate Leucippe and her values from the rest of the characters. This in turn has the effect of elevating her to a higher status than her companions;

she provides the one example of purity in a treacherous world. However, it can also operate to undermine Leucippe; her morals seem incongruous in isolation.

Second, if we read Clinias' 'common maxims' with respect to Leucippe's behaviour, they too colour our reception of her protests. He offers the following advice on the role of speech in seduction:

Σὺ μηδὲν μὲν εἴπῃς πρὸς τὴν παρθένον Ἀφροδίσιον, τὸ δὲ ἔργον ζήτει πῶς γένηται σιωπῇ. Παῖς γὰρ καὶ παρθένος ὅμοιοι μέν εἰσιν εἰς αἰδῶ· πρὸς δὲ τὴν τῆς Ἀφροδίτης χάριν κἂν γνώμης ἔχωσιν, ἃ πάσχουσιν ἀκούειν οὐ θέλουσι· τὴν γὰρ αἰσχύνην κεῖσθαι νομίζουσιν ἐν τοῖς ῥήμασι. Γυναῖκας μὲν γὰρ εὐφραίνει καὶ τὰ ῥήματα· παρθένος δὲ τοὺς μὲν ἔξωθεν ἀκροβολισμοὺς τῶν ἐραστῶν εἰς πεῖραν φέρει καὶ ἄφνω συντίθεται τοῖς νεύμασιν. ἐὰν δὲ αἰτήσῃς τὸ ἔργον προσελθών, ἐκπλήξεις αὐτῆς τὰ ὦτα τῇ φωνῇ, καὶ ἐρυθριᾷ καὶ μισεῖ τὸ ῥῆμα καὶ λοιδορεῖσθαι δοκεῖ· κἂν ὑποσχέσθαι θέλῃ τὴν χάριν, αἰσχύνεται. Τότε γὰρ πάσχειν νομίζει τὸ ἔργον, ὅτε μᾶλλον τὴν πεῖραν ἐκ τῆς τῶν λόγων ἡδονῆς ἀκούει.

Take care not to use erotic language to the girl: it is the act that you should aim to achieve, and in silence. Boys and maids are equally shy: even if they are inclined towards the pleasures of Aphrodite, they do not want to hear about what they are undergoing. They think that the shame lies in talking about it. Now mature women, *they* enjoy talking about it, but a maiden is different. She puts up with the border skirmishes of reconnoitring lovers, and tends to acquiesce suddenly with a nod; but if you mount a full-scale assault, and ask her outright to perform the act, you will stun her ears with your voice. She will blush, condemn your words, and consider them an affront. Even if she is willing to promise you gratification, she will be ashamed to do so. You see, the pleasure she derives from your words leads her to think that she is actually experiencing the act, and not simply listening to your attempts. (1.10.2–4)

In this passage Clinias lays down the law about language, gender and sexual status. According to these cultural codes, a person's sexual status determines their relationship to language. The *pais* and the *parthenos* take affront rather than pleasure at verbal references to sex; they are compromised merely by listening to accounts of 'the pleasures of Aphrodite'. Women – *gunaikes* – on the other hand, take pleasure in the words, εὐφραίνει ... τὰ ῥήματα. Clinias posits a direct correlation between sexual activity and speech. The axis of differentiation is that of age or experience rather than gender – both boys and girls feel disconcerted by sex talk. However, it is the girl who is the focus of Clinias' advice as he sets out the programme for Clitophon's seduction of Leucippe.

The view that a female's speech was influenced by and in turn indicative of her sexual experience is enshrined in the linguistic double meaning of the Greek word *stoma*, meaning both oral and genital mouth or lips. Giulia Sissa documents medical writings that chart the paralleling of and interaction between the two orifices.[100] Galen, for example, compared the clitoris to the uvula, for the clitoris protects the uterus from the cold in the same way that the uvula protects the trachea. The logic runs that a female who opens one of her mouths is thought to open the other. Loose talk suggests sexual promiscuity.[101] Conversely, sexual activity will affect a woman's speech. For a *parthenos*, as Clinias states, taking pleasure in sexual words is almost to perform a physical consummation; it is collusion, complicity. The suggestion of sex is an approximation to the act itself.[102]

After his pronouncements on the differing pleasures in erotic speech enjoyed by adolescents and adults, Clinias continues with the following statement on a maiden's behaviour:

Κἂν μὲν προσῇ τις συνθήκη τῆς πράξεως, πολλάκις δὲ καὶ ἑκοῦσαι πρὸς τὸ ἔργον ἐρχόμεναι θέλουσι βιάζεσθαι δοκεῖν, ἵνα τῇ δόξῃ τῆς ἀνάγκης ἀποτρέπωνται τῆς αἰσχύνης τὸ ἑκούσιον.

And if you obtain some guarantee of action, often, when they come to the act, even if they are still willing, they want it to look as if they have been forced, seeking to deflect the charge of shameful consent by claiming coercion. (1.10.6)

The belief that girls dissemble, pretending not to want sexual attentions when in reality they do, has a long history in Graeco-Roman literature.[103] But it is in the sex manual that this becomes an explicit philosophy. The *praeceptor* in Ovid's *Ars Amatoria* suggests that the lover should mix kisses with his wheedling words, whether or

---

[100] Sissa (1990), 53–67, 166–7.
[101] Cf. Hanson and Armstrong (1986); Nemesianus, *Eclogues* 4.11 and Soranus, *Gynaecology* 3.1.7; see Brown (1988), 101–2, n. 81; and the rich material and discussion in Gleason (1995), 82–102. More broadly on the gendering of speech in the archaic and Classical periods, see the essays collected in Lardinois and McClure (2001), especially McClure's introduction.
[102] A striking example of a virgin's inability to speak about desire is preserved in a fragment of the Ninus romance: see Morales (1999).
[103] I have discussed this in greater detail in relation to Pseudo-Theocritus, *Idylls* 27 and Musaeus' *Hero and Leander* in Morales (1999).

not the woman wishes to give them. If she fights and admonishes the lover:

> It's all right to use force: that sort of force goes down well with the girls: what in fact they love to yield they'd often rather have stolen. Rough seduction delights them, the audacity of near rape is a compliment – so the girl who could have been forced yet somehow got away unscathed may feign delight but in fact feels sadly let down. (*AA* 1.673–8; cf. also *Amores* 1.5)

Woman's unwillingness to have sex has no place in this rapist's charter, which appropriates her expressions of dissent to signify the contrary: consent.[104] Conversely, a woman's ostensible gladness at not having been forced is inverted to evince her disappointment. As Richlin writes, 'The pupil here is led to believe that women do have emotions with which to enjoy the experience, but there is apparently no way to tell for sure . . . The deletion of women's voice here is even more thorough than in the tale of Philomela.'[105]

Clinias does not go to the same extremes as Ovid; he advises Clitophon not to use force if the maiden remains obstinate, as she is not yet sufficiently softened. However, both Ovid and Clinias argue that maidens typically express consent as dissent. If consent, intrinsic to the act of seduction, is fashioned as dissent then it is impossible to draw with any certainty the boundary between seduction and rape, between *peitho* and *bia*. Later in the narrative, Clitophon interprets Leucippe's response to his advances as conforming to this pattern of behaviour. He reads her show of dissent as willing compliance:

> Καὶ ἅμα λέγων τὴν χεῖρα βιαιότερον περιέβαλλον καὶ ἐφίλουν ἐλευθεριώτερον· ἡ δὲ ἠνείχετο, κωλύουσα δῆθεν.
>
> With these words, I clasped her more forcibly and began to kiss more freely. She acquiesced, with a show of resistance. (2.7.7)

Κωλύουσα δῆθεν is an imprecise phrase. Δῆθεν usually has the sense of 'I suppose', or 'doubtless', often with an ironic overtone, like the Latin *scilicet*. It is used (normally in a ὡς clause) to signify pretence, and this is the sense which translators have brought out.[106]

---

[104] A scenario dramatised in *Amores* 1.5.   [105] Richlin (1992c), 169.
[106] Winkler has 'with only a token resistance'; 'while pretending to resist' (Gaselee); 'en résistant, du moins en apparence' (Garnaud).

That this is Clitophon's subjective evaluation is highlighted by his admission, a few lines later, that he does not know how Leucippe felt. A serving maid disturbs the couple kissing and they spring apart. Clitophon comments:

ἐγὼ μὲν ἄκων καὶ λυπούμενος, ἡ δὲ οὐκ οἶδ' ὅπως εἶχεν.

I was unwilling and suffering, she – well, I do not know what her emotions were. (2.8.1)

Power is, above all else, the right to define reality. Leucippe is denied this right; her consent is redefined, for the sake of reputation no less, as dissent. If consent is fashioned as dissent then, conversely, dissent can easily be read as consent. This is what happens in the pictorial representations of violence, which can be read as ciphers for Leucippe. As has been noted, Andromeda is depicted in terms that enhance her attractiveness, through her terror. In the *ekphrasis* of Europa, the reactions of Europa's companions suggest that she has been forcibly abducted, which is consistent with most other versions of the myth, but Europa herself is conveyed without sign of any protest.

Of course, Clinias' advice concerning a maiden's unwillingness ever to be seen consenting to sex, even when she does desire it, is offered in the context of aiding Clitophon to seduce Leucippe and with their relationship in mind, not in anticipation of Thersander's attempted seduction. I am not suggesting that Leucippe's aria in defence of her virginity is designed to be read as the inverse – an expression of consent, or desire for a relationship with Thersander. Rather, the paradigmatic and paraded fashioning of women's expressions of dissent as consent, theorised in Clinias' *sententia*, undermines both of these concepts and renders Leucippe's expressions of them if not meaningless, then questionable. The reader comes to Leucippe's speech at the end of the novel having already absorbed the message that you cannot take a girl's expression of unwillingness to grant sexual favours at face value. Leucippe is given strong words of refusal, and yet her vocabulary for expressing dissent has already been neutralised. This raises the question as to whether there can be a place for a 'good virgin' in a novel which presents itself as, amongst other things, an erotic handbook.

This leads to my third point, that the analogic representations of Leucippe (Leucippe as figured through ekphrastic, mythic and oneiric representations and as revealed through the phoenix) and the experiences of sexual exposure and violence which Leucippe undergoes, both literally and vicariously (during her 'epilepsy', and the first two scenes of *Scheintod*), taint Leucippe and, more specifically, compromise her *parthenia*. Presumably, Leucippe considers herself a virgin because she has not had intercourse. That physical penetration is the criterion for losing one's virginity is implied in the exchange at 8.6.15–8.7.1. Having explained how the virginity test works, the priest of Artemis expresses concern that Leucippe does not act precipitously. If she is a *parthenos* then there is nothing to fear, but he tentatively suggests that this might not be the case:

εἰ δὲ οὐ, αὐτοὶ γὰρ ἴστε οἷα εἰκὸς ἐν τοσαύταις αὐτὴν ἐπιβουλαῖς γενομένην ἄκουσαν . . .

if not – after all, you yourselves know full well what is likely to have happened to one who found herself, albeit unwillingly, caught up in the midst of so many intrigues . . . (8.6.15)

Leucippe refuses to let the priest finish his sentence and boldly asserts her resolution to stand trial. He congratulates her, not only for her *sophrosune* but for her *tuche* (8.7.1). The priest's words suggest that *parthenia* is a physical condition which could be lost against one's will, taken by force, and that it is not just Leucippe's moral character which has preserved her virginity but also good luck. However, there is little consensus in ancient thought about what constitutes *parthenia* and loss of *parthenia*.[107] Indeed, there are other moments in the novel which appear to recognise this difficulty. At 2.28.2 Leucippe says: Εἰ παρθενίας ἔστι τις δοκιμασία, δοκίμασον, 'If there be a test for virginity, apply it to me.' In his letter to Leucippe, Clitophon writes: μαθήσῃ τὴν σήν με παρθενίαν μεμιμημένον, εἴ τις ἔστι καὶ ἐν τοῖς ἀνδράσι παρθενία, 'learn that I have imitated your virginity, if there be a male equivalent of virginity' (5.20.5). At 8.5.7 he says: Εἴ τις ἄρα ἔστιν ἀνδρὸς παρθενία, ταύτην κἀγὼ μέχρι τοῦ παρόντος πρὸς Λευκίππην ἔχω, 'If there be such a thing as virginity in a man, I have retained it up to the

---

[107] See Sissa (1990).

present day, as far as Leucippe is concerned.' These lines convey the inexactitude and inscrutability of *parthenia*. Uncertainty about whether the condition exists in men prompts consideration of what it means in women. Is *parthenia* an absolute state or can it be viewed, as Clitophon presents it, with qualification?

This subject was hotly debated by several writers, roughly contemporaneous with Achilles Tatius. Seneca's *Controversiae* 1.2 argues the case of the 'Prostitute Priestess':

> A virgin was captured by pirates and sold; she was bought by a pimp and made a prostitute. When men came to her, she begged for money. When she failed to get a donation from a soldier who came to her, he struggled with her and tried to use force; she killed him. She was accused, acquitted and sent back to her family. She seeks a priesthood.

The law states: 'A priestess must be chaste and of chaste parents, pure and of pure parents.' The orators' arguments mainly pivot upon what constitutes chastity and purity. Similarities of situation and theme between this rhetorical exercise and the 'virgin despite all odds' scenes in some of the Greek novels have been noted,[108] and the lines of argument taken by the declaimers can be of help to us in assessing the representation of Leucippe. Some orators are for the maiden's ordination, arguing that to have preserved her chastity even in a brothel, she must be divinely protected (1.2.17–21), and commenting on her dignity and pride (1.2.17). As we have seen, this is one perspective from which to view Leucippe; as an almost holy figure, distinguished by her pride and dignity, like a martyr. However, other orators question her chastity, for reasons which include the following. Publius Vinicius, 1.2.3: 'I should call you unfit for the priesthood if you had merely passed through a brothel', 'every part of her body was inspected – and handled'; Cestius Pius, 1.2.7: 'You offered yourself, a girl in a brothel: even if nobody raped you, the place itself did so' (*iam te ut nemo violaverit, locus ipse violavit*). These suggest that it is not solely sexual intercourse, or even physical contact with a man which defines loss of chastity, but that the girl is also defiled by her environment. This could equally be said about Leucippe; her *parthenia* is compromised

---

[108] Kérenyi (1927), Haight (1936), ch. 4; Richlin (1996). On *Controv.* 1.2 and protocols of declamation, see Richlin (1992a), 16–18.

by the company of sexually aggressive men and by the eroticised 'environment' of the narrative. Thersander points out that she loves an adulterer and spent many nights in the company of pirates and concludes that far from being a *parthenos*, she is a whore: ἐγὼ μέν σε καὶ πεπορνεῦσθαι δοκῶ, 'I reckon you are a whore' (6.20.3); Παρθένος; ... ὦ τόλμης καὶ γέλωτος ..., A virgin? ... What audacity! How amusing!' (6.21.3); τὸ δὲ τῆς ψευδοπαρθένου ταύτης ἑταίρας ..., 'this fake virgin, this whore' (8.3.3). The orator Publius Asprenas declares: 'No woman is chaste enough if an enquiry has to be held about her' (1.2.10). This is an opinion which seems to be shared by Leucippe's mother, Pantheia, who rejects the very idea of having Leucippe's virginity tested, for the shame which having the event witnessed would bring:

'"Ἔτι καὶ τοῦτο", ἔφη ἡ Πάνθεια, "λείπεται, ἵνα καὶ μετὰ μαρτύρων δυστυχῶμεν."

'That', said Pantheia, 'would cap it all – that our misfortune should be witnessed publicly too.' (2.28.3)

Leucippe's insistence that Sosthenes bear witness to her mistreatment, and the public examination of her virginity, were exactly what Pantheia wanted to avoid. Μαρτύρησον at 6.20.3 is a ringing reminder of μετὰ μαρτύρων at 2.28.3. Her absence from the latter half of the novel is striking. It is significant that Leucippe's father is present for the virginity test and marriage celebrations, but not her mother.

Several of the concepts of chastity discussed by the orators in Seneca's declamation are shared by certain important Christian thinkers and, given that we are invited to view Leucippe's speeches as 'martyr' speeches, it is appropriate that we consider her position from a Christian perspective. Desiring sex, even if she has not practised it, is enough to make a virgin no longer a virgin, according to Patristic thought, as R. Howard Bloch relates:

Yet, as the Fathers make abundantly clear, it is not enough merely to be chaste. The distinction between virgins in mind and chastity of the body is emphasised throughout, and there is no difference between desire and the act. Rather, the act is defined by the mental state of the actor.[109]

---

[109] Bloch (1989), 116. A view also articulated by one of the declaimers in Seneca's *Controversiae* 6.8, in the case of 'The Vestal Virgin's Verse'.

As desire inheres in the gaze, it is enough to look or to be looked at for a girl to lose her virginity. Cyprian, commenting on virgins in a state of undress at the public baths writes: 'Virginity is unveiled to be marked out and contaminated.'[110] Tertullian asserts: 'Seeing and being seen belong to the self-same lust' and 'every public exposure of a virgin is (to her) a suffering of rape'.[111] It is clear that for a girl to remain a virgin she must not desire or be desired, look or be looked at, criteria by which all the heroines of the Greek novels would fail badly. According to Tertullian, virginity needs strictly to be policed, 'For a virgin ceases to be a virgin from the time when it becomes possible for her not to be one.'[112] As has been argued, there are plenty of possibilities for Leucippe's virginity to be compromised. Even if we do not judge Leucippe by the harsh standards of Cyprian and Tertullian, it is clear from the arguments used in the *controversia* that Leucippe's purity would not necessarily go unquestioned by readers of Achilles Tatius and that some might see her as defiled by the very narrative which constructs her.

Thersander's repeated accusation that Leucippe is a whore is part of that defilement. In addition to the references already mentioned, Thersander makes the charge as part of his case that Leucippe should undergo a virginity test. He publicly laments the time when 'whoremongers (οἱ πορνοβοσκοί) desecrate sacred embassies, when whores (αἱ πόρναι) pollute the most holy of our temples' (8.8.3). Later in the same speech he suggests that Leucippe is an *akolastos*, because she is a runaway slave, and even suggests that the priest of the temple might have enjoyed a threesome with her and Clitophon: 'The abode of Artemis has become a bedroom for adulterers, for a whore! Such things hardly happen in a penny brothel!' (ἡ τῆς Ἀρτέμιδος οἰκία μοιχῶν γέγονε καὶ πόρνης θάλαμος. ταῦτα μόλις ἐν χαμαιτυπείῳ γίνεται, 8.8.11–12). He again refers to her as a whore (τὴν πόρνην) in his written

---

[110] Cyprian, 'The Dress of Virgins', *Treatises* 47. This and the following quotations from Christian writers are quoted in Bloch (1989), whose discussion of virginity has been helpful here. See also Brown (1988).

[111] Tertullian, *On the Veiling of Virgins* 4.28 and 4.29. Cf. Matthew 5.28: 'Whosoever looks on a woman to lust after her has committed adultery.'

[112] *On the Veiling of Virgins* 4.34.

statement at 8.11.2. The only real prostitute who features in the novel is the woman who is dressed in Leucippe's clothes by the pirates and decapitated in her stead. She remains unnamed and we learn of her existence and her part in the trick only towards the end of the novel; the two factors conspire to make her insignificant. She is necessary for a plot device, but is expendable; to the readers as well as the pirates. No one expresses outrage at the report of this woman's death. Like the prostitutes whom Clitophon mentions he has visited (but remains inexperienced in *eros*), this prostitute does not really 'count'. However, in Leucippe's narration of her death, she does not call the woman a *porne* or speak dismissively of her, but rather describes her as 'an unfortunate woman (γυναῖκα.. κακοδαίμονα), one of those who make money by selling Aphrodite's wares' (8.16.1). The details about how the prostitute was conned into thinking she was to marry one of the pirates, and how he pretended to be interested in her provide just a glimpse, albeit shortlived, of poignancy and sympathy for this 'poor woman' (τῆς ταλαιπώρου γυναικὸς, 8.16.2). In the stratagem, where Leucippe and the woman swapped clothes, Leucippe for a brief time 'was' a prostitute, but she was a prostitute who retained her virginity.

Paradoxically, the more Leucippe protests her virginity, the more she draws attention to her sexual self. The constant parade of the sexual, even in order to deny exercising it, operates to equate Leucippe with sexuality. The strong accentuation of both sexuality and chastity in the portrayal of Leucippe and their moral irreconcilability makes her a difficult character to read and has caused scholars some anxiety. Kérenyi notes the parallels between the uneasy juxtaposition of sexuality and chastity in Leucippe's case and its recurrence in other novels and martyr tales and in Seneca's *Controversiae* 1.2. He concludes that the recurrence of the theme and its transposability into different settings give it the status of a legend, rather than an original story or historical account. He argues, as does Merkelbach, the other major proposer of the *Mysterientexte* approach, that the tension between sexuality and chastity arises because the legend originates in the religious myth of Io and Isis, an idea which, decades later, has been reconsidered and developed by Laplace.¹¹³ Laplace's expansion of Kérenyi's thesis is ingenious in its teasing out of allusions in the narrative to Aeschylus' *Prometheus Bound* and other versions of the Io myth, but ultimately has to work hard to convince that, in this emphatically intertextual narrative, the myth of Io and Isis has greater prominence and importance than the many other myths featured.

Charles Segal proposes a structuralist reading which interprets the narrative as a series of 'doublets and complementarities'.¹¹⁴ He reads the novel as staging the two sides of the female archetype, the sexual and the virginal woman, which are embodied in the goddesses Aphrodite and Artemis, and reflected in the characters Melite and Leucippe. Segal interprets Leucippe's character as an extension of this doubling:

In addition to the complementary roles of the female figures, Achilles Tatius also employs a pattern of doublets within the adventures of the main heroine herself. Beside the virginal Leucippe, who must, of course, remain pure to the end for the long-postponed consummation of her union with Clitophon, there is, as it were, another Leucippe who is threatened with physical violation and at several points seems actually to undergo such violation.¹¹⁵

He argues that there are 'two Leucippes':

the pure Leucippe who survives intact and the image of the sexually initiated (violated) Leucippe from whom the heroine is carefully separated by acts of ritual or quasi-ritual sacrifice. Each time, Leucippe is reborn, as it were, as the chaste virgin.¹¹⁶

However, it is not at all evident that the two aspects of Leucippe, her sensuality and virginity, are as clearly delineated as Segal implies. In fact, far from the narrative oscillating between a virginal Leucippe and a sexual Leucippe who are carefully demarcated, the two aspects coexist within the same character. This is an important distinction because it is in the simultaneous and paradoxical representation of these two aspects within the one character that the tension and the titillation lies. Seeing the character as being split

---

¹¹³ Kérenyi (1927), Merkelbach (1962), 115, n. 2 and Laplace (1983a).
¹¹⁴ Segal (1984), 83.   ¹¹⁵ Ibid., 84.   ¹¹⁶ Ibid., 85.

into 'two Leucippes' does not allow full play to the interface of the two aspects within the character.

The strong accentuation of both sexuality and chastity in Leucippe does not need to be explained with reference to mythic predecessors, religious rites or narrative structural patterns. The concomitant chastity and sensuality of Leucippe needs no further explanation than the acknowledgement that it is a potent and enduring (male) fantasy.[117] Leucippe is not *either* a virgin *or* a whore, nor at some times a virgin and at others a whore, but a virgin/whore, with the one aspect overlaying the other. It is the tension between the heroine's sanctity and the suggestion of that sanctity being defiled which is erotic.

The 'virgin whore' is a standard trope of popular literature. There are various configurations of this fantasy. One version involves women who were once whores rehabilitated into classy virgins. One of the speeches in Libanius' *Progumnasmata* concerns the ethopoieia 'What speech would a prostitute who has been chaste (πόρνη σωφρονήσασα) utter?'[118] This woman is imagined shunning Aphrodite and applying herself to Athena's 'decency' (ἐπιείκεια). She is a tart-with-a-heart, straight out of New Comedy, sister of the 'reformed' prostitute Chrysis in Menander's *Samia*.[119] Sometimes, classy virgins are reduced to the status of common whores, for example in the Herodotean tales of King Rhampsinitos' (unnamed) daughter who, as part of her father's subterfuge to trap a thief, was installed in a room 'with instructions to accept all men indiscriminately' (*Histories* 2.121), and Cheops' daughter, prostituted by her father for money (2.126).[120]

In other versions classy virgins are forced into prostitution, but by dint of their own extraordinary ingenuities remain virgins. Seneca's 'Prostitute Priestess' is one of this type, as is Xenophon of Ephesus' Anthia, who is sold into prostitution but feigns epilepsy

---

[117] On this fantasy in Musaeus' *Hero and Leander*, see Morales (1999).
[118] See Hawley (1995), 265–6.
[119] On prostitutes in New Comedy, see Henry (1985). Virgin girls are captured and sold into prostitution in Plautus, *Curculio* 213; *Persa* 656; *Poenulus* 100–1 and *Rudens* 664–76.
[120] There are suggestions that Aphrodite and/or Isis appeared as prostitutes. See Henrichs (1972), 20–1 and Burkert (1983), 160 n. 117: 'In Abydus, there was even a shrine of "Aphrodite the whore" who, in spite of her name, was duly worshipped and had a festival.' However, the evidence is thin, to say the least.

to fool the brothel-keeper and keep her virginity.[121] The scenario is developed in the late fifth- or early sixth-century CE novel *The Story of Apollonius of Tyre*, whose heroine Tarsia, after many a misadventure, finds herself in a brothel in Mytilene in the service of a pimp who worships the god Priapus. Tarsia sweet-talks her clients not only into sparing her virginity, but also into giving her money to buy her freedom from the brothel. In one scene, Tarsia is sent to 'entertain' a man who, unbeknown to her, is her father, Apollonius. She introduces herself as follows: 'Greetings, whoever you are, and be cheerful. I am not some impure woman (*aliqua . . . polluta*) come to console you, but an innocent virgin who keeps my virginity intact in the midst of moral shipwreck (*innocens virgo quae virginitatem meam inter naufragium castitatis inviolabiliter servo*, A40). Her description of herself articulates the paradox of the virgin/whore: 'I walk among filth, but I am unaware of filth . . . Now I have been sold to a pimp but I have never tarnished my honour' (*Per sordes gradior, sed sordis conscia non sum . . . Lenoni nunc vendita numquam violavi pudorem*, A41).

Leucippe is in this mould. Margaret Williamson's comparison of her with de Sade's heroine Justine is in many ways an apposite one.[122] In her discussion of Justine and her cinematic successor, Marilyn Monroe, Angela Carter writes:

The theory of the sentimental image of the Good Bad Girl is that she has the appearance of a tart and an air of continuous availability but, when the chips are down, she would never stoop to sell herself.[123]

In her consummate desirability Leucippe has the appearance of a tart; in her repeated self-exposure, literally or through projected images, and in the inevitability that she will end up in situations where she is actively lusted after, Leucippe has the air of continuous availability. When the chips are down it is inconceivable that she would stoop to sell herself, that she would seize the initiative and barter her virginity for Clitophon's life, or use her physical attractiveness to manipulate Thersander. It is not difficult to imagine the Leucippe of the beginning of the novel taking action, but the later

---

[121] In Apuleius, Charite is abducted by robbers who plan to sell her to a brothel-keeper but she is rescued by her fiancé: *Met.* 7.9.5.
[122] Williamson (1986).   [123] Carter (1979), 66.

Leucippe is active only in glorifying her status as a passive victim. The fantasy which Leucippe embodies is that of the Good Bad Girl, virgin whore, prostitute priestess, *porne sophronesasa*.

The Good Bad Girl does not take pleasure in the overt articulation of desire, nor is she given the opportunity to express her consent or dissent to sexual activity, without distortion. Thus Clinias' *sententia* on the voice of the *parthenos*, in part a self-fulfilling prophecy, appears to be borne out in the representation of Leucippe. What, then, of grown women whom Clinias portrays as the inverse of inexperienced maidens? Does Melite take pleasure in words?

Sweet-talking Melite

Melite is the honey in Clitophon's 'swarm of stories'. She is so positioned not merely by nomenclature, but also by her role as the antagonist. She plays Rose Red to Leucippe's Snow White, Jane Russell to Leucippe's Marilyn. Unlike the protagonist, the antagonist is of secondary importance in the narrative hierarchy. This is not Melite's novel, we do not expect the narrative climax to be the celebration of *her* marriage. This makes her important, yet ultimately expendable. It is perhaps the antagonist's expendability which fosters the reader's expectation that she will be more interesting than the usually conformist and 'safe' protagonist. Typically it is the sidekick, not the star, who has the sweetest moments.

Melite is wealthy, powerful, from the city, married and though young, relatively experienced. Such women figure in the other Greek novels; from the gentle queen in Chariton to the wicked Arsace in Heliodorus.[124] It is a cliché that the older, independent, sexually mature woman poses a threat to the chastity of the hero. The woman who not merely threatens but takes the hero's virginity is Lykainion in Longus' *Daphnis and Chloe*, and it is she who most closely resembles Melite. Lykainion's sexual encounter with Daphnis is described quite specifically as a pedagogical

---

[124] In so far as Melite comes from Ephesus and, for a while, believes her husband to be dead, she also resembles the Ephesian widow in Petronius, *Satyrica* 111–12. Neither character mourns her husband deeply. For a comparison of Melite with Judith, see Pervo (1991), 155–9.

experience: 'Give youself to me as a pupil,' offers Lykainion, 'and as a favour to those Nymphs I will teach you' (3.17). Daphnis willingly participates in his 'erotic education' (*erotikes paidagogias*). Achilles Tatius is less explicitly didactic than Longus, but the reader who comes to *Leucippe and Clitophon* with knowledge of *Daphnis and Chloe* might anticipate Melite to be not only a sexual predator, but a pedagogue and a figure of authority.

'[A]s a work of art no other character in the Greek Romances can compare with that of Melitta', writes Wolff.[125] His comment is appropriate, for it is as a work of art that Melite is first introduced. Satyrus reports Aphrodite's handiwork:

Γυναῖκα γὰρ ἐξέμηνεν ἐπ' αὐτῷ πάνυ καλήν, ὥστε ἂν ἰδὼν αὐτὴν εἴποις ἄγαλμα, Ἐφεσίαν τὸ γένος, ὄνομα Μελίτην.

She has driven a woman crazy for him – a woman of such great beauty that you would think her a statue if you saw her. Her family is from Ephesus, and her name is Melite. (5.11.5)

Clitophon has already encountered a woman who is compared to a statue, in his dream, earlier at 4.1.6:

Ἐδόκουν γὰρ τῇ παρελθούσῃ νυκτὶ ναὸν Ἀφροδίτης ὁρᾶν καὶ τὸ ἄγαλμα ἔνδον εἶναι τῆς θεοῦ.

on the previous night, I had dreamt I saw a temple of Aphrodite, with the goddess's cult statue within.

The woman prohibits Clitophon from entering the temple but counsels him to wait a while until the time when she will not only let him enter but also make him a priest of the goddess. At the time Clitophon (and no doubt the reader reading the novel for the first time) interprets the dream as symbolising that he would have to wait before having intercourse with Leucippe, just as Leucippe's dream advised her to postpone relations with Clitophon, who would later become her husband (4.1.4). Now, however, comes the realisation that it is *Melite* who serves Aphrodite and it is she who resembles a statue. Reinterpreting Clitophon's dream, coupled with the generic expectation that the 'older woman' will attempt to seduce the younger man, fosters the expectation that Clitophon will soon

[125] Wolff (1912), 154.

'cross her threshold'. Comparing Melite to a statue also emphasises her status as a desirable object, her potent 'to-be-looked-at-ness'. Indeed, Clitophon's description of her also appeals to the visual, focusing on the texture and colour of skin and hair in an almost tactile surveillance, ending with an affirmation of his pleasure in looking at her:

Ἦν δὲ τῷ ὄντι καλή, καὶ γάλακτι μὲν ἂν εἶπες τὸ πρόσωπον αὐτῆς κεχρῖσθαι, ῥόδον δὲ ἐμπεφυτεῦσθαι ταῖς παρειαῖς. Ἐμάρμαιρεν αὐτῆς τὸ βλέμμα μαρμαρυγὴν Ἀφροδίσιον· κόμη πολλὴ καὶ βαθεῖα καὶ κατάχρυσος τῇ χροιᾷ, ὥστε ἔδοξα οὐκ ἀηδῶς ἰδεῖν τὴν γυναῖκα.

She truly was beautiful: you would have said that her face was daubed with milk, and that roses grew in her cheeks. Her brilliant eyes scintillated with erogenous sparkle, and her hair was thick, long, and golden in colour. It was not without a certain feeling of pleasure that I beheld the woman. (5.13.1–2)

Melite is portrayed in terms that conform to the dominant metaphorics of the gaze (statues and food) which were used to depict Leucippe. The phrase τὸ βλέμμα μαρμαρυγή further associates her with Aphrodite, whose eyes are described as 'sparkling' (ὄμματα μαρμαίροντα) at *Iliad* 3.397.

However, unlike Leucippe, Melite is shown looking back. She is so sick with desire for Clitophon that she does not eat and Clitophon tells us, in a crucial phrase, 'she did nothing but gaze upon me': πάντα δὲ ἔβλεπέ με (5.13.3). His explanation of Melite's behaviour reinforces the active nature of her desire: Οὐδὲν γὰρ ἡδὺ τοῖς ἐρῶσι πλὴν τὸ ἐρώμενον, 'Nothing is sweet to lovers other than the beloved' (5.13.3). This is followed by an analysis of how beauty enters the lover's eyes and impresses an image of the beloved on the soul of the lover, like a photograph, which further constructs Melite's gaze as an active agent. Clitophon's reaction to Melite's desire is, significantly, couched in objectifying terms, with another comparison of Melite to a work of art:

Λέγω δὴ πρὸς αὐτὴν συνείς· "'Ἀλλὰ σύ γε οὐδενὸς μετέχεις τῶν σαυτῆς, ἀλλ' ἔοικας τοῖς ἐν γραφαῖς ἐσθίουσιν." Ἡ δέ, "Ποῖον γὰρ ὄψον", ἔφη, "μοι πολυτελὲς ἢ ποῖος οἶνος τιμιώτερος τῆς σῆς ὄψεως;" Καὶ ἅμα λέγουσα κατεφίλει με, προσιέμενον οὐκ ἀηδῶς τὰ φιλήματα· εἶτα διασχοῦσα εἶπεν· "Αὕτη μοι τρυφή."

I understood this, and said to her: 'Come on, you have not touched your food. You look like someone eating in a painting.' 'Yes, but what extravagant provisions, what wine could be worth more to me than the vision of you?' With these words, she began to kiss me, and I accepted her kisses with no small pleasure. Then she drew apart. 'That', she said, 'is what I call sustenance.' (5.13.5)

When ogling Leucippe, Clitophon is described as eating no more than a person in a dream. In a phrase that recalls this episode and pointedly subverts it, it is the woman, Melite, who is described as eating no more than someone in a image.

Both images of objectification, that of statue and consumption, are used by Clitophon to reduce and commodify Leucippe. Melite, in her relationship with Clitophon, takes these metaphors and re-appropriates them. She breaks the logic of female objectification by men; she gazes at Clitophon. Moreover, her gaze is an objectifying one; she uses the two metaphors of commodification which are normatively, both in Achilles and other writings, used by men about women, thereby undermining the established polarity, and the gendered hierarchy valorised by it. At 6.1.3 Melite compares Clitophon, who has dressed in woman's clothes to escape from prison, to a picture of Achilles. That a woman should liken a man to a work of art is a subversion of the dominant scopic order. Furthermore, Melite's comparison echoes Clitophon's comparison of Leucippe with a painting of Selene (1.4.3), which serves to highlight the reversal of gender roles and viewing relations. At 5.22.5, Melite complains of Clitophon's reluctance to consummate their affair:

Ἔοικα δὲ εἰκόνος ἐρᾶν· μέχρι γὰρ τῶν ὀμμάτων ἔχω τὸν ἐρώμενον.

It is like loving a statue: I get no more than ocular satisfaction from my beloved.

She again envisages Clitophon as a work of art and she appropriates the metaphorics of the gaze. In the passage at 5.13.5, the linguistic play between *to opson*, 'food', and *he opsis*, 'sight', blurs the distinction between eating and viewing, thereby reinforcing the potency of the consuming gaze and Melite's assumption of active spectatorship.

Through the figure of Melite the text constructs a female viewing subject, a factor which complicates readings of Achilles which focus exclusively upon the male gaze and its objectification of the female characters.[126] There is a place in this narrative for a 'voyeuristic moment' controlled by a woman. However, it is significant that the narrative perspective is not upon the object of Melite's gaze; we still have no glimpse of Clitophon's physical appearance. The focus is upon Melite's looking, not on what she looked at. As Bazin comments on the heroines of *film noir*: 'The object of the shot is not what she is looking at, nor even her look; it is: *looking at her looking.*'[127] With Melite the male abrogates the subjectivity of his gaze and becomes the object of her gaze. However, this reversal is censored at the point of objectification; spectatorial desire to see the male body exposed is given no gratification.

Melite also demonstrates a formidable command of language throughout the narrative. Unlike Leucippe, who is manipulated by her very own words, Melite is in control of her speech. She cracks jokes, punning pointedly on *kenotaphion* and *kenogamion* at 5.14.4.[128] In contrast to Leucippe, whose words are intercepted and overheard, most of Melite's communication is direct. One particularly striking example of Melite's manipulation of language is an episode on board her ship when she tries to persuade Clitophon to sleep with her. She describes the ship using metaphors of female fertility:

Ἐμοὶ μὲν γὰρ δοκεῖ τὰ παρόντα γάμων εἶναι σύμβολα· ζυγὸς μὲν οὗτος ὑπὲρ κεφαλῆς κρεμάμενος, δεσμοὶ δὲ περὶ τὴν κεραίαν τεταμένοι. Καλά γε, ὦ δέσποτα, τὰ μαντεύματα· ὑπὸ ζυγὸν ὁ θάλαμος, καὶ κάλοι δεδεμένοι. Ἀλλὰ καὶ πηδάλιον τοῦ θαλάμου πλησίον· ἰδοὺ τοὺς γάμους ἡμῶν ἡ Τύχη κυβερνᾷ . . . Λιγυρὸν δὲ συρίζει περὶ τοὺς κάλους καὶ τὸ πνεῦμα· ἐμοὶ μὲν ὑμέναιον ἄγειν δοκεῖ τὰ τῶν ἀνέμων αὐλήματα. Ὁρᾷς δὲ καὶ τὴν ὀθόνην κεκυρτωμένην ὥσπερ ἐγκύμονα γαστέρα· δεξιόν μοι καὶ τοῦτο τῶν οἰωνισμάτων· ἔσῃ μοι ταχὺ καὶ πατήρ.

It seems to me that our surroundings betoken marriage, this yoke dangling above our heads and the bonds taut around the yardarm. The omens are good, my master: a bridal suite lying under a yoke and ropes bound tight. Even the rudder is close to the bridal suite: see, Fortune is piloting our marriage! . . .The breeze is whistling sweetly around the rigging: it seems to me that the wind's pipings are leading the wedding-hymn. See how the sail billows out like a pregnant belly. I take even this as a favourable omen: you will soon father me a child, too. (5.16.4–6)

---

[126] E.g. Montague (1992). [127] Bazin, quoted in Doane (1987a), 100.
[128] On this pun and more generally on *kenogamion* and *gamos* in Achilles Tatius, see Liviabella Furiani (1988).

Normally, this sort of language is used pejoratively, as in an amatory epigram by Meleager:

> Οὐκέτι, Τιμάριον, τὸ πρὶν γλαφυροῖο κέλητος
> πῆγμα φέρει πλωτὸν Κύπριδος εἰρεσίην·
> ἀλλ' ἐπὶ μὲν νώτοισι μετάφρενον, ὡς κέρας ἱστῷ,
> κυρτοῦται, πολιὸς δ' ἐκλέλυται πρότονος·
> ἱστία δ' αἰρωρητὰ χαλᾷ σπαδονίσματα μαστῶν·
> ἐκ δὲ σάλου στρεπτὰς γαστρὸς ἔχει ῥυτίδας·
> νέρθε δὲ πάνθ' ὑπέραντλα νέως, κοίλη δὲ θάλασσα
> πλημμύρει, γόνασιν δ' ἔντρομός ἐστι σάλος.

No longer, Timo, do the timbers of your spruce corsair hold out against the strokes of Cypris' oarsmen, but your back is bent like a yardarm lowered, and your grey forestays are slack, and your relaxed breasts are like flapping sails, and the belly of your ship is wrinkled by the tossing of the waves, and below she is all full of bilge-water and flooded with the sea, and her joints are shaky. (*Pal. Anth.* 5.204.1–8)

In Meleager's poem, nautical metaphors are used to degrade the woman, Timo. Her bodily parts are compared, one by one, to parts of the ship; they are fetishised through figurative language. The female body is anatomised with vast symbols, a ship's sails, yardarm, the sea, but is itself an absent referent; it is reduced in this process. To understand the symbolism, the reader must make certain mental connections, for example he or she is prompted to think through the possible connotations of 'bilge-water', and it is in these associations that the humour and the invective lies.[129] (A modern analogy might be the use of motoring vocabulary to describe women: 'she needs a good servicing', 'trade her in for a new model', etc.)

Melite uses similar figurative language, but to different ends. Most importantly, she anatomises herself, her own body. She is the absent referent, she defines her own reality. In Meleager, a woman's body is symbolised as a ship (love-boat). In Achilles Tatius, a ship is symbolised as a woman's body. It is also symbolised as a man's body, if we see innuendo in *pedalion*, 'rudder'.[130] Melite takes the usual pattern of comparison (woman symbolised as painting, meadow, peacock, temple, rose, etc.) and inverts it.

---

[129] Cf. Theognis 457–60. [130] As Ewen Bowie kindly pointed out to me.

She not only defines her own reality, but that of Clitophon, whose mode of transport has suddenly been transformed into a giant sexual icon, from which there is no escape. Figurative language is not merely descriptive, but prescriptive, extending our perceptual models of the world to make us see something *as* something else. For Meleager, the ship's sails symbolise sagging breasts; for Melite, they symbolise a fertile belly. For Melite, language is a tool of seduction; through language, she acts.

5

CONCLUSION

This book has attempted to advance our understanding of Achilles Tatius' *Leucippe and Clitophon* through close attention to its literary and visual contexts, its narrative structure and 'digressions', its intertexts and moral attitudes, and its constructions of gender. It has been concerned to scrutinise Achilles' obsessions with the eye, and in so doing to question the dialogic potential of the novel for feminism.

One conclusion which might be drawn is that the novel is ambivalent. I do not mean a weak version of ambivalence, in which the meaning of stories dissolves into a postmodern mist of ludicity and playfulness. Rather, I mean a stronger version of ambivalence: 'the state of holding on to more than one story at the same time'.[1] One story is that summed up by Photius' epigram:

> Bitter love, but virtuous life
> Is the story that Clitophon tells
> The most virtuous life of Leucippe
> Astonishes everyone. How she was beaten,
> Shaved and abused,
> And greatest of all, having died three times, endured.
> If you too wish to be virtuous, my friend,
> Do not look at the sights that frame the image,
> But first learn the outcome of the tale,
> For it joins in marriage those who loved wisely.

> Ἔρωτα πικρόν, ἀλλὰ σώφρονα βίον
> ὁ Κλειτοφῶντος μὲν παρεμφαίνει λόγος·
> ὁ Λευκίππης δὲ σωφρονέστατος βίος
> ἅπαντας ἐξίστησι, πῶς τετυμμένη
> κεκαρμένη τε καὶ κατηχρειωμένη,
> τὸ δὴ μέγιστον, τρὶς θανοῦσ' ἐκαρτέρει.
> εἴπερ δὲ καὶ σὺ σωφρονεῖν θέλῃς, φίλος,

[1] Johnson (1998), 2.

μὴ τὴν πάρεργον τῆς γραφῆς σκόπει θέαν,
τὴν τοῦ λόγου δὲ πρῶτα συνδρομὴν μάθε·
νυμφοστολεῖ γὰρ τοὺς ποθοῦντας ἐμφρόνως.[2]

Read in the context of the other novels, a strategy that necessarily tends towards homogenising them, Achilles Tatius validates civic ideals and promotes (Stoic) conjugal ethics. This book is sensitive to some of the ways in which we might extend a Stoic approach to the novel, but argues that this is too limited a reading. It is only one story. I have traced other interpretations of Achilles Tatius' novel suggested by its various conspicuous relations with other genres and texts: Platonic philosophy, the mime, *controversiae*, and *epithalamium*. One of the recurrent considerations of this book, for example, has been to explore the Phoenicianness of these 'Phoenician Tales' and to chart some of the ways they reflect and manipulate stereotypes of Phoenicia.

Another conclusion is that the key to how we read *Leucippe and Clitophon* lies in the weight we give the ending. Critics who argue that Achilles Tatius and the other erotic novels 'should be read as acts of "legitimation"' whose adventures 'valorize the civic ideal' stress the endings of the novels over and above the *parerga*.[3] Episodes of attempted rape and blithe adultery are subordinated to the 'love and marriage' finale. Those who advance the opposite view, that *Leucippe and Clitophon*, like the other novels, is 'the enemy of the Civic',[4] explicitly downplay the importance of the endings. Thus Doody argues:

> The point of the ancient novel is not its ending. Closure is not really telos, though the ending of any novel interprets afresh for us what has gone before. The novel resides in the experience in which we are involved along the way.[5]

Achilles Tatius complicates critical perspectives on closure by making the ending a particular problem, as Chapters 2 and 3 of this study have discussed, by not returning to the opening frame nor explaining who the unnamed narrator is and why Clitophon is alone and unhappy. I have argued that this lacuna is anticipated by

---

[2] The epigram is contained (part and whole) in two thirteenth-century manuscripts and is also found in the *Palatine Anthology* (9.203), where it is attributed to Photius or Leon the Philosopher.
[3] Swain (1996), 60–1.   [4] Doody (1996), 471.   [5] Doody (1996), 61.

CONCLUSION

a narrative pattern of frustrated knowledge. Moreover it makes it even harder to privilege the 'outcome of the tale' when it is not clear what that outcome is. The novel's moral agenda is hermeneutically inseparable from its literary structure.

This book has throughout urged a very different way of reading from that prescribed by Photius' epigram. It has insisted that we look at the *parergos thea* in some depth. This different methodology, refusing to exclude or underplay 'digressions' – *ekphrasis*, *sententia*, *blason* and spectacle, descriptions of the mechanics of vision and of exotic *thaumata* – will recoup different stories. One focus has been on the many sententious statements in *Leucippe and Clitophon*. Drawing on rhetorical theories of *sententiae* and analysing their form, content, focalisation and relations within the narrative, I have argued that their most important role is to lay down the law about gender and ethnicity, even if those laws are on occasion undercut with irony. The broader aim here has been to contribute to a narratology of *sententiae*, and to insist once more that whether and how to read intratextually are, in part, political choices.[6]

Looking at the *parergos thea* has other ramifications. It refuses to disavow the scenes of violence inflicted on women, most of which are cordoned off in dreams and *ekphraseis*. I have attempted to chart the various manifestations of misogyny in Achilles Tatius, while at the same time giving consideration to those elements in the novel which provide rich material for resistant or renegade readings.[7] Voice and gaze, I have argued, function as 'technologies of gender', principles that organise male and female experience differently. The metaphorics of the gaze in this novel, symptomatically of Greek literature in general, envisage women as food and works of art. Some of the theoretical descriptions of the mechanics of vision depict the process as a mutual activity. However, this is not borne out in the practice. I have discussed how, when characters are described as gazing and being gazed at, agency in the viewing process is inconsistent. Sometimes the male characters are

---

[6] The project of Sharrock and Morales (2000). Swain (1996) is particularly dismissive of narratological approaches to the novel which he represents as depoliticised.
[7] On 'renegade reading'; cf. Boardman (1994). On 'resistant' readings of Ovid, see Richlin (1992c).

active agents in the viewing process, at other times their agency (and thus responsibility) is surrendered to their eyes (as if acting independently of them) and to external forces. This has implications beyond our appreciation of Achilles Tatius. It can be read as part of a tenacious tradition of mitigating male violence. Leucippe, the object of the men's attentions, is presented as having no control over her beauty, yet is held responsible for its actions. It is hard not to read this as part of a *longue durée* of 'blaming the victim'.

Melite, however, offers some challenge to these ideologies, so it is fitting that this study should end with her. I have shown how the minor characters in *Leucippe and Clitophon* should be read not just as 'personalities', but as representations of different ways of viewing and reading the world. Melite represents the possibility of a different way of interacting in the world, an alternative to the norm.[8] Her abuse of the chastity test is the most obvious example of her subversive appeal, undermining as it does societal values of fidelity and marriage and Leucippe's strict adherence to them. It is only by playing down Melite, her liaison with Clitophon, and her flaunting of her adultery by cheating on the test that one can entertain the suggestion that '[the ideal novels] support the belief that ... sex outside marriage was now no longer sanctioned and that the security of the city was felt to depend on what Musonius calls the "rampart" (*peribolê*) of marriage'.[9] Rather, the comic crafting of Melite's scenes, which militate against the values of chastity and fidelity, are designed to have a greater impact than Clitophon's rather banal report of his marriage to Leucippe at the close of the novel's previous chapter.

Melite's appropriation of the tools of male agency, metaphor and gaze, cannot 'undo' their misogynist use elsewhere in the novel. But what it can do is jeopardise the illusion that control of language and sight are exclusively male prerogatives. It sets up the possibility of a different scopic order, an alternative way of reacting to and regarding the world. The very fact that the female gaze is represented is itself a radical gesture. It is radical because it negates fixity and, as a corollary, undermines any totalising reading of visuality.

---

[8] 'Melite scompliglia le carte': Cresci (1978), 74.
[9] Swain (1996), 122; cf. Veyne (1978).

CONCLUSION

Against this it could be argued that, by including this challenge to the dominant order, and by locating it in the antagonist who is lower down the hierarchy of characters, the narrative effectively co-opts the challenge. Co-option is a neutralising dynamic, which operates to assimilate and render impotent the radical potential of the female gaze.[10] This is yet another strategy that the narrative deploys to put women in their place. However, it is one thing to assume that the novel is determined in ideological ways and projects certain ways of reading, and another to assume that those projections work. A phenomenological reading might still privilege the pleasures offered by Melite's story, despite the sidelining of her character by the narrative.

It is the novel's ambivalence, its holding on to more than one story at the same time, which makes it important for feminism. All literature is, to some degree or another, 'the place where impasses can be kept and opened for examination, where questions can be guarded and not forced into a premature validation of the available paradigms'.[11] But the ancient Greek novels, and Achilles Tatius in particular, perform interrogations of culture in a particularly active way. I have traced the ways in which *Leucippe and Clitophon* can be read as a narrativised *controversia*. The novels give the silenced women in the *controversiae* a voice and move towards a more casuistical ethic (though one still a long way off the particularised narratives of the realist novel). As narrativised *controversiae* the novels are constitutively contestatory. They have liberatory potential. It is a potential that is, I argue, realised in crucial ways, in so far as it challenges literary and moral orthodoxies. However, there is a deeper level of conservatism at work in the novel. It reinforces, aggressively and flamboyantly, misogynist perspectives on women, even if, and as, it also threatens masculinities. One might say that Achilles, like Achilles in the picture recalled by Melite is like a man dressed in woman's clothes: unsettling, uncanny, and potentially subversive, but ultimately androcentric.

---

[10] On co-option, see Graff (1989).
[11] Johnson (1998), 13.

REFERENCES

Adam, J. (1963) *The Republic of Plato*, 2nd edn, 2 vols. Cambridge.
Adams, C. (1990) *The Sexual Politics of Meat*. Cambridge.
Adams, J. (1982) *The Latin Sexual Vocabulary*. London.
Alexiou, M. (1977) 'A critical reappraisal of Eustathios Macrembolites' *Hysmine and Hysminias'*, *BMGS* 3: 23–43.
Altheim, F. (1948) *Roman und Dekadenz. Literatur und Gesellschaft im ausgehenden Altertum*, vol. 1: 13–47. Halle.
Alvares, J. (1993) 'The Journey of Observation in Chariton's 'Chaireas and Callirhoe''. Diss. Austin, Texas.
Anderson, G. (1979) 'The Mystical Pomegranate and the Vine of Sodom: Achilles Tatius 3.6', *AJPh* 100: 516–18.
(1982) *Eros Sophistes – Ancient Novelists at Play*. Chico, CA.
(1984) *Ancient Fiction: The Novel in the Graeco-Roman World*. London.
(1988) 'Achilles Tatius: a New Interpretation', in Beaton (1988a), 190–3.
(1989) 'The *Pepaideumenos* in Action: Sophists and their Outlook in the Early Empire', *ANRW* 2.33.1: 79–208.
(1993) *The Second Sophistic: A Cultural Phenomenon in the Roman Empire*. London.
(1997) 'Perspectives on Achilles Tatius', *ANRW* 2.34.3 Sprache und Literatur: 2278–99.
Archer, L., Fischler, S. and Wyke, M. eds. (1994) *Women in Ancient Societies: An Illusion of the Night*. Basingstoke and London.
Ardener, S. ed. (1975a) *Perceiving Women*. London.
(1975b) 'Sexual Insult and Female Militancy', in Ardener (1975a), 29–53.
Arendt, H. (1970) *On Violence*. London.
Aubet, M.-E. (1987) *The Phoenicians and the West*. Cambridge.
Austin, N. (1994) *Helen of Troy and Her Shameless Phantom*. Cornell.
Avotins, I. (1980) 'Alexander of Aphrodisias on vision in the atomists', *CQ* 30: 429–54.
Bakhtin, M. (1973) *Problems of Dostoevsky's Poetics*, transl. R. W. Rotsel. Ann Arbor, Mich.
(1981) *The Dialogic Imagination: Four Essays*, ed. M. Holquist; transl. M. Holquist and C. Emerson. Austin, Texas.
(1984) *Rabelais and his World*, transl. H. Iswolsky. Bloomington.
Bal, M. (1995) 'Reading the Gaze: The Construction of Gender in "Rembrandt"', in Melville and Readings (1995), 147–73.

REFERENCES

Barns, J. W. B. (1965) 'Egypt and the Greek Romance', in *Akten des 8. Kongress fur Papyrologie*, ed. H. Gerstinger. *Mitteilungen aus der Papyrussammlung der Nationalbibliothek in Wien*, n.s. 5. Vienna: 29–36.

Baron, D. (1986) *Grammar and Gender*. New Haven and London.

Barthes, R. (1974) *S/Z*, transl. R. Miller. London. (= *S/Z*. Paris, 1970).
— (1975) *The Pleasure of the Text*, transl. R. Miller. New York. (= *Le Plaisir du texte*. Paris, 1973.)
— (1986) *The Rustle of Language*, transl. R. Howard. Oxford. (= *Le Bruissement de la langue*. Seuil, 1984.)

Barton, C. A. (1993) *The Sorrows of the Ancient Romans: The Gladiator and the Monster*. Princeton.
— (2002) 'Being in the Eyes: Shame and Sight in Ancient Rome', in Fredrick (2002a), 216–35.

Bartsch, S. (1989) *Decoding the Ancient Novel: The Reader and the Role of Description in Heliodorus and Achilles Tatius*. Princeton.
— (1994) *Actors in the Audience: Theatricality and Doublespeak from Nero to Hadrian*. Cambridge.
— (2000) 'The Philosopher as Narcissus: Vision, Sexuality, and Self-Knowledge in Classical Antiquity', in Nelson (2000), 70–97.

Baslez, M.-F., Hoffman, P. and Trédé, M. eds. (1992) *Le Monde du Roman Grec, Actes du colloque international tenu à l'Ecole normale supérieure (Paris 17–19 décembre 1987)*. Etudes de Littérature Ancienne 4. Paris.

Baudelaire, C. (1964) *The Painter of Modern Life and Other Essays*, transl. J. Mayne. London.

Baudrillard, J. (1990) *Seduction*, transl. B. Singer. Basingstoke. (= *De la Séduction*. Paris, 1980.)

Beacham, R. C. (1991) *The Roman Theatre and its Audience*. London.

Beagon, M. (1992) *Roman Nature. The Thought of Pliny the Elder*. Oxford.

Beard, M. (1993) 'Looking (Harder) for Roman Myth: Dumézil, Declamation and the Problems of Definition', in F. Graf ed. *Colloquium Rauricum* 3 (1993), 44–64.

Beard, M. and Henderson, J. (1998) 'With this body I thee worship: Sacred Prostitution in Antiquity', in Wyke (1998), 56–79.
— (2001) *Classical Art from Greece to Rome*. Oxford.

Beaton, R. ed. (1988a) *The Greek Novel AD 1–1985*. London.
— (1998b) 'The Greek Novel in the Middle Ages', in Beaton (1988a), 134–43.

Beck, H.-G. (1976) 'Marginalia on the Byzantine Novel', in Reardon (1976), 59–74.

Bellen, H. (1971) *Studien zur Sklavenflucht im römischen Kaiserreich*. Wiesbaden.

Benhabib, S. (1994) 'Feminism and the Question of Postmodernism', in Polity Press ed. (1994): 76–92.

Bennington, G. (1985) *Sententiousness and the Novel. Laying down the Law in Eighteenth-Century French Fiction*. Cambridge.

Berger, J. (1972) *Ways of Seeing*. London.
 (1980) *About Looking*. New York.
Bertrand, J.-M. (1988) 'Les Boukoloi ou le Monde à l'Envers', *REA* 90: 139–49.
Bettini, M. (1992) *Il ritratto dell'amante*. Torino.
 (1999) *The Portrait of the Lover*, transl. L. Gibbs. Berkeley.
Bevan, D. ed. (1989) *Literary Gastronomy*. Amsterdam.
Bielohlawek, K. (1940) 'Gastmahls-und Symposionlehren bei griechischen Dichtern', *WS* 58: 11–30.
Billault, A. (1990) 'L'inspiration des ekphraseis d'œuvres d'art chez les romanciers grecs', *Rhetorica* 8.2: 153–60.
 (1991) *La Création romanesque dans la littérature grecque à l'époque imperiale*. Paris.
Blackham, H. J. (1985) *The Fable as Literature*. London and Dover, New Hampshire.
Bloch, R. H. (1989) 'Chaucer's Maiden's Head: "The Physician's Tale" and the Poetics of Virginity', *Representations* 28, Fall 1989: 113–34.
Bloom, A. (1991) *The Republic of Plato*, translation, notes and essay. Basic Books, USA.
Boardman, K. (1994) '"The Glass of Gin": Renegade Reading Possibilities in the Classic Realist Text,' in Mills (1994), 199–217.
Bobzien, S. (1998) *Determinism and Freedom in Stoic Philosophy*. Oxford.
Bonaria, M. ed. (1965) *Romani Mimi*. Rome.
Bonnet, C. (1988) *Melqart: Cultes et mythes de l'Héraclès Tyrien en Méditerranée*. Namur.
Boorsch, J. (1967) 'About some Greek romances', *YFS* (1967), 72–88.
Borthwick, E. K. (1980) 'A Note on some Unusual Greek Words for eyes', *CQ* (1980), 252–6.
Bowersock, G. W. (1969) *Greek Sophists in the Roman Empire*. Oxford.
 ed. (1974) *Approaches to the Second Sophistic*. Pennsylvania.
 (1994) *Fiction as History: Nero to Julian*. Berkeley.
Bowie, E. L. (1974) 'Greeks and their Past in the Second Sophistic', in Finley (1974), 166–209.
 (1982) 'The Importance of Sophists', *YCS* 27: 29–60.
 (1985) 'The Greek Novel', in Easterling and Knox (1985): 683–99.
 (1989) 'The Greek Novel', in Easterling and Knox (1989), 123–39.
 (1991) 'Hellenism in Writers of the Early Second Sophistic', in S. Saïd ed., ΕΛΛΗΝΙΣΜΟΣ: *Quelques jalons pour une histoire de l'identité grecque, Actes du colloque de Strasbourg*, Leiden (1991), 186–94.
 (1994) 'The Readership of the Novels in the Ancient World', in Tatum (1994), 435–59.
 (1998) 'Phoenician Games in Heliodorus' *Aithiopika*', in Hunter (1998), 1–18.
Bowie, E. L. and Harrison S. J. (1993) 'The Romance of the Novel', *JRS* 83: 159–78.
Boyle, A. J. (1987) *Seneca's Phaedra*. Leeds.

ed. (1990) *The Imperial Muse*, vol. 2. Berwick.
(2003) 'Introduction: Reading Flavian Rome', in Boyle and Dominik (2003), 1–68.
Boyle, A. J. and Dominik, W. J. eds. (2003) *Flavian Rome: Culture, Image, Text* Leiden.
Bradley, M. (in preparation) 'Concepts of Colour in Ancient Rome', PhD. thesis. Cambridge.
Branham, B. (1989) *Unruly Eloquence: Lucian and the Comedy of Traditions.* Cambridge, Mass.
ed. (2002) *Bakhtin and the Classics*. Evanston.
Branigan, E. (1984) *Point of View in the Cinema: A Theory of Narration and Subjectivity in Classical Film.* Berlin.
Braun, M. (1938) *History and Romance in Graeco-Oriental Literature.* Oxford.
Braund, D. and Wilkins, J. eds. (2000) *Athenaeus and his World: Reading Greek Culture in the Roman Empire.* Exeter.
Bremmer, J. (1991a) 'Walking, Standing and Sitting in Ancient Culture', in Bremmer and Roodenburg (1991b), 15–35.
Bremmer, J. and Roodenburg, H. eds. (1991b) *A Cultural History of Gesture.* Cambridge.
Brennan, T. (1996a) '"The Contexts of Vision" from a Specific Standpoint', in Brennan and Jay (1996b), 217–30.
Brennan, T. and Jay, M. eds. (1996b) *Vision in Context. Historical and Contemporary Perspectives on Sight.* London.
Briant, P. (1976) '"Brigandage", dissidence et conquête en Asie achéménide et hellénistique', *DHA* 2: 163–258.
Briquel-Chatonnet, F. (1992) 'L'image des Phéniciens dans les romans grecs', in Baslez, Hoffman and Trédé (1992), 189–98.
Britton, C. (1992) *The Nouveau Roman: Fiction, Theory and Politics.* Basingstoke.
Bronfen, E. (1992) *Death, Femininity and the Aesthetic.* Manchester.
Brooks, P. (1995) *The Melodramatic Imagination.* New Haven and London.
(1993) *Body Work: Objects of Desire in Modern Narrative.* Cambridge, Mass.
Brown, P. (1988) *The Body and Society.* New York.
Brown, S. (1991) *Late Carthaginian Child Sacrifice.* Sheffield.
Brunt, P. A. (1994) 'The Bubble of the Second Sophistic', *BICS* 39: 25–52.
Bryson, N. (1983) *Vision and Painting: The Logic of the Gaze.* London.
(1988) 'The Gaze in the Expanded Field', in Foster (1988), 87–113.
(1990) *Looking at the Overlooked.* London.
(1994) 'Philostratus and the Imaginary Museum', in Goldhill and Osborne (1994), 255–83.
Bryson, N., Holly, M. A, and Moxey, K. eds. (1994) *Visual Culture: Images and Interpretations.* Hanover, New Hampshire.
Buci-Glucksmann, C. (1986) *La Folie du voir: de l'esthétique baroque.* Paris.
Burke, K. (1953) *Counter-Statement.* Berkeley.

Burkert, W. (1983) *Homo Necans. The Anthropology of Ancient Greek Sacrificial Ritual and Myth*, transl. P. Bing. Berkeley.
Burrus, V. (1987) *Chastity as Autonomy. Women in the Stories of the Apochryphal Acts*. Lewiston.
Burton, J. B. (1998) 'Reviving the Pagan Greek Novel in a Christian World', *GRBS* 39: 179–216.
Burton, W. (1597) *The Most Delectable and Plesant Historye of Clitophon and Leucippe . . . Nowe Newlie Translated into English by W. B.* London.
Bush, R. (1928) 'Musaeus in English Verse', *MLN* 43: 101–4.
Butler, J. (1990) *Gender Trouble: Feminism and the Subversion of Identity*. New York and London.
Buxton, R. (1980) 'Blindness and Limits: Sophokles and the Logic of Myth', *JHS* 100: 22–37.
Bychkov, O. (1999) 'ἡ τοῦ κάλλους ἀπορροή: A Note on Achilles Tatius 1.9.4–5, 5.13.4', *CQ* 49: 339–42.
Cairns, D. L. (1993) *Aidos. The Psychology and Ethics of Honour and Shame in Ancient Greek Literature*. Oxford.
Calame, C. (1991) *Poetics of Eros in Ancient Greece* (= *I Greci e l'eros*, transl. J. Lloyd.) Princeton.
Cameron, A. (1991) *Christianity and the Rhetoric of Empire: The Development of Christian Discourse*. Berkeley.
Cantarella, E. (1992) *Bisexuality in the Ancient World*, transl. C. O' Cuileanain. New Haven and London.
Carson, A. (1986) *Eros the Bittersweet*. Princeton.
Carter, A. (1979) *The Sadeian Woman*. London.
Carter, J. B. and Morris, S. P. eds. (1995) *The Ages of Homer: A Tribute to Emily Townsend Vermeule*. Austin, Texas.
Cartledge, P. (1990) 'Fowl Play: a Curious Lawsuit in Classical Athens (Antiphon XVI, frr. 57-9 Thalheim)', in Cartledge, Millett and Todd (1990), 41–61.
(1998) *Democritus*. London.
Cartledge, P., Millett, P. and Todd, S. eds. (1990) *Nomos: Essays in Athenian Law, Politics and Society*. Cambridge.
Cartledge, P., Millett, P. and von Reden, S. eds. (1998) *KOSMOS: Essays in Order, Conflict and Community in Classical Athens*. Cambridge.
Cataudella, Q. (1954) 'Giovanni Crisostomo nel Romanzo di Achille Tazio', *La Parola del Passato* 9: 25–40.
Caws, M. A. (1981) *The Eye in the Text: Essays on Perception, Mannerist to Modern*. Princeton.
(1989) *The Art of Interference. Stressed Readings in Verbal and Visual Texts*. Cambridge.
ed. (1991) *City Images: Perspectives from Literature, Philosophy and Film*. New York.
Chambers, R. (1984) *Story and Situation, Narrative Seduction and the Power of Fiction*. Manchester and Minnesota.

REFERENCES

Cizek, E. (1973) 'La diversité des structures dans le roman antique', *St. Clas.* 15: 115–24.

Clark, E. A. (1984) *The Life of Melania the Younger*. Lewiston.

Cline, R. H. (1972) 'Heart and Eyes', *Romance Philology* 25.3: 263–97.

Clover, C. J. (1992) *Men, Women, and Chainsaws: Gender in the Modern Horror Film*. London.

Coates, P. (1991) *The Gorgon's Gaze: German Cinema, Expressionism and the Image of Horror*. Cambridge.

Coleman, K. (1990) 'Fatal Charades: Roman Executions Staged as Mythological Enactments', *JRS* 80: 44–73.

Conca, F. (1969) 'I Papiri di Achille Tazio', in *Rendiconti dell'Istituto Lombardo Classe di Lettere, Scienze Morali e Storiche* 103: 649–77.

Copjec, J. (1994) *Read my Desire*. Boston, Mass.

Coward, R. (1984) *Female Desire*. London.

Cowie, E. (1984) 'Fantasia', *m/f* 9: 78–84.

Crane, W. G. (1937) *Wit and Rhetoric in the Renaissance*. New York.

Crary, J. (1991) *Techniques of the Observer: On Vision and Modernity in the Nineteenth Century*. Cambridge, Mass.

Cresci, L. R. (1978) 'La figura di Melite in Achille Tazio', *Atene e Roma* 23: 74–82.

Cribiore, R. (2001) 'The Grammarian's Choice: the Popularity of Euripides' *Phoenissae* in Hellenistic and Roman Education', in Too and Livingstone (2001), 241–59.

Cunningham, I. (1987) *Herodae Mimiambi. Cum Appendice Mimorum Papyraceorum*. Leipzig.

Dallenbach, L. (1989) *The Mirror in the Text*, transl. J. Whiteley, with E. Hughes. Chicago.

Davies, S. L. (1980) *The Revolt of the Widows: The Social World of the Apochryphal Acts*. Carbondale and Edwardsville.

Davis, L. (1987) *Resisting Novels. Ideology and Fiction*. London.

de Bolla, P. (1995) 'The Visibility of Visuality: Vauxhall Gardens and the Siting of the Viewer', in Melville and Readings (1995), 282–95.

DeJean, J. (1987) 'Female Voyeurism; Sappho and Lafayette', *Rivista di Letterature moderne e comparate* 40: 201–15.

Delahaye, H. (1921) *Les Passions des Martyrs et les Genres Littéraires*. Brussels.

de Lauretis, T. (1987) *Technologies of Gender*. Basingstoke.

Delhay, C. (1990) 'Achille Tatius Fabuliste?', *Pallas* 36: 117–31.

de Perot, J. (1911) 'Die Vorgänge im Heiligtum der Artemis zu Ephesus bei Achilles Tatios und in der Abtei daselbst bei Shakespeare', *Germanisch-Romanische Monatsschrift* 111: 247–8.

Denyer, N. ed. (2001) *Plato Alcibiades*. Cambridge.

Detienne, M. and Vernant, J.-P. (1978) *Cunning Intelligence in Greek Culture and Society*. Hassocks, Sussex.

Dickie, M. (1991) 'Heliodorus and Plutarch on the Evil-Eye', *CPh* 86: 17–29.

Diggle, J. (1972) 'A Note on Achilles Tatius', *CR* 22: 7.
Doane, M. A. (1987a) *The Desire to Desire. The Woman's Film of the 1940's*. Basingstoke.
  (1987b) 'The "Woman's Film": Possession and Address', in Gledhill (1987), 283–98.
  (1991) *Femmes Fatales*. London and NY.
Donovan, J. (1999) *Women and the Rise of the Novel, 1405–1726*. New York.
Doody, M. A. (1996) *The True Story of the Novel*. London.
Dörrie, H. (1938) 'Die griechischen Romane und das Christentum', *Philologus* 93: 273–6.
Dover, K. J. (1965) 'The Date of Plato's Symposium', *Phronesis* 10: 2–20.
Downey, G. (1941) 'Ethical Themes in the Antioch Mosaics', *Church History* 10: 367–76.
Duchemin, J. ed. (1983) *Visages du destin dans les mythologies*. Paris.
Durham, D. B. (1938) 'Parody in Achilles Tatius', *CPh* 33: 1–19.
Dyck, A. R. (1986) *Michael Psellus: The Essays on Euripides and George of Pisidia and on Heliodorus and Achilles Tatius*. Vienna.
Easterling, P. and B. Knox eds. (1985) *The Cambridge History of Classical Literature*, vol. 1. Cambridge.
  eds. (1989) *The Cambridge History of Classical Literature*, vol. 1, part 4: 'The Hellenistic Period and the Empire'. Cambridge. (First published as part of *The Cambridge History of Classical Literature*, vol. 1. Cambridge, 1985.)
Edwards, C. (1993) *The Politics of Immorality in Ancient Rome*. Cambridge.
  (1997) 'Self-Scrutiny and Self-Transformation in Seneca's Letters', *G&R* 44.1: 23–38.
Edwards, D. (1987) 'The New Testament and the Ancient Romance: A Survey of Recent Research', *PSN* 17: 9–14.
Egger, B. M. (1988) 'Zu den Frauenrollen im griechischen Roman: Die Frau als Heldin und Leserin', *GCN* 1: 33–66.
  (1990) 'Women in the Greek Novel: Constructing the Feminine'. Diss., University of California – Irvine.
  (1994) 'Looking at Chariton's Callirhoe', in Morgan and Stoneman (1994), 31–48.
Ellis, H. (1934) *Man and Woman: A Study in Secondary and Tertiary Sexual Characteristics*. London.
Elsner, J. (1991) 'Visual Mimesis and the Myth of the Real: Ovid's Pygmalion as Viewer', *Ramus* 20.2: 154–68.
  (1992) 'Pausanias: A Greek Pilgrim in the Roman World', *Past and Present* 135: 3–29.
  (1993) 'Seductions of Art: Encolpius and Eumolpus in a Neronian Picture Gallery', *PCPS* 39: 30–47.
  (1994) 'From the Pyramids to Pausanias and Piglet: Monuments, Travel and Writing', in Goldhill and Osborne (1994), 224–54.
  (1995) *Art and the Roman Viewer*. Cambridge.

ed. (1996a) *Art and Text in Roman Culture*. Cambridge.

(1996b) 'Naturalism and the Erotics of the Gaze: Intimations of Narcissus', in Kampen (1996a), 247–61.

(1998) *Imperial Rome and Christian Triumph*. Oxford.

(2000a) 'Caught in the Ocular: Visualising Narcissus in the Roman World', in Spaas (2000), 89–110.

(2000b) 'Between Mimesis and Divine Power: Visuality in the Greco-Roman World', in Nelson (2000), 45–69.

(2001) 'Describing Self in the Language of Other: Pseudo (?) Lucian at the Temple of Hierapolis', in Goldhill (2001), 123–53.

Elsner, J. and Sharrock, A. R. (1991) 'Re-viewing Pygmalion', *Ramus* 20.2: 149–82.

Elsom, H. E. (1992) 'Callirhoe: Displaying the Phallic Woman', in Richlin (1992b), 212–30.

Engel, H. (1985) *Die Susanna-Erzählung*. Göttingen.

Esrock, E. J. (1994) *The Reader's Eye: Visual Imaging as Reader Response*. Baltimore.

Fantham, E. (1972) *Comparative Studies in Republican Latin Imagery*. Toronto.

(1989) 'Mime: The Missing Link in Roman Literary History', *CW* 82: 153–63.

Faris, W. B. (1991) 'The Labyrinth as Sign', in Caws (1991), 33–41.

Feldherr, A. (1998) *Spectacle and Society in Livy's History*. California.

Ferrari, G. (1987) *Listening to the Cicadas. A Study of Plato's Phaedrus*. Cambridge.

Finley, M. I. ed. (1974) *Studies in Ancient Society*. London.

Foley, H. P. ed. (1981) *Reflections of Women in Antiquity*. New York and London.

Fortenbaugh, W. W. and Gutas, P. eds. (1992) *Theophrastus: His Psychological, Doxographical, and Scientific Writings*. New Brunswick/London.

Foster, H. ed. (1988) *Vision and Visuality*. Seattle.

Foucault, M. (1986) *The Care of the Self: The History of Sexuality*, vol. 3, transl. R. Hurley, London. (= *Le Souci de Soi*. Paris, 1984.)

(1989) *The Order of Things: An Archaeology of the Human Sciences*. London. (= *Les Mots et les Choses*. Paris, 1966.)

Fowler, D. P. (1991) 'Narrate and Describe: the Problem of Ekphrasis', *JHS* 81: 25–35.

(1997) 'Second Thoughts on Closure', in Roberts, Dunn and Fowler (1997), 3–22.

Foxhall, L. and Salmon, J. eds. (1998) *Thinking Men: Masculinity and its Self-Representation in the Classical Tradition*. London and NY.

Frede, D. (2003) 'Stoic Determinism', in B. Inwood ed. *The Cambridge Companion to Stoicism*: 179–205.

Fredrick, D. ed. (2002a) *The Roman Gaze: Vision, Power, and the Body*. Baltimore, Maryland.

(2002b) 'Introduction: Invisible Rome', in Fredrick (2002a), 1–30.

Freedberg, D. (1989) *The Power of Images: Studies in the History and Theory of Response*. Chicago.
Freedman, B. (1991) *Staging the Gaze – Postmodernism, Psychoanalysis and Shakespearean Comedy*. Ithaca.
French, R. (1994) *Ancient Natural History*. London.
Frend, W. H. C. (1965) *Martyrdom and Persecution in the Early Church*. Oxford.
Freud, S. (1919) 'On the Uncanny', in Strachey (1856–1939) vol. 9, 217–52.
Frontisi-Ducroux, F. (1994) *Du Masque au visage: aspects de l'identité en Grèce ancienne*. Paris.
 (1996) 'Eros, Desire, the Gaze' in Kampen (1996a), 81–100.
Frontisi-Ducroux, F. and Vernant, J. B. (1997) *Dans L'œil du Miroir*. Paris.
Frye, N. (1976) *The Secular Scripture. A Study of the Structure of Romance*. Cambridge, Mass.
Fusillo, M. (1988) 'Textual Patterns and Narrative Situations in the Greek Novel', *GCN* 1: 17–31.
 (1989) *Il Romanzo Greco: Polifonia ed Eros*. Venice.
 (1990a) 'Le conflit des émotions: un topos du roman grec érotique', *Museum Helveticum* 47: 201–21.
 (1990b) 'Il testo nel testo: la citazione nel romanzo greco', *MD* 25: 27–48.
 (1991) *Naissance du Roman*. Paris. (= *Polifonia ed Eros*, transl. M. Abrioux.)
 (1997) 'How Novels End: Some Patterns of Closure in Ancient Narrative', in Roberts, Dunn and Fowler (1997), 209–27.
Galy, J.-M. and Thievel, A. eds. (1994) *La Rhétorique grecque: Actes du colloque 'Octave Navarre' 1992*. Nice.
Gamman, L. and Marshment, M. eds. (1988) *The Female Gaze*. London.
Gandelman, C. (1991) *Reading Pictures, Viewing Texts*. Bloomington.
Garland, L. (1990) '"Be Amorous, But Be Chaste . . .": Sexual Morality in Byzantine Learned and Vernacular Romance', *BMGS* 14: 62–120.
Garnaud, J.-P. (1991) *Achille Tatius d'Alexandrie. Le Roman de Leucippé et Clitophon*. Paris.
Garson, R. W. (1978) 'Works of Art in Achilles Tatius' *Leucippe and Clitophon*', *Acta Classica* 21: 83–6.
Gaselee, S. (1984) *Achilles Tatius*. First edn 1917. Loeb Classical Library, London and Cambridge, Mass.
Genette, G. (1987) *Seuils*. Paris.
Gesner, C. (1970) *Shakespeare and the Greek Romance: A Study of Origins*. Lexington.
Gianotti, G. F. (1996) 'Forme di consumo teatrale: mimo e spettacoli affini', in Pecere and Stramaglia (1996), 265–92.
Gigli, D. (1978) 'Alcune nuove concordanze fra Nonno ed Achille Tazio', in Livrea and Privitera (1978), 431–6.
Gill, C. (1973) 'The Sexual Episodes in the *Satyricon*', *CP* 68: 172–85.
 (1993) 'Plato on Falsehood – not Fiction', in Gill and Wiseman (1993), 38–87.

REFERENCES

Gill, C. and Wiseman, T. P. eds. (1993) *Lies and Fiction in the Ancient World*. Exeter.

Gleason, M. (1995) *Making Men*. Princeton.

Gledhill, C. ed. (1987) *Home Is Where the Heart Is: Studies in Melodrama and the Woman's Film*. London.

Goldhill, S. D. (1991) *The Poet's Voice: Essays on Poetics and Greek Literature*. Cambridge.

(1994) 'The Naive and Knowing Eye: Ecphrasis and the Culture of Viewing in the Hellenistic World', in Goldhill and Osborne (1994), 197–223.

(1995) *Foucault's Virginity: Ancient Erotic Fiction and the History of Sexuality*. Cambridge.

(1996) 'Refracting Classical Vision: Changing Cultures of Viewing', in Brennan and Jay (1996b), 15–28.

(1998) 'The Seductions of the Gaze: Socrates and his Girlfriends', in Cartledge, Millett and von Reden (1998), 105–24.

ed. (2001a) *Being Greek Under Rome. Cultural Identity, the Second Sophistic and the Development of Empire*. Cambridge.

(2001b) 'The Erotic Eye: Visual Stimulation and Cultural Conflict', in Goldhill (2001a), 154–94.

(2002) *Who Needs Greek? Contests in the Cultural History of Hellenism*. Cambridge.

Goldhill, S. D. and Osborne, R. eds. (1994) *Art and Text in Ancient Greek Culture*. Cambridge.

eds. (1999) *Performance Culture and Athenian Democracy*. Cambridge.

Gorden, G. S. ed. (1912) *English Literature and the Classics*. Oxford.

Gould, J. (1989) *Herodotus*. London.

Graff, G. (1989) 'Co-optation', in Veeser (1989), 168–81.

Grainger, J. D. (1991) *Hellenistic Phoenicia*. Oxford.

Greenblatt, S. (1991) *Marvellous Possessions. The Wonder of the New World*. Oxford.

Gregory, J. (1985) 'Some Aspects of Seeing in Euripides' *Bacchae*', *G&R* 32: 23–31.

Griffin, J. (1985) *Latin Poets and Roman Life*. London.

Grigson, G. (1976) *The Goddess of Love*. London.

Grooten, A. (1991) 'Coming to Your Senses... On the Scopic Order and Woman's Disorder', in Hermsen and van Lenning (1991), 208–27.

Gross, K. (1992) *The Dream of the Moving Statue*. Ithaca and London.

Grosz, E. (1990) *Jacques Lacan: A Feminist Introduction*. London.

Grottanelli, C. (1987) 'The Ancient Novel and Biblical Narrative', *QUCC* 27: 7–34.

Guida, A. 'Nuovi Testimoni di Longo e Achille Tazio', *Prometheus* 7: 1–10.

Gunderson, E. (2003) 'The Flavian Amphitheatre: All the World as Stage', in Boyle and Dominik (2003), 637–58.

Guthrie, W. K. C. (1975) *A History of Greek Philosophy*, vol. 4. Cambridge.

Hägg, T. (1971) *Narrative Technique in the Ancient Greek Romances: Studies of Chariton, Xenophon of Ephesus and Achilles Tatius*. Stockholm.
— (1983) *The Novel in Antiquity*. Oxford.
Haight, E. (1936) *Essays on Ancient Fiction*. New York.
— (1943) *Essays on the Greek Romances*. New York.
— (1945) *More Essays on the Greek Romances*. New York.
Hall, E. (1989) *Inventing the Barbarian*. Oxford.
— (1995) 'The Ass with Double Vision: Politicising an Ancient Greek Novel', in Margolies and Joannou (1995), 47–59.
Halperin, D., Winkler, J. J. and Zeitlin, F. I. eds. (1990) *Before Sexuality: the Construction of Erotic Experience in the Ancient Greek World*. Princeton.
Hanson, A. and Armstrong, D. (1986) 'The Virgin's Neck: Aeschylus' *Agamemnon* 245 and Other Texts', *BICS* 33: 97–100.
Harden, D. (1962) *The Phoenicians*. London.
Harding, S. and Hintikka, M. B. eds. (1983) *Discovering Reality: Feminist Perspectives on Epistemology, Metaphysics, Methodology, and Philosophy of Science*. D. Reidel Publishing Company.
Harlan, E. C. (1965) 'The Description of Paintings as a Literary Device and Its Application in Achilles Tatius'. Diss., University of Columbia.
Harrison, S. J. (1989) 'Two notes on Achilles Tatius', *Philologus* 133: 153–4.
Hartog, F. (1988) *The Mirror of Herodotus: The Representation of the Other in the writing of history*, transl. J. Lloyd. Berkeley. (= *Le Miroir d'Herodote*. Paris, 1980.)
Harvey, E. D. (1992) *Ventriloquised Voices. Feminist Theory and English Renaissance Texts*. London.
Havelock, E. (1963) *Preface to Plato*. Cambridge, Mass.
Hawley, R. 'Female Characterization in Greek Declamation', in Innes, Hine and Pelling (1995), 255–67.
Heath, J. (1992) *Actaeon, The Unmannerly Intruder – The Myth and its Meaning in Classical Literature*. New York.
Heath, M. (1989) *Unity in Greek Poetics*. Oxford.
Hedrick, C. W. (1998) 'Conceiving the Narrative: Colors in Achilles Tatius and the Gospel of Mark', in Hock, Chance and Perkins (1998), 177–97.
Hefferman, C. F. (1988) *The Phoenix at the Fountain. Images of Woman and Eternity in Lactantius's Carmen de Ave Phoenice and the Old English Phoenix*. London and Toronto.
Heffernan, J. A. W. (1993) *The Museum of Words: The Poetics of Ekphrasis from Homer to Ashbery*. Chicago.
Heinze, R. (1899) 'Petron und der griechische Roman', *Hermes* 34: 494–519.
Heiserman, A. R. (1977) *The Novel before the Novel*. Chicago.
Henderson, J. (1991) *The Maculate Muse: Obscene Language in Attic Comedy*, 2nd edn. New York.
Henrichs, A. (1972) *Die Phoinikika des Lollianos*. Bonn.
Henriques, F. (1962) *Prostitution and Society*. New York.

Henry, M. M. (1985) *Menander's Courtesans and the Greek Comic Tradition*. Frankfurt.

(1992) 'The Edible Women: Athenaeus "Concept of the Pornographic"', in Richlin (1992b), 250–68.

(2000) 'Athenaeus, the Ur-Pornographer', in Braund and Wilkins (2000), 503–10.

Herbert, R. L. (1988) *Impressionism: Art, Leisure and Parisian Society*. New Haven.

Hermsen, J. J. and van Lenning, A. eds. (1991) *Sharing the Difference: Feminist Debates in Holland*. London.

Hesk, J. P. (2000) *Deception and Democracy in Classical Athens*. Cambridge.

Hewitt, N., O'Barr, J. and Rosebaugh, N. eds. (1996) *Talking Gender: Public Images, Personal Journeys and Political Critiques*. North Carolina.

Hoar, N. (1992) 'Genderlect, Powerlect and Politeness', in Perry, Turner and Sterk (1992), 69–77.

Hock, R. F., Chance, J. B. and Perkins, J. eds. (1998) *Ancient Fiction and Early Christian Narrative*. Society of Biblical Literature. Atlanta, Ga.

Hodges, A. (1638) *The Loves of Clitophon and Leucippe, A Most Elegant History, Written in Greeke by Achilles Tatius and now Englished*. Oxford.

Holquist, M. (1990) *Dialogism. Bakhtin and his World*. London.

Holzberg, N. (1995) *The Ancient Novel*, transl. C. Jackson-Holzberg. London. (= *Der Antike Roman*. Munich, 1986.)

hooks, bell (1992) *Black Looks: Race and Representation*. Boston, Mass.

Hopkinson, N. ed. (1994) 'Studies in the *Dionysiaca* of Nonnos', *PCPS* suppl. vol. 17.

Hopwood, K. (1998) 'All that may become a man: the bandit in the ancient novel', in Foxhall and Salmon (1998), 195–204.

How, W. W. and Wells, J. (1912) *A Commentary on Herodotus*, vol. 1. Oxford.

Hubaux, J. and Leroy, M. (1939) *Le Mythe du Phénix dans les littératures grecque et latine*. Liège.

Hubbard, T. K. (2002) 'Pindar, Theoxenus, and the Homoerotic Eye'. *Arethusa* 35 no. 2 Spring 2002: 255–96.

Huet, P.-D. (1670) *Traité de l'origine des romans*, repr. 1942, ed. A. Kok. Amsterdam.

Hughes, D. D. (1991) *Human Sacrifice in Ancient Greece*. London.

Hughes Fowler, B. (1989) *The Hellenistic Aesthetic*. Bristol.

Hunter, R. L. (1983) *A Study of Daphnis and Chloe*. Cambridge.

(1989) *Apollonius of Rhodes: Argonautica Book III*. Cambridge.

(1992) 'Writing the God: Form and Meaning in Callimachus, Hymn to Athena', *MD* 29: 9–34.

(1993) Review of M. Fusillo's *Naissance du roman* and D. Teske's *Der Roman des Longos als Werk der Kunst: Untersuchungen zum Verhaltnis von Physis und Techne in 'Daphnis und Chloe'*, in *JHS* 113: 201–2.

(1994) 'History and Historicity in the Romance of Chariton', *ANRW* 2.34.2: 1055–86.

(1996) 'Education at the Margins. Response to J. R. Morgan, "*Erotika Mathemata*: Greek Romance as Sentimental Education"', in Sommerstein and Atherton (1996), 191–205.

(1997) 'Longus and Plato', in Picone and Zimmermann (1997), 15–28.

ed. (1998) *Studies in Heliodorus*, PCPS suppl. vol. 21.

Imbert, C. (1980) 'Stoic Logic and Alexandrian Poetics', in Schofield, Burnyeat and Barnes (1980), 182–216.

Innes, D., Hine, H. and Pelling, C. eds. (1995) *Ethics and Rhetoric. Classical Essays for Donald Russell on his Seventy-Fifth Birthday*. Oxford.

Ioppolo, A. M. (1990) 'Presentation and Assent: A Physical and Cognitive Problem in Early Stoicism', *CQ* 40.2 (1990), 433–49.

Irigaray, L. (1985) *This Sex Which Is Not One* transl. C. Porter. Ithaca.

Irwin, E. (1974) *Colour Terms in Greek Poetry*. Toronto.

Jacobs, F. (1821) *Achillis Tatii Alexandrini de Leucippes et Clitophontis amoribus libri octo*. Lipsiae.

Jay, M. (1988) 'Scopic Regimes of Modernity', in Foster (1988), 3–23.

(1993) *Downcast Eyes. The Denigration of Vision in Twentieth-Century French Thought*. Berkeley.

(1996) 'Vision in Context: Reflections and Refractions', in Brennan and Jay (1996b), 1–14.

Jeffreys, S. (1993) *The Lesbian Heresy: A Feminist Perspective on the Lesbian Sexual Revolution*. London.

Jenks, C. ed. (1995a) *Visual Culture*. London and New York.

ed. (1995b) 'The Centrality of the Eye in Western Culture: An Introduction', in Jenks (1995a), 1–25.

ed. (1995c) 'Watching Your Step: the History and Practice of the Flâneur', in Jenks (1995a), 142–60.

Jennison, G. (1937) *Animals for Show and Pleasure in Ancient Rome*. Manchester.

Jocelyn, H. D. (1980) 'A Greek Indecency and its Students: ΛΑΙΚΑΖΕΙΝ', *PCPS* 26: 12–66.

Johansen, T. K. (1997) *Aristotle on Sense-Organs*. Cambridge.

Johns, C. (1982) *Sex or Symbol: Erotic Images of Greece and Rome*. London.

Johnson, B. (1998) *The Feminist Difference: Literature, Psychoanalysis, Race, and Gender*. Boston, Mass.

Jonas, H. (1954) 'The Nobility of Sight', in *Philosophy and Phenomenological Research* 14: 507–52.

Jordanova, L. (1989) *Sexual Visions: Images of Gender in Science and Medicine between the Eighteenth and Twentieth Centuries*. London and New York.

Kampen, N. B. ed. (1996a) *Sexuality in Ancient Art*. Cambridge.

(1996b) 'Omphale and the instability of gender', in Kampen (1996a), 233–46.

Kaplan, A. E. (1983) 'Is the Gaze Male?', in Snitow, Stansell and Thompson (1983), 309–27.

(1997) *Looking for the Other: Feminism, Film, and the Imperial Gaze*. London.

Kappeler, S. (1986) *The Pornography of Representation*. Minneapolis.

REFERENCES

Kaster, R. A. (2001) 'Controlling Reason: Declamation in Rhetorical Education at Rome', in Too and Livingstone (2001), 317–37.

Keitel, E. (1991) 'The Non-Appearance of the Phoenix at Tacitus *Annals* 6.28', *AJP* 120.3: 429–42.

Keller, E. F. and Grontkowski, C. R. (1983) 'The Mind's Eye', in Harding and Hintikka (1983), 207–24.

Kelly, D. (1992) *Telling Glances. Voyeurism in the French Novel.* New Jersey.

Kendall, R. and Pollock, G. eds. (1991) *Dealing with Degas: Representations of Women and the Politics of Vision.* London.

Kennedy, D. (1993) *The Arts of Love.* Cambridge.

Kennedy, G. A. (1999) *Progymnasmata: Greek Textbooks of Prose Composition Introductory to the Study of Rhetoric.* Fort Collins, privately published.

Kérenyi, K. (1927) *Die griechische-orientalische Romanliteratur in religionsgeschichtlicher Beleuchtung.* Tübingen.

Kermode, F. (1979) *The Genesis of Secrecy: On the Interpretation of Narrative.* Cambridge, Mass.

King, H. (1986) 'Agnodike and the profession of medicine', *PCPS* 32: 53–77.

Kofman, S. (1991) *Freud and Fiction.* Cambridge.

Kokolakis, M. (1959) 'Pantomimus and the Treatise Περὶ Ὀρχήσεως', *Platon* 10: 3–56.

Konstan, D. (1994) *Sexual Symmetry: Love in the Ancient Novel and Related Genres.* Princeton.

Kornfeld, W. (1972) 'Prostitution Sacrée', in *Supplément au Dictionnaire de la Bible*, fasc. 47, cols. 1358–9.

Kost, K. (1971) *Musaios. Hero und Leander.* Bonn.

Krasner, J. (1992) *The Entangled Eye: Visual Perception and the Representation of Nature in Post-Darwinian Narratives.* Oxford.

Krier, T. M. (1990) *Gazing on Secret Sights: Spencer, Classical Imitation, and the Decorums of Vision.* Ithaca and London.

Kuch, H. ed. (1989a) *Der antike Roman: Untersuchungen zur literarischen Kommunikation und Gattungsgeschichte.* Berlin.

ed. (1989b) 'Die "Barbaren" und der antike Roman', *Das Altertum* 35: 80–6.

La Belle, J. (1988) *'Herself Beheld'. The Literature of the Looking Glass.* Ithaca.

Lacan, J. (1977) *The Four Fundamental Concepts of Psychoanalysis*, ed. J.-A. Miller, transl. A. Sheridan. London.

Laplace, M. (1980a) 'Sur un Lieu Commun d'Achille Tatius', *REG* 93: 515–19.

(1980b) 'Les Légendes Troyennes dans le "Roman" de Chariton, Chaireas et Callirhoe', *REG* 93: 83–125.

(1983a) 'Légende et fiction chez Achille Tatius: les personnages de Leucippé et d'Io', *Bulletin de l'Association Guillaume Budé* October 1983: 311–18.

(1983b) 'Achilleus Tatios, *Leucippé et Clitophon*: P. Oxyrhynchos 1250', *ZPE* 53: 53–9.

(1983c) 'Achille Tatius, *Leucippé et Clitophon* 2.14.8: sur un fleuve prétendument Ibérique', *L'Antiquité Classique* 52: 243–5.

(1988a) 'Etudes sur le roman d'Achille Tatius, Leucippé et Clitophon'. Diss. Paris.
(1988b) 'Achilleus Tatios, Leucippé et Clitophon 3.21.3. L'Oracle des "Bouviers" du Nil', *ZPE* 74: 97–100.
(1991) 'Achille Tatius, Leucippé et Clitophon: des Fables au Roman de Formation', *GCN* 4: 35–56.
(1993) 'A Propos du P. Robinson-Coloniensis d'Achille Tatius, Leucippé et Clitophon', *ZPE*: 43–56.
(1994) 'La parole et l'action chez Euripide, Platon et Achille Tatius: sur la séduction du paradoxe et du revirement romanesques', in Galy and Thievel (1994), 233–58.
Laqueur, T. (1986) 'Orgasm, generation, and the politics of reproductive biology', *Representations* 14: 1–41.
Lardinois, A. and McClure, L. (2001) *Making Silence Speak. Women's Voices in Greek Literature and Society*. Princeton.
Lausberg, H. (1960) *Handbuch der literarischen Rhetorik*. Munich.
Leach, E. W. (1988) *The Rhetoric of Space. Literary and Artistic Representations of Landscape in Republican and Augustan Rome*. Princeton.
Leclant, J. (1960), 'Astarté à cheval d'après les représentations égyptiennes', *Syria* 37 (1960): 1–67.
Lejeune, A. (1948) *Euclide et Ptolémée, deux stades de l'optique géométrique grecque*. Louvain.
(1948) *La'Optique de Claude Ptolémée dans la version latine d'après l'arabe de l'émir Eugène de Sicile*. Leiden.
Leppin, H. (1992) *Histrionen: Untersuchungen zur sozialen Stellung von Buhnekunstlern im Westen des romischen Reiches zur Zeit der Republik und des Principats*. Bonn.
Létoublon, F. (1993) *Les Lieux Communs du Roman. Stéréotypes Grecs d'Aventure et d'Amour*. Leiden.
Levi, D. (1944) 'The Novel of Ninus and Semiramis', *PAPhS* 87: 420–8.
(1947) *Antioch Mosaic Pavements*. Princeton.
Levine, A.-J. ed. (1991) *Women Like This: New Perspectives on Jewish Women in the Greco-Roman World*. Atlanta.
Lightfoot, J. L. (2003) *Lucian: On the Syrian Goddess*. Oxford.
Lindberg, D. C. (1976) *Theories of Vision From Al-Kindi to Kepler*. Chicago and London.
Littlewood, A. R. (1977) 'The Romantic Paradise', in Reardon (1977), 34–6.
Liviabella Furiani, P. (1985a) 'Achille Tazio 8.9.9. sgg e Platone, *Leggi* 12.961 A-B: Un Esempio di Imitazione e Deformazione', *Prometheus* 11: 179–82.
(1985b) 'Religione e letteratura nel "racconto" di sacrifici umani presso i romanzieri greci d'amore', in *Filosofia della natura e pensiero religioso, Quaderni dell'Istituto di Filosofia dell'Università di Perugia* 11: 87–119.
(1988) '*Gamos* et *kenogamion* nel romanzo di Achille Tazio', *Euphrosune* 16: 271–80.

(1989) 'Di donna in donna. Elementi "femministi" nel romanzo greco d'amore', in Liviabella Furiani and Scarcella (1989), 43–106.

(2002) 'Il corpo nel romanzo di Achille Tazio', *AN* 1: 134–51.

Liviabella Furiani, P. and Scarcella, A. eds. (1989) *Piccolo Mondo Antico*. Perugia.

Livrea, E. and Privitera, G. A. eds. (1978) *Studi in onore di Anthos Ardizzoni*. Rome.

Lloyd, G. E. R. (1983) *Science, Folklore and Ideology*. Cambridge.

Long, A. A. ed. (1966) 'Thinking and Sense-Perception in Empedocles: Mysticism or Materialism', *CQ* 16: 256–76.

— ed. (1971) *Problems in Stoicism*. London.

— ed. (1974) *Hellenistic Philosophy*. London.

— ed. (1996) *Stoic Studies*. Cambridge.

Lovejoy, A. O. and Boas, G. (1935) *Primitivism and Related Ideas in Antiquity*. Baltimore.

Lowe, N. J. (2000) *The Classical Plot and the Invention of Western Narrative*. Cambridge.

Machamer, P. K. and Turnbull, R. G. eds. (1978) *Studies in Perception: Interrelations in the History of Philosophy and Science*. Columbia/Columbus.

Maclean, M. (1988) *Narrative as Performance. The Baudelairean Experiment*. London.

MacQueen, B. (1990) *Myth, Rhetoric and Fiction. A Reading of Longus' 'Daphnis and Chloe'*. Lincoln, Nebr. and London.

Maeder, D. (1991) 'Au Seuil des Romans Grecs: Effets du réel et effets de création', *GCN* 4: 1–33.

Maehler, H. (1976) 'Der Metiochus-Parthenope Roman', *ZPE* 23: 1–20.

Malamud, M. (1990) 'Making a Virtue of Perversity: the Poetry of Prudentius', in Boyle (1990), 274–98.

Margolies, D. and Joannou, M. eds. (1995) *Heart of a Heartless World. Essays in Cultural Resistance in Memory of Margot Heinemann*. London.

Marrou, H.-I. (1956) *A History of Education in Antiquity*. London.

Matsen, R. P., Rollinsen, P. and Sousa, M. eds. (1990) *Readings in Classical Rhetoric*. Illinois.

Mayne, J. (1993) *Cinema and Spectatorship*. London.

McCarty, W. (1989) 'The Shape of the Mirror: Metaphorical Catoptrics in Classical Literature', *Arethusa* 22: 161–90.

McClure, L. (1999) *Spoken Like a Woman. Speech and Gender in Athenian Drama*. Princeton.

McConnell-Ginet, S., Borker, R. and Furman, N. eds. (1980) *Women and Language in Literature and Society*. Praeger, USA.

McDermott, H. (1989) *Novel and Romance: The 'Odyssey' to 'Tom Jones'*. Basingstoke.

McGill, S. C. (2000) 'The Literary Lives of a *Scheintod*: Clitophon and Leucippe 5.7 and Greek Epigram', *CQ* 50: 323–6.

McHale, B. (1987) *Postmodern Fiction*. New York and London.
McKay, P. A. (1963) 'Klephtika', *G&R* 10: 147–52.
McKeown, J. (1979) 'Augustan elegy and mime', *PCPS* 25: 71–84.
McLeod, A. M. G. (1969) 'Physiology and Medicine in a Greek Novel', *JHS* 89: 97–105.
Melville, S. and Readings, B. eds. (1995) *Vision and Textuality*. Basingstoke.
Merkelbach, R. (1962) *Roman und Mysterium in der Antike*. Munich and Berlin.
Metz, C. (1974) *Language and Cinema*. The Hague.
Meyering, T. C. (1989) *Historical Roots of Cognitive Science: The Rise of Cognitive Theory of Perception from Antiquity to the Nineteenth Century*. Dordrecht.
Mignogna, E. (1993) 'Europa o Selene? Achille Tazio e Mosco o il Ritorno dell' "Inversione"', *Maia* 45: 177–83.
　(1995) 'Roman und *Paradoxon*: Die Metamorphosen der Metapher in Achilleus Tatios' *Leukippe und Kleitophon*', *GCN* 6: 21–37.
　(1996a) 'Narrativa greca e mimo: il romanzo di Achille Tazio', *SIFC* 14, fasc. 2. Florence.
　(1996b) 'Il Mimo "Leucippe". Un ipotesi su PBerol inv. 13927 [Pack2 2437]', *Rivista di Cultura Classica e Medioevale* 38: 161–6.
　(1997) 'Leucippe in Tauride (Ach. Tat. 3, 15–22): mimo e "pantomimo" tra tragedia e romanzo', in *MD* 38: 225–36.
Miles, R. ed. (1999) *Constructing Identities in Late Antiquity*. London.
Millar, F. (1983) 'The Phoenician Cities: A Case-Study of Hellenisation', *PCPS* 29: 55–71.
Miller, J. (1990) *Seductions: Studies in Reading and Culture*. London.
Mills, S. (1994) *Gendering the Reader*. Hemel Hempstead.
Moger, A. S. (1982) 'That Obscure Object of Narrative', *YFS* 63: 129–38.
Molesworth, C. (1991) 'The City: Some Classical Moments', in Caws (1991), 12–30.
Molinié, G. (1982) *Du Roman Grec Au Roman Baroque*. Toulouse.
Montague, H. (1992) 'Sweet and Pleasant Passion: Female and Male Passion in Ancient Romance Novels', in Richlin (1992b) 231–49.
Morales, H. L. (1995) 'The Taming of the View: Natural Curiosities in *Leukippe and Kleitophon*', *GCN* 6: 39–50.
　(1996) 'The Torturer's Apprentice: Parrhasius and the Limits of Art', in Elsner (1996a), 182–209.
　(1997) 'A Scopophiliac's Paradise: Vision and Narrative in Achilles Tatius'. Diss., University of Cambridge.
　(1999) 'Constructing Gender in Musaeus' *Hero and Leander*', in Miles (1999), 41–69. London.
　(2000) 'Sense and Sententiousness in the Ancient Greek Novels', in Sharrock and Morales (2000), 67–88.
　(forthcoming) 'The ancient novels and the history of sexuality' in Whitmarsh (forthcoming).

Morgan, J. R. (1982) 'History, Romance and Realism in Heliodorus', *CA* 1: 221–65.
  (1993) 'Make-Believe and Make Believe: the Fictionality of the Greek Novels', in Gill and Wiseman (1993), 175–229.
  (1994) 'Daphnis and Chloe: Love's Own Sweet Story', in Morgan and Stoneman (1994), 64–79.
  (1995) 'The Greek Novel: Towards a Sociology of Production and Reception', in Powell (1995), 130–52.
  (1996a) 'The Ancient Novel at the End of the Century: Scholarship since the Dartmouth Conference', review article in *CP* 91: 63–73.
  (1996b) '*Erotika Mathemata*: Greek Romance as Sentimental Education', in Sommerstein and Atherton (1996), 163–89.
Morgan, J. R. and Stoneman, R. eds. (1994) *Greek Fiction: The Greek Novel in Context*. London.
Morgan, T. (1998) *Literate Education in the Hellenistic and Roman Worlds*. Cambridge.
Morris, I. ed. (1994) *Classical Greece: Ancient Histories and Modern Archaeologies*. Cambridge.
Moscati, S. (1968) *The World of the Phoenicians*. London.
Most, G. W. (1989) 'The Strangers' Stratagem: Self-Disclosure and Self-Sufficiency in Greek Culture', *JHS* 109: 114–33.
Mugler, C. (1960) 'La lumière et la vision dans la poésie grecque', *REG* 73: 40–73.
Mulvey, L. (1975) 'Visual Pleasure and Narrative Cinema', *Screen* 16.3: 6–18.
  (1981) 'Afterthoughts on "Visual Pleasure and Narrative Cinema" inspired by King Vidor's *Duel in the Sun* (1946)', *Framework* 15/16/17 (1981): 12–15.
  (1989) *Visual and Other Pleasures*. Basingstoke.
Musurillo, H. ed. (1954) *Acts of the Pagan Martyrs. Acta Alexandrinorum*. Oxford.
  ed. (1972) *The Acts of the Christian Martyrs*. Oxford.
Myerowitz, M. (1992) 'The Domestication of Desire: Ovid's *Parva Tabella* and the Theater of Love', in Richlin (1992b): 131–55.
Napolitano, F. (1983–4) 'Leucippe nel Romanzo di Achille Tazio', *Annali della Facoltà di Lettere e Filosofia della Università di Napoli* 26: 85–101.
Nelson, R. S. ed. (2000) *Visuality Before and Beyond the Renaissance*. Cambridge.
Newby, Z. (2002) 'Reading Programs in Greco-Roman Art: Reflections on the Spada Reliefs', in Fredrick (2002a): 110–48.
Nimis, S. (1994) 'The Prosaics of the Ancient Novel', *Arethusa* 27.3: 387–411.
  (1998) 'Memory and Description in the Ancient Novel', *Arethusa* 31.1: 99–122.
  (1999) 'The Sense of Openendedness in the Ancient Novel', *Arethusa* 32.2: 215–38.
Nolan, E. P. (1990) *Now Through a Glass Darkly. Specular Images of Being and Knowing from Virgil to Chaucer*. Ann Arbor.

Nutting, H. C. (1922) 'Oculos Effodere', *CP* 17: 313–18.
Ogle, M. B. (1913) 'The Classical Origin and Tradition of Literary Conceits', *AJP* 34: 125–52.
  (1920) 'The Lover's Blindness', *AJP* 41: 240–52.
Olender, M. (1985) 'Aspects de Baubo: Textes et contextes antiques', *RHR* 1: 3–55, an abridged translation of which appears as 'Aspects of Baubo: Ancient Texts and Contexts', in Halperin, Winkler and Zeitlin (1990), 83–113.
Onians, J. (1980) 'Abstraction and Imagination in Late Antiquity', *Art History* 3: 1–24.
Orlandini, M. (1993) 'Note sul romanzo greco: il paesaggio urbano tra retorica e storiografia', *A&R* 38: 57–78.
Orr, L. (1991) *Problems and Poetics of the Nonaristotelian Novel*. London and Toronto.
O'Brien, D. (1970) 'The Effect of a Simile: Empedocles' Theories of Seeing and Breathing', *JHS* 90: 140–79.
O'Sullivan, J. N. (1978) 'Notes on the Text and Interpretation of Achilles Tatius 1', *CQ* 28: 324.
  (1980) *A Lexicon to Achilles Tatius*. Berlin and New York.
Osborne, R. (1986) 'The Viewing and Obscuring of the Parthenon Frieze', *JHS* 107: 98–105.
  (1994a) 'Framing the Centaur: Reading Fifth-Century Architectural Sculpture', in Goldhill and Osborne (1994), 52–84.
  (1994b) 'Looking On – Greek Style. Does the Sculpted Girl Speak to Women Too?', in Morris (1994), 81–96.
  (1997) 'Men Without Clothes: Heroic Nakedness and Greek Art', in Wyke (1997), 504–28.
Owens, E. J. (1991) *The City in the Greek and Roman World*. London.
Pacteau, F. (1994) *The Symptom of Beauty*. London.
Padel, R. (1992) *In and Out of the Mind: Greek Images of the Tragic Self*. Princeton.
Page, C. (1991) 'The Truth about Lies in Plato's Republic', *AncPhil*. 11: 1–33.
Page, D. (1951) *A New Chapter in the History of Greek Tragedy*. Cambridge.
Panayotakis, C. (1995) *Theatrum Arbitri. Theatrical Elements in the 'Satyrica' of Petronius*. Leiden.
Parker, H. (1992) 'Love's Body Anatomized: The Ancient Erotic Handbooks and the Rhetoric of Sexuality', in Richlin (1992b), 90–111.
Parker, P. (1987) *Literary Fat Ladies*. London.
Patnaik, E. (1989) 'The Succulent Gender: Eat Her Softly', in Bevan (1989), 59–74.
Pearcy, L. T. (1978) 'Achilles Tatius, *Leucippe and Clitophon* 1.14–15 – An Unnoticed Lacuna?', *CP* 73: 233–5.
Pearson, L. C. (1909) 'Phrixus and Demodice', *CR*: 255–7.
Pecere, O. and Stramaglia, A. eds. (1996) *La Letteratura di Consumo nel Mondo Greco-Latino*. Cassino.

REFERENCES

Perkins, J. (1995) *The Suffering Self: Pain and Narrative Representation in the Early Christian Era*. London.
Pernot, L. (1983) 'Chance et Destin dans la Rhétorique Epideictique Grecque à l'Epoque Impériale', in Duchemin (1983), 121–9.
Perry, B. E. (1967) *The Ancient Romances: A Literary-Historical Account of their Origins*. Berkeley.
Perry, L. A. M., Turner, L. H., and Sterk, H. M. eds. (1992) *Constructing and Reconstructing Gender: The Links among Communication, Language and Gender*. New York.
Pervo, R. I. (1987) *Profit with Delight. The Literary Genre of the Acts of the Apostles*. Philadelphia.
  (1991) 'Aseneth and her Sisters: Women in Jewish Narrative and in the Greek novels', in Levine (1991), 145–60.
Phillimore, J. S. (1912) 'The Greek Romances', in Gorden (1912), 87–117.
Picone, M. and Zimmerman, B. eds. (1997) *Der antike Roman und seine mittelalterliche Rezeption*. Basel.
Plazenet, L. (1997) *L'Ebahissement et la délectation. Réception comparée et poétiques du roman grec en France et en Angleterre aux XVIe et XVIIe siècles*. Paris.
Plepelits, K. (1996) 'Achilles Tatius' in Schmeling ed. (1996): 387–416.
  (1980) *Achilleus Tatios. Leukippe und Kleitophon*. Stuttgart.
Polity Press ed. (1994) *The Polity Reader in Gender Studies*. Cambridge.
Pollard, J. (1977) *Birds in Greek Life and Myth*. London.
Pollitt, J. J. (1974) *The Ancient View of Greek Art: Criticism, History, and Terminology*. New Haven and London.
Pollock, G. (1991) 'The Gaze and the Look: *Women with Binoculars* – A Question of Difference', in Kendall and Pollock (1991), 106–30.
Potter, D. (1993) 'Martyrdom as Spectacle', in Scodel (1993), 53–88.
Powell, A. ed. (1995) *The Greek World*. London.
Powell, J. U. (1933) *New Chapters in the History of Greek Literature*, vol. 3. Oxford.
Pratt, M. L. (1992) *Imperial Eyes. Travel Writing and Transculturation*. London.
Pratt, L. H. (1993) *Lying and Poetry from Homer to Pindar*. Ann Arbor.
Prendergast, C. (1991) 'Framing the City: Two Parisian Windows', in Caws (1991), 179–95.
Prier, R. (1989) *Thauma Idesthai: The Phenomenology of Sight and Appearance in Archaic Greek*. Tallahassee, Florida.
Quet, M.-A. (1992) 'Romans grecs, mosaiques romaines', in Baslez, Hoffmann and Trédé (1992), 125–60.
Quiggin, E. C. ed. (1913) *Essays and Studies Presented to William Ridgeway*. Cambridge.
Radford, J. ed. (1986) *The Progress of Romance: The Politics of Popular Fiction*. London.
Raeder, J. (1983) *Priene: Funde aus einer griechischen Stadt*. Berlin.

Rattenbury, R. M. (1926) 'Chastity and chastity ordeals in ancient Greek romances', *PLL* 1: 59–71.
　(1933) 'Romance: Traces of Lost Greek Novels', in Powell (1933), 211–57.
　(1956) Review of Vilborg (1955), *CR* 6: 229–33.
Reardon, B. P. (1971) *Courants littéraires grecs des IIe et IIIe siècles après J.-C.* Paris.
　ed. (1977) *Erotica Antiqua*. Acta of the International Conference on the Ancient Novel. Bangor, Maine.
　(1989) *The Collected Ancient Greek Novels*. Berkeley.
　(1991) *The Form of Greek Romance*. Princeton.
　(1994) 'Achilles Tatius and Ego-Narrative', in Morgan and Stoneman (1994), 80–96.
Reich, H. (1974) *Der Mimus*. Leipzig.
Reeve, M. D. (1971) 'Hiatus in the Greek Novelists', *CQ* 21: 514–39.
　(1981) 'Five Dispensable Manuscripts of Achilles Tatius', *JHS* 101: 114–15.
Reynolds, R. (1946) 'The Adultery Mime', *CQ* 40: 77–84.
Richlin, A. (1992a) *The Garden of Priapus: Sexuality and Aggression in Roman Humor*. New York.
　ed. (1992b) *Pornography and Representation in Greece and Rome*. Oxford.
　(1992c) 'Reading Ovid's Rapes', in Richlin (1992b), 158–79.
　(1996) 'How Putting the Man in Roman Put the Roman in Romance', in Hewitt, O'Barr and Rosebaugh (1996), 14–35.
Richlin, A. and Rabinowitz, N. S. eds. (1993) *Feminist Theory and the Classics*. Oxford.
Rispoli, G. M. (1985) *L'Artista sapiente. Per una storia della fantasia*. Naples.
Rist, J. M. (1969) *Stoic Philosophy*. Cambridge.
Roberts, D. H., Dunn, F. M. and Fowler, D. eds. (1997) Princeton.
Roberts, J. A. (1991) *The Shakespearean World: Geography, Genus and Gender*. Lincoln, Nebr. and London.
Roberts, M. (1989) *The Jeweled Style. Poetry and Poetics in Late Antiquity*. Ithaca and London.
Robertson, D. S. (1913) 'The authenticity and date of Lucian *De Saltatione*', in Quiggin (1913), 180–5.
Rohde, E. (1914) *Der griechische Roman und seine Vorläufer*. 4th edn, 1960. Leipzig.
Romm, J. (1992) *The Edges of the Earth in Ancient Thought: Geography, Exploration, and Fiction*. Princeton.
Rommel, H. (1923) *Die naturwissenschaftlich-paradoxographischen Exkurse bei Philostratos, Heliodoros und Achille Tatios*. Stuttgart.
Roscher, W. H. (1890) *Über Selene und Verwandtes*. Leipzig.
Rose, H. J. (1928) *A Handbook of Greek Mythology*. London.
Rose, M. A. (1979) *Parody/Meta-Fiction*. London.
Rose, P. W. (1993) 'The Case for Not Ignoring Marx in the Study of Women in Antiquity', in Richlin and Rabinowitz (1993), 211–37.

Rouveret, A. (1989) *Histoire et Imaginaire de la Peinture Ancienne*. Rome.
Rowland, B. (1978) *Birds with Human Souls. A Guide to Bird Symbolism*. Knoxville, Tennessee.
Russell, D. ed. (1990) *Antonine Literature*. Oxford.
Russell, D. A. and Wilson, N. G. eds. (1981) *Menander Rhetor* (translation and commentary). Oxford.
Rutherford, I. 1997 'Kalasiris and Setne Khamwas: A Greek Novel and Some Egyptian Models', *ZPE* 117: 203–9.
Saïd, S. (1994) 'The City in the Greek Novel', in Tatum (1994), 216–36.
Sanchez, M. B. (1981) 'Notas sobre el texto de Aquiles Tacio', *Habis* 12: 65–70.
(1992) 'Egito en la Novela Griega Antiqua', *Habis* 3: 197–215.
Sandbach, F. H. (1971) 'Phantasia Kataleptike', in Long (1971), 9–21.
Sandy, G. (1982) *Heliodorus*. Boston.
(1989) *The Story of Apollonius, King of Tyre*, transl. in Reardon (1989), 736–72.
Sandy, G. (1994) 'New Pages of Greek Fiction', in Morgan and Stoneman (1994), 130–45.
(1996) 'The Heritage of the Ancient Greek Novel in France and Britain', in Schmeling (1996), 735–73.
Scarcella, A. M. (1987) 'Caratteri e Funzione delle gnomai in Achille Tazio', *Euphrosune* 15: 269–80.
Scarry, E. (1985) *The Body in Pain: the Making and Unmaking of the World*. Oxford.
Schissel von Fleschenberg, O. (1913) *Entwicklungsgeschichte des griechischen Romanes im Altertum*. Halle.
(1942) 'Digenes Akritas und Achilleus Tatios', *Neophilologus* 27: 143–8.
Schmeling, G. ed. (1996) *The Novel in the Ancient World*. Leiden.
Schmitz, T. (1997) *Bildung und Macht: Zur sozialen und politischen Funktion der zweiten Sophistik in der griechischen Welt der Kaiserzeit*. Munich.
Schofield, M. (1991) *The Stoic Idea of the City*. Chicago.
Schofield, M., Burnyeat, M. and Barnes, J. eds. (1980) *Doubt and Dogmatism*. Oxford.
Schwartz, E. (1896) *Fünf Vorträge über den griechischen Roman*. Berlin.
Schwartz, J. (1976) 'Achille Tatius et Lucian de Samosate', in Reardon (1977), 81–90.
Scobie, A. ed. (1973a) *More Essays on the Ancient Romance and its Heritage*. Meisenheim.
Scobie, A. ed. (1973b), 'Barbarians in the Greek Romances', in Scobie (1973a), 19–34.
Scodel, R. ed. (1993) *Theater and Society in the Classical World*. Michigan.
Sedelmeier, D. (1959) 'Studien zu Achilleus Tatios', *WS* 72: 113–43.
Sedley, D. N. (1992) 'Empedocles' Theory of Vision and Theophrastus' De Sensibus', in Fortenbaugh and Gutas (1992), 20–31.
Segal, C. (1984) 'The Trials at the end of Achilles Tatius' *Clitophon and Leucippe*: doublets and complementaries', *SIFC* 77: 83–91.

(1995) 'Spectator and Listener', in Vernant (1995), 184–217.
Siebers, T. (1983) *The Mirror of Medusa*. Berkeley.
Selden, D. L. (1994) 'Genre of Genre', in Tatum (1994), 39–64.
Sharrock, A. R. (1991) 'Womanufacture', *JRS* 81: 36–49.
    (1994) *Seduction and Repetition in Ovid's Ars Amatoria 2*. Oxford.
    (2000) 'Intratextuality: Texts, Parts and (W)holes in Theory', in Sharrock and Morales (2000), 1–39.
    (2002) 'Looking at Looking: Can you Resist a Reading?', in Fredrick (2002a), 265–95.
Sharrock, A. R. and Morales, H. L. eds. (2000) *Intratextuality: Greek and Roman Textual Relations*. Oxford.
Shaw, B. (1984) 'Bandits in the Roman Empire', *Past and Present* 105: 3–52.
Shorrock, R. (2001) *The Challenge of Epic: Allusive Engagement in the Dionysiaca of Nonnus*. Leiden/Boston/Koln.
Siegel, R. E. (1970) *Galen on Sense Perception*.
Simon, G. (1988) *Le Regard, l'être et l'apparence dans l'optique de l'antiquité*. Paris.
Silverman, K. (1992) *Male Subjectivity at the Margins*. New York and London.
    (1996) *The Threshold of the Visible World*. New York and London.
Sissa, G. (1990) *Greek Virginity*. Cambridge, Mass.
Slater, N. 'Vision, Perception, and Phantasia in the Roman Novel', in Picone and Zimmerman (1997), 89–105.
    (1998) 'Passion and Petrification: the Gaze in Apuleius', *CP* 93: 18–48.
Smith, A. M. (1999) *Ptolemy and the Foundations of Ancient Mathematical Optics*. Philadelphia. (= *Transactions of the American Philosophical Society* 89.3.)
Smith, M. (1975) 'On the Wine God in Palestine', *Salo Wittmayer Jubilee Volume*, American Academy for Jewish Research (1975): 815–29.
Smith, R. (1889) *The Loves of Clitopho and Leucippe*. London.
Snare, G. (1989) *The Mystification of George Chapman*. Durham and London.
Sniader Lanser, S. (1981) *The Narrative Act: Point of View in Prose Fiction*. Princeton.
Snitow, A. B., Stansell, C. and Thompson, S. eds. (1983) *Powers of Desire*. New York.
Soder, R. (1932) *Die apokryphen Apostelgeschichten und die romanhafte Literatur der Antike*. Stuttgart.
Sommerstein, A. H. (1990) *Lysistrata* (edition and notes). Warminster.
Sommerstein, A. H. and Atherton, C. eds. (1996) *Nottingham Classical Literature Studies* 4.
Soulez-Luccioni, A. (1974) 'Le Paradigme de la vision de soi-même dans l'Alcibiade majeur', *Revue de Métaphysique et de Morale* 79: 196–222.
Spaas, L. ed. (2000) *Echoes of Narcissus*. New York and London.
Spearing, A. C. (1993) *The Medieval Poet as Voyeur*. Cambridge.
Spencer, N. ed. (1995) *Time, Tradition and Society in Greek Archaeology*. London.

REFERENCES

Spender, D. (1980) *Man Made Language*. London.
Stacey, J. (1994) *Hollywood Cinema and Female Spectatorship*. London.
Stallybrass, P. and White, A. (1986) *The Politics and Poetics of Transgression*. London.
  (1992) 'Transvestism and the "body beneath"', in Zimmerman (1992), 64–83.
Stam, R. (1992) *Reflexivity in Film and Literature From Don Quixote to Jean-Luc Godard*. Columbia.
Steel, L. (1995) 'Challenging Preconceptions of Oriental "Barbarity" and Greek "Humanity": Human Sacrifice in the Ancient World', in Spencer (1995), 19–27.
Stehle, E. S. (1990) 'Sappho's Gaze: Fantasies of a Goddess and Young Man', *differences* 2.1: 88–125.
Steiner, D. T. (1995) 'Stoning and Sight: A Structural Equivalence in Greek Mythology', in *CA* 14.1: 193–211.
  (2001) *Images in Mind. Statues in Archaic and Classical Literature and Thought*. Princeton.
Steiner, G. (1969) 'The Graphic Analogue from Myth in Greek Romance', *Illinois Studies in Language and Literature* 58: 123–37. (= *Classical Studies Presented to Ben Edwin Perry*. Chicago.)
Steiner, W. (1988) *Pictures of Romance: Form against Context in Painting and Literature*. Chicago.
Stephens, S. A. (1994) 'Who read ancient novels?', in Tatum (1994), 405–18.
Stephens, S. A. and Winkler, J. J. eds. (1995) *Ancient Greek Novels: The Fragments*. Princeton.
Steussy, M. J. (1993) *Gardens in Babylon: Narrative and Faith in the Greek Legends of Daniel*. Atlanta.
Stewart, A. (1997) *Art, Desire, and the Body in Ancient Greece*. Cambridge.
Stewart, S. (1984) *On Longing: Narratives of the Miniature, the Gigantic, the Souvenir, the Collection*. Baltimore.
  (1991) *Crimes of Writing: Problems in the Containment of Representation*. Oxford.
Still, J. and Worton, M. (1993) *Textuality and Sexuality. Reading Theories and Practices*. Manchester.
Stinton, T. C. W. (1976) 'Si Credere Dignum Est: Some Expressions of Disbelief in Euripides and Others', *PCPS* 22: 60–89.
Stonehill, B. (1988) *The Self-Conscious Novel: Artifice in Fiction from Joyce to Pynchon*. Philadelphia.
Strachey, J. ed. (1856–1939) *The Standard Edition of the Complete Psychological Works of Sigmund Freud*. London.
Sturken, M. and Cartwright, L. (2001) *Practices of Looking: An Introduction to Visual Culture*. Oxford.
Suleiman, S. R. (1986) *The Female Body in Western Culture*. Cambridge, Mass.
Sullivan, J. P. (1968) *The 'Satyricon' of Petronius: A Literary Study*. London.

Swain, S. (1996) *Hellenism and Empire. Language, Classicism, and Power in the Greek World AD 50–250*. Oxford.

Synnott, A. (1993) *The Body Social. Symbolism, Self and Society*. London.

Tait, J. (1994) 'Egyptian Fiction in Demotic and Greek', in Morgan and Stoneman (1994), 203–22.

Tambiah, S. J. (1969) 'Animals are Good to Think and Good to Prohibit', *Ethnology* 8: 423–59.

Tannen, D. (1991) *You Just Don't Understand: Women and Men in Conversation*. London.

(1994) *Gender and Discourse*. Oxford.

Tanner, T. (1979) *Adultery in the Novel*. Baltimore.

(1992) *Venice Desired*. Oxford.

Tatum, J. (1989) *Xenophon's Imperial Fiction: On the Education of Cyrus*. Princeton.

ed. (1994) *The Search for the Ancient Novel*. Baltimore.

Taylor, C. C. W. (1999) *The Atomists: Leucippus and Democritus*. Toronto.

Thorne, B., Kramarae, C. and Henley, N. eds. (1983) *Language, Gender and Society*. Rowley, Mass.

Tomlinson, R. (1992) *From Mycenae to Constantinople. The Evolution of the Ancient City*. London.

Too, Y. L. (1996) 'Statues, Mirrors, Gods: Controlling Images in Apuleius', in Elsner (1996), 133–52.

Too, Y. L. and Livingstone, N. eds. (2001) *Pedagogy and Power: Rhetorics of Classical Learning*. Cambridge.

Toynbee, J. M. C. (1973) *Animals in Roman Life and Art*. London and Southampton.

Trapp, M. B. (1990) 'Plato's *Phaedrus* in Second-Century Greek Literature', in Russell (1990), 141–73.

Underwood, E. A. ed. (1953) *Science, Medicine, and History: Essays on the Evolution of Scientific Thought and Medical Practice*. London.

Van Dijk, J. G. M. (1996) 'The Function of Fables in Graeco-Roman Romance', *Mnemosyne*, 49.5.

Van Hoof, A. J. L. (1988) 'Ancient Robbers: Reflections behind the Facts', *AncSoc* 19: 105–24.

van Hoorn, W. (1972) *As Images Unwind: Ancient and Modern Theories of Visual Perception*. Amsterdam.

Vasaly, A. (1993) *Representations. Images of the World in Ciceronian Oratory*. Berkeley.

Veeser, H. ed. (1989) *The New Historicism*. London.

Vessey, D. W. T. (1991–3) 'Thoughts on "The Ancient Novel" or What Ancients? What Novels?', *BICS* 38: 144–61.

Vernant, J.-P. (1998) *La Mort dans les yeux*. Paris.

(1991) *Mortals and Immortals. Collected Essays*, ed. F. I. Zeitlin. Princeton.

ed. (1995) *The Greeks*, transl. C. Lambert and T. L. Fagan. Chicago.

Veyne, P. (1978) 'La famille et l'amour sous le haut-empire romain', *Annales ESC* 33: 35-63.
Veyne, P. (1990) 'La Providence Stoïcienne intervient-elle dans l'Histoire?', *Latomus* 49: 553-74.
Vickers, N. J. (1986) 'This Heraldry in Lucrece' Face', in Suleiman (1986), 209-22.
Vilborg, E. (1955) *Achilles Tatius. Leucippe and Clitophon.* Stockholm.
  (1962) *Achilles Tatius. Leucippe and Clitophon. A Commentary.* Goteborg.
Vogliano, A. (1938) 'Un papiro di Achille Tazio', *SIFC* 15: 121-30.
von Dobschutz, E. (1902) 'Der Roman in der altchristlichen Literatur', *Deutsche Rundschaum* 111: 87-106.
von Fritz, K. (1953) 'Democritus' Theory of Vision', in Underwood (1953), 53-68.
von Reden, S. and Goldhill, S. (1999) 'Plato and the Performance of Dialogue', in Goldhill and Osborne (1999), 257-89.
von Staden, H. (1978) 'The Stoic Theory of Perception and its "Platonic" critics', in Machamer and Turnbull (1978), 96-136.
Walden, J. W. H. (1894) 'Stage Terms in Heliodorus' *Aethiopica*', *HSCP* 5: 1-43.
Walker, A. (1992) 'Eros and the Eyes in the *Love-Letters* of Philostratus', *PCPS* 38: 132-48.
Watson, G. (1988) *Phantasia in Classical Thought.* Galway.
Webb, R. (1999) 'Ekphrasis Ancient and Modern: the Invention of a Genre', *Word and Image* 15: 7-18.
  (2001) 'The Progymnasmata as Practice', in Too and Livingstone (2001), 289-316.
Wesseling, B. (1988) 'The Audience of the Ancient Novel', *GCN* 1: 67-79.
Whitmarsh, T. (1999) 'The Writes of Passage: Cultural Initiation in Heliodorus', in Miles (1999), 16-40.
  (2001) *Greek Literature and the Roman Empire. The Politics of Imitation.* Oxford.
  ed. (forthcoming) *The Cambridge Companion to the Ancient Novel.* Cambridge.
Wiersma, S. (1990) 'The Ancient Novel and its Heroines: a Female Paradox', *Mnemosyne* 43: 109-23.
Wilhelm, F. (1902): 'Zu Achilles Tatius', *RhM* 57: 55-75.
Williams, L. (1989) *Hard Core: Power, Pleasure, and the 'Frenzy of the Visible'.* Berkeley.
  ed. (1995) *Viewing Positions: Ways of Seeing Film.* New Brunswick, NJ.
Williamson, M. (1986) 'The Greek Romance', in Radford (1986), 23-43
Willis, W. H. (1990) 'The Robinson-Cologne Papyrus of Achilles Tatius', *GRBS* 31: 73-102.
Wilson, N. G. (1983) *Scholars of Byzantium.* London.
Wilson, P. (2000) *The Athenian Institution of the Khoregia. The Chorus, the City and the Stage.* Cambridge.

REFERENCES

Winkler, J. J. (1974) 'In Pursuit of Nymphs: Comedy and Sex in Nonnos' "Tales of Dionysus". Diss. Austin, Texas.

(1980) 'Lollianos and the Desperadoes', *JHS* 100: 155–81.

(1985) *Auctor and Actor: A Narratological Reading of Apuleius' Golden Ass.* Berkeley.

(1989) 'Achilles Tatius *Leucippe and Clitophon*', in Reardon (1989), 170–284.

(1990) *The Constraints of Desire.* London and New York.

(1994) 'The Invention of Romance', in Tatum (1994), 23–38.

Winter, I. J. (1995) 'Homer's Phoenicians: History, Ethnography or Literary Trope?', in Carter and Morris (1995), 247–71.

Wiseman, T. P. (1979) *Clio's Cosmetics: Three Studies in Greco-Roman Literature.* Leicester.

(1985) *Catullus and his World: A Reappraisal.* Cambridge.

Wolff, S. L. (1912) *Greek Romances in Elizabethan Fiction.* Columbia.

Wyke, M. (1994) 'Woman in the Mirror: The Rhetoric of Adornment in the Roman World', in Archer, Fischler and Wyke (1994), 134–51.

(1997) *Gender and the Body in Mediterranean Antiquity, Gender and History* 9. Oxford.

ed. (1998) *Gender and the Body in the Ancient Mediterranean.* Oxford.

Yatromanolakis, Y. (1990) *Leukippe kai Kleitophon*, text, transl. and commentary. Athens.

Zanker, G. (1981) 'Enargeia in the Ancient Criticism of Poetry', *RhM* 124: 297–311.

Zeitlin, F. I. (1982) 'Cultic Models of the Female: Rites of Dionysus and Demeter', *Arethusa* 15: 129–53.

(1990) 'The Poetics of Eros: Nature, Art and Imitation in Longus' *Daphnis and Chloe*', in Halperin, Winkler and Zeitlin (1990), 417–64.

(1994) 'The Artful Eye: Vision, Ecphrasis and Spectacle in Euripidean Theatre', in Goldhill and Osborne (1994), 138–96.

Zimmerman, S. ed. (1992) *Erotic Politics. Desire on the Renaissance Stage.* London.

Zola, E. (1928) *Le Roman Expérimental.* Paris.

INDEX LOCORUM

ACHILLES TATIUS

Leucippe and Clitophon
1.1–1.3	37
1.1.2	54 n. 64
1.1.3	138
1.1.8	43
1.2.2–3	51–2, 111
1.3	48
1.3.4–5	52
1.4.2–3	38, 104, 156
1.4.4–5	131–5, 172
1.5.5–7	80–1, 178
1.6.1–2	166
1.6.5	123
1.6.6	78–82
1.7.4	43
1.8.7	64 n. 90
1.8.8	43
1.9.3–5	154
1.9.4–5	130–5
1.10.1	6, 154
1.10.2–4	208
1.10.6	208
1.10.7	62
1.10.11	59
1.12	42
1.13.4	43 n. 28
1.15.1–8	39, 138, 184
1.15.6	43 n. 28
1.16.1	81, 185
1.16.2	62, 185
1.16.3	190
1.17.3	54
1.17.3–5	43 n. 25
1.19.1–3	39, 81, 189–90
1.19 5–6	184
2.1.2–3	192
2.2	47, 50
2.3.3	165
2.7.7	210
2.8.1	211
2.11.2ff.	141–2
2.11.4	49

2.13.2	89
2.14.1–2	43 n. 25, 49 n. 50
2.15.3–4	45, 56, 64 n. 90
2.16.2	90–1
2.18.3–4	62
2.19.2	39
2.20.1	84–5
2.21.1–5	87
2.21.7	148
2.22.1	198
2.23.1	84
2.23.3	43 n. 28, 65, 86, 124
2.23.4–5	125
2.28.1	62
2.28.2	212
2.28.3	214
2.29.1–5	201
2.30.1	86, 206
2.36.1	126
2.36.3	64 n. 90
2.36.4	82 n. 138
2.37.5–10	75, 149–50, 153
2.38.1	153
2.38.2	198
3.4.2	179
3.6.1	43 n. 25
3.6.3	174, 176
3.7.3–4	176
3.7.5	148 n. 139, 175
3.7.7–8	176
3.7.8	43, 174–7
3.8.4	176
3.8.7	175
3.10.5	175
3.11.2	201
3.13.3	43
3.15.5	35
3.15.6	56, 172
3.15–20	167–9
3.16.3	172, 175
3.18.5	172
3.20.5–7	172–3
3.25	190–8
3.25.7	87 n. 149

INDEX LOCORUM

4.1.2–3	125	7.5.3	43 n. 28
4.1.3–5	206	7.16.4	131 n. 92
4.1.5	125	8.2.1–3	83
4.1.6–8	221	8.3.3	214
4.1.7	126	8.4.1–2	162
4.3.1–2	157, 197–9	8.5.2–3	56
4.4.4	43 n. 28	8.5.7	212
4.8.1–2	126–7	8.5.9 ff.	180
4.14.9	115	8.6	193
4.17	195–6	8.6.10	181
5.1.1–6	100–6	8.6.15–8.7.1	212
5.3.3	201	8.8.3	215
5.3.4–5.4.2	178–80, 180	8.8.5–6	57
5.5.1	180	8.8.11–12	215
5.5.2	115	8.9.1	65
5.5.6–8	180	8.9.9	52 n. 61
5.7.8	43	8.10.9	76
5.7.9	181	8.13.3	181
5.11.5	221	8.16.1–2	216
5.13.1–2	222	8.17.3	62
5.13.3	222		
5.13.4	131–5		
5.13.5	222–3		
5.16.4–6	224–5		
5.16.7	5		
5.19.2	62 n. 84		
5.19.5–6	202		
5.20.5	212		
5.21	42 n. 23		
5.22.5	223		
5.23.5–7	83		
5.23.7	59		
5.27.1	59		
5.27.2	207		
5.27.4	6, 99		
6.1.3	61, 223		
6.3.1	63, 139		
6.4.2	201		
6.6.2–4	135–40, 161–5		
6.6.3	105		
6.7.1–7	136–40		
6.7.8–9	162		
6.15.4	201		
6.16.1–6	201		
6.16.4–6	62		
6.18.2–3	79–80		
6.19.1–19	117–21, 128		
6.20	83, 199		
6.20.3	214		
6.21.2	83, 199		
6.21.3	57, 83, 214		
6.22.2–3	205		
6.22.4	200		
7.4.1–5	129		

ACTS OF SS PERPETUA AND FELICITY

21.9–10	205 n. 97

AELIAN

De nat. animal.

3.47	187–8

AESCHYLUS

Agamemnon

240	27 n. 110

ALEXANDER

De sensu

24.14	133–4

ANTH. LAT.

902.3	32 n. 130

PS.-APOLLODORUS

2.4.3	28 n. 118

APULEIUS

Metamorphoses

7.9.5	219

INDEX LOCORUM

ARISTIDES QUINTILIANUS

De Musica
2.8.30   22–3

ARISTOPHANES

Eccl.
12   191 n. 67

ARISTOTLE

Poetics
1454b   22
De Caelo
303a6   134
442a29   134
Rhetoric
2.21.9   113 n. 64
2.21.12   107 n. 43

ARRIAN

Discourses on Epictetus
3.24   203

ATHENAEUS

Deipnosophistae
9 397C   199
13 375A   89 n. 154
13 561C   105 n. 36
13 574E   89 n. 154
13. 605F4–10   33
14 655B   191 n. 68

CASSIUS DIO

Roman History
58.4–5   33 n. 136

CHARITON

1.1.3   66 n. 93
1.11.6   85 n. 113
2.6.3   162 n. 14
2.10.3   114
3.2.4   114, 160 n. 11
3.2.16   161
4.19   160
5.3.1   160
5.3.2   114, 116–17
5.5.6   116, 160 n. 11
6.4.5   121–2
6.6.7   116–17

CICERO

De. Orat.
3.26.101   111

CLEMENT OF ALEXANDRIA

Protrepticus
2.21 = Orph. *Fr.*
52 (Kern)   27 n. 111

CYPRIAN

Treatises
47   215

DIO CHRYSOSTOM

Olympic Discourse
2   62 n. 85

EPICTETUS

Handbook
17   63 n. 87

EURIPIDES

Hecuba
521–69   27 n. 110
568–70   195
Phoenician Women
1023   52

GALEN

De simplic. medicam.
12.10–14   192

HEBREW BIBLE

1 Kings 2:5, 33   43 n. 25
2 Kings 23:13   43 n. 25

HELIODORUS

1.26.6   114
4.3.1   66
5.29.4   114
10.41.4   149

INDEX LOCORUM

HERODOTUS

2.121–6	218
3.104.2–7	55 n. 70
4.9	52

HESIOD

Theogony

295–305	52

Works and Days

57–8	64 n. 90

HORACE

Satires

2.2.26	62 n. 85

HOMER

Iliad

2.478	64 n. 90
2.673–4	66 n. 93
3.397	222
10.435	64 n. 90
10.436–7	45 n. 34
16.823	64 n. 90
20.234–5	64 n. 90
21.203–384	66 n. 93

Odyssey

6.102–4	121–2

JUVENAL

7.420–1	32 n. 130

LIVY

1.58.9	203

LONGINUS

On the sublime

15.1–2	90
43.5	191

LONGUS

2.7.1	54 n. 65
2.7.7	155–6
2.37	181
3.17	221
3.19	156
4.11.2	84

LUCIAN

De Dea Syria

4	45–6
82	72

De Hist. Conscrib.

10	141

Erotes (of Pseudo-Lucian)

53	123

Pseudol.

1.28	191 n. 69

LYCOPHRON

Alexandra

1.844–5	28 n. 117

MENANDER

frg. 568 = K–A 791	19–21

MENANDER RHETOR

399.15–16	185–6
401.27–402.10	185–6
404.8–10	186

NONNUS

Dionysiaca

1.531–2	106
5.587–621	106 n. 39
7.210–18	106 n. 39
11.101–2	105
42.47–81	106
42.454–5	105–6

OPPIAN

Halieutica

1.578	189 n. 62

OVID

Ars amatoria

1.219–28	185

Metamorphoses

4.789ff.	28 n. 118
4.794–8	163

INDEX LOCORUM

PAUSANIAS

3.26.1	43 n. 26
9.28.2	55 n. 70
9.34.1	28 n. 117

PERSIUS

1.18	31 n. 130

PHILO

FGrH 3c 2.790
F2.31	43 n. 26

PHILOSTRATUS

Apoll. Tyan.
2.30	139
6.19	92–3
Epistle 12	131 n. 91
Epistle 26	23–5, 27
Epistle 32	25 n. 103

Imagines
1.15	166
1.29.3	176

PINDAR

frg. 123 S–M	22 n. 97

Olympian Odes
2.9–10	142

PLATO

Alcibiades I
132c–d	14–15

Laws
12 961a–b	52 n. 61

Meno
76c–d	132

Phaedrus
229b–230a	53
250d	132
251b	132
255c1–3	25 n. 103, 51
255d	132

Republic
414 b ff.	55
450b	51

Symposium
180d–182a	52, 127 n. 84

Theaetetus
149a–151d	155

188b	91
191b	91
193a	91

Timaeus
91d6ff.	187 n. 54

PLINY

10.2.5	193

PLUTARCH

Moralia
De lib. educ.
10C	59

Conjug. praecept.
142D	24 n. 102

Mul. virtut.
247F–248D	27 n. 113

Quaest. Rom.
284A	191

De sollert. anim.
991F	187

Peri poluprag.
515D	85
518C	85
519C	86–7

PRUDENTIUS

Peristephanon
3.131–45	205 n. 96

QUINTILIAN

Institutio Oratoria
1.9.3	108
8.5	107 n. 43
8.5.3	108
8.5.8	113
8.5.28	111
8.5.32 and 34	143
11.3.75–7	139–40

SENECA

Controversiae
Preface to
Book 7 (2)	70 n. 105
1.2	216
1.7	200 n. 84
6.8	214 n. 109

INDEX LOCORUM

Suasoriae
1.7   121

SENECA

Epistles
14.6   205 n. 95
33.4   111
33.5   138–40
94   107 n. 44
Phaedra
735   203

ST AUGUSTINE

City of God
4.10   169 n. 28
Confessions
1.16   81–2

ST BASIL

To Young Men on Reading Greek Literature
7.5–7   59

STRABO

17.1.6–10   101

STRATO

AP 11.22.2   189 n. 61

SUDA

s.v. Ἀχιλλεύς
Στάτιος   4 n. 18, 4 n. 19

TACITUS

Annals
6.28   190 n. 64

TERENCE

Eunuch
585ff.   82

TERTULLIAN

On the Veiling of Virgins
428–9   215

THEODORUS PRISCIANUS

Euporista
2.11.34   79 n. 136

THEON

2.118   90

THEOPHRASTUS

Characters
11.1–2   27
De sensibus
12   133

THE STORY OF APOLLONIUS KING OF TYRE

A40–1   219

THUCYDIDES

2.43.1   105 n. 33

XENOPHON

Memorabilia
3.11.1–4   25–7
Symposium
8.9–10   126
8.15–16   126

XENOPHON OF EPHESUS

5.7.1ff.   199
5.15.3   149 n. 141

GENERAL INDEX

Achilles (the hero), 61
  on Scyros, 76
  on Scyros, painting of, 61, 223, 231
  on Scyros, pantomime of, 73
Achilles Tatius
  author, 4
  name, 4
  see also *Leucippe and Clitophon*
Adams, C., 33
Adams, J., 31–2 n. 130
Addison Roberts, J., 187
Aeschylus, 27 n. 110, 141
Agnes, 205
Agnodike, 27 n. 113
aidos, 22–3, 162
akolasia, 75, 88–9, 94
Alcibiades, 89
Alexandria, 100–6
Alpheus and Arethusa, 185–6
anasurmos, 27–8; see also exhibitionism
ancient novel
  and genre, 1–2
  and martyrologies, 204
  'origins' of, 6
  readership of, 2–5
Anderson, G., 1, 38 n. 6, 51, 86, 100, 104
Andromeda, see *ekphrasis* of Andromeda and Perseus
animals, descriptions of, 184–99
Aphrodite, 42
Aphthonius, 107 n. 43
Apollo and Daphne, 80–1, 178, 181–2
Apuleius, 12, 44 n. 31, 72, 219
Arendt, H., 173
Argos Panoptes, 141
Aristophanes, 64–7
Aristotle, 17, 22, 107 n. 43, 187
ars amatoria, 74–5, 152–6, 185
Artemidorus, 187
Artemis, 206
Astarte, 37, 42–8
Athenaeus, 33, 67 n. 96, 89 n. 154, 105 n. 36, 191 n. 68
atomism, 16, 133–5

autopsy, 89, 101, 103

Baal, 43 n. 24
Babrius, 148
Bakhtin, 70
Bal, M., 34 n. 141
Barthes, R., 108, 112, 156
Barton, C., 170 n. 30
Bartsch, S., 36, 38 n. 6, 39–40, 47, 96–8, 147, 173, 177, 182
Baubo, 27
Baudrillard, J., 128–9
Bennington, G., 108, 111
Berger, J., 30, 198
Bettini, M., 39–40
Billault, A., 110 n. 54
blason, 138–40
Bloch, R., 214
Boorsch, J., 144
boukoloi, 114, 141
Bowersock, G., 204 n. 92
Bowie, E., 1, 3
Bremmer, J., 22
Brennan, T., 29 n. 122
bricolage, 99
Briquel-Chattonet, F., 49
Britton, C., 99
Brooks, P., 170
Brown, P., 204 n. 91
Buci-Glucksmann, 140
Burke, K., 99

Cadmus, 50, 55 n. 71
Cairns, F., 162 n. 13
Calligone, 40, 52, 90
Callisthenes, 78, 88–94
Candaules, 9, 10 n. 46
cannibalism, 50
Carter, A., 219
Cassius Dio, 33 n. 136
casuistry, 69–70
Caws, M., 99, 143
Charicles, 152
Charikleia, 114

265

Chariton, *Callirhoe*, 57, 85 n. 143, 111, 114, 121–2, 160–1
Charmides (character in *L&C*), 56, 114, 126–7, 157, 197–9
chastity, 7, 47,
chastity test, 68
Clement of Alexandria, 33 n. 137, 131 n. 93, 133
Clinias, 59, 75, 107, 130–1, 152–6, 208–9
clod, *see* Egyptian clod
Clover, C., 31 n. 129
Coates, P., 46–7
Conops, 56, 78, 84–7, 141, 148
controversiae, 68–71, 200
Copjec, J., 30
Coward, R., 188
Cowie, E., 150
Cresci, R., 230
curiosity, *see polupragmosune*
Cyclops, 86

Dali, S., 143
Daphne, *see* Apollo and Daphne
deaths, false (*Scheintode*), 43, 72, 167–9, 173–5, 192–3
de Bolla, P., 32
de Lauretis, T., 23, 33
della Croce, A., 7
Demeter, 27
Democritus, 16, 133
de Rochemaure, J., 7
de Sade, M., 219
desire
 and frustration, 117–30
 at first sight, 156–65
Diggle, J., 42 n. 23
digression, 41, 96–151
Dionysius, 114
Dionysus, festival of, 50, 204 n. 92
Doane, M., 30
Doody, M., 3, 12 n. 53, 76, 104 n. 33, 159, 163, 171, 228
doubleness, motif of, 43
dreams, 52–3, 93 n. 165, 169, 182–4

Egger, B., 2, 3, 113, 160
Egyptian clod, 43
Egyptian ox, 45 n. 34
Egyptian priest, 87 n. 149
ekphrasis, 36, 90, 92, 97, 120, 138–40, 182–4
 of Andromeda and Perseus, 87, 148 n. 139, 174–7, 182, 211
 of Calligone's necklace, 141–2
 in *Daphnis and Chloe*, 37
 of Europa, 37, 38–48, 61, 87, 138, 176, 211
 in Lucian, *On the Hall*, 20
 of Philomela, Tereus and Procne, 115, 178–80
 of Prometheus, 174–7
Elagabalus, 72 n. 113
Elephantis, 75
Elsner, J., 8, 29, 46 n. 36
Elsom, H., 170, 172
enargeia, 90
Empedocles, 17 n. 78, 132–3, 135
Encolpius, 86
ending of the novel, 8, 144–5, 228–9
endings of books, 200
ephebic initiation ritual, 62 n. 84
Epictetus, 58, 63, 203
Epicurus, 16
epithalamium, 185–6
eros, 117–21
Eshmun, 43 n. 24
Esrock, E., 28, 34 n. 140
ethnocentrism, 114–17, 168; *see also* Phoenicians, stereotypes of
ethopoieia, 68
Eulalia, 205
Euripides, *Iphigenia in Tauris*, 72
Europa 37–48, 50, 87, 186; *see also ekphrasis*, of Europa
exhibitionism, 28, 34
 and fantasy of empowerment, 160
 see also anasurmos
exposure, 24, 195–7
expurgation of the text, 7
eye
 as icon, 140–3
 as metaphor, 142
 associated with phallus, 31
 Evil Eye, 12

fables, 86–7; *see also* Phaedrus
false perception, 91–2; *see also* Plato, *Theaetetus*
flâneur, 103
form, in literature, 99–151
fountains, 138
Fredrick, D., 31 n. 128
Frontisi-Ducroux, F., 8, 32
Fusillo, M., 39, 48 n. 46, 86 n. 145

Galen, 22 n. 95, 209
Gandelman, C., 13

GENERAL INDEX

Garland, L., 5 n. 22
Garnaud, J.-P., 39 n. 10, 193
Garson, R., 97 n. 8
Gaselee, S., 39, 96
gaze
  'the assaultive gaze', 31 n. 129
  the consumptive gaze, 32–4, 165–6
  definitions of, 29–35
  and ethnicity, 23
  and glance, 34
  homoerotic, 22 n. 97
  'the imperial gaze', 30
  lesbian, 22 n. 97
  and look, 35
  the oppositional gaze, 27
  as a 'technology of gender', 23
genre, and effeminacy, 75–6
Gnathon, 84, 88
gnome, 97; *see also sententia*
gnomologia, 107
gods, omnivoyence of, 22
Goldhill, S., 8, 33 n. 137, 34 n. 139, 55 n. 67, 131 n. 93, 174 n. 36
Gorgias (character in *L&C*), 56, 66
Gregory, J., 89

Hägg, T., 121
Hartog, F., 89, 101–2
Heath, J., 105 n. 37
Hedrick, C., 110 n. 54
Hefferran, J., 28 n. 113, 183 n. 46
Heimarmene, 63–4
Helen of Troy, 9
Heliodorus, *Ethiopian Tales*, 12, 49, 65–6, 96, 112, 114, 149
Henry, M., 33 n. 137
Hérembert, J., 8
Hermagoras, 97
Herodotus, 101, 190
heroes, passivity of, 58–9
Hesiod, 64 n. 90
hippopotamus, 197–9
Hodges, A., 111–12, 194
Holzberg, N., 2 n. 9
Homer, 64–7, 81–2, 122, 222
hooks, b., 23 n. 99
Hopwood, K., 168 n. 27
Hubbard, T., 22 n. 97
human sacrifice, 168–9
Hunter, R., 127 n. 84
hupokrisis, 67–8
hyperrealism, 128–30
hypertext, 69

identity
  and ways of seeing, 18–21
Io
  myth of, 67 n. 98, 141
  and Isis, 216–17
Irene, 204–5
Irigaray, L., 30 n. 127

James, Henry, 103
Jay, M., 29 n. 123
Jenks, C., 103
John Chrysostom, 65 n. 91
Johns, C., 32
Johnson, B., 227, 231
Juvenal, 32 n. 130

Kappeler, S., 34, 198
Kepler, J., 29
Kérenyi, K., 216–17
khoregos, Clitophon as, 63
King, H., 27
Konstan, D., 72 n. 116, 158
Krasner, J., 183–4

labyrinth, 103
Laplace, M., 51–2, 57, 87, 141
letters, 202–3
Leucippe and Clitophon
  Christian appropriation of, 5
  and comedy, 66–7
  date of novel, 5, 190 n. 64
  as epithalamium, 185–6
  and genre, 7
  manuscript tradition of, 39 n. 10, 40
  reception in Byzantine writers, 6
  reception in late antiquity, 6
  relations with mime and pantomime, 68–77
  as 'philosophical' novel, 50–60
  as *Phoinikika* (*Phoenician Tales*), 48–50
  sixteenth- and seventeenth-century adaptations of, 7, 112
  see also Achilles Tatius
Leucippus, 16, 133, 135
Lindberg, D., 16
Livia, 33 n. 136
Lloyd, G., 186
Lollianus, 50, 72
Longinus, 90, 191
Longus, *Daphnis and Chloe*, 42 n. 23, 46, 54 n. 65, 84, 111, 114, 149, 155–6, 181, 207, 221
Lowe, N., 41 n. 22

GENERAL INDEX

Lucian
 De Dea Syria, 45–6
 De Domo, 20–9
 De Hist. Conscrib., 141
 De Saltatione, 67–8, 72, 77
 Erotes (of Pseudo-Lucian), 123, 148
 Onos, 72
Lucretia, 203
Lucretius, 16
Lykainion, 156, 220–1

Maeder, D., 53 n. 63, 55
Magritte, 142
marriage, 58; see also ending of the novel
Marsyas, 170
Martial, 75
martyrs, 203–5
McClure, L., 191
McDermott, H., 96–7, 144
meadows, 25, 39
Medusa, 27–8, 159, 163, 170–1, 176–7, 182
Melite, 3, 47, 56–7, 59–61, 68, 113 n. 64, 131, 202, 206–7, 220–6, 230–1
Menander, 19–21, 41 n. 22, 66, 218
Menander Rhetor, 185–6
Menelaus, 172–3
Merkelbach, R., 87, 141, 216–17
metaphors
 birth as metaphor, 154–5
 eye as metaphor, 142
 and Melite, 221–6
 nautical, 224–6
 peacock as metaphor, 185
 theatrical, 62–3
 for *thumos* and *eros*, 118–21
 for vision, 31–4; involving food, 32–4, 165–6; involving statues and works of art, 33–4; involving violence, 158–64
Metiochus and Parthenope, 12, 74
metrology, 101
Metz, C., 30
Mignogna, E., 71, 168 n. 24
Millar, F., 50
mime, 68–77
 artists, 72, 172
 Charition mime, 72
 'Leucippe' mime, 71–2
 see also Publilius Syrus
mimesis, 92–3
mirrors, 13–15, 71 n. 111, 77, 130–2, 134
 literary mirroring, 79–81
Moger, A., 151
Morgan, J., 108

mosaic from Antioch, *iv*, 11–18, 71 n. 111, 74
Most, G., 144–67
Mulvey, L., 30, 31
Musaeus, 6, 131 n. 90
mystery-text, 76, 87
mythology, 178–84

names
 'motivated' names, 56, 66–7
 of prostitutes, 67
Napolitano, F., 206 n. 99
narcissus, 136–8
necklace, Calligone's, 141–2
Newby, Z., 20 n. 87
Nicostratus, priest of Artemis, 64–7, 180
Nimis, S., 36, 41–2, 46 n. 40, 69, 104 n. 33, 145
Ninus romance, 11, 209 n. 102
Niobe, 56, 170–1
Nonnus, *Dionysiaca*, 33, 105–6
nouveaux romanciers, 102, 128

Odysseus, 55 n. 67
Olender, M., 27
opsis, subjectivity and objectivity of, 18–20
optical theory, 15–17, 29–35; see also atomism *and* vision
orgasm, 75, 149–50, 152–3
Orr, L., 111
Ovid, 75, 152–6, 163, 210

Pacteau, F., 138–9, 156–7
paederasts, 152
paideia, 21, 49, 65, 82, 89
Pan, 180–2
pan-pipes, story of, 180
Pantheia, 62, 85–6, 169
pantomime, 68–77
 'Achilles on Scyros', 73
 and 'snuff' drama, 168
Parker, H., 74
Parker, P., 138
Parrhasius, 25
Parthenope, 74
Pasiphae, 43 n. 26
peacock, 62, 141, 185, 190
Pelops, 158
Perkins, J., 57–60
Perry, B., 2 n. 9, 96
Persius, 31 n. 130
Petronius, 12, 71 n. 110, 72, 84, 86, 112 n. 62, 168, 201–2, 220 n. 124

268

GENERAL INDEX

Phaedrus, 148
phantasia, 20, 89–94, 202
Philaenis, 75
Philo, 131 n. 93, 187
Philomela, 115, 182, 201, 210
philosophers, 57
Philostratus, 23–9, 31–2, 120, 139, 190
Phoenicia/Phoenicians
   'Phoenician lie', 55–6
   Phoenician perspective, 42
   Phoenician Tales, 48–50
   phoinix, 49
   stereotypes of, 48–50, 55–6, 116, 168–9, 191–2; *see also* ethnocentrism
phoenix, 87 n. 149, 190–8
Photius, 227–9
Phryne, 27–8 n. 113
physiognomics, 22–3
Plato
   Alcibiades I, 14–15
   Charmides, 197 n. 81
   Meno, 132
   Phaedrus, 17–18, 25 n. 103, 32, 52–3, 66, 132
   Protagoras, 17
   Republic, 17, 51, 55
   Symposium, 52, 127 n. 84, 145
   Theaetetus, 17, 91–2, 155
   Timaeus, 16–17, 132, 187 n. 54
   on vision, 14–18, 91–2, 132–3, 197 n. 82
Plazenet, L., 112
Pliny, 187, 193
Plutarch, 18–29, 24 n. 102, 27 n. 113
Polemo, 22 n. 96
polupragmosune, 84–7, 194
Polybius, 101
pornography, 76
progumnasmata, 97–9, 114, 120, 218
Prometheus, *see ekphrasis*, of Prometheus
'prosaics', 36
prostitute
   accusations of being a, 215–16
   Aphrodite and Isis as prostitutes, 218 n. 120
   Melortis, 89
   'Prostitute Priestess', 213–14
   Timo, 225
   unnamed, 216
   see also virgin/whore
prostitution
   temple-prostitution, 44, 47, 49, 153
   Anthia sold into, 198 n. 82
   names of women in, 67

Providence, 63
Psellus, Michael, 61 n. 81
Ptolemy, 15
Publilius Syrus, 112, 203
purple, discovery of, 49
Pygmalion, 27 n. 110

Quintilian, 107 n. 43, 108, 113, 139–40, 143–4

rape
   attempted, of Syrinx, 181–2
   of Medusa, 163
   of Philomela, 178–80
   threat of, 162
   see also ekphrasis, of Europa, *and* Apollo and Daphne
Rattenbury, R., 97 n. 8
readership of the novel, 2–5
   gendering of, 73–6
reading, teleological approaches to, 36ff.
realism, 83–4, 94, 108; *see also* hyperrealism
Reardon, B., 54, 87, 97, 169
reception of the novel, 5–7; *see also Leucippe and Clitophon*
Richlin, A., 34, 69, 121, 210
Rohde, E., 2 n. 9
Romm, J., 55 n. 69
Rowland, B., 190 n. 63

Saïd, S., 102
Sappho, 22 n. 97
Satyrus, 84 n. 141, 148, 172–3
Scarcella, A., 110 n. 54, 115
Scarry, E., 173
scopophilia, 34
'Second Sophistic', 5–6
Sedelmeier, D., 36 n. 3
Segal, C., 217
Selden, D., 43–4,
Selene, 38–48, 156
Semonides, 187, 201
Seneca the Elder, 68, 121
Seneca the Younger, 58, 113 n. 64, 138–9, 203
sententia, 96–151
sexuality, debate on, 52, 148
Sharrock, A., 98
sight
   Greek vocabulary of, 34–5
   love at first, 156–65
Silverman, K., 30, 34 n. 141
Sissa, G., 209

269

Socrates
  and Clitophon, 57, 59
  in Xenophon's *Memorabilia*, 25–6, 105
Soder, R., 204 n. 91
Sophocles, *Oenomaus*, 158
Sostratus, 89
spectacle, 199–220
speech, 199–220, 224–6
Stephens, S., 79 n. 135
Stewart, A., 8
Stewart, S., 128
St Galaktion, 5
Stoicism, 57–60, 92–3, 132–3
Strabo, 101–2
Susannah and the elders, 202
Swain, S., 228, 230
syllepsis, 43, 93
Synnott, A., 21

temple at Sidon, 45
Tereus, 115, 178–80
Theagenes, 49, 65–6
Theano, 24 n. 102
theatricality, 60–77
Thecla, 203–4
Theodorus Priscianus, 79 n. 136
Theodote, 25–6, 31–2
Theon, 90, 97 n. 9, 107 n. 43
Theophrastus, 27, 133
Thersander, 65, 79–84, 93 n. 165, 113 n. 65, 115, 135–7, 199–202, 215
thumos, 117–21
Trapp, M., 51
Tristram Shandy, 96
Tyche, 62–4
Tyrian wine, 49

uncanny (*unheimlich*), 46–7, 104, 187

viewing
  and characterisation, 77–95
  and empowerment, 156–65
  as penetrative, 31–2
  as subjective, 42

  see also atomism, gaze, *opsis*, optical theory, *polupragmosune*, vision, visualities, visual masking
viper, and sea eel, 185, 188–9
virginity, 83–4, 203–20
  ritual defloration of, 168–9
  test, 180, 193–5, 212
virgin/whore, 218–20
vision
  atomists' theories of, 133–5
  Aristotle on, 17, 134
  dynamics of in Antioch mosaic, 11–18
  Ptolemy's theories of, 15
  Stoic theories of, 15–16, 92–3, 132–3
  Galen on, 15–16
  Plato on, 15–18, 91–2, 132–3
  the mechanics of, 130–5
  see also gaze, *opsis*, optical theory, *polupragmosune*, visualities, visual masking, voyeurism
visualities, ancient and modern, 29–35, 159
'visual masking', 183–4
voyeurism, 105–6
  'of exactitude', 128–9
  see also anasyrmos, exhibitionism, *polupragmosune*, scopophilia

Walker, A., 25 n. 103
weapons
  the display of, 172–84
  of mime-artist, 72
  of Perseus, 43, 174–7, 182
Williams, L., 30
Williamson, M., 94, 219
Winkler, J., 145, 168 n. 27
Wolff, S., 221

Xenophon, *Memorabilia*, 25–7, 32
Xenophon of Ephesus, *Ephesian Tales*, 52, 57, 111, 203, 218–19

Zeno, 105 n. 36, 132–3
Zola, E., 83